P9-CSA-208

DATE DUE

MAR 3 1990

FEB 06 '90

OCT 24 '93

RT'D OCT 04 '93

GAYLORD

PRINTED IN U.S.A.

A BIBLIOGRAPHY OF CALVINIANA 1959—1974

STUDIES IN MEDIEVAL AND REFORMATION THOUGHT

EDITED BY

HEIKO A. OBERMAN, Tübingen

IN COOPERATION WITH

E. JANE DEMPSEY DOUGLASS, Claremont, California
LEIF GRANE, Copenhagen
GUILLAUME H. M. POSTHUMUS MEYJES, Leiden
ANTON G. WEILER, Nijmegen

VOLUME XV

DR. D. KEMPFF

— A BIBLIOGRAPHY OF CALVINIANA
1959—1974

LEIDEN
E. J. BRILL
1975

A BIBLIOGRAPHY OF CALVINIANA

1959 - 1974

BY

DR. D. KEMPFF

LEIDEN
E. J. BRILL
1975

#2930466

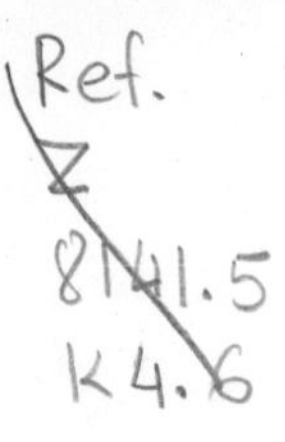

BX
9418
K46

Also published in series:
Wetenskaplike bydraes van die P.U. vir C.H.O.
Reeks F. Instituut vir die Bevordering van Calvinisme
F3. Versamelwerke, Nr. 3

ISBN 0 86990 213 X

ACKNOWLEDGEMENT

The financial assistance of the *Human Sciences Research Council of South Africa* in connection with the research for this work is hereby acknowledged. Opinions expressed in this work or conclusions reached are those of the author and must in no instance be regarded as a reflection of the opinions and conclusions of the *Human Sciences Research Council.*

Inquiries in connection with the *Wetenskaplike Bydraes* must be addressed to:
The Institute for Advancement of Calvinism.
Potchefstroom University for C.H.E., Potchefstroom,
Transvaal, 2520. Republic of South Africa.

Copyright 1975 by E. J. Brill, Leiden, Netherlands.
All rights reserved. No part of this book may be reproduced or translated in any form, by print, photoprint, microfilm, microfiche or any other means without written permission from the publisher.

Printed by the Potchefstroom Herald (Pty) Ltd., P.O. Box 156,
Potchefstroom 2520, Transvaal, Republic of South Africa.

TABLE OF CONTENTS

398961

ALUMNI MEMORIAL LIBRARY
Creighton University
Omaha, Nebraska 68178

PREFACE

"Omnes aliquid novi ex Africa"

Most probably few scholars will expect a bibliography of this size on a European reformer from the African continent. Once again however, the above-mentioned Latin proverb has been proved true, you can always expect something novel from this "dark" continent. Some explanation of this exceptional "spark of light" from South Africa necessitates a brief preface.

The Institute for the Advancement of Calvinism

The aim of the Institute for the Advancement of Calvinism (established some ten years ago at Potchefstroom) is to encourage research on Calvin and Calvinism. In order to attain this end one of its first tasks was a bibliographical study to ascertain the amount of research material which had become available after the previous bibliography compiled by W. Niesel up to 1959. The result of this enquiry, which has continued over the last five years, is contained in the present bibliography. The sincere wish of the I.A.C. is that this bibliography will render valuable service to Calvinologists all over the world and stimulate scientific research about Calvinism.

International co-operation

This 1959—1974 bibliography should be regarded as the first contribution of the I.A.C. towards international Calvin-research. Our Institute is firmly convinced of the absolute necessity of international co-operation in this field. It has already established contact with various similar organizations and institutions throughout the world and it will be glad to get into touch with institutions and persons of the same interest in future. To facilitate this contact a brief introduction may be appropriate.

Bibliographical research by the I.A.C.

Building upon the material contained in this bibliography the I.A.C. is publishing in Afrikaans a series of Calvin causeries which is indispensable to students and interested readers. These causeries are annotated bibliographies mainly of books and articles available in the Ferdinand Postma Library of the University of Potchefstroom on for instance the following subjects: Calvin's view on Scripture, state and the law, state and church, ethics, music, education, culture, economics, science, ecclesiastical ecumenical relationships, church government and church discipline, pastoral care, his attitude towards missionary work, eccesiastical councils, his doctrine about God, anthropology etc.

The preparation of these causeries by different authors is made possible by the Calviniana collection available in the Library of the University of Potchefstroom. A continuous effort is made to enlarge this collection, already of a high standard. The I.A.C. will therefore be very willing to exchange publications on a mutual basis or to be informed not merely about recent publications but also about valuable older stuff available. We are especially interested keeping our existing collection of doctor's and masters' theses up to date.

Publications of a different nature

Apart from the abovementioned causeries the I.A.C. issues three other types of publications.

The first is a pamphlet series on important issues. These pamphlets on topical matters, composed and duly elucidated from a Calvinist-Biblical point of view by authorities in their respective fields, appear monthly. Nearly one hundred numbers have thus far been published. About 3 500 of these studies are sent monthly to recipients in Southern Africa and various countries. To increase the number of readers some of these pamphlets will be issued in English in future.

The second is a brochure series which provides for a more extensive discussion from a Calvinistic point of view of different topics, e.g. the Calvinist and art; human rights; dramatic art, film and T.V. In these series are also included studies on different aspects of Calvinistic thought.

The third type of publication by our Institute comprizes our efforts towards international co-operation. The I.A.C. aspires to publish more comprehensive works at least every five years containing the contributions of Calvinists throughout the world. Two volumes of this nature entitled *Die atoomeeu — „In U Lig"* (The atomic age in the light of the Word of God) and *Reformasie en Revolusie* (Reformation and Revolution) were published in 1969 and 1974 respectively. Most probably the next volume will contain the acts of an international Calvinistic conference (on the various aspects of tertiary education) to be held at Potchefstroom towards the end of 1975.

Other activities

In an extensive research programme, which will be carried out during the next decade, we shall try to ascertain the impact of Calvinism on the South African society. In this project the links between South African and European Calvinism will be traced. In addition to the Reformational heritage of the 16th century, its background will be studied as far back as the Pre-Reformation, Late Mediaeval and even Patristic period.
The I.A.C. does not aim to revive the past in an anachronistic way with the help of historical research. Because of many possible deviations during the four centuries of Calvinistic thought it is important, however, to get to the primogenitor. We regard the study of the original sources as of the utmost importance. The idea is not to canonise the thought of Calvin, but to build on the firm foundation of most of his ideas which clearly echo Biblical revelation.

In the different ways briefly described above the I.A.C. endeavours, by means of unswerving loyalty to Scripture, to be a tower of light of the Calvinistic life and world view in the contemporary darkening world.

Hopefully, we work and pray under the same motto as that of Calvin's Geneva: *Post tenebras lux!*

B. J. van der Walt,
Director: I.A.C.

The Potchefstroom University for Christian Higher Education,
Potchefstroom 2520, Republic of South Africa.

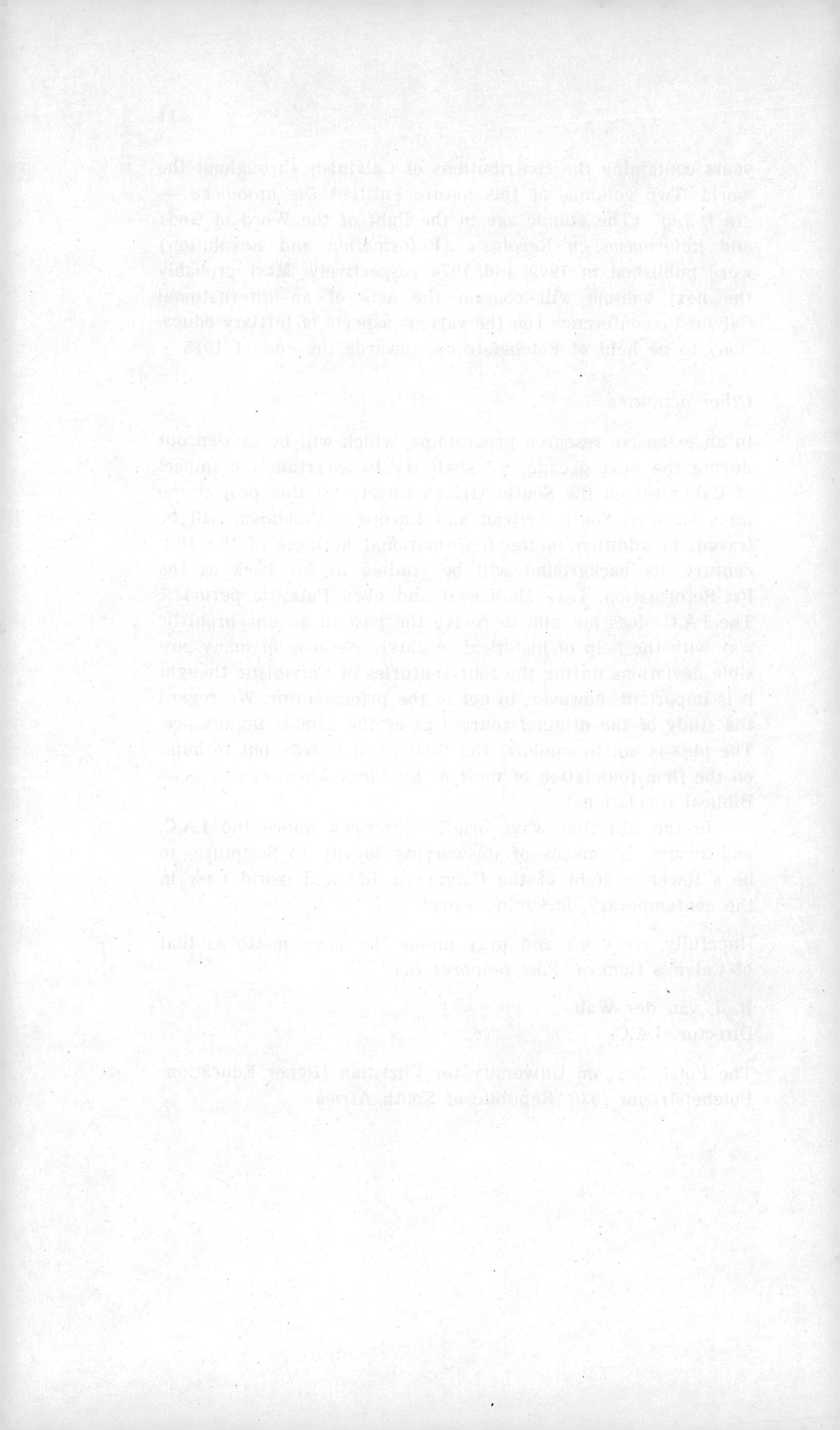

INTRODUCTION

It has been said more than once that interest in, and the study of Calvin and his influence are waning and will soon come to an end. But, strangely enough, the way things have gone, has been in the opposite direction: books and articles regularly flow from the presses and in September 1974 a congress of Calvin-scholars was held in Amsterdam. It is apparent that the many items mentioned by *Erichson* (Bibliographa Calviniana) and *Niesel* (Calvin-Bibliographie, 1900—1959) have been accompanied or followed by numerous others. Some periodicals have given bibliographical surveys of limited scope. Smaller or larger bibliographical studies have also appeared (particulars to be found on pp. 24—26). All of these serve to prove that Calvin or Calviniana is far from obsolete. All relevant bibliographical information has been taken into consideration and, where necessary, grateful use has been made of it.

Because interest in Calviniana has not come to a standstill but has actually increased, research in this field seemed necessary. The intention was to produce a Calviniana-bibliography as comprehensive as possible, taking all relevant material into account. The following points can be mentioned regarding the design for the research and content of this work:

1 Items published before 1900 (and not reprinted) were not included, as other skilled hands are at work gathering those particulars.

2 Originally the intention was that this bibliography be *post-Niesel,* starting from 1959. The research, however, made in clear that Niesel's work ommitted important items, e.g. quite a number of theses produced in the U.S.A. and France. Therefore an attempt was made to cover the ground from 1900.

3 Certain delays inevitably arose and this work is published later than was originally intended, viz. 1972. This made it possible to incorporate items after 1972 and as far as possible into 1974.

4 It became apparent that it was necessary to include besides

publications by and on Calvin also works by and on fellow-reformers of Calvin's and/or people directly influenced by him or his work. This does eliminate *Luther* cum suis and also *Zwingli* c.s., save when there was a contact with Calvin c.s. But included are *Beza, Farel, Knox* (centre-figures in the Reformation Monument in Geneva) as also are *Bucer, Knox, a Lasco,* a.o.

5 History has shown that the influence of Calvin c.s. extended over countries and centuries. Items published after 1900 (see 1) which deal with this influence up to the year 1650 (i.e. just past the time of the Westminster Assembly) have been entered in this work, while items after 1650 were included only when this influence in a country or matter is specifically mentioned.

6 For the reasons mentioned this is intended as a *Calviniana*-bibliography. As regards Calvin himself the research was as wide and thorough as possible and it includes items before 1959 as completely as was possible. As for as the broader Calviniana (contained in the second part) were concerned, relevant items found were duly entered.

7 I had the choice of including either too much or too little, depending where the decisive line was drawn. It was decided rather to err per excessum than per defectum, thus making this work of value for more than just specializing students.

8 Grateful acknowledgement must be made of the aid of several libraries where research was done and of persons who also helped. A special word of thanks goes to the library and staff of the Potchefstroom University for Christian Higher Education for assistance given.

Regarding the method of presentation the following has to be taken into consideration:

1 The items themselves have not been numbered so as to leave scope for additions as near as possible to date of publication.

2 To facilitate usage, the contents have been divided into as many sections and sub-sections as the material required and as seemed necessary. The table of contents can be used as a guide.

3 If a specific item actually is at home in several sections,

it is repeated wherever necessary and therefore there are no cross-references (except in section-headings).

4 Items in collective works are entered in such a way that the full title is mentioned with every article.

5 *Thesis* is used as a common denominator and not in a specific sense. Therefore it can include anything from a treatise (for Baccalaureus) right up to a thesis for a doctorate.

6 Items are entered as far as possible in the language of publication, but the language of reference is English. Some problems did arise in instances of orthography and the nearest possible spelling was used.

I sincerely trust that this bibliography will not only represent the results of the study of Calvin and Calviniana but that it may also stimulate further study in this field, thus serving the true God in Jesus Christ.

D. Kempff.
1975, May.

I CALVIN.

1.1. OWN WORKS:

Catechism, etc.

CALVIN, Jean. Brève instruction chrétienne. Adaptation en français moderne par Pierre Courthial. Paris, Les Bergers et les Mages [1958?] 82 p.

CALVIN, Jean. Catechism, 1538. Tr. and annotated by Ford Lewis Battles. Pittsburgh, Pittsburgh Theological Seminary, 1972. 62, 62p.

CALVIN, Jean. The catechisme; or, Manner to teache children the Christian religion. Amsterdam, Theatrum Orbis Terrarum, 1968. 167 p. (English experience, its record in early printing books published in facsimile, no. 46). Original t.-p.: The catechisme; or, Manner to teache children the Christian religion, wherin the minister demandeth the question and the childe maketh answere. By John Crespin, 1556.

CALVIN, Jean. [Catechismus Ecclesiae Genevensis. Gaelic. 1962] Adtimchiol an chreidimh; the Gaelic version of John Calvin's Catechismus Ecclesiae Genevensis. A facsimile reprint, including the prefixed poems and the Shorter catechism of 1659, with notes and glossary, and an introd., ed. by R. L. Thomson. Edinburgh, Oliver & Boyd, for the Scottish Gaelic Texts Society, 1962. 264 p. (Scottish Gaelic texts, v. 7).

CALVIN, Jean. Christliche Unterweisung (Instruction et confession de foi dont on use en l'église de Genève) Der Genver Katechismus von 1537, übers. von L. Schuckert. Hamburg, Furche, 1963. 78 p. (Furche-Bücherei, Bd. 217).

CALVIN, Jean. Deux congrégations et exposition du catéchisme, Première réimpression de l'édition de 1563 avec une introd. et des notes, par Rudolph Peter. Paris, Presses universitaire de France, 1964. 49 p. (Cahiers de la Revue d'histoire et de philosophie religieuses, 38).

Commentaries on Bible books.

CALVIN, Jean. Calvin's commentaries: the Pentateuch (sic) v. 1 [Repr. of Calvin Translation Society ed.] Grand Rapids, Associated Publishers and Authors, 1971.

CALVIN, Jean. Calvijn over Genesis 1—3. Vlaardingen, Bolland, 1968.

CALVIN, Jean. A commentary on Genesis. Tr. and ed. by John King (Repr.) London, Banner of Truth Trust (1965, 1847) 2 v. in 1. (A Geneva series commentary).

CALVIN, Jean. (Verklaring van de Bijbel) Genesis (herdr.) Goudriaan, De Groot, 1970. 2 v.

CALVIN, Jean. Le livre de la Genèse. Texte établi par André Malet, avec la collaboration de Pierre Marcel et de Michel Reveillaud. Genève, Labor et Fides, 1962, 687 p. (His Commentaires sur l'Ancien testament, 1).

CALVIN, Jean. Calvin's commentaries: Joshua and the Psalms, v. 2 [Repr. of Calvin Translation Society, ed.] Grand Rapids, Associated Publishers and Authors, 1971.

CALVIN, Jean. (Verklaring van de Bijbel) Het boek der Psalmen. Goudriaan, De Groot, 1970, 2 v.

CALVIN, Jean. Commentary on the Psalms, tr. by Arthur Golding. Rev. and ed. by T. H. Parker. London, James Clarke (1965) 4 v.

CALVIN, Jean. Calvin's commentaries: Isaiah, v. 3 [Repr. of Calvin Translation Society ed.] Grand Rapids, Associated Publishers and Authors, 1971.

CALVIN, Jean. Calvin's commentaries: Ezekiel and Daniel, v. 5. [Repr. of Calvin Translation Society ed.] Grand Rapids, Associated Publishers and Authors, 1971.

CALVIN, Jean. A commentary on Daniel (Tr. by Thomas Myers, repr.) London, Banner of Truth Trust, 1966 (1852/3) 2 v. in 1.

CALVIN, Jean. (Verklaring van de Bijbel) De kleine profeten (bd.) 2: Joël, Amos, Obadja. Goudriaan, De Groot, 1972. 381 p.

CALVIN, Jean. Calvin's commentaries: the Minor Prophets, v. 6. [Repr. of Calvin Translation Society ed.] Grand Rapids, Associated Publishers and Authors, 1972.

CALVIN, Jean. New Testament commentaries [New tr.] Editors: David W. Torrance [and] Thomas F. Torrance. Grand Rapids, Mich., Eerdmans (1959-'72) 12 v. Also published by Oliver & Boyd, Edinburgh.

CALVIN, Jean. (Verklaring van de Bijbel) De evangelieën van Mattheus, Markus en Lukas in onderlinge overeenstemming gebracht. Goudriaan, De Groot, 1971. 3 v.

CALVIN, Jean. Calvin's commentaries: the Gospels, v. 7 [Repr. of Calvin Translation Society ed.] Grand Rapids, Associated Publishers and Authors, 1972.

CALVIN, Jean. Auslegung der Evangelien-Harmonie, übers. van Hiltrud Stadtland-Neumann und Gertrud Vogelbusch. Neukirchen, Verlag des Erziehungsvereins (1966) 457 p. (His Auslegung der Heiligen Schrift. Neue Reihe, Bd. 12, 1).

CALVIN, Jean. Auslegung des Johannes-Evangeliums, übers. von Martin Tiebesius und Hans Christian Petersen. Neukirchen, Verlag des Erziehungsvereins (1964) 496 p. (His Auslegung der Heiligen Schrift. Neue Reihe, Bd. 14).

CALVIN, Jean. (Verklaring van de Bijbel) Het evangelie van Johannes. Goudriaan, De Groot, 1971. 875 p.

CALVIN, Jean. (Verklaring van de Bijbel) De handelingen der Apostelen. Goudriaan, De Groot, 1970. 2 v.

CALVIN, Jean. Auslegung des Römerbriefe und Korinthierbriefe, bearb. und übers. von G. Graffman, H. J. Haarbeck (und) O. Weber. Neukirchen, Verlag des Erziehungsvereins, 1960. 604 p. (His Auslegung der Heiligen Schrift. Neue Reihe, Bd. 16).

CALVIN, Jean. Uitlegging op den zendbrief van Paulus aan de Romeinen en op den eersten en tweeden zendbrief van Paulus aan de Corinthiërs. Naar de uitgaven der oude hollandsche oversetting van J. D., in de tegenwoordige spelling door A. M. Donner. Goudriaan, De Groot, 1972. Reprint of 1888—1889 ed.

CALVIN, Jean. Épître aux Romains. Genève, Labor et Fides (1960) 380 p. (His commentaries, t. 4).

CALVIN, Jean Épîtres aux Galates, Ephésiens, Philippiens et Colossiens. Genève, Labor et Fides (1965) 407 p. (His Commentaires, t. 6).

CALVIN, Jean. Uitlegging op den zendbrief van Paulus aan de Galaten, op de zendbrieven van Paulus aan de Efesiërs, Filippensen en Colossensen, en op den eersten en tweeden zendbrief van Paulus aan de Thessalonicensen. Naar de uitgaven der oude hollandsche oversetting van J. D., in tegenwoordige spelling door A. M. Donner. Goudriaan, De Groot, 1972. Reprint of 1890 ed.

CALVIN, Jean. John Calvin's sermons on Ephesians. London, Banner of Truth Trust, 1974. 705 p. Adapted in modern English from the Arthur Golding translation of 1577.

CALVIN, Jean. Auslegung der kleinen Paulinische Briefe. Unter Mitarbeitung von H. J. Barenings [u.a.] Neukirchen, Verl. des Erziehungsvereins, 1963. 635 p. (His Auslegung der Heiligen Schrift. Neue Reihe, Bd. 17).

CALVIN, Jean. Uitlegging van de pastorale brieven; opnieuw vert. uit het Latijn naar de uitg. van Baum, Cunitz en Reuss, door H. Schroten. Kampen, Kok, 1966. 309 p. (His Kommentaren op de zendbrieven).

CALVIN, Jean. La epistola del apostel Pablo a los Hebreos; el comentario de Juan Calvino del original Latin, y ed. Ingle's por Juan Owen. Al castellano por Louis Torres y Márquez. Mexico, Fuente, 1960. 372 p.

CALVIN, Jean. A zsidókhoz írt levél magyarázata. Függelék: 1. Három prédikáció Melkisédek történetéröl. 2. A. 110. zsoltar magyarázata [von] Kálvin János (Fordította. Szabó András. A fordítást átdolgozta és függelékkel ellátta: Nagy Barna) Budapest (Kiadja a Református Zsinati Iroda Satjóoztálya) 1965. 255 p. (Református egyházi könyvtár, 27) Original title: Commentarii in epistolam ad Hebraeos.

Institution.

CALVIN, Jean. Calvin im zwanzigsten Jahrhundert [von] Hermann Unger. (Schwetzinger, Schwetzinger Verlagsdruckerei, 1950) 93 p. (In his Unterweisung in der christlichen Religion).

CALVIN, Jean. Calvin's Institutes. Notes by Robert Dunzweiler [Repr. of Beveridge ed.] Grand Rapids, Associated Publishers and Authors, 1971.

CALVIN, Jean. A Calvin treasury; selections from the Institutes of the Christian religion. Tr. by Ford Lewis Battles. Ed. by William F. Keesecker. Introd. by T. F. Torrence London, SCM (c1963) 143 p. (Living church books).

CALVIN, Jean. A compend of the Institutes of the Christian religion. Ed. by Hugh T. Kerr. Philadelphia, Westminster Press (1964) 228 p. Also published by Lutterworth Press, London (repr. 1965).

CALVIN, Jean. Instituce uceni, krestánského nabozenstvi. Prel., úvodem a poznámkami opatril F. M. Dobiáš. Praha, Komenského evangelická fakulta bohoslovecká, 1951. 342 p. (Spisy Komenského evangelické fakulty bohoslovecké. Rada A, sv. 16) Translation of Institution christianae religionis.

CALVIN, Jean. Institusie; of, Onderwysing in die Christelike godsdiens. Opnuut in Afr. vert. en verkort weergegee deur A. Duvenage. (Potchefstroom, Pro Rege, 1967) 550 p.

CALVIN, Jean. Institutes of the Christian religion. Ed. by John T. Mc. Neill. Tr. by Ford Lewis Battles, in collaboration with the ed. and a committee of advisers. London, SCM, 1961. 2 v. (Library of Christian Classics, v. 20, 21) Also pub. by Westminister, Philadelphia.

CALVIN, Jean. The Institutes of the Christian religion. Tr. from the Latin into simple modern Eng., by Joseph Pitts Wiley. With the pref. to the original ed. (1920) by H. Tydeman Chilvers, and a new introd., by J. I. Packer. London, Sovereign Grace Union, 1966. 196 p.

CALVIN, Jean. Institution de la religion chrestienne. Ed. critique avec introd., notes et variantes, pub. par Jean-Daniel Benoit. Paris, Vrin, 1957-'63. 5 v. facsim. (Bibliothèque des textes philosophiques).

CALVIN, Jean. Institution de le religion Chréstienne. Ed. nouv. (2 ed., par Jean Cadier) [et al] Genève, Société Calviniste de France; International Society for Reformed Faith and Action (1967) 4 v.

CALVIN, Jean. Institution de la religión christiana. Traducida y publicada pör Cipriano de Valera en 1597; reeditarda por Luis de Usoz y Rio en 1858; nueva ed. rev. en 1967. Rijswijk, Stichting Uitgave Reformatorische Boeken [1968] 2 v. (1262 p.).

CALVIN, Jean. Institution of the Christian religion; embracing almost the whole sum of piety and whatever is necessary to know the doctrine of salvation, Basel, 1536. Facsim. of 1536 ed. Now Englished completely for the first time by Ford Lewis Battles. Pittsburgh, Pittsburgh Theological Seminary, 1969. 514 p.

CALVIN, Jean. Instituzioni della religione christiana di Giovanni Calvino. A cura di Giorgio Tourn. Torino, UTET [1971] 2 v. (1804 p.)

CALVIN, Jean. John Calvin; the darkened intellect **(In:** Classical statements on faith and reason. Ed. and with an introd. by Eddie L. Miller. New York, Random House, 1970. p. 70—82) (Selections from Institutes of the Christian religion).

CALVIN, Jean. Juan Calvino, Institucion de la religion Christiana. Tr. de Ciperiano de Valera (con. introd. por B. Forster Stockwell) Buenos Aires, La Aurora (1952-'60) 2 v.

CALVIN, Jean. Unterricht in der christlichen Religion. Institutio Christianae religionis. Nach der letzten Ausg. übers. und bearb. von Otto Weber (2. durchges. Aufl. der einbändigen Ausg. Neukirchen) Neukirchener Verl., 1963. 1238 p.

Letters.

CALVIN, Jean. Johannes Calvins Lebenswerk in seinen Briefen; eine Auswahl von Briefen Calvins in deutscher Übersetzung von Rudolf Schwarz (2 Aufl.) Neukirchen Kreis Moers, Neukirchener Verl. 1961-'62. 3 v. (1310 p.).

CALVIN, Jean. Juan Calvino; Repuesta al cardenal Sadoleto. (Rijswijk) Fundación editorial de literatura reformada (1964) 70 p.

CALVIN, Jean. Kalvin levelei a nőkhöz [Letters to women] Tr.: P. Pruzsinszky. Budapest, 1909. 198 p.

CALVIN, Jean. [Letter to Mme. Besson, 10 June, 1542. With Eng. tr. prepared by Samuel Terrien, 1953] 3 1. Unpublished manuscript.

CALVIN, Jean. Letters of John Calvin. Comp. and ed. by Jules Bonnet. New York, Franklin, 1973. 4 v. Reprint of 1855—1858 ed. (Burt Franklin research and source works series. Philosophy and religious history monographs, 16).

CALVIN, Jean. Les lettres à Jean Calvin de la collection Sarrau. Publiées avec une notice sur Claude et Isaac Sarrau par Rodolphe Peter et Jean Rott. Paris, Presses Universitaires de France, 1972 (Cahiers de la Revue d'histoire et de philosophie religieuses, no. 43).

CALVIN, Jean. Letters of John Calvin. Compiled from the original manuscript and edited with historical notes by Jules Bonnet. New York, Franklin [1973]. 4 v. facs. (Burt Franklin research & source works series. Philosophy and religious history monographs, 116). Reprint, Edinburgh & Philadelphia editions, 1855—58.

CALVIN, Jean. A Reformation debate; Sadoleto's letter to the Genevans and Calvin's reply. Ed. with an introd., by John C. Olin. New York, Harper and Row [1966] 136 p. (Harper torchbooks, TB 1239 G).

REFORMATORENBRIEFE: Luther; Zwingli; Calvin. Unter Mitarb. von H. Delius und G. W. Locher hrsg. von G. Gloede. Neukirchen-Vluyn, Neukirchener Verl. 1973, 431 p. „Calvin": p. 315—432.

Selections.

CALVIN, Jean. Alle Tage tut Gott sein Werk (Zitate [aus verschiedenen deutschen Ausg. von Calvins Werken]. Auswahl von Heinrich Bödeker) Wüppertal, Müller (1963) 40p.

CALVIN, Jean. Calvin, homme d'église. Oeuvres choisies du réformateur et documents sur les Eglises réformées du 16e siècle. 2 ed. Genève, Labor et fides (1971) 322 p.

CALVIN, Jean. Calvin m'a dit. Textes sur la souffrance humaine choisis et présentes par Denise Hourticq. Saint-Maur, L'Echo, 1964. 91 p.

CALVIN, Jean. Calvin on election and damnation (**In:** Renaissance, reformation and absolutism 1400—1600. Ed. by Thomas G. Barnes & Gerald D. Feldman. Boston, Little Brown; 1972. p. 101—106). (A documentary history of modern Europe).

CALVIN, Jean. Calvino, antologia. Presentacion selección por M. Guitérrez Marín. Barcelona, Producciones Editoriales del Nordeste, 1971.

CALVIN, Jean. Forms of prayer to be used in private houses. Edinburgh, St. Andrew Press, 1961. 22 p. (The Porch Library).

CALVIN, Jean. Glossaire; dictionnaire des locutions obscures et des mots vieillis qui se rencontrent dans les oeuvres de Jehan Calvin. Genève, Slatkine, 1968. 42 p. Réimpression de l'édition anonyme de Paris, 1855.

CALVIN, Jean. Il problema della salvezza nell' età della riforma della chiesa (**In:** Religione. A cura di Mario Miegge. Firenze, Sansoni, 1965. p. 541—549) [Institutes of the Christian religion. Selections].

CALVIN, Jean. Johannes Calvin und die Kirche. Ein Lesebuch mit Texten und Themen. Eingeleitet und ausgewählt von Udo Smidt. Stuttgart, Evangelisches Verlagswerk, 1972. 120 p.

CALVIN, Jean. John Calvin; selections from his writings. Ed. with an introd., by John Dillenberger. Garden City, N.Y., Anchor, 1971, 590 p.

CALVIN, Jean. Leben aus dem Glauben. Einl. von Otto Weber. Konstanz, Christliche Verlagsanstalt, 1959. 141 p. (Konstanzer Taschenbuch, Nu. 6).

CALVIN, Jean. Modlitby Jana Kalvina. Praha, Kalich (1948) 109 p.

CALVIN, Jean. Ny Fianan 'ny Kristiana. Nadikan'i pasteur Ch. Ranaivo, Tananarive, Impr. Tananarivieme, 1948. 54 p.

CALVIN, Jean. Pensées de Calvin sur la prière. Genève, Kündig & Fils, 1908. 28 p.

CALVIN, Jean. The piety of John Calvin; an anthology illustrative of the spirituality of the reformer of Geneva. Selected, tr. and ed. by Ford Lewis Battles. Pittsburgh, Pa., Pittsburgh Theological Seminary, 1969. 190 p.

CALVIN, Jean. A Reflection Book introduction to the writings of John Calvin. Selected and ed. by Hugh T. Kerr. New York, Association Press (1960) 124 p. (Association Press reflection book).

CALVIN, Jean. Stemmen uit Genève; preken, artikelen, brieven, enz. van Johannes Calvijn. Meeuwen, Gereformeerde Bibliotheek, 1967. v.

CALVIN, Jean. The sum of the Christian life; the denial of ourselves **(In:** Values in conflict; Christianity, marxism, psychoanalysis, existentialism. Ed. by Victor Comerchero. New York, Appleton-Century-Crofts, 1970. p. 137—148) [Institutes of the Christian religion. Selections].

CALVIN, Jean. À la rencontre de Jean Calvin. Textes et documents réunis, par Bernard Gagnebin. Genève, Georg (1964) 81 p.

Sermons.

CALVIN, Jean. Calvin's Saturday morning sermon on Micah 6 : 6—8; tr. by A. D. Lewis. **Scottish journal of theology,** 23: 166—182, 1970.

CALVIN, Jean. Het gepredikte Woord. Preeken van Johannes Calvijn. Vert. door J. Douma en W. H. van der Vegt. 2e dr. Franeker, Wever [1965?] 3 v.

CALVIN, Jean. John Calvin; four sermons **(In:** 20 centuries of great preaching; an encyclopedia of preaching. Ed. by Clyde E. Fant, Jr. and William M. Pinson, Jr. Waco, Tex., Word Books, 1971. v.2, p. 131-181.

CALVIN, Jean. Predigten über das 2. Buch Samuelis, hrsg. van Hanns Rückert. Neukirchen Kreis Moors, Neukirchener Verl., 1961. 786 p. **(His** Supplementa Calviniana, 1).

CALVIN, Jean. [Preken over Job] Meeuwen, Gereformeerde Bibliotheek, 1967 — v. **(His** Stemmen uit Genève bundel 7, 9, 11, 13, 14, 16, 17 18, 19—)

CALVIN, Jean. Sermones de libris Jérémie, cap. 14—18 et Threnorum, cap. 1. Ad fidem Genavensis et Parisiensis manuscriptorum, ed. Rud. Peter. Neukirchen, Neukirchener Verl. 1971. 250 p. **(His** Supplementa Calviniana, 6).

CALVIN, Jean. Sermons sur le Livre de Michée, publiés par Jean Daniel Benoit. Neukirchen, Neukirchener Verl. 1964. 262 p. **(His** Supplementa Calviniana, 5).

CALVIN, Jean. Sermons sur le Livre d'Esaie, Chapitres 13—29, publiés par Georges A. Barrois. Neukirchen, Neukirchener Verl. 1961. **(His** Supplementa Calviniana, 2).

Tracts, treatises, works.

CALVIN, Jean. Academic discourse (All Saints' Day, 1553) Tr. and annotated by D. Cooper and Ford Lewis Battles. **Hartford quarterly,** 6: 76—85, 1965.

CALVIN, Jean. Avertissement contre l'astrologie. Traité des reliques. Suivis du Discours de Théodore de Bèze sur la vie et la mort de Maître J. Calvin. Paris, Colin (1962) 138 p. (Bibliotheque de Cluny. Le trésor). Also published by Ed. d'art Mazenod, 1965.

CALVIN, Jean. Calvin's commentary on Seneca's De Clementia. With introd. tr. and notes; by Ford Lewis Battles and André Malan Hugo. Leiden, Published for the Renaissance Society of America, by Brill, 1969. 140, 448 p. (Renaissance text series, 3).

CALVIN, Jean. Concerning the eternal predestination of God. Tr. with an introd. by J. K. S. Reid. London, Clarke (1961) 191 p.

CALVIN, Jean. La connaissance religieuse. Étude d'histoire et de dogmatique. Paris, Fischbacher, 1970. 64 p.

CALVIN, Jean. Consensus Tigurinus (1549) Tr. by I. D. Bunting. **Journal of Presbyterian history,** 44: 45—61, 1966.

CALVIN, Jean. Ioannis Calvini Opera quae supersunt omnia. Ad fidem editionum principum et authenticarum ex parte etiam codicum manu scriptorum, additis prolegomenis literariis, annotationibus criticis, annalibus calvinianis indicibusque novis et copiosissimis. Ed.: Guilielmus Baum, Eduardus Cunitz, Eduardus Reuss. New York, Johnson Reprint, 1964. 59 v. in 58.

CALVIN, Jean. Johannes Calvin; aus der Frühzeit und Lehre vom dreieinigen Gott. Ausgewählt und übers. von Joachim Rogge (Original text und deutsche übers.) Berlin, Evangelische Verlagsanstalt, 1964. 112 p.

CALVIN, Jean. Johannes Calvin: der Schriftausleger, der Prediger, der Reformator, der Mensch. Ausgewählt und übers von Joachim Rogge (Original text und deutsche übers.) Berlin, Evangelische Verlagsanstalt, 1964. 144p.

CALVIN, Jean. Johannes Calvin; zur Lehre von der Kirche, über die Prädestination, die Sakramentslehre, über Staat und Kirche. Ausgewählt und übers. von Joachim Rogge (Original text und deutsche übers.) Berlin, Evangelische Verlagsanstalt, 1964. 160 p.

CALVIN, Jean. Kalvin János Müvei [small treatises by Calvin.] Tr.: S. Ceglèdi [et al.] Papa, 1908.

CALVIN, Jean. Preface to the homilies of Chrysostom; tr. by J. H. McIndoe.**Hartford quarterly,** 5: 19—26, 1965.

CALVIN, Jean. La religione individuale, a cura di Piero Jahier. Lanciano, Carabba, 1912. 139 p.

CALVIN, Jean. So spricht Calvin (Bearb. von Ursula von Mangoldt) München, 1956. 125 p. (Lebendige Quellen zum Wissen um die Ganzheit der Menschen).

CALVIN, Jean. Three French treatises (Traité des reliques; Traité de la Cêne; Excuse aux nicodemites) Ed. by F. M. Higman. London, Athlone Press, 1970. 171 p. (Athlone Renaissance library).

CALVIN, Jean. Tractaat der reliquieën. Zeer nuttige aankondiging van het grote profijt dat de Christenheid zal hebben, als zij zich ontdoet van alle heilige en religieuse voorwerpen... (herdr.) 's-Gravenhage, Uitzicht, 1965. 61 p.

CALVIN, Jean. Traité des reliques. Le discours contre la papauté qui et à Rome [par] M. Luther. Première traduction en français par Pierre Jundt. Paris, Mazenod, 1964. 177 p. (Les ecrivains célèbres. Oeuvres, 43).

CALVIN, Jean. Tratados breves (por) Juan Calvino. La Santa Cena. Carta al cardenal Sadoleto (Trad. du français) Buenos Aires, La Aurora, 1959. 137 p. (Obras clasicas de la Reforma, 18).

CALVIN, Jean. Von Gott bezwungen; eine Hörfolge von Johannes Kuhn [Sprecher] Uwe- Jens Pape (u.a.) Regie: Gottfried Wolf [Phonodisc] Stuttgart, Verl. Junge Gemeinde Schwinghammer, 1964. 12 in. 33⅓ rpm. (Credo (Reihe 2)).

CALVIN, Jean. Vorrede von Johannes Calvin, 1563, zu Genesis, zürcher Übersetzung. Original Farbholzschnitte: Carl Heinz Kliemann. Berlin, Vogt, 1962. 111 p.

CALVIN, Jean. Witchcraft and the reformation **(In:** Witchcraft in Europe, 1100—1700; a documentary history. Ed., with an introd., by Alan C. Kors and Edward Peters. Philadelphia, University of Pennsylvania Press, 1972. p. 202—212). [Institutes of the Christian religion. Selections].

CALVIN, Jean. Zur Unmöglichkeit des Krieges und Möglichkeit des Religionenkrieges. Aus Predikten: Samuel. **Reformierte Kirchenzeitung,** 106: 52—53, 1965.

Japanese and Korean translations

CALVIN, Jean. [Geneve Catechism] Tr. by H. Toyama. Tokyo, Protestant Publishing, 1963.

CALVIN, Jean. [Commentaries on the Bible]. Tokyo, Protestant Pub. Co., 1959—. Comprising: Psalms, 3v. [of 4], 1970—'72; John, 2v., 1963—'65; Acts, 2v., 1973, 1968; Romans, 1959; I Corinthians, 1960; II Corinthians, 1963; Galathians and Ephesians, 1962; Philippians, Colossians and Thessalonians, 1970; Peter, Jude and I—III John, 1963.

CALVIN, Jean. [Institutes] Tr. by Nobuo Watanabe. Tokyo, Protestant Pub. Co., 1962—'65. 7v.

CALVIN, Jean. [Calvin's Selected writings: Letters to the lovers of Jesus Christ]. Tr. by Nobuo Watanabe. Tokyo. Protestant Pub. Co., 1959. (Christian classics, no. 8).

CALVIN, Jean. [Calvin's theological tracts] Tr. by Y. Akagi. Tokyo, Protestant Pub. Co., 1967.

CALVIN, Jean. Calvin's Institutes Book I. Beveridge edition. Tr. by Ch. H. Han & B. Ey. Shin. Seoul, Word of Life Press, 1964. 373 p. [In Korean].

CALVIN, Jean. A compend of Calvin's Institutes, comp. by H. Kerr. Tr. by J. S. Rhee. Seoul, CLSK, 1974 (6th impr.), 273 p. [In Korean].

1.2 WORKS ABOUT CALVIN: GENERAL

Bibliographies.

ARCHIV FÜR REFORMATIONSGESCHICHTE. Beiheft; Literaturbericht, v. 1, 1972.

AUBERT, Fernand. Un Calvin peu connu de la Collection Maillart-Gosse. **Genava,** 12: 172—174, 1934.

BAINTON, Roland Herbert. Bibliography of the Continental Reformation. Chicago, American Society of Church History, 1935. "The Reformation in French Switzerland": p. 36—44, 2nd. ed. rev. and enl. (Hamden, Conn.) Archon Books, 1972.

BOLDRINI, Marcello. Una indagine statistica del Secolo, XVI: II Trattato delle Reliquie di Giovanni Calvino. **Giornale degli economisti e Rivista di Statistica,** 54: 250—253, 1924.

BRUSSELS. Centre National de Bibliographie. Les bibliographies, I: Jean Calvin. Bruxelles, 1964. 21 l.

CABEEN, D. C. A critical bibliography of French literature, II: The sixteenth century. Ed. by Alexander H. Schutz. Syracuse, Syracuse Univ. Press, 1956. "Calvin." p. 195—204.

CIORANESCO, Alexandre. Bibliographie de la littérature française du seizième siècle. Collaboration et préface: V. L. Saulnier. Paris. Klincksieck, 1959. Jean Calvin: p. 165—182.

DE KLERK, Peter. Calvin bibliography 1972. **Calvin theological journal,** 7 (2) 221—250, 1972.

DE KLERK, Peter. Calvin bibliography, 1973. **Calvin theological journal,** 9 (1) 38—73, 1974.

DE KLERK, Peter. Calvin bibliography 1974. **Calvin theological journal,** 9 (2): 210—240, 1974.

DE KOSTER, Lester Roland. Living themes in the thought of John Calvin; a bibliographical study. Ann Arbor, University Microfilms, 1969. 564 l. Thesis—University of Michigan. 1964.

ERICHSON, A fred. ed. Bibliographia Calviniana; catalogus chronologicus operum Calvini. Catalogus systematicus operum quae sunt de Calvino cum indice auctorum alphabetica [Repr.] Nieuwkoop, De Graaf, 1960 (1900).

FRAENKEL, Peter. Petit supplement aux bibliographies calviniennes, 1901—1963. **Bibliotheque d'Humanisme et Renaissance,** 33 (2) 385—414, 1971.

GRAPPE Georges. La vie littéraire: Jean Calvin. **L'Opinion,** 4: 177—179, 1911.

INTERNATIONAL COMMITTEE OF HISTORICAL SCIENCES. Commission Internationale d'Histoire Ecclésiastique Comparée. Bibliographie de la Reforme: 1450—1648; ouvrages parus de 1940 à 1955. Leiden, Brill, 1960-v. Contents — fasc. 1. Allemagne, Pays Bas. 3 ed., 1964. - fasc. 2. Belgique, Suède, Norvège. Danemark, Irlande, Etats-Unis d'Amerique. 1960-fasc. 3. Italie, Espagne, Portugal. 1961.-fasc. 4. France Angleterre, Suisse. 1963 — fasc. 5. Pologne, Hongrie, Tchécoslovaquic, Finlande. 1965. — fasc. 6. Au'riche. 1967.

KEMPFF, Dionysius. Bibliografie van Suid-Afrikaanse Calviniana. Potchefstroom, Potchefstroomse Universiteit vir Christelike Hoër Onderwys, 1973. 53 p. (Wetenskaplike bydraes van die P.U. vir C.H.O. Reeks F2. Instituut vir die bevordering van Calvinisme. Calvyncauserieë, nr. 2).

KRANZ, Gisbert. Europas christliche Literatur, 1500—1960. Aschaffenburg, Pattloch, 1961. "Calvin", p. 33—35.

KUNITZ, Stanley Jasspon & COLBY, Vineta. European authors, 1000—1900; a biographical dictionary of European literature. New York, Wilson, 1967. Calvin: p. 140—142.

LEONARD, Emile G. Bibliographie Calvinienne abrégeé. **Revue de theologie et d'action evangeliques,** 3: 405—424, 1943.

MORPHOS, P.O. & FRAUTSCHI, R. L. Literature of the Renaissance [in] 1961-'63. **Studies in philology,** 59: 341—343, 1962; 60: 351—354, 1963; 61: 353—355, 1964.

NICOLE, Roger. Some notes towards a biblography of John Calvin. **Gordon review,** 5: 174—181, 1959; 6: 21—28, 1960. **(Also in:** American Theological Library Association. Summary of proceedings (of the) ninth annual conference. New York, 1955. p. 6—19).

NIESEL, Wilhelm. Calvin-Bibliographie, 1901—1959. München, Kaiser, 1961. 120 p.

PARIS. Bibliothéque Nationale Catalogue des ouvrages de Calvin conservés au Département des Impremés. Paris, Imprimerie Nationale, 1905. 30 p.

PETER, Rodolphe. Notes de bibliographie calvinienne a propos de deux ouvrages récents [1] F. L. Battles & A. M. Hugo: Calvin's commentary on Seneca's De Clementia [2] Eugénie Droz: Chemins de l'hérésie; textes et documents (v. 1) **Revue d'histoire et de philosophie religieuses,** 51 (1) 79—87, 1971.

PETER, Rodolphe. Oeuvres de Calvin publieés à Genève entre 1550 et 1600. **Bibliotheque d'Humanisme et Renaissance,** 31 : 181—183, 1969.

PIPKIN, H. Wayne. A. Zwingli bibliography. Pittsburgh, Pa., Clifford E. Barbour Library, Pittsburgh Theological Seminary (c1972). 157 p. (Bibliographia tripotamopolitana, no. 7).

ROWE, Kenneth E. Calvin bibliography. Madison, N. J., Drew Univ., 1967. 67 p.

SCHMIDT, Albert Marie. Calviniana, 1936—1937. **Foi et vie,** 38 : 358—364, 1937.

SMID, T. D. Enkele bibliografische opmerkingen betreffende Calvijn en zijn commentaar op Jeremia. **Gereformeerd theologisch tijdschrift,** 61 : 156—165, 1961.

SMID, T. D. Some bibliographical observations on Calvin's Sermons sur le livre de Job. **Free University quarterly,** 7 : 51—56 1960/61; **Het Boek, N.R.,** 24 : 365—367, 1936/37.

SPENCE, T. H. Brief bibliography of Presbyterian history; John Calvin. **Religion in life,** 25: 603—604, 1956.

STUPPERICH, Robert. Die Zwingli- und Calvin-Forschung der letzten zwei Jahrzehnte im deutschen Sprachgebiet. **Archiv für Kulturgeschichte,** 42: 108—126, 1960.

TYLENDA, Joseph N. Calvin bibliography, 1960—1970. **Calvin theological journal,** 6: 156—193, 1971.

Calvin: Biographical details.

BAINTON, Roland Herbert. Women of the Reformation in Germany and Italy. Minneapolis, Minn., Augsburg Pub. House, 1971. "Renée of Ferrara, 1510—1575": p. 234—251.

BENOIT, Jean Daniel. La conversion de Calvin [Discours prononcé à Montauban, le 14 November 1909] Vals-les-Bains, 1909.

BEZEMER, C. Beslissende jaren in het leven van Calvijn. **Hervormd weekblad — de Geref. Kerk,** 84: 13—14, 1972/73.

BONNET, Jules. Idelette de Bure. **Société de l'histoire du protestantisme français. Bulletin** 102 (4) 636—646, 1956.

BOSMAN, I. Vroue van die Hervorming; tydgenote van Calvyn. **Woord en daad,** 6 (20) 7, 1961.

BUSCARLET, Daniel. La joie de Calvin. **La revue reformée,** 15 (60) 48—55, 1964.

CADIER, Jean. La conversion de Calvin. **Société de l'histoire du protestantisme français. Bulletin,** 116 (1—3) 142—151, 1970.

CADIER, Jean. Les maladies de Calvin et ses relations avec les médicins montpelliérains. **Monspeliensis hippocrates,** 1 (2) 6—12, 1958.

CAZALET, William G. Calvin and his friends. **Huguenot Society of London. Proceedings,** 13 (2) 262—272, 1924.

CLAVIER, Henri. Calvin à Strasbourg 1538—1541. **Protestantische Rundschau** 15 : 81—88, 1938.

d'ASSONVILLE, Victor Edouard. Die vrou van Calvyn. **Die Gereformeerde Vroueblad,** 25 (1) 7—9, 1970.

D'ENTREVES, C. La fuga di Calvino attraverso il col Durand. **Augusta praetoria,** 3 : 238—242, 1950.

DIVITA, James J. The Italian sojourn of John Calvin: 1536. **Italian quarterly,** 14 : 85—111, 1971.

DOSKER, Henry E. The story of Calvin's life **(In:** Calvin celebration by the Presbytery of Louisville. Addresses delivered at the celebration of the 400th anniversary of the birth of John Calvin. Louisville, Kent., 1909. p. 13—22).

DOSKER, Henry E. The youth of Calvin. **The Banner,** 44 : 240—241; 259—260; 277—278; 309—311; 326—327; 341—343; 357—358; 373—374, 1909.

DOUMERGUE, Emile. Calvin, un grand français. **Foi et vie,** 12: 683—685, 1909.

DOUMERGUE, Emile. Le caractère de Calvin; l'homme, le système, l'église, l'état; réimpr. de l'd. de Paris 1921. Genève, Slatkine, 1970. 178 p.

DRESSEL, L. C. Calvyn se troue sorg; vroue van die Hervorming: Idelette. **Die Voorligter,** 30 (5) 20, 1967.

DREYER, Marie. Idelette; vrou van Calvyn **Die Hervormer,** 50 (2) 14—15, 1959.

DROZ, Eugénie. Chemins de l'hérésie; textes et documents I. Genève, Slatkine Repr., 1970. "Jean Calvin à Bâle:" p. 89—130.

DROZ, Eugénie. Chemins de l'hérésie. textes et documents, III Genève, Slatkine Repr., 1944. "Une correspondante inconnue de Calvin: Madame de Laubespine", p. 30—60.

DUDON, Paul. Quand et comment Calvin est-il devenu protestant? **Recherches de sciences religieuses,** 14 : 411—428, 1924.

FORD, Harry Pringle. John Calvin; an outline biography. **The Interior,** 40 (2030): 512f., 1909.

GAGNEBIN, Bernard. Faux autographes de Calvin. **Musées de Genève,** 12, no 6, 1955.

GALLICET - CALVETTI Carla. L'umanesimo di Giovanni Calvino a quattrocento anni dalle morte. **Vita e pensiero** 47: 496—504, 1964.

GANOCZY, Alexandre. Le jeune Calvin. Genèse et évolution de sa vocation réformatrice. Mit einer Einl. von Joseph Lortz. Wiesbaden, Steiner, 1966. 382 p. (Veröffentlichungen des Instituts für Europäische Geschichte, Mainz, Bd. 40. Abt. Abendländische Religionsschichte).

GOOD, James Isaac & RICHARDS, Geo W. Life pictures of John Calvin for young and old. Philadelphia, Heidelberg Press, 1909. 32 p.

HANEKOM, Tobias Nicolaas. Rondom die sterfbed van Calvyn. **Nederduitse Gereformeerde teologiese tydskrif,** 5 (4) 212—219, 1964.

HASLER, R. A. Influence of David and the Psalms upon John Calvin's life and thought. **Hartford quarterly,** 5 : 7—18, 1965.

HEMPHILL, Charles R. The times of Calvin **(In:** Calvin celebration by the Presbytery of Louisville. Addresses delivered at the celebration of the 400th anniversary of the birth of John Calvin. Louisville, Kent., 1909. p. 3—11).

HUNTER, A. Mitchell. The erudition of John Calvin. **Torch and trumpet,** 4 (4) 6—10, 1954.

JOOSTE, Josef Petrus. Calvyn se jeug, 1509—1536. **Die Bondsbode,** 17 (24) 12—15, 1965.

KELLER, Adolf. Calvin in Strassburg. **Christliche Welt**, 52: 935, 1938.

KROMMINGA, Diedrich Hinrich. Calvin's courage in his ministry. **The Banner,** 69 : 607, 1934.

KROMMINGA, Diedrich Hinrich. Crises in Calvin's career. **The Banner,** 78 : 894—895, 1943.

KROMMINGA, John H. Reflections on the life of Calvin. **The Banner,** 88: 1319, 1953.

LANG, August. Die Bekehrung Johannes Calvins. Neudr. der Ausg. 1897. Aalen, Scientia, 1971. 57 p. (Studien zur Geschichte der Theologie und der Kirche 11, 1).

LECERF, Auguste. L'apogeé et la mort de Calvin. **Foi et vie** 36: 301—314, 1935.

LE MAIRE, J. De l'influence de l'Université d'Orléans sur la conversion de Calvin. **Societé archéologique et historique de l'Orleanais. Bulletin trimestriel, N.S.,** 1: 328—332, 1959/60.

LITTELL, Franklin Hamlin. What Calvin learned at Strassburg **(In:** The heritage of John Calvin. Ed. by John H. Bratt. Grand Rapids, Eerdmans, 1973. p. 74—86) (Heritage Hall Lectures, 1960—1970) (Heritage Hall publication, no. 2).

McNEILL, John Thomas. Calvin the man. **Christianity today,** 8 (17) 777—779, 1964.

MARCEL, Pierre. L'humilité de Calvin. **Societé de l'histoire du protestantisme français. Bulletin,** 110: 175—185, 1965.

MENTON, Henry C. John Calvin, lawyer. **North American review,** 190: 212—221, 1909.

MESNARD, Pierre. Jean Calvin, étudiant au droit, à Orléans **(In:** Actes du Congrès sur l'ancienne Université d' Orléans (XIIIe-XVIIIc siècles) Orléans, Bourdon-Blanc, 1962, p. 81—91.)

NAUTA, Doede. Nogmaals de zeilende Calvijn. **Centraal weekblad voor de Gereformeerde Kerken in Nederland,** 16 (19) 2, 1968.

NIJENHUIS, Willem Calvijns "subita conversio", notities bij een hypothese. **Nederlands theologisch tijdschrift,** 26 (3/4) 248—269, 1972.

PALM, Franklin Charles. Calvinism and the religious wars. New York, Fertig, 1971 (c1932) 117 p. "Calvin and Geneva", p. 3—33.

PANNIER, Jacques. Les années d'études et l'evolution religieuse de Luther et de Calvin. **Foi et vie,** 26: 857—865, 1923.

PANNIER, Jacques. Calvin étudiant au Quartier Latin. **Foi et vie,** 36: 257—269, 1935.

PANNIER, Jacques. Calvin étudiant et privée de Calvin, 1538—1541. **Societé de l'histoire du protestantisme français. Bulletin,** 87: 360—367, 1938.

PAULUS, N. Calvins Lebensende und die Jesuiten. **Germania,** 18, 1901.

PINAULT, Jean. Calvijn's afscheidswoorden tot de predikanten. **Centraal weekblad voor de Gereformeerde Kerken in Nederland,** 12 (19) 5, 1964.

PONCET, Antonin. La maladie de Calvin, par Antonin Poncet et René Leriche. (Paris) Masson (n.d.) 10 p. (Extrait des Bulletins et memoires de la société médicale des hôpitaux de Paris, séance du 3 avril 1909).

PRINSLOO, B. Weerskante aan die brand; lewe van Calvyn. **Die Bondsbode,** 11 (89) 5—6; 8; 10, 1959.

REY, A. Note sur l'origine liégenoise d'Idelette de Bure. **Société de l'histoire du protestantisme belge. Bulletin,** 1922: 111—117.

RICHARDS, William Rogers. Traits of Calvin's personality. **The Interior,** 40 (2030) 517—518, 1909.

RIESER, Ewald. Calvin; Franzose, Genfer oder Fremdling? Untersuchung zum Problem der Heimatliebe bei Calvin. Zürich, Schmidberger, 1968. 136 p. Thesis — Zürich, 1968.

ROUSSEL, Bernard. Le jeune Calvin. **Revue d'histoire et de philosophie religieuses,** 48 (1) 54—59, 1968.

RUMOER rond de zeilende Calvijn. **Centraal weekblad voor de Gereformeerde Kerken in Nederland,** 16 (17) 7, 1968.

SAVARY, Léon. Calvin bewacht die Stadtmauer. **Merian,** 16 (1) 87—89, 1963.

SENARCLENS, Jacques de. Le jeune Calvin. **Revue de theologie et de philosophie, N.S.,** 16 (1) 56—60, 1967.

SPRENGER, Paul. Das Rätsel um die Bekehrung Calvins. Neukirchen, Buchhandlung des Erziehungsvereins, 1960. 100 p. (Beiträge zur Geschichte und Lehre der Reformierten Kirche, 11. Bd.).

STUTTERHEIM, J. F. Die bekering van Calvyn. **Die Brug,** 13 (7) 5—6, 1964.

SUTHERLAND, Nicola Mary. Calvin's idealism and indecision **(In:** Salmon, J. H. M., ed. The French wars of religion; how important were religious factors? Boston, Heath, 1967. p. 14—24).

TESTAMENT van Johannes Calvyn; soos opgestel op 25 April 1564. **Die Kerkblad,** 67 (1750) 8—9, 1964.

VAN DER MOLEN, Gezina Hermina Johanna. Idelette van Buren, de vrouw van Calvijn. **Christelijk vrouwenleven,** 23 (4) 117—; (5) 153—, 1939.

VAN DER WALT, S. C. Die huwelik van Calvyn. **Die Bondsbode,** 11 (92) 11; 14, 1959.

VAN ITTERZON, G. P. Het laatste levensjaar van Calvijn. **Hervormd weekblad — de Geref. Kerk,** 75: 257—259, 1963/64; **De Reformatie,** 39 (35) 275—276, 1964; **Gereformeerd weekblad,** 19 (48) 358—359, 1964.

WEICK, J. D. Idelette von Büren, die Gattin Johannes Calvins. **Der Mennonit** 12: 101-, 1964.

Celebrations, portraits, etc.

ALLIER, Jacques. "Journée Calvin" à Noyon, dans la salle de fêtes de l'hotel de ville, le samedi 23. Mai 1964. **Sócieté de l'histoire du protestantisme français. Bulletin,** 110: 186—191, 1964.

ALLIER, Jacques. Le 4° centenaire de la mort de Calvin. Manifestation au siège de la Société de l'histoire du protestantisme français, le vendredi 22.5. 1964. **Sócieté de l'histoire du protestantisme français. Bulletin,** 110: 157—159, 1964.

ANNIVERSAIRE (400e) de la mort de Jean Calvin. Programme des manifestations. Nouv. Brèves: Calvinisme, evangélisation et prosélytisme. **La revue reformée,** 56, 1964.

AUBERT, Fernand. Un portrait de Calvin jeune. **Societé de l'histoire du protestantisme français. Bulletin,** 85: 55—56, 1936.

BARTH, Karl. Fragments grave and gay. Ed. by Martin Rumscheidt. Tr. by Eric Mosbacher. London, Fontana Library, 1971. "Thoughts on the 400th anniversary of Calvin's death." p. 105—110.

BARTH, Karl. Calvin als Theologe; zum 450. Geburtstag Calvins am 10. Julie 1959. **Evangelisch-lutherische Kirchenzeitung,** 13: 205—206, 1959.

BARTH, Karl. Zum Todestag Calvins. **Evangelische Theologie,** 24: 225—229, 1964.

BENOIT, Jean Daniel. L'année 1559 dans les annales calviniennes. **Revue d'histoire et de philosophie religieuses,** 39: 103—116, 1959.

BIÉLER, André. A propos du quatrième centenaire de la mort de Jean Calvin. **Musées de Genève,** 5: 2—6, 1964.

BILDNISSE Calvins und Zwinglis. **Christliches Kunstblatt,** 51: 253, 1909.

BORNKAMM, Heinrich. Calvin; der grosse Menschenbilder der Reformation. Zum 400. Todestag am 27 Mai. **Sonntagsblatt,** 20: 15, 1964.

BORNKAMM, Heinrich. Calvin. Zum 400. Todestage am 27. Mai 1964. **Ruperto-Carola,** 16 (35) 139—143, 1964.

BROWNSON, M. A. The Calvin celebration in Geneva, and Calvin's city as it is today; personal impression. **Journal of Presbyterian history,** 5 (4) 164—174, 1909.

CALVIN quarter-centenary. Service held in the Church of St. Giles, Edinburgh, May 21, 1909; in commemoration of the 400th anniversary of the birth of John Calvin. London, Blackwood, 1909.

CALVINISMUS und Luthertum. Zum 450. Geburtstag Johannes Calvins. **Kirchenblatt für evangelisch — lutherische Gemeinden,** 109 (7) 115—117; (8) 138—141, 1959.

CALVIJN herdacht in geboorteland (Speciale postzegel in Noyon; tentoonstelling in Parijs) **Centraal weekblad voor de Gereformeerde Kerken in Nederland,** 12 (22) 5, 1964.

CALVYN; na 450 jaar! **Die Kerkbode,** 84 (1) 4, 1959.

CALVYN-JUBILEUM; boodskappe uit verskillende lande. **Woord en daad,** 4 (6) 1, 1959.

CASTIGLIONE, Tommaso Riccardo. Presenza italiena a Ginevra. Il IV centenario dell'Università di Calvino. **Protestantesimo** 14: 231—236. 1959.

COETZEE, Petrus Johannes. Calvyn se ouditorium weer 'n vuurtoring in 'n donker wêreld. **Die Kerkblad,** 64 (1605) 2, 1961.

DELTEIL, Frank. IVe centenaire de la mort de Calvin. **Societé de l'histoire du protestantisme français. Bulletin,** 110: 144—147, 1964.

DOUMERGUE, Paul. Le centenaire de Calvin à Genève. **Foi et vie,** 12: 429—436, 1909.

DREYER, Johannes Gerhardus Martinus. Calvynseëls. **Die Hervormer,** 55 (5) 17, 1964.

DUDDE, W. A. Calvin anniversary at Geneva. **Christian century,** 76: 882—883, 1959.

DUVENAGE, A. Calvyn-herdenking, 1564—1964; Calvyn en die gemeente. **Gereformeerde Kerk in Suid-Afrika. Almanak,** 90: 154—157, 1964.

FABER, Jelle. Drie decennia dienst [Calvin] **De Reformatie,** 39: 261—262; 269—270; 277—278, 1964.

FAST, Heinold. Gott allein die Ehre. Zum 450. Geburtstag von Johannes Calvin. **Junge Gemeinde,** 12 (7) 102, 1959.

GALLICET-CALVETTI, Carla. L'umanesimo di Giovanni Calvino a quattrocento anni della morte. **Vita e pensiero,** 47: 496—504, 1964.

GEERDES, L. K. A pilgrimage to Calvin's birthplace. **The Banner,** 94 (3) 32, 1959.

GEISENDORF, Samuel. Calvin et la clémence [poem] Pour le jubilé de Calvin (1909) [4] p.

GENEVA. Bibliotheque Publique. 400 ans d'iconographie calvinienne, 1564—1964. Exposition organisée par Paul Chaix, avec la collaboration du musée historique de la Réformation. (Geneva, 1964) 11 1.

HAMILTON, W. H. Four-hundredth anniversary [Calvin]. **Scots magazine,** 13: 369—374, 1936.

HAMMING, M. Het Nijmegen van Frankrijk [re Noyon] **Gereformeerd weekblad,** 11: 42, 1955/56.

HANEKOM, Tobias Nicolaas. Die ouditorium van Calvyn. **Die Kerkbode,** 84 (1) 10—12; 15, 1959.

HÄNNY, K. Ein neuentdecktes Calvinbildnis. **Schweizer Sammler,** 9: 65, 1935.

HAVERKAMP, William. Calvijn-herdenking. **De Wachter,** 97 (16) 5; 13, 1964.

HESSELINK, John. Where Calvin lived and worked; reflections. **Reformation review,** 15 (5) 23—28, 1962.

HOMRIGHAUSEN, E. G. The Calvin year. **Theology today.** 19: 377—78, 1959.

HOYOIS, E. Pourquoi commemorer Jean Calvin en Belgique. **Les cahiers calvinistes,** 2 (4) 15—18, 1960.

HUGO, André Malan. Calvyn-herdenking. **Die Kerkbode,** 84 (1) 6—9, 1959.

HUGO VAN DALEN, W. S. Johannes Calvyn herdacht, 1509—1564. Overweging tussen dankbaarheid en onbehagen. **Pennoen,** 9: 4—6, 1964.

JACOBS, Paul. Johannes Calvin; zum 450. Geburtstag des Genfer Reformators. **Evangelische Welt,** 13 (13) 369—372, 1959.

KELLER, Adolf. Das Reformationsdenkmal in Genf. **Christliches Kunstblatt,** 51: 132—149, 1909.

KEMPFF, Dionysius. Calvyn-herdenking. **Die Kerkblad,** 67 (1747) 3; (1749) 2, 1964.

KEMPFF, Dionysius. Johannes Calvyn; 27 Mei 1564—27 Mei 1964. **Die Kerkblad,** 67 (1750) 2—4, 1964.

KLOOSTER, Fred H. The Calvin jubilee at Frankfurt. **Torch and trumpet,** 9 (8) 20—22, 1960.

KRITISCHER Nachtrag zu den Calvin-Jubiläen in Genf. **Freidenker,** 42: 78—79, 1959.

KROON, K. H. Calvijnherdenking, 1959. **Groene Amsterdammer,** 11/7/59.

KRUSCHE, Werner. Ein brennendes Herz für die Kirche; zum 450. Geburtstage Johannes Calvin am 10. Juli. **Zeichen der Zeit,** 13: 294—297, 1959.

KUIJT, P. Calvijn, na 400 jaar herdacht in zijn leven, zijn geschriften, zijn theologie. Gouda, Christelijke Kweekschool, De Driestar, 1964. 27 p. (Koop de waarheid en verkoop ze niet, 17e jg., no. 1).

LARDANS, Daniel R. Genève à l'heure de Calvin. Fêtes commémoratives de la naissance du Reformateur, 1509—1559. Genève, 31 Mai au juin, 1959. Genève, s.à.r.l.) (1959) Contents: photographs.

LEWIS, David. Genfer Feiern beweisen Calvins Modernität. **Der deutsche Hugenott,** 29 (1) 2—4, 1965.

McNEILL, John Thomas. Calvin after 400 years. **Christian century,** 81: 702—704, 1964.

NAUTA, Doede. Een Calvijn-congres. **Centraal weekblad voor de Gereformeerde Kerken in Nederland,** 22 (40) 7, 1974.

NAUTA, Doede. Het sterfjaar van Calvijn. **Centraal weekblad voor de Gereformeerde Kerken in Nederland, 12** (19) 1; 3, 1964.

NEET, H. E. Eine Zitadelle der Reformation; Genf gedenkt des strengen Calvin. **Christ und Welt,** 12 (23) 8, 1959.

PAGEL, Arno. Gott allein die Ehre! Zum 450. Geburtstag von Johannes Calvin. **Die Jugendhilfe,** 57: 235—240, 1959.

PANNIER, Jacques. A Strasbourg il y a quatre siècles; 31 Mars 1939 (Notice sur Calvin) (Carrieres — sous — Possy) La Cause, 1938. 16 p. (Voix de La Cause, Cahier 14/15).

PAP, Istvan & KOVATS, Istvan. Kálvin jubileumí emlékkönyv [Jubilee] Budapest, 1910.

PETER, Rodolphe & ROTT, Jean. Exposition Jean Calvin. Strasbourg, Bibliotheque Nationale et universitaire. **Revue d'histoire et de philosophie religieuses,** 45 (1) 128—155, 1965.

POLMAN, Andries Derk Rietema. Calvijnherdenking te Kampen; Luther en Calvijn. **De Bazuin,** 102 (24) 2, 1959.

POTGIETER, Frederick Johannes Mentz. Calvyn ná 400 jaar. **Nederduitse Gereformeerde teologiese tydskrif,** 5 (3) 129—131, 1964.

Le QUATRIÈME centenaire de la mort de Calvin. Soirée culturelle à Paris au temple du Saint-Esprit, le lundi 25 Mai 1964. **Societé de l'histoire du protestantisme français. Bulletin,** 110: 207—218, 1964.

SCHIPPERS, Reinier. Hervormingsdag 1959; uit het antwoord van Calvijn aan kardinaal Sadoleto. **Belijden en beleven.** 17 (5) 1, 1959.

SCHLIER, R. Diaspora der Christeinheit; Calvin, Jahr 1959. **Die evangelische Diaspora,** 30: 249—254, 1959/60.

SCHORER, Jean. Genf feiert Johann Calvin. **Freies Christentum,** 11: 87—89, 1959.

STAUFFER, Richard. L'hommage à Calvin des Universités de Strasbourg et Berne. **Societé de l'histoire du protestantisme français. Bulletin,** 112: 223—235, 1966.

STICHING „Calvynmuseum" opgericht. **Centraal weekblad voor de Gereformeerde Kerken in Nederland,** 14 (14) 7, 1966.

STUTTERHEIM, J. F. Die Calvynherdenkings in Frankryk en Switserland. **Die Hervormer,** 50 (5) 10; 14, 1959.

TREURNICHT, Andries Petrus. Gedenkposseëls tere ere van Calvyn. **Die Kerkbode,** 93 (26) 829, 1964.

TREURNICHT, Andries Petrus. Die sterfjaar van Calvyn. **Die Kerkbode,** 93 (23) 733, 1964.

VAN DER MUNNIK, J. H. Johannes Calvijn; zijn 450e geboortedag. **Vriend des huizes,** 6: 256—259, 1959.

VAN HALSEMA, Emo. By de Calvijnherdenking. **De Wachter,** 92 (27) 4—5, 1959.

VAN HALSEMA, Emo. Vier honderd jaar geleden, 5 Juni 1959. **De Wachter,** 92 (43) 4—5, 1959.

VROEGINDEWEY, W. Johannes Calvijn; Hervormingsdag, 31 Oktober 1517. Huizen (Bout) [s.j.] 16 p.

WENDEL, Francois. Allocution d'ouverture. **Revue d'histoire et de philosophie religieuses,** 44 (4) 267—269, 1964.

WOLF, Ernst. Calvin, 1564—1964. **Stimme der Gemeinde,** 16: 329—332, 1964.

ZABORSZKY, J. A. I. Calvijn-monument in Boedapest. **Centraal weekblad voor de Gereformeerde Kerken in Nederland,** 12 (31) 2, 1964.

ZEEDEN, Ernst Walter. Johannes Calvin. Zu seinem 400. Todestage am 27. Mai 1564. **Oberrheinische Pastoralblatt,** 65: 138—151, 1964.

Commentaries and studies on books concerning Calvin.

AEBERHARDT, W. Erstausgabe von Calvins Jesajakommentar. **Schweizerisches Gutenberg Museum/ Musée Gutenberg Suisse,** 40: 9—12, 1954.

BAUCHY, I. H. Le nom de Calvin a la salle des thesis. **Societé archéologique et historique de l'Orleanais. Bulletin,** 4: 118, 1966.

BRAK, W. Herlevende Calvijnstudie in Frankrijk. **Gereformeerd weekblad,** 11 (19) 149—150, 1955.

BüSSER, Fritz. Supplementa Calviniana. **Zwingliana,** 12 (9) 683—686, 1968.

COETZEE, Carel Frederik Christoffel. Calvyn en die Skrif. Potchefstroom, Potchefstroomse Universiteit vir Christelike Hoër Onderwys, 1973. 27 p. (Wetenskaplike bydraes van die P.U. vir C.H.O. Reeks F2. Instituut vir die bevordering van Calvinisme. Calvyncauserieë, nr. 1).

DEMURA, Akira. Calvin studies in Japan. **The North-East Asia journal of theology,** 1 (1) 118—125, 1968.

DICKENS, Arthur Geoffrey. Recent books on Reformation and counter reformation. **Journal of ecclesiastical history,** 19 (2) 219—226, 1968.

DU PLESSIS, Lourens Martinus. Calvyn oor die staat en die reg. Potchefstroom, Potchefstroomse Universiteit vir Christelike Hoër Onderwys, 1974. 143 p. (Wetenskaplike bydraes van die P.U. vir C.H.O. Reeks F2. Instituut vir die bevordering van die Calvinisme. Calvyncauserieë, nr. 3).

GRAZZINI, G. Letteratura dei "Raccolti" di Calvino. **Letterature moderne,** 9: 621—637, 1959.

GROSCLAUDE, Pierre. La place de Calvin dans la littérature français. **Societé de l'histoire du protestantisme français. Bulletin,** 110: 160—174, 1964.

HALL, Basil. The Genevan tradition [Re: new works on influence of Calvin and Geneva on other reformers to the end of the 16th century] **Journal of ecclesiastical history,** 20: 111—116, 1969.

HENRY, Carl Ferdinand Howard. Calvin research in this century. **Christianity today,** 9 (25) 1290, 1965.

HIGMAN, Francis Montgomery. The style of John Calvin in his French polemical treatises. (London) Oxford Univ. Press, 1967. 191 p. (Oxford modern languages and literature monographs).

NIJENHUIS, Willem. Tien jaar Calvijn-onderzoek, 1950—1960. **Vox theologica,** 31: 57—69, 1961.

PARKER, Thomas Henry Louis. Calvini opera sed non omnia. **Scottish journal of theology,** 18 (2) 194—203, 1965.

PETER, Rodolphe. Calviniana et alia (nouveaux compléments au repertoire des imprimes genevois de 1550 à 1660) **Bibliotheque d'humanisme et renaissance,** 34 (1) 115—123, 1972.

PETER, Rodolphe. Les éditions de 1562 de l'Institution de la religion chrestienne de Calvin. **Revue d'histoire et de philosophie religieuses,** 54: 31—48, 1974.

PETER, Rodolphe. Jean Calvin prédicateur; notice bibliographique à propos d'un ouvrage récent. **Revue d'histoire et de philosophie religieuses,** 52: 111—117, 1972.

PONTHIEUX, A. Un des plus anciens documents noyonnais concernant Calvin (1536) **Societé de l'histoire du protestantisme français. Bulletin,** 76: 407—411, 1927.

RICHTER, Mario. Recenti studi calviniani (1960—1966) **Rivista di storia e letteretura religiosa,** 3: 99—130 1967.

SALLEY, Claudia Louise. A French humanist's chef-d'oeuvre: The commentaries on Seneca's De clementia, by John Calvin. **Renaissance papers,** 1967: 41—53.

SAVIGNAC, Jean de. Une réédition du De Clementia de Jean Calvin. **La revue reformée,** 21 (84) 39—46, 1970.

SCHOLL, Hans. Ein neuer Zweig in der Calvin-Forschung [Re: Ganoczy: Le jeune Calvin, a.o.] **Kirchenblatt für die reformierte Schweiz,** 124 (7) 97—100, 1968; 124 (8) 114—116, 1968.

SCHWARZ, R. Calvin-Literatur; cine Nachlese. **Kirchenblatt für die reformierte Schweiz,** 25 (28) 1909.

SMELLIE, Alexander. The Reformation in its literature. London & New York, Melrose, [1925] 320 p. Lectures VII & VIII: "Calvin".

STRASSER, Otto Erich. Bücher zum Calvin-Jubiläum **Kirchenblatt für die reformierte Schweiz,** 115: 148—150, 1959.

STRASSER, Otto Erich & WIESER, Gottlob. Neue Calvin-Literatur. **Kirchenblatt für die reformierte Schweiz,** 115: 342—344, 1959.

TEDESCHI, John A. & WILLIS, Edward David. Two Italian translations of Beza and Calvin. **Archiv für Reformationsgeschichte,** 55: 70—74, 1964.

TOURN, Giorgio. Studi Calviniani. **Protestantesimo,** 23: 11—32, 1968.

VAN HALSEMA, Emo. McNeil over Calvijn. **De Wachter,** 92 (44) 4—5, 1969.

VERVLIET, H. D. L. A Calvin catechism printed in 1561 at Paris by Pierre Hamon, Philippe Danfrie and Jean Le Royer **(In:** Studia bibliographica in honorem Herman de la Fontaine Verwey. Under the editorship of S. van der Woude. Amsterdam, Hertzberger, 1966, 1968, p. 370—374).

Das WERK Johannes Calvins im Neukirchener Verl. **Reformierte Kirchenzeitung,** 102: 337—338, 1961.

WIESER, Gottlob. Die Drucklegung von Calvins Predigten; eine Aufgabe für den reformierten Weltbund. **Kirchenblatt für die reformierte Schweiz,** 111: 121—122, 1955.

WIESER, Gottlob. Zur Calvin-Literatur der letzten 50 Jahre. **Kirchenblatt für die reformierte Schweiz,** 115: 217—218, 1959.

Fiction and drama.

BARR, Gladys (Hutchinson) The master of Geneva; a novel based on the life of John Calvin. New York, Rinehart & Winston (1961) 252 p.

BROWN, William & DEN, James. The mountains [a play about Calvin in opposition to Servetus. Grand Rapids, Calvin College, n.d.] 21 1.

DE ROVER, Piet Adriaan. Calvijn, de reus uit Noyon; levensroman. Aalten, De Graafschap, 1962. 191 p.

GERSTNER, Edna. Idelette; a novel based on the life of Madame John Calvin. Grand Rapids, Zondervan [1963] 160 p.

HOLKEBOER, Lois. City of God [a play about John Calvin. Grand Rapids, Calvin College, n.d.] 54 1.

KORT, Wesley A. The open prison [a play about John Calvin. Grand Rap:ds, Calvin College, n.d.] 37 1.

LEROY, F. Voortvarend en oprecht. Goes, Oosterbaan & Le Cointre, 1959. 192 p.

McGINLEY, P. Reformers and Puritans; two sides of Calvin [Poems] **American scholar,** 29: 53—54, 1959/60.

PFENNINGER, Arthur. Pour l'honneur de Dieu; le drama de la vie de Calvin. Adaptation française par Edmond Duméril. [St.-Germain — en — Laye] (Societé Calviniste) (1961) 56 p. (La Revue réformée, no. 41, no. XI, 1960/1).

THARAUD, Jérôme & THARAUD, Jean. La chronique des frères ennemis. Paris, Plon (c1929) 288 p.

VAN AMMERS-KÜLLER, Jo. Het scharlaken wambuis; roman uit de tijd van Johannes Calvijn. Amsterdam, Engelhard, Van Embden (1955) 301 p.

General discussions of Calvin's life and work.

ALBERIGO, Guiseppe. La Riforma Protestante. Milano, Garzanti, 1959. "Giovanni Calvino." p. 188—240.

ALLIER, Jacques. Le rayonnement de Calvin. **La revue reformée,** 15 (60) 37—41, 1964.

ANDERSON, Charles S. The Reformation; then and now. Minneapolis, Augsburg (1966) "The storm moves sou^th; J. Calvin." p. 43—55.

AUGUSTIJN, Cornelis. Calvijn. Den Haag, Kruseman (1966) 127 p. (Helden van de geest, 41).

BACH, Wilhelm Carl. Johann Calvin. Bielefeld, 1909.

BAINTON, Roland Herbert. La lotta per la libertà religiosa. Bologna, Il Mulino, 1969. "Calvin:" p. 54—71.

BAINTON, Roland Herbert. The travail of religious liberty: nine biographical studies. Philadelphia, Westminster 1951. "Calvin". p. 54—71. Also published by Lutterworth, London, 1953.

BAKER, Nathan Larry. A brief introduction to the life and thought of John Calvin. Fort Worth, Tex., Southwestern Baptist Theological Seminary, 1966.

BALZAC, Honoré de. Der Terrorist Calvin. **Die christliche Frau,** 1 (4) 25—29, 1953/54.

BARTH, J. D. Het Calvinistisch beginsel in deszelfs wording door Calvijn. Woerden, Mulder (1926) 136 p.

BAUDRILLART, André. Calvin, Calvinisme (In: Dictionnaire de Théologie Catholique Paris, 1923. t.II. col. 1377—1422).

BAUMAN, Clarence. Gewaltlosigkeit im Täufertum. Eine Untersuchung zur theologischen Ethik des oberdeutschen Täufertums der Reformationszeit. Leiden, Brill, 1968. "Calvin": p. 326—331. (Studies in the history of Christian thought, 3) Thesis, Bonn.

BEARD, Charles. The Reformation of the 16th Century in its relation to modern thought. Lectures delivered at Oxford and in London in April, May and June, 1883. 2nd ed. Williams and Norgate, 1885. Ann Arbor, University of Michigan Press, 1962. "Calvin." p. 242—261.

BEISIEGEL, K. Calvin, der Christ, Theologe, Kirchenmann und Politiker. **Der Evangelist,** 110: 314—315, 1959.

BÉKÉSI, A. Kálvin a népért [Calvin for the people] **Református egyház,** 2: 449, 1959.

BELLOC, Hilaire. How the Reformation happened. London, Cape [1954, 1928] "Calvin": p. 121—143.

BERGIER, Jean François. Calvin **(In:** — I protagonisti della storia universale. Milano, Compagnía Ed. Internazionali, 1966. p. 477—504).

BESTER, G. R. C. Johannes Calvyn; die mens. **Die Voorligter,** 26 (12) 20, 1963.

BÈZE, Theodore de. A discource wrytten by M. Theodore de Beza, conteyning in briefe the historie of the life and death of Maister John Calvin, with the testament and laste will of the saide Calvin, and the catalogue of his books that he hath made. Turned out of Frenche into Eng. by I. S. London, Imprinted for H. Denham for L. Harrison, 1564. [Amsterdam, Theatrum Orbis Terrarum; New York, Da Capo Press, 1972] IV. (unpaged) (The English experience, its record in early printed books published in facsimile, no. 433).

BIRNSTIEL, J. G. Calvin als Mann des Gemüts. **Schweizerisches Protestantenblatt,** 32 (27) 215—216, 1909.

BÖDEKER, Heinrich. Das glühende Herz; Johannes Calvin's Leben für Gott und Menschen. Gladbeck, Schriftenmissions-Verl., 1964. 60 p.

BOISSET, Jean. Les chrétiens séparées de Rome; de Luther à nos jours. Paris, Presses Universitaires de France, 1970. La deuxième generation des reformateurs: "Calvin". p. 71—96. (SUP. L'Historien. 3).

BOISSET, Jean. Histoire du protestantisme. Paris, Presses Universitaires de France, 1970. "Calvin:" p. 52—59. (Que sais-je? 427).

BOISSONNAS, Henri. Le vrai visage de Calvin. **Genava,** 10: 72—83, 1962.

BONTOUX, G. Louis Veuillot et les mauvais maîtres des XVIe, XVIIe, et XVIIIe siècles: Luther, Calvin, Rabelais, Molière, Voltaire, Rousseau, les Encyclopèdistes et libres penseurs. Paris, Perrin, 1919. "Calvin": p. 32—47.

BOWIE, Walter Russell. Men of fire; torch bearers of the Gospel. New York, Harper, 1961. "Calvin": p. 145—156.

BOYER, Charles. La formation de Calvin. **Doctor Communis,** 25: 85—104, 1972.

BRASELMANN, Werner. Der Gehorsam des Calvin **(In:** Der mündige Christ. Hrsg. von Heinrich Giessen, u.A. Stuttgart, Kreuz, 1956. p. 57—60).

BRATT, John Harold. John Calvin; our spiritual father. **The Banner,** 94 (7) 4—5, 1959.

BRATT, John Harold. The life and work of John Calvin **(In:** The rise and development of Calvinism; a concise history. Ed., by John H. Bratt. Repr. Grand Rapids, Eerdmans, 1971 (1964) p. 9—26).

BREZZI, Paolo. Le origini del protestantesimo. Roma, "Ut unum sint" 1961. "Calvino e il suo movimento": p. 148—174 (Ut unum sint, 1).

BRONOWSKI, Jacob & MAZLISH, Bruce. The Western intellectual tradition, From Leonardo to Hegel. Freeport, Books for Libraries Press, 1971. "Calvin": p. 91—99.

BROOME, John. Calvin & Zwingli. Harpenden, Gospel Standard Baptist Trust, 1972. "John Calvin": p. 1—10.

BRUNETIÈRE, Ferdinand. Das Werk Calvins. **Das Wort in der Zeit,** 3: 981—999, 1936.

CADIER, Jean. Calvin. Paris. Presses universitaires de France, 1966. 161 p. (Mythes et réligions, 58).

CADIER, Jean. Calvin sa vie, son oeuvre avec un exposé de sa philosophie [et un choix de textes de Calvin] Paris, Presses universitaires de France, 1967. 114 p. (SUP philosophes).

CADIER, Jean. The man God mastered; a brief biography of John Calvin. Tr. from the French, by O. R. Johnston (Repr.) London, Inter-varsity Fellowship (1964) 187 p.

CALVIN et les Genevois, par un citoyen de Genève — sans parti pris — réponse à la publication du "Monistenkreis" de Genèva, au nom de "quelques personnes qui se préparent a glorifier le célebre Picard". Genève, Libraire Kündig, 1908. 20p.

CAUGHEY, Frank McClure. The sources of the thought and teaching of John Calvin. Pittsburgh, 1937. Thesis — University of Pittsburgh.

CHIMINELLI, Piero. Il Calvinismo. Milano Istituto editoriale Galileo, 1948. 214 p. (Le religioni dell' umanità, 19).

CHUN, Kyung Yun. The life and theological thought of Calvin. (Seoul) Sin-Kyo Chul Pan Sa, 1959- v. In Korean.

COETZEE, Petrus Johannes. Johannes Calvyn; God se gawe. **Die Kerkblad,** 61 (1504) 1—2, 1959.

CRISTIANI, Leon. Calvino et il calvinismo **(In:** Piolanti, A., ed. Il protestantesimo ieri e oggi. Roma, Ferrari [1958] p. 90—107).

DAMBORIENA, Prudencio. Fe catolica e iglesias y sectas de la Reforma. Madrid, Razon y Fe, 1961. "Calvino, y religion reformada": p. 111—138.

DANNENFELDT, Karl H. The church of the Renaissance and Reformation; decline and reform from 1300 to 1600. Saint Louis, Concordia (c1970) "Calvin": p. 91—103. (Church in history series).

DATEMA, S. Uit het leven en werken van Johannes Calvijn; een goed krijgsknecht van Jezus Christus. Rotterdam, Zwagers [ca. 1909] 50 p.

DE HARTOG, Arnold Hendrik. Calvijn. Baarn, Hollandia [n.d.] 48 p. (Groote dogmatici, ser. 1, no. 3).

DELUMEAU, Jean. Naissance et affirmation de la Réforme. Paris, Presses universitaires de France, 1965 "Calvin": p. 110—133. (Nouvelle Clio. L'histoire et ses problèmes, 30).

DE WEERD, H. In de branding der reformatie. Amsterdam, Kirchner (1951) "Calvijn": p. 115—193.

DEWITT, John. John Calvin, the man. **Princeton theological review,** 7: 369—380, 1909.

DE ZEEUW, Pieter. Johannes Calvijn 1509—1564. **Belijden en beleven,** 18 (51) 6; (52) 6; (53) 6, 1961.

DE ZEEUW, Pieter. Johannes Calvijn, de hervormer van Genève. 's-Gravenhage, Willem de Zwijgerstichting, 1965. 102 p.

DILLENBERGER, John. An introduction to John Calvin **(In:** Calvin, Jean. John Calvin; Selections from his writings. Garden City, N.Y., Anchor, 1971. p. 1—20).

DOBIÁŠ, František M. Calvin, Luther, Hus. **Communio viatorum,** 10 (4) 259—268, 1967.

DOOYEWEERD, Herman. Calvijn als bouwer. **Polemios,** 2 (22) (23) 1947.

DOSKER, Henry E. The story of Calvin's life **(In:** Calvin celebration by the Presbytery of Louisville. Addresses delivered at the celebration of the 400th anniversary of the birth of John Calvin. Louisville, Kent., 1909, p. 13—22).

DOUMERGUE, Émile. Jean Calvin; les hommes et les choses de son temps (Repr..) Genève, Slatkine, 1969 (1899—1927).

DREYER, Johannes Gerhardus Martinus. Johannes Calvyn. **Die Hervormer,** 50 (2) 3—4, 1959.

DU PLESSIS, Jacobus Stephanus. Johannes Calvyn; sy historiese betekenis. **Die Kerkblad,** 67 (1750) 6—7, 1964.

DUVENAGE, A. Calvyn; die groot hervormer. **Die Kerkblad,** 61 (1519) 9; 11; 22, 1959.

DUVENAGE, Schalk Carel Willem. Calvyn breek die mensgemaakte skanse om die Heilige Skrif af **(In:** Potchefstroomse Universiteit vir Christelike Hoër Onderwys. Instituut vir die bevordering van Calvinisme. Die atoomeeu; in U lig. Potchefstroom, 1969. p. 23—34).

ELTON, Geoffrey Rudolph. Europa im Zeitalter der Reformation, 1517—1559. Übersetzung [von Reformation Europe, 1517—1559] durch Jürgen Schwarz. Hamburg, Siebenstern Taschenbuch, 1971. "Calvin": V. 2, p. 187—214.

ELTON, Geoffrey Rudolph. Reformation Europe, 1517—1559. London, Collins [1963—1967] "Calvin": p. 210—238. (Fontana history of Europe).

ENGELBRECHT, Barend Jacobus. Calvyn as die grondlegger van die Reformatoriese leer. **Die Hervormer,** 50 (2) 12—13; 16—17; 20, 1959.

EVANS, John. Bywyd ac athrawiaeth John Calfin, gyda detholion lawer o'i waith. Caernarfon, O'Brien Owen, 1909. 111 p.

FARRINGTON, Evelyn Maude (White) Calvin as a literary artist. Belfast, 1945. Thesis (M.A.) — Queen's Univ. of Belfast, 1945.

FARRINGTON, Evelyn Maud (White) Calvin, the modern man. Belfast, Belfast News Letter, 1953. 50 p.

FARRIS, A. L. Significance of John Calvin. **Evangelical churchman,** 55: 377—378, 1959.

FEBVRE, Lucien Paul. Au coeur religieux du XVIe siècle. Paris, Sevpen, 1957. Crayon de Jean Calvin: p. 251—267. Also in Portuguese in: **Revista de historia,** 5 (12) 254—267, 1952.

FONCKE, R. Johannes Calvijn als wonderdoener. **Koninklijke Vlaamse Academie voor Taal- en Letterkunde. Verslagen en mededelingen,** 8, 9, 10: 331—343, 1959 **(Also in:** De Nederduitse 16e eeuwse kroniek, door Johan Oldecop van Hildesheim).

FRY, Charles George. John Calvin; theologian and evangelist. **Christianity today** 115 (2) 59—62, 1970.

FUHRMANN, Paul Traugott. Why Calvin? [n.p., 196-?] 13 p.

GERRISH, Brian Albert. John Calvin (**In:** Gerrish, Brian Albert, ed. Reformers in profile. Philadelphia, Fortress Press (1967) p. 142—164).

GERRISH, Brian Albert. John Calvin and the meaning of reformation (repr.) **Maccormick quarterly,** 21: 114—122, 1967.

GLOEDE, Günter. Johannes Calvin, Reformator und Sammler der zweiten Generation (**In:** Oekumenische Profile; Bruckenbauer der einen Kirche. Hrsg. von G. Gloede (u.a.) Stuttgart, Evangelische Missionsverl., 1961. v. I., p. 51—61).

GLOEDE, Günter. Johannes Calvin; Wortführer des Protestantismus. 4-Aufl. Glessen, Brunnen-Verl. (c1959) 84 p. (Zeugen des gegenwärtigen Gottes, 139—140).

GRAZIA, Gennaro di. Il protestantesimo; nella storia della chiesa. Napoli, Giannini, 1958. "Giovanni Calvino [a.o.]" 271—307.

The GREAT reformer. **Time, 73 (24)** 54—55, 1959.

GREEN, Vivian Hubert Howard. Renaissance and Reformation; a survey of European history between 1450 and 1600. Londcn, Arnold, 1964 [Chapter X, 2, 3; Chapter XV, 2: Calvin, Calvinism, influence of Calvin, the Huguenots].

GRIEB, O. Johannes Calvin und sein Werk. **Neue Blätter aus Süd-Deutschland für Erziehung und Unterricht,** 1909: 129—146.

GROSSMANN, Eberhard. Beiträge zur psychologischen Analyse der Reformatoren Luther und Calvin. Basel 1958. 36 p. Also in **Monatschrift für Psychiatrie und Neurologie,** 132: 274—290, 1956. And in **Confinia psychiatrica,** 1: 17—30, 1958.

HALASKI, Karl. Das Bild Calvins. **Kirchenblatt für die reformierte Schweiz,** 112: 70—72, 1956.

HALL, Basil. John Calvin, humanist and theologian. Rev. ed. (London) Historical Ass., 1967 (c1956). 39 p. (Historical Association, London, General Series, no. 33)

HALLDEN, Erik. Arvet från Calvin? [Heritage of Calvin?] **Tro och liv,** 6: 250—256, 1968.

HAMERSMA, T en DU TOIT, Jacob Daniël. Johannes Calvijn, vader der Gereformeerde kerken; zijn leven en beginselen. Potchefstroom, Gereformeerde Studenten Corps "Veritas Vincet", 1909. 106 p.

HARBISON, Elmore Harris. The Christian scholar in the age of the Reformation. New York, Scribner, c1956 "Calvin": p. 137—164.

HARBISON, Elmore Harris. History and destiny (repr.) **Theology today,** 21: 395—409, 1965.

HARKNESS, Georgia Elma. Calvin and his tradition (**In:** Anderson, William Ketcham, ed. Protestantism; a symposium (Repr.) Freeport, N.Y. Books for Libraries Press (1969, c1944) p. 52—66) (Essay index reprint series).

HARPER, Howard V. Profiles of Protestant saints. Foreword by Richard Cardinal Cushing. New York, Fleet Press, 1968. "John Calvin": p. 17—28.

HAUSS, Friedrich. Väter der Christenheit; 4. Ausg. Wuppertal, Brock-haus, 1973. "Johannes Calvin (1509—1564)": p. 171—179.

HAVERKAMP, William. Calvijn als mens. **De Wachter,** 99 (5) 5; 13, 1966.

HESSELINK, I. John. Catholic character of Calvin's life and work (repr.) **Reformation review,** 19: 13—19, 1965.

HEYNS, Johan Adam. Johannes Calvyn. **Hugenote-Vereniging van Suid-Afrika. Bulletin,** 3: 6—8, 1965.

HILL, David C. Messengers of the King. Illus. by Paul Konsterlie. Minneapolis (1968) "Calvin": p. 35—41.

HILLERBRAND, Hans Joachim. Christendom divided; the protestant reformation. New York, Corpus Publications, 1971. "John Calvin": p. 99—115.

HILLERBRAND, Hans Joachim. Men and ideas in the sixteenth century (2nd print) Chicago, Rand McNally (1969) "Calvin": p. 81—85. (Rand McNally European history series).

HILLERBRAND, Hans Joachim. **ed.** The Protestant Reformation. London, MacMillan, 1968. "Calvin": p. 153—221. (Documentary history of Western civilization).

HOLMQUIST, Hjalmar Fredrik. Luther, Loyola, Calvin i deras reformatoriska genesis; en kyrkhohistorisk parallellteckning. Lund, Gleerup, 1912. 160 p. Thesis — Lunds universitet.

HOLWERDA, Pieter. John Calvin; a good soldier of Jesus Christ. **The Banner,** 79: 1016, 1944.

Un HOMME du XVIe siècle: Calvin. 1509—1564. **Cahiers français,** 40: 12—15, 1959.

HOMMES, Nicolaas Jan. Een machtige rede over Calvijn. **Gereformeerd weekblad,** 11: 101—102, 1955/56.

HOMMES, Nicolaas Jan. Een spotprent op Calvijn. **Gereformeerd weekblad,** 12: 221—222; 228—229, 1956/57.

HOOGSTRA, Jacob T. **ed.** Juan Calvino profeta contemporanéo. Antología ordenada por temas. Ed. por Jacob T. Hoogstra. Grand Rapids, Mich., TSELF, 1973.

HOURTICQ, Denise. Calvin, mon manist, Redner und Schriftsteller [Tr. from Calvin, mon ami] **Die Hugenottenkirche,** 17 (6) 33—35, 1964.

HOURTICQ, Denise. Calvin, mon ami (histoire de la Réforme racontée aux jeunes) Genève, Editions Labor et fides (1970, c1963) 107 p.

HUGHES, Philip Edgecumbe. John Calvin; the man who God subdued (**In:** Puritan and Reformed Studies Conference, 10th London, 1959. "How shall they hear", a symposium. (Southampton) 1960. p. 5—10).

HUGUET, E. De omgangstaal bij Calvijn, vert. door S. Eringa. **Gereformeerd theologisch tijdschrift,** 23: 433—452, 1922/23.

INGWERSEN, Gesina. Johannes Calvijn. (illus.: Tadema) Amsterdam Bijbel Kiosk-Vereeniging (s.j.) 20 p.

ISERLOH, Erwin. Johannes Calvin; Persönlichkeit und Werk (**In:** Handbuch der Kirchengeschichte, Bd. 4: Reformation, katholische. Reform und Gegenreformation. Hrsg. von Hubert Jedin. Freiburg, Herder, 1967. p. 376—405).

IWAND, Hans Joachim. Nachgelassene Werke, IV: Gesetz und Evangelium. München, Kaiser, 1964. "Calvin": p. 359—393.

JELINEK, Emil. Kalwin w gronie reformatorów. **Jednota,** 8: 6—8, 1964.

JOHANNES Calvyn. **Woord en daad,** 8 (41) 1—3, 1965.

JOHNSON, Thomas Cary. John Calvin; who was he? Of what sort was he? What did he do for the world? **Union Seminary quarterly review,** 21 (2) 108—136, 1909/10.

JOHNSON, W. Guy. Calvin. **Churchman,** 50: 30—41, 1936.

JOHNSTON, O. R. Calvin the man **(In:** Puritan and Reformed Studies conference, 15th. London, 1964. Able ministers of the New Testament; papers read. (London, 1965) p. 19—35).

JONES, William M. Reformers from Wittenberg, Strasbourg, Zurich and Geneva in England: 1547—1549. **Hiff review,** 27: 69—73, 1970.

KAEGI, Werner. Jacob Burkhardt über Calvin. **Neue zürcher Zeitung,** 60 (2231) 1964.

KAMPHUIS, J. Zicht op Calvijn [door] J. van Genderen e.a.: boekbespreking. **De Reformatie,** 41: 53—54; 61—63, 69—70; 76—78; 85—86, 1965/66. **(Also in:** Kamphuis, J. Onderweg aangesproken; beschouwingen over kerk, confessie en cultuur. Groningen, Vuurbaak, 1968. p. 158—186).

KEIZER, P. K. Calvin. **(In:** Dutchmen's views on some Christianity questions; with an introd. of H. Colijn [Ed. by the Calvinist Movement in Holland] Kampen, Kok, 1939. p. 38—43.

KEMPFF, Dionysius. Calvyn en sy tyd. **Die Kerkblad,** 67 (1772) 2—3, 1964.

KIK, Jacob Marcellus. Church and state; the story of two kingdoms. New York, Nelson, 1963. "Calvin": p. 71—85.

KNOX, George William. The intellect of Calvin. **The Interior,** 40 (2030) 518—520, 1909.

KODAIRA, N. [Calvin]. Tokyo, United Church Press, 1967 [In Japanese].

KRECK, Walter. Parole et esprit selon Calvin. **Revue d'histoire et de philosophie religieuses,** 40 (3) 215—228, 1960.

KRUGER, M. A. Johannes Calvyn. **Die Bondsbode,** 11 (89) 1—3, 1959.

KUIPER, Herman, Surprises in Calvin. **The Banner,** 96 (2) 19, 22; (4) 6—7, 1961.

KUROSAKA, K. [Calvin studies]. Tokyo, Protestant Pub. Co., 1973. [In Japanese].

KUYPER, H. H. Kerkgeschiedenis; de invloed van Calvijn, cursus 1931/1932. [s.pl., 1932?] 64 1.

KUYPER, H. H. Zuid-Afrika; reisindrukken. Amsterdam, De Herout, 1925. "Lezing over Calvijn": p. 177—191.

LANG, A. Zwingli, Butzer, Calvin als Männer der Weltliteratur. **(In:** Cohn, G. Universitätsfragen und Erinnerungen. Stuttgart, Enke. 1918. p. 7—38).

LANG, August. Zwingli, Butzer, Calvin als Männer der Weltliteratur **(In:** Die religiöse Entwicklung der Menschheit im Spiegel der Weltliteratur. Hrsg. von L. Weber. Gütersloh, Bertelsmann, 1901. p. 277—299).

LANGHOFF, H. Der verkannte Calvin **(In:** Rogge, J. Johannes Calvin, 1509—1564; eine Gabe zu seinem 400 Todestag. Berlin, Evangelische Verlagsanhalt (1963) p. 47—71).

LANSDALE, Marya Hornor. The human side of Calvin. **Century illustrated magazine,** 56: 454—464. 1909.

LEONARD, Emile G. Histoire générale du protestantisme. Paris, Presses universitaire de France, 1961. "Calvin": p. 258—311.

LEONARD, Emile G. A history of Protestantism, ed. by H. H. Rowley [Tr. of Histoire générale du Protestantisme] London, Nelson, 1965. Calvin: p. 292—351.

LIEBETRAUT, Friedrich. Johann Calvin, 1509—1564. **Kirchenblatt für die reformierte Schweiz,** 8 (2) 43—45, 1951.

LINDEBOOM, Antonius Margarites. Hallo jongelui, vandaag over Calvijn. **Gereformeerde weekblad,** 19 (10) 61—62, 1963.

LLEWELLIN, Frederick George. Reformers and the Reformation. London, Jakeman & Carner, 1921. "Calvin": p. 65—117.

LOHSE, Bernhard. Calvin als Reformator, **Luther,** 35: 102—117, 1964.

LORTZ, Joseph. Johannes Calvin und die Reformation in Genf **(In:** Kleine Reformationsgeschichte; Ursachen, Verlauf, Wirkung. Von Joseph Lortz und Erwin Iserloh. Freiburg, Herder, 1971 (1969) p. 182—195) (Herder-Bücherei, Bd. 342).

L'OSTALIER, L. Armoiries de Calvin. **Chercheurs et curieux,** 5 (52) 421—422, 1955.

LUZZI, Giovanni. Giovanni Calvino. **Fede e vita,** 1: 181—186, 1909.

MAAS, Hermann. Johannes Calvin, 1509—1564 **(In: Philipp Melanchton.** Gedenkschrift zum 400. Todestag des Reformators, 19. April 1560/1960. Hrsg. von Georg Urban. 2. erw. Aufl. Bretten, 1960. p. 109—111).

MACGIFFERT, Arthur Cushman. Protestant thought before Kant [Repr.] New York, Harper, 1962 (c1961, c1911) "Calvin", p. 81—99. (Harper torch books, 93).

MACKENZIE, Donald. John Calvin. **The Presbyterian register,** 16: 89—99, 1934.

MACKINNON, James. Calvin and the Reformation. New York, Russel, 1962. 302 p.

MARICHAL, Walter M. L'homme Calvin. **Les cahiers calvinistes,** 6/7 (24) 7—13, 1965.

MASNAI, László. Kálvin Jànos as Ige fényeben [Johannes Calvin im Lichte des Wortes] **(In:** Kalvin és a kálvinismus; tanulmányok. Az Institutio négyszázadik évfordulójára irták a Debreceni M. Kir. Tisza István — Tudomány — egyetem Református Hittudományi Karának tanarai és doctorai. Debrecen, Debrecen Szabad Királyi Város és a Tiszántúli Református Egyhazkerület Konyvnyomda — Vállalata, 1936. p. 22—32).

MATTHEWS, Walter Robert. John Calvin **(In:** Hearnshaw, Fossey, John Cobb, ed. The social and political ideas of some great thinkers of the Renaissance and the Reformation; a series of lectures delivered at King's College, University of London. With a pref. by Ernest Barker; repr. New York, Barnes & Noble, 1967. p. 193—215).

MEETER, H. Henry. John Calvin; the great reformer. **The Banner,** 94 (28) 6—7, 1959.

MERLE D'AUBIGNE, Charles. John Calvin; the man and his times **(In:** Calvin memorial addresses, delivered before the General Assembly at Savannah, May 1909, in observance of the birth of John Calvin. Richmond, Va., Presbyterian Committee of Publication (n.d.) p. 261—280).

MEIJERINK, H. J. Vreemdelingschap naar de Schriften. IX, 15: Calvyn. **De Reformatie, 45 (40)** 317—318, 1970.

MIDDENDORP, Willem. Der Bote seines Königs. **Reformatio,** 8: 259—260, 1959.

MÖNCH, W. Calvin; ein religiöse und politische Charakterkopf aus dem Zeitalter der französischen Renaisance. **Geistige Arbeit,** 1: 3, 1937.

MOOS, R. W. von. Begegnung mit Calvin. **Central blatt,** 76: 652—659. 1936.

MORII, M. [Calvin]. Tokyo, Maki, 1964. [In Japanese].

MOSSE, George Lachmann. The Reformation; 3rd ed. New York, Holt, Rinehart and Winston (c1963) "Calvin": p. 57—80. (Berkshire studies in European history).

MURALT, Leonhard von. Johannes Calvin **(In:** Der Historiker und die Geschichte; ausgewählte Aufsätze und Vorträge (Festgabe für Leonhard von Muralt. Hrsg.: Fritz Büsser, Hanno Helbling und Peter Stadler) Zürich, Verlag Berichthaus, 1960. p. 97—101).

NEAL, Fred Warner. John Calvin; the man and his ministry. **(In:** A symposium: John Calvin. On the occasion of the 450th anniversary of his birth and the 400th anniversary of the final edition of the Institutes. Three addresses delivered to the Memphis Presbytery. Memphis, Tenn., 1959. p. 15—23).

NEILSON, George Alexander. Twelve Reformation heroes. London, Pickering & Inglis, 1960. "Calvin": p. 67—73.

NEUSER, Wilhelm Heinrich. Calvin. Berlin, De Gruyter, 1971. 121 p. (Sammlung Göschen, Bd. 3005).

NEWMAN, A. H. The Calvinism of Calvin. **Review and expositor,** 6 (10) 562—566, 1909.

NIJENHUIS, Willem. Ecclesia Reformata; studies on the Reformation. Leiden, Bril, 1972. "Calvin's life and work in the light of the idea of tolerance": p. 115—129, (Kerkhistorische bijdragen, dl. 3).

OLIN, John C. Calvin **(In:** New Catholic Encyclopedia. New York, McGraw-Hill, 1966. v. 2, 1087—90).

OLSON, Bessie Goldie. John Calvin; a great statesman. Chicago, Van Kampen, c1946. 47 p. (Hall-of-fame series).

PABLO, Jean de. Wahrheit gegen Dichtung. Berlin, Hugenottenmuseum, 1964. 6 p. (Sonderdruck aus **Die Hugenottenkirche,** 17 (6) 1964).

PAISLEY, Ian R. K. Three great reformers. (Belfast, Puritan) [1968] "Calvin": p. 15—30.

PARIS, James. Ouvriers et champions de la réformé en Suisse. Neuchâtel, Delachaux & Niestle, 1917. 93 p. "Esquisse publiée á l'occasion de jubilé de la Réformation, sous les auspices de la Conference des églises réformées de la Suisse et dédiée par elle aux Protestants suisses." "Jean Calvin, organisateur de l'église de Genève et du protestantisme français," p. 61—78.

PARKER, Thomas Henry Louis. The Church of England and Calvin. [An appreciation of Calvin as statesman and theologian]. **Theology,** 31: 91—94, 1950.

PARKER, Thomas Henry Louis. Portrait of Calvin. Tr. by Ch. Ch. Kim. Seoul, CLSK 1960. 137 p. [In Korean].

PERRIRAZ, Louis. Histoire de la théologie reformée française. Neuchâtel, Messeiler, 1961. "Calvin": t.

4 p. 17—36; "Le calvinisme": t.4, p. 36—68.

PICOT, Albert. Portrait de Calvin. **Les cahiers protestants,** 43: 52—85, 1959.

PONT, A. D. Johannes Calvyn; 'n lewensskets. **Die Hervormer,** 52 (11) 5—6; 18—19, 1962.

PONT, A. D. Oor die kerkhervormer Johannes Calvyn. **Nederduitsch Hervormde Kerk van Afrika. Almanak,** 1965: p. 30—37.

POTGIETER, Frederick Johannes Mentz. Ernstige verdraaiing in geskiedenishandboek vir hoërskole: het Calvyn mense na die brandstapel gestuur? **Roeping,** 17 (3) 3; (4) 10, 1969.

POTGIETER, J. H. L. S. Johannes Calvyn. **Lantern,** 9: 154—165, 1959.

PRAAMSMA, Louis. Calvin and his contributions to the Reformation. **Torch and trumpet,** 14 (6) 4—6, 1964.

PRAAMSMA, Louis. Calvin as man and as Christian. **Torch and trumpet,** 7: 6—9, 1959.

PREUSS, H. Calvin und seine Gesetzgebung. **Kirchliche Zeitschrift,** 60: 321—326, 1936.

PRINS, Pieter. Etwas über Calvin und Calvinismus. Huldreich Zwingli (von J. E. Goudappel) Hendrik de Cock (von F. Dresselhuis) 3 Vorträge (Serfhennersdorf) Selbstverl. des altreformierten Jünglingsblattes, 1934. "Calvin": p. 3—14.

PRÜFER, A. Albrecht. Calvins Sprache. **Die Hugenottenkirche,** 19 (11) 49—50; (12) 53—54, 1966.

PRUZSINSZKY, P. Kálvin János. **Református egyház,** 1, 1909.

RAMM, Bernard. Varieties of Christian apologetics. Grand Rapids, Mich., Baker, 1961. "Calvin": p. 163—178.

RAWLINS, A. J. B. Die denker van Genève. **Die Voorligter,** 27 (5) 12, 1964.

REED, Richard Clark. Calvin's contribution to the Reformation **(In:** Calvin memorial addresses, delivered before the General Assembly at Savannah, May 1909, in observance of the birth of John Calvin. Richmond, Va., Presbyterian Committee of Publication. [n.d.] p. 15—36).

REID, William Stanford. Calvin's interpretation of the Reformation. **Evangelical quarterly,** 29: 4—22, 1957.

REID, William Stanford. The Genevan revolutionary. **Evangelical quarterly,** 32 (2) 66—78, 1960.

REITSMA, Carl J. John Calvin. **The Presbyterian guardian,** 41: 12—13, 1972.

RHEE, Jong-Sung. Calvin's life and thought. Seoul, Presbyterian Board of Education, 1968. 222 p. [In Korean].

RILLIET, Jean Horace. Calvin, 1509—1564. Paris, Fayard, 1963. 283 p. (Les temps et les destins).

RITTER, Gerhard. Die neugestaltung Europas im 16 Jahrhundert. Die kirchlichen und staatlichen Wandlungen im Zeitalter der Reformation und der Glaubens. Kämfe, Tempelhof (c1950) "Calvin": p. 186—198.

ROBINSON, William Childs. The Reformation; a rediscovery of grace. Michigan, Eerdmans (c1962) "Calvin": 96—118.

ROGGE, Joachim. Aus Calvins Schriften und Briefen, sowie aus Zeugnissen seiner Zeitgenossen, zusammen gestelt und übers. **(In:**

Rogge, J. Johannes Calvin, 1509—1564; eine Gabe zu seinem 400. Todestag. Berlin, Evangelische Verlagsanhalt (1963) p. 98—153).

ROTT, Jean. Documents strasbourgeois concernant Calvin. **Revue d'histoire et de philosophie religieuses,** 44 (4) 290—331, 1964. **(Also in:** Regards contemporians sur Jean Calvin. Actes du colloque Calvin, Strasbourg, 1964. Paris, Presses Universitaires de France, 1965. p. 28—73) (Cahiers R.H.P., 39).

RÜCKERT, Hanns. Einleitung **(In:** Predigten über das 2. Buch Samuelis, von Johannes Calvin. Hrsg. von Hanns Rückert. Neukirchen Kreis Moers, Neukirchener Verl. der Buchhandlung des Erziehungsvereins, 1961. p. vii—xxxix) (Supplementa Calviniana, 1).

RÜCKERT, Hanns. Vorträge und Aufsätze zur historischen Theologie. Tübingen, Mohr (Siebeck) 1972. "Calvin": p. 165—173.

RUST, Hans. Johann Kalvin. Leipzig, Quelle Meyer, 1926. 48 p. (Religionskundliche Quellenbücherei).

SANFILIPPO, Paolo. Calvino. Firenze, Comandi, 1935. 87 p.

SÄNGER, Walter. Zum Reformationsfest; ein Mann der sein Herz Gott opferte: Johannes Calvin, 1509—1564. **Der evangelische Religionslehrer an der Berufsschule,** 9—10: 21—27, 1953.

SAVIGNAC, Jean de. Un Calvin trop peu connu. **Les cahiers calvinstes,** 16 (5) 9—14, 1963.

SCHALK. Adolph. Catching up with Calvin and Zwingli. **U.S. Catholic & jubilee,** 35: 19—26, 1970.

SCHLIER, Richard. Calvins Bedeutung für die evangelischen Glaubensgenossen in der Zerstreuung zur Zeit der Gegenreformation. **Die evangelische Diaspora,** 27: 226—238, 1956/57. **(Also in:** Um Diaspora-Dienst und Diaspora-Fragen; Bruno Geissler dem Achtzigjährigen. Hrsg. von P. W. Gennrich. Kassel, 1958. p. 196—209).

SCHMIDT, Albert Marie. John Calvin and the Calvinistic tradition. Tr. by Ronald Wallace. New York, Harper (1960) 192 p. (Men of wisdom, M.W. 10).

SCHNEIDER, Arthur. Blick in das Herz Calvins. **Die Wartburg,** 34: 261—270, 1935.

SCHOLTEMEIJER, Herman. Johannes Calvyn: die stryder vir die eer van God. 2e dr. Potchefstroom, Pro Rege, 1973. 102 p.

SENYATSI, Charles Phuti. Bophelo bja Jean Calvin. Bloemfontein, N.G. Sendinguitg. (pref. 1970) 69 p.

SINGER, Charles Gregg. John Calvin; his roots and fruits. Philadelphia, Presbyterian and Reformed Pub. Co., 1967. 70 p. (International library of philosophy and theology. Philosophical and historical studies series) **(Also in:** Encyclopedia of Christianity, V. II).

SMITH, Samuel David. John Calvin and worldly religion. **Lexington theological journal,** 3: 65—74, 1968.

SMYTH, Thomas. Complete works; v. 3. New ed., rev. and ed. Philadelphia, Presbyterian Board of Publication, 1908. "Calvin and his enemies; a memoir of the life, character and principles of Calvin": p. 319—403.

SOMMER, Carl Ernst. Johannes Calvin, 1509—1564. **Der Evangelist,** 110: 315—316, 1959.

STAEDTKE, Joachim. Giovanni Calvino; formazione e realizzazione. Tr. [of Johannes Calvin] par A. Frioli. Roma, Edizioni: Paoline, 1971. (Storia e personalità, 20).

STAEDTKE, Joachim. Johannes Calvin; Erkenntnis und Gestaltung. Göttingen, Musterschmidt-Verl. (c1969) 114 p. (Persönlichkeit und Geschichte, Bd. 48).

STALKER, James. Calvin as reformer and his ideals **(In: Service held by the General Assemblies of the Church of Scotland and the United Free Church of St. Giles, Edinburgh, in commemoration of the fourth hundreth anniversary of the birth of John Calvin. Edinburgh, 1909. p. 27—36).

STAUFFER, Richard. Calvins Menschlichkeit. Zürich, EVZ (c1964) 71 p. (Theologische Studien, Hft. 79).

STAUFFER, Richard. L'humanité de Calvin. Neuchâtel, Delachhaux & Niestle, 1964. 68 p. (Cahiers theologiques, 51).

STAUFFER, Richard. L'humanité de Calvin. **Societé de l'histoire du protestantisme français. Bulletin,** 110: 152—156, 1964.

STAUFFER, Richard. The humanness of John Calvin. Nashville, Abingdon, 1971 96 p.

STEELE, Wilbur Fletcher. Calvin the heretic. **Methodist review,** 91: 551—561, 1909.

STEIGER, Manfred. Über die literarische Bedeutung Calvins. **Reformatio,** 8 (5/6) 357—361, 1959.

STEINMETZ, Max. Johann Calvin; Mensch, Werk, Wirkung. **(In:** Weite Welt und breites Leben; Festschrift der Universitätsbibliothek der Friedrich Schiller-Universität, Jena, zum 80. Geburtstag von prof. dr. Karl Bulling, am 24 Juli 1965. Leipzig, Bibliographisches Institut, 1965. p. 251—264) (Zentralblatt für Bibliothekwesen. Beihft. 82).

STEPHAN, Raoul. Gestalten und Kräfte des französischen Protestantismus. Aus den Franz von Gerda Onken-Joswick und Franz Oesterwitz. Mit einer Vorw. von Marc Boegner. München, Claudius-Verl., 1967. 369 p. Der Weg Calvins. **(Also in: Der deutsche Hugenott,** 31 (3) 66—73; 31 (4) 99—108, 1967).

STRASSER, Erich. Die Weltoffenheit Calvins **(In:** Universität Bern. Johannes Calvin. Akademische Feier der Universität Bern zu seinem 400. Todestag. Bern, Haupt, 1965. p. 7—19) (Berner Universitätsschriften, Hft. 13).

STRASSER-BERTRAND, O. E. Johannes Calvin **(In:** Schmidt, W. Gestalten der Reformation. Wuppertal, Jugenddienst-Verl. (1967) p. 87—95).

STRONG, J. Selden. The essential Calvinism. Boston, Pilgrim Press (1909) "Calvin": p. 19—134.

STUPPERICH, Robert. Geschichte der Reformation. (München) Deutscher Taschenbuch Verl. (1967) "Calvin": p. 230—244.

TAYLOR, Henry Osborn. Thought and expression in the sixteenth century. 2nd ed., rev. (repr.) New York, Ungar, 1959 (1920) "Calvin": v. 1., p. 384—427.

TAZELAAR, J. P. Johannes Calvijn; de man van Genève. **De Spiegel,** 3 (40) 319; (43) 338, 1904.

TAZELAAR, J. P. Johannes Calvijn; een boekje voor de Zondagschool. Heusden, Meerburt, 1909. 24 p.

THEMUDO LESSA, Vicente. Calvino, 1509—1564, sua vida sua obra. Sao Paulo, Casa Editôra Presbiteriana, 1969.

TILLICH, Paul. Vorlesungen über die Geschichte des christlichen Denkens. Teil 1: Urchristentum bis

Nachreformation. Hrsg. und übers. von Ingeborg C. Henel, Stuttgart, Evangelisches Verlagswerk, 1971. "Johannes Calvin": p. 275—289. Original title: A history of Christian thought, ed. by Carl E. Braaten. New York, Harper & Row, 1968.

TODD, John M. Reformation. Garden City, N.Y., Doubleday, 1971. "France, Switzerland and Calvin to 1542": p. 275—313.
"Europe 1532—64; from the Peace of Nuremberg to the death of Calvin": p. 314—328.

TOWNS. Elmer L. The Christian hall of fame. Grand Rapids, Baker Book House, 1971. "John Calvin, 1509—1564" p. 52—55.

TRANDA, Bogdan. Po czterech wieach. **Jednota,** 8: 4—5, 1964.

TRAUB, Hellmut. Calvin; der Herrscher **(In:** Motive des Glaubens; eine Ideengeschichte des Christentums in 18 Gestalten [Hrsg. von Johannes Lehmann] Hamburg, Furche-Verl. (1968) p. 111—117).

TROCMÉ, Etienne. Une révolution mal conduite. **Revue de l'histoire des religions,** 39 (2) 160—168, 1959.

VANCE, James I. John Calvin, the citizen (and other contributions on Calvinism, by D. B. Brummitt, J. Victor and F. W. Perkins) **Religious digest,** 2 (5) 49—60, 1936.

VAN DE POL, Willem Hendrik. World Protestantism [Tr.: Het wereldprotestantisme] New York, Herder & Herder, 1964. "Calvin": p. 126—186.

VAN DER VYVER, Gert Christoffel Petrus. Calvyn in historiese perspektief. **Die Kerkblad,** 67 (1772) 3—4, 1964.

VAN DER WALT, B. Johannes Calvyn; donker bladsye uit die geskiedenis van Calvyn; Calvyn die leidsman van martelare; die karikatuur van Calvyn. **Die Bondsbode,** 16 (19) 4—5, 1964.

VAN HALSEMA, Thea (Bouma) Meet John Calvin. **The Banner,** 94 (16) 32; (17) 20; (18) 18; (19) 20; (20) 20; (22) 15, 1959.

VAN TIL, Cornelius. Calvin as controversialist. **Torch and trumpet,** 9 (3) 5—9, 1959.

VENTER, Erasmus Albertus. Calvyn en die Calvinisme. Bloemfontein, SACUM, 1972. 53 p.

VIÉNOT, John. Histoire de la Réforme Française des origines à l'Edit de Nantes. Paris, Fishbacher, 1925. "Calvin": p. 177—206.

VIERNEISEL, E. J. Johannes Calvin. **Hochland,** 38: 195—206 [1941?].

VINAY, Valdo. La riforma protestante. Brescia, Paideia, 1970. 479 p. "Giovanni Calvino e la riforma nella Svizzera francese": pp. 139—200 (Biblioteca di cultura religiosa, 20).

VUATAZ, Roland. Calvin face à la musique de son temps. Genève, 1968. 148 l. Thesis-Genève.

WALKER, Williston. John Calvin; the organiser of reformed Protestantism, 1509—1565 (With a bibliographical essay by J. T. McNeill) New York, Schocken Books, 1969. 456 p.

WALTY, J. N. Bulletin d'histoire des doctrines; la Reforme au XVIe siècle: Calvin, Bucer, Erasme, Zwingli. **Revue des sciences philosophiques et théologiques,** 53 (1) 114—139; (2) 341—367, 1969.

WATANABE, K. [Calvin and Calvinists] Tokyo, Komine, 1971 [In Japanese].

WEBER, Otto. Johannes Calvin; Gestalter der Kirche. **Der evangelische Erzieher,** 12: 1—11, 1960.

WEBER, Otto. Die Treue Gottes in der Geschichte der Kirche. Neukirchen, Neukirchener Verl. des Erziehungsvereins, 1968. "Johannes Calvin; Gestalter der Kirche": p. 1—18. (Beiträge zur Geschichte und Lehre der reformierten Kirche, 29).

WENCELIUS, Léon. Trois pionniers de l'humanisme français au XVIe siècle. Mainz, Kupferberg [1948] 50 p. (Universitas Maguntina; Reden und Aufsätze, 6).

WHALE, John Seldon. The Protestant tradition; an essay in interpretation. Cambridge, University Press, 1962. "Calvin": p. 119—171.

WIESER, Gottlob. Calvin als Leiter der Kirche. **Kirchenblatt für die reformierte Schweiz,** 115: 242—246, 1959.

WITT-GUIZOT, François Jean Henry de. Pour la foi et pour la patrie; études et discours. Paris, 1912. "A propos de Calvin": p. 123—135.

WOLF, Ernst. Calvins Stellung innerhalb der Reformation und ihrer Theologie. **Die Evangelische Kirche in Deutschland,** 21: 7—12, 1960.

WOLF, Ernst. Johannes Calvin. **Der deutsche Hugenott,** 22: 66—75, 1958.

WOLF, Ernst. Der sehr unbequeme Reformator. Zum 400. Todestag Calvins. **Junge Kirche,** 25: 308—314, 1964.

WOODS, D. W. John Calvin; his place in history. **Lutheran quarterly.** 39: 552—565, 1909.

WOUDSTRA, Marten H. Johannes Calvijn; in volle zin katholiek. **Church and nation.** 3: 65, 1958.

ZILKA, F. Jan Kalvín; zivot a dílo. Ke c tyrstaleté památce jeho narození napsal F. Zilka. V. Praze, Comenia, 1909. 117 p. (Comenium, 20).

ZIMMERMAN, Karl. Johannes Calvin. **Freies Christentum,** 16: 79—81, 1964.

Theology: General and smaller subjects.

AINSLEE, James Lyon. The doctrine of orders in the Reformed Churches in the 16th and 17th centuries. Edinburgh, 1935. 285 p. Thesis — Edinburgh Univ., 1935.

AKAGI, Y and KURAMATSU, I. [Theology of Luther and Calvin] Tokyo, United Church Press, 1964. [In Japanese].

BARTH, Karl. Calvin als Theologe. **Theologische Literaturzeitung.** 84: 241—244, 1959; **Deutsches Pfarrerblatt,** 59: 241—242, 1959; **Reformatio,** 8: 317—318, 1959.

BRILLENBURG WURTH, Gerrit. Calvyn en die koninkryk van God. **Die Kerkblad,** 62 (1570) 6—7, 13, 1960.

BRILLENBURG WURTH, Gerrit. Calvijn en het koninkrijk Gods. **De Bazuin,** 102 (25) 1—2, 1959.

BROWN, Francis. Calvin as a theologian. **Century illustrated magazine,** 56: 465—467, 1909.

CARBONNIER, Jean. Droit et théologie chez Calvin **(In:** Universität Bern. Johannes Calvin. Akademische Feier der Universität Bern zu seinem 400. Todestag. Bern, Haupt, 1965. p. 18—31) (Berner Universitätsschriften, Hft. 13).

COCHRANE, Arthur C. John Calvin and nuclear war. **Christian century,** 79: 837—839; 1039, 1962.

COURVOISIER, Jaques. Calvin und die Juden; zu einem Streitgespräch **(In:** Calvin und die Juden; ihr Gegenüber vom Apostelkonzil bis heute. Hrsg. von W.-D. Marsch und K.

Thieme. Mainz, 1961. p. 141—146).

CRISTIANI, Léon. L'insurrection protestante; l'église de 1540 à 1623. Paris, Fayard, 1961. Calvin: Chapter 5. (Je sais, je crois, 76).

CRISTIANI, Léon. The revolt against the church; tr. by R. F. Trevett. London, Burns & Oates. c1962. 142 p. (Faith and Fact books, v. 77).

CRISTIANI, Léon. La rivolta protestante; tr. by G. Auletta. Catania, Paoline. 1962. 174 p.

FROST-CHRISTENSEN, Rose-Marie. Calvin og teokratiet. **Dansk teologisk tidsskrift,** 34: 256—284, 1971.

FRYE, Roland Mushat. God, man and Satan; patterns of Christian thought and life in Paradise lost, Pilgrim's progress and the great theologians. Princeton, Princeton Univ. Press, 1960. 184 p.

GAFFIN, Richard B. Calvin and the sabbath. Chestnut Hill, Pa., 1962. 234 1. Thesis- Westminster Theological Seminary.

GANOCZY, Alexandre. Calvin; théologien de l'église et du ministère. 445 p. (Unam sanctam, 48).

GEORGE, A. R. The theology of Calvin. **Expository times,** 63 (12) 375—376, 1951/52.

GRENSTED, L. W. The theology of Calvin. **Church quarterly review,** 155 (317) 406—407, 1954.

HALL, Charles A. M. With the spirit's sword; the drama of spiritual warfare in the theology of John Calvin. Richmond, Va., John Knox Press (c1968) 227 p. (Basel studies of theology, no 3) Thesis — Basel.

HESSELINK, I. John. Calvin und Heilsgeschichte **(In:** Oikonomia. Heilsgeschichte als Thema der Theologie. Oscar Cullmann zum 65. Gebürtstag gewidmet. Herausgeber: Felix Christ. Hamburg, Reich, 1967. p. 163—170)

JAMES, William Stanley. The significance of the category of form in the theology of John Calvin. Edinburgh, 1951. 258 l. Thesis — Edinburgh, Univ., 1951.

JOHNSON, Robert Clyde. Authority in Protestant theology. Philadelphia, Westminister, 1959. "Calvin": p. 42—62.

KITAMORI, K. [Theology of the Reformation] Tokyo, Protestant Pub. Co., 1960. [In Japanese].

KLOOSTER, Fred H. John Calvin; the theologian. **Torch and trumpet,** 9 (1) 4—6, 18, 1959.

KORTH, K. Johann Calvin und seine Theologie. **Die Christenlehre,** 17: 100—116, 1964.

KRUSCHE, Werner. Die Theologie Calvins **(In:** Rogge, J. Johannes Calvin, 1509—1564; eine Gabe zu seinem 400. Todestag, Berlin, Evangelische Verlagsanstalt (1963) p. 27—46).

KUIJT, P. Calvijn's Bijbelse theologie in 't kort. Gouda, Christelijke Kweekschool „De Driestar", 1964. 12 p. (Bibliotheek "Koop de waarheid en verkoop ze niet", 17e jg. no. 7).

LA VALLEE, Armand Aimee. Calvin's criticism of scholastic theology. Cambridge, Mass., 1967. 319 1. Thesis-Harvard Univ.

LEITH, John Haddon. Calvin's polemic against idolatry **(In:** Soli Deo Gloria; New Testament studies in honor of William Childs Robinson. Ed. by J. Mc. Dowell Richards. Richmond, Va., John Knox Press, 1968. p. 111—124).

LEITH, John Haddon. John Calvin;

theologian of the Bible. **Interpretation,** 25 (3) 329—345, 1971.

LEWIS, E. Ridley. Calvin and tradition. **Theology,** 23: 220—222, 1942.

LITTLE, David. The theology of order; a study in the relation between theological and social organizational formulations in the thought and practices of John Calvin [Cambridge, Mass, 196-?] 57 1.

LOCHER, Gottfried Wilhelm. Calvin spricht zu den Juden. **Theologische Zeitschrift,** 23 (3) 180—196, 1967.

MINTON, Henry Collin. Calvin the theologian **(In:** Calvin memorial addresses, delivered before the General Assembly at Savannah, May 1909, in observance of the birth of John Calvin. Richmond, Va., Presbyterian Committee of Publication (n.d.) p. 37—56).

MÜLLER, Jacobus Johannes. Sektebeskouing deur Calvyn. **Die Voorligter,** 27 (10) 11, 1964.

MÜLLER, Jacobus Johannes. Die sekte-beskouing van Calvyn. **Nederduitse Gereformeerde teologiese tydskrif,** 5 (3) 159—167, 1964.

MURRAY, John. Calvin as theologian and expositor. [London] 1964. 12 p. (Annual lecture of the Evangelical Library, 1964).

NIESEL, Wilhelm. Die Theologie Calvins. Tr. by J.-S. Rhee. Seoul, CLSK, 1974. 300 p. [In Korean].

NUOVO, Victor Lawrence. Calvin's theology; a study of its sources in classical antiquity. New York, 1964. 212 1. Thesis-Columbia Univ.

OBERMAN, Heiko Augustinus. Extra dimension in the theology of Calvin. **Journal of ecclesiastical history,** 21 : 43—64, 1970.

OBERMAN, Heiko Augustinus. Infinitum capax finiti. Kanttekeningen bij de theologie van Calvijn. **Vox theologica,** 6 : 165—174, 1965.

PACKER, James Innell.. Calvin the theologian. **International reformed bulletin,** 2 (4) 15—25, 1959 **(Also in:** Duffield, G.E., ed. John Calvin. Apleford, Courtenay (1966) p. 149—175) (Courtenay studies in Reformation theology, 1).

PARTEE, Charles Soul in Plato Platonism, and Calvin. **Scottish journal of theology,** 22 (3) 278—296, 1969.

PATERSON, W. P. The theology of Calvin. **(In:** Service held by the General Assemblies of the Church of Scotland and the United Free Church of St. Giles, Edinburgh, in commemoration of the fourth hundreth anniversary of the birth of John Calvin. Edinburgh, 1909. p. 37—55).

PELKONEN, J. Peter. The teaching of John Calvin on the nature and function of the conscience. **Lutheran quarterly,** 21 (1) 74—88, 1969.

REID, John Kelman Sutherland. Diakonia in the thought of Calvin **(In:** Service in Christ; essays presented to Karl Barth on his 80th birthday. Ed. by J. I. McCord and T.H.L. Parker. London, Epworth, 1966. p. 101—109) Also published by Eerdmans, Grand Rapids.

REUTER, Karl. Das Grundverständnis der Theologie Calvins, unter Hinbeziehung ihrer geschichtlichen Abhängigkeiten (Neukirchen-Vluyn) Neukirchener Verl., 1963- v. (Beiträge zur Geschichte und Lehre der Reformierten Kirche, 15 Bd.).

ROTTENBURG, Isaac C. Calvin and world upheaval. **Reformed** review, 13 : 23—29, 1959.

SAXER, Ernst. Aberglaube, Heuchelei und Frömmigkeit; eine Untersuchung zu Calvins reformatorischer Eigenart. Zürich, Zwingli (c1970) 290 p. (Studien zur Dogmengeschichte und systematischen Theologie, Bd. 28) Thesis-Zürich.

SCHULZE, Martin. Meditatio futurae vitae; ihr Begriff und ihre herrschende Stellung im System Calvins; ein Beitrag zum Verständnis van dessen Institutio. Aalen, Scientia, 1971. (Leipzig, 1901) 89 p. (Studien zur Geschichte der Theologie und der Kirche, Bd. 6, Hft. 4).

SCHÜTZEICHEL, Heribert. Die Glaubenstheologie Calvins. München, Heuber, 1972. 276 p. (Beiträge zur ökumenischen Theologie, Bd. 9).

STOB, Henry. John Calvin on doctrine and life. **Reformed journal,** 9 : 14, 1959.

SUBILIA, Vittorio. Liberta e dogma secondo Calvino e secondo i riformati italiani **(In:** Roma, Facolta Valdesi di Teologica. Ginevra et l'Italia; recolta di studi promossa dalla Facolta Valdesi di Teologica di Roma a cura Delio Cantimori [et al] Firenze, Sansoni [1959] p. 191—214) (Bibliotheca Storica Sansoni, 34).

TAVARD, George Henri. Holy Writ or Holy Church; the crisis of the Protestant Reformation. New York, Harper, 1959. "Calvin": p. 98—111.

TENTLER, Thomas Nathaniel. The problem of anxiety and preparation for death in Luther, Calvin and Erasmus. Cambridge, Mass., 1961. "Calvin": p. 67—106. Thesis — Harvard Univ., Cambridge.

THOMAS, George Hasson. Revelation, faith and doctrine; a study based on the theology of John Calvin, Friedrich Schleiermacher and Karl Barth. Ann Arbor, University Microfilms, 1961. "Calvin": p. 3—98. Thesis—Vanderbilt Univ., Nashville, Tenn.

TILLEY, A. The literature of the French Renaissance. Cambridge, University Press, 1904. I Ch. 9—"Calvin".

VAN GELDER, Herman Arend Enno. The two reformations in the 16th century; a study of the religious aspects and consequences of Renaissance and Humanism. Den Haag, Nijhoff, 1961. "Calvin": p. 267—273.

VAN GENDEREN, J. Calvijns dogmatisch werk **(In:** Zicht op Calvijn [door] J. van Genderen [e.a.] Amsterdam, Buijten & Schipperheijn, 1965. p. 9—46) (Christelijk perspectief, dl. 7).

VASADY, Bela. The main traits of Calvin's theology [in Hungarian] Grand Rapids, Mich., Eerdmans, 1951. 43 p.

VISSER, Anna Jippe. Calvijn en de Joden. 's-Gravenhage, Boekencentrum [1963?] 26 p. (Miniaturen, no 2) (Bijlage van het maandblad **Kerk en Israel,** 17 (5) 1963).

WALKER, William Garnett. The doctrine of the ascension of Christ in Reformed theology. Nashville, Tenn., 1968. Calvin, p. 11—79. Thesis — Vanderbilt Univ. Nashville, Tenn.

WALZER, Michael. Exodus 32 and the theory of holy war; the history of a citation. **Harvard theological review,** 61 : 1—14, 1968.

WARFIELD, Benjamin Breckinridge. Calvin as a theologian and Calvinism today. London, Evangelical Press (1969) 32 p.

WEBB, R. A. Calvin; exegete and theologian **(In:** Calvin celebration by the Presbytery of Louisville. Addresses delivered at the celebration of the 400th anniversary of the birth of John Calvin. Louisville, Ken., 1909. p. 23—33).

WENDEL, Francois. Calvin; the

origins and development of his religious thought. Tr. by Philip Mairet (3rd impression. London) Collins (1969, c1963) 383 p. (Fontana library. Theology and philosophy).

WENDEL. Francois. Calvin; Ursprung und Entwicklung seiner Theologie (Die übers. in Deutsche besorgte Walter Kickel) Neukirchen-Vluyn, Neukirchener Verl. des Erziehungsvereins (c1968) 339 p. Original title: Calvin, Sources et evolution de sa pensée religieuse.

WHITNEY, Harold J. The theology of Calvin for today. Grand Rapids, Zondervan, 1959. 203 p.

WISKERKE, J. R. Calvijn en de doperse leer van „zieleslaap" en „zieledood." **De Reformatie,** 36 (7) 49—50; (8) 57—59, 1960.

WISKERKE, J. R. Calvijn over „paradijs" en „hemel". **De Reformatie,** 36 (11) 81—82; (12) 89—90, 1960.

WISKERKE, J. R. De substantie van de substantie-ellende III, 6: Mislukt beroep op Calvijn. **De Reformatie,** 42 (13) 101, 1967.

WOUDSTRA, Marten H. Calvijn over „het Calvinisme" **Church and nation,** 3: 131, 1959.

1.3. WORKS ABOUT CALVIN: VARIOUS SUBJECTS.

Art.

CHRISTEN, Ernest. Calvin et l'art. **Almanach Jean Calvin,** 46—50, 1936.

DE VRIES, S. J. Calvin's attitude towards art and amusement **Calvin forum,** 17(6): 101—107; 1952.

DOUMERGUE, Émile. L'art et le sentiment dans l'oeuvre de Calvin; trois conférences prononcées à Genève dans la salle de la Reformation [et] à Lausanne dans le temple de Saint-Francois en avril 1902. Genève, Slatkine Repr., 1970 (1902) 85 p.

DUBOSE, Lucius Beddinger. The transcendent vision; Christianity and the visual arts in the thought of John Calvin. Louisville, 1965. 176 1. Thesis — Louisville. Presbyterian Theological Seminary.

GENEUX, Paul L'esthétique de Calvin. **Les cahiers protestants,** 30: 387—401, 1946.

LESLIE, Robert Homer. Music and the arts in Calvin's Geneva; a study of the relation between Calvinistic theology and music and the arts, with special reference to the Cent-cinquante pseaumes (1583) of Pascal de l'Estocart. Montreal, 1969. 395, 415 1. Thesis, McGill Univ., Montreal.

ROTHUIZEN, Gerard Theodoor. Calvijn en de cultuur. **Centraal weekblad voor de Gereformeerde Kerken in Nederland,** 12 (19) 2, 1964.

ROTHUIZEN, Gerard Theodoor. Calvijn en de kunst. **Centraal weekblad voor de Gereformeerde Kerken in Nederland,** 18 (9) 6, 1970.

WENCELIUS, Léon. Les réformateurs et l'art. **Societé de l'histoire du protestantisme français. Bulletin,** 117 (1—3) 11—37, 1971.

Baptism see Sacraments.

Bible: authority and inspiration of the Scripture.

ALLISON, Leon McDill. The doctrine of Scripture in the theology of John Calvin and Francis Turretin. Princeton, N. J. 1958. 106 1. Thesis-Princeton Theological Seminary.

ASHLEY, Clinton Matthew. John Calvin's utilization of the principle of accomodation and its continuing significance for an understanding of biblical language. Fort Worth, Tex., 1972. 222 1. Thesis—Southwestern Baptist Theological Seminary.

BATES, G. Typology of Adam and Christ in John Calvin. **Hartford quarterly,** 5: 42—57, 1965.

BÉKÉSI, A. Kálvin, mint irásmagyarázó (Calvinus exegeticus) **Theologiai szemle,** 2: 273—279, 1959.

BESSE, Georges. Saint Augustin dans les oeuvres exégètiques de Jean Calvin. Recherches sur l'autorité reconnue à saint Augustin par Calvin en matière d' exégèse **Revue des etudes Augustiniennes,** 6: 161—172, 1960.

BOOT, Izaäk. De allegorische uitlegging van het Hooglied voornamelijk in Nederland; een onderzoek naar de verhouding tussen Bernard van Clairvaux en de nadere reformatie. Woerden, Zuijderduijn, 1971. "De hoogliedinterpretatie bij Luther, Calvijn en Beze": p. 93—126. Thesis—Utrecht.

BOUT, H. Calvijn en het Oude Testament. **Theologia reformata,** 3: 6—31, 1960.

BRUBAKER, Lauren Edgar. A study of John Calvin's doctrine of revelation. New York, 1942. 168 1. Thesis-Union Theological Seminary, New York.

CALLADINE, Daniel. L'unité des deux testaments dans la théologie de Calvin. Paris, 1949. 140 1. Thesis-Faculté libre de théologie protestante de Paris.

COETZEE, Carel Frederik Christoffel. Calvyn en die skopus van die Skrif. **Woord en daad,** 15 (137) 16—17; (138) 8—9, 1974.

COETZEE, Carel Frederik Christoffel. Die skopus van die Skrif by Calvyn; 'n dogmatiese verkenning van sekere hoofstukke uit die Institusie van Calvyn. Potchefstroom, 1972. 139 1. Thesis- P.U. vir C.H.O., Potchefstroom.

DEAN, Eric Thomas. Calvin and Barth on Scripture and tradition. Chicago, 1959. 165 p. Thesis- University of Chicago.

DEAN, Eric Thomas. Relation between Scripture and tradition; theoretical statements by Calvin and Barth. **Encounter,** 23: 277—291, 1962.

DEMSON, D. E. Calvin's theology of the Word of God; an examination of the Christocentic character of Calvin's theology, with reference to his teaching concerning man's knowledge of God, the providence of God, the law of God, and the life of the Christian man. [Oxford, 1964?] Thesis-Oxford University.

DU TOIT, Andries Bernardus. Calvyn as Bybelverklaarder. **Die Kerkbode,** 108 (17) 571—572; 574, 1971.

EDWARDS, Charles Eugene. Calvin on inerrant inspiration; excerpts from authorities. **Bibliotheca sacra,** 88: 465—475, 1931.

FLOOR, Lambertus. Calvyn se hermeneutiek in sy betekenis vir ons tyd. **In die Skriflig,** 4 (14) 3—20, 1970.

FORSTMAN, H. Jackson. Word and spirit, Calvin's doctrine of Biblical authority. Stanford, Calif., Stanford Univ. Press, 1962. 178 p.

GALLUS, Tibor. Der Nachkomme der Frau in der altlutheranischen Schriftauslegung (Ein Beitrag zur Geschichte der Exegese von Gen. 3 : 15) T.I.: Der Nachkomme der Frau — Gen. 3: 15 — in der Schriftauslegung von Luther, Zwingli und Calvin. Klagenfurt, Corinthia, 1964, 172 p.

GARNET, P. Some aspects of John Calvin's New Testament exegesis as seen in his commentary on the Epistle to the Romans. [Sheffield, 1962/63?] Thesis- Sheffield.

GAUTERON, Ellis. L'autorité de la Bible d'après Calvin. Montauban (Orphelius Imprimeurs) 1902. 92 p. Thesis- Faculté de théologie protestante, Montauban.

GILBERT, J. H. The Bible of Calvin. **Biblical world,** 27: 344—347, 1906.

GORDON, Cecil Earle. A critical and comparative examination of the idea of revelation in the theology of John Calvin and Karl Barth. New York, 1939. 136 1. Thesis-Union Theological Seminary, New York.

GREIJDANUS, Seakle. Prof. Dr. J. A. Cremer's boek over Calvijns schriftbeschouwing en behandeling. **Gereformeerd theologisch tijdschrift,** 27 (9) 353—366, 1926/27.

GRIN, E. L'unité des deux testaments selon Calvin. **Theologische Zeitschrift,** 17: 175—187, 1961.

GROENEWALD, Evert Philippus. Calvyn en die Heilige Skrif. **Nederduitse Gereformeerde teologiese tydskrif,** 5 (3) 131—141, 1964.

HAROUTUNIAN, Joseph. Calvin as biblical commentator **(In:** Calvin, Jean. Commentaries. Newly tr. and ed. by Joseph Haroutunian, in collaboration with Louis Pettibone Smith. London, S.C.M. (1958) p. 15—50) (Library of Christian classics, v. 23).

HOOK, W. J. Calvin on the authority of the Word of God. [Dublin? 1964/65?] 80 l. Thesis- Trinity College, Dublin.

HUGHES, Philip Edgecumbe. Inspiration of Scripture in the English reformers, illuminated by John Calvin. **Westminister theological journal,** 23: 129—150, 1961.

ISTAFANOUS, Abd-el-Masih. Calvin's doctrine of Biblical authority. Princeton, N. J., 1963. 243 1. Thesis- Princeton Theological Seminary.

KEESECKER, William F. The wisdom of the Psalms; selections and expositions based on commentary by John Calvin. New York, World Pub. Co. [1970] 60 p. (World inspirational books).

KRAUS, Hans Joachim. Calvins exegetische Prinzipien. **Zeitschrift für Kirchengeschichte,** 79 (3) 329—341, 1968.

KRAUS, Hans Joachim. Vom Leben und Tod in den Psalmen; eine Studie zu Calvins Psalmkommentar **(In:** Leben angesichts des Todes; Beiträge zum theologischen Problem des Todes. Helmut Thielicke zum 60. Geburtstag. Tübingen, 1968. p. 27—46).

LEATH, J. O. John Calvin's method of interpreting the New Testament. **Methodist quarterly review,** 78: 105—113, 1929.

LILLEY, Alfred Leslie. Religion and revelation; a study of some moments in the effort of Christian theology to define their relations, being the Paddock lectures of 1931. London, Society for promoting christian knowledge [1932] "Calvin": p. 79—.

MARICHAL, Walter M. Calvin et l'écriture sainte. **Les cahiers calvinistes,** 22 (12) 7—16 1964.

MARKARIAN, John Jacob. The Calvinistic concept of the Biblical revelation in the theology of B.B. Warfield. Madison, N. J., 1963. 261 1. Thesis- Drew Univ. Madison, N. J.

MICKELSON, John K. The relationship between the Commentaries of

John Calvin and his Institutes and the bearing of that relationship on the study of Calvin's doctrine of Scripture. **Gordon Review,** 5 (4) 155—168, 1959.

MIEGGE, Mairo. I talenti messi a profitto. L'interpretazione della paraboli dei denari affidati ai servi dalla Chiesa antica a Calvino. Urbino, Argalià editore (1969) 142 p. (Pubblicazioni dell' Università di Urbino) Testi e saggi a cura dell' Istituto di Filosofia.

MONSMA, Timothy M. The Bible as spectacles in Calvin's apologetics. Grand Rapids, 1962. 105 l. Thesis-Calvin Seminary.

MURRAY, John. Calvin on scripture and divine sovereignty. Grand Rapids, Mich., Baker Book House (c1960) 71 p.

NICOLE, J. M. Calvin, homme de la Bible. **Revue de theologie et d'action évangéliques,** 3: 310—327, 1943. **(Also in:** Bourilly, E., ed. Calvin et la Réforme en France. Ed. rev. (No. spécial de la revue "Etudes evangeliques, 1964 Aix-en-Provence". p. 42—59.))

NIJENHUIS, Willem. Paulus en Calvijn **(In:** De dertiende apostel en het elfde gebod; Paulus in de loop der eeuwen. Onder red. van G. C. Berkouwer en H. A. Oberman. Kampen, Kok, 1971. p. 88—101) **(Also in: Rondom het Woord,** 13: 82—95, 1971).

ORR, James. Calvin's attitude towards and exegesis of the Scriptures **(In:** Calvin memorial addresses, delivered before the General Assembly at Savannah, May 1909, in observance of the birth of John Calvin. Richmond, Va., Presbyterian Committee of Publication [n.d.] p. 89—106).

PACKER, James Innell. Calvin; a servant of the Word **(In:** Puritan and Reformed Studies, Conference, 15th, London, 1964. Able ministers of the New Testament; papers read at conference, Dec. 1964. [London, 1965] p. 36—55).

PARKER, Thomas D. The interpretation of Scripture, I: a comparison of Calvin and Luther on Galatians. **Interpretation,** 17: 61—75, 1963.

PARKER, Thomas Henry Louis. Calvin, the biblical expositor. **Churchman,** 78: 23—31, 1964. **(Also in:** Duffield, G. E., ed. John Calvin. Appleford, Courtenay [1966] p. 176—189) (Courtenay studies in Reformation theology, 1).

PARKER, Thomas Henry Louis. Calvin's New Testament Commentaries. London, SCM, 1971. 208 p.

PARKER, Thomas Henry Lewis. The sources of Calvin's New Testament. **Zeitschrift für Kirchengeschichte,** 73: 272—289, 1962.

PETER, Rodolphe. Calvin and Louis Bude's translation of the Psalms **(In:** Duffield, G. E., ed. John Calvin. Appleford, Courtenay [1966] p. 190—209) (Courtenay studies in Reformation theology, 1).

PRAAMSMA, Louis. Calvin on Scripture. **Torch and trumpet,** 9 (4) 4—7, 1959.

PRUST, Richard C. Was Calvin a biblical literalist? **Scottish journal of the theology,** 20 (3) 312—328, 1967.

PURY, Roland de. Pour marquer les distances; simple note une exégèse de Calvin et de Luther. **Foi et vie,** 65 (1/2) 42—45, 1966.

RAY, R. Witness and Word. **Canadian journal of theology.** 15: 14—23, 1969.

REED, Richard Clark. The gospel as taught by Calvin. Richmond, Va.,

Presbyterian Committee of Publications [n.d.] 157 p.

REID, John Kelman Sutherland. The authority of Scripture; a study of the Reformation and post-Reformation understanding of the Bible. London, Methuen [1957] "Calvin": p. 29—55.

RICKABAUGH, Homer Tyndale. Calvin's witness to the Bible as religious authority. Richmond, Va., Union Theological Seminary, 1962. 176 1. Thesis- Union Theological Seminary, Richmond, Va.

RICKER, Marilla M. The four gospels. East Aurora, N.Y., The Roycrofters, 1911. "Calvin": p. 77—94.

RUSSEL, S. H. Calvin and the messianic interpretation of the Psalms. **Scottish journal of theology,** 21 (1) 37—47, 1968.

SCHELLONG, Dieter. Calvins Auslegung der synoptischen Evangelien. München, Kaiser, 1969. 343 p. (Forschungen zur Geschichte und Lehre des Protestantismus, 10. Reihe, Bd. 38).

SCHULZE, Ludolf Ferdinand. Die Skrifbeskouing van die Reformatore. **In die Skriflig,** 4 (13) 28—43, 1970.

SPENCER, Robert E. A comparative examination of the idea of revelation in the theology of John Calvin and Karl Barth. New York, 1964. 102 1. Thesis- The Biblical Seminary in New York.

STADTLAND-NEUMANN, Hiltrud. Evangelische Radikalismen in der Sicht Calvins; sein Verständnis der Bergpredigt und der Aussendungsrede, Matth. 10 (Neukirchen-Vluyn) Neukirchener Verl., 1966. 155 p. (Beiträge zur Geschichte und Lehre der Reformierten Kirche, Bd. 24).

STEVENS, James D. Calvin's interpretation of Romans 12. Dallas, Tex., Dallas Theological Seminary, 1971. 48 1. Thesis- Dallas Theological Seminary.

VAN DER WALT, F. Calvyn oor die hermeneutiese reël ten opsigte van nuuskierigheid en spekulasie. **In die Skriflig,** 6 (23) 36—38, 1972.

VAN RENSBURG, S. P. Calvyn as eksegeet. **Die Hervormer,** 50 (2) 7—8, 1959.

VERHOEF, Pieter Adriaan. Luther and Calvin's exegetical library. **Calvin theological journal** 3 (1) 5—20, 1968.

VISCHER, Wilhelm. Calvin, exégète de l'Ancien Testament. **Etudes theologiques et religieuses,** 40 (4) 213—231, 1965.

WALCHENBACH, John Robert. The influence of David and the Psalms on the life and thought of John Calvin. Pittsburgh, 1969. 105 1. Thesis- Pittsburgh Theological Seminary.

WALLACE, Ronald S. Calvin the expositor. **Themelios,** 2 (1) 32—37, 1963; **Christianity today,** 8 (17) 782—784, 1964.

WATTERSON, Aulton Douglas, Jr. The view of the inspiration of the Bible in Martin Luther and John Calvin. Louisville, 1958. 110 1. Thesis- Southern Baptist Theological Seminary, Louisville.

WOOD, Arthur Skevington. The principles of biblical interpretation; as enunciated by Irenaeus, Origen, Augustine, Luther and Calvin. Grand Rapids, Zondervan, 1967. "Calvin": p. 85—96.

WOUDSTRA, Marten H. Calvin's dying bequest to the church; a critical evaluation of the commentary on Joshua. Grand Rapids, Mich., Calvin Theological Seminary, (pref.

1960) 46 p. (Calvin Theol. Sem., Monograph series, 1).

Christ and Christology.

COSTE, Henri. Le probleme de l'incarnation dans les chaptires 6 à 17 du livre II de l'Institution de la religion chrétienne. Quelques aspects de la christologie de Calvin Genève, 1949. 125 1. Thesis- Genève.

DE WIT, J. De grootste fout in Calvijns leer. Commentaar over het boek van G. C. Berkouwer: De persoon van Christus. (Hardinxveld Giessendam) [1967] 118 p.

DOMINICÉ, Max. Connaisance de Jésus-Christ [d'après Calvin] **Foi et vie,** 32: 597—612, 1930.

DU TOIT, Daniël A. „Neergedaal ter helle. . .”; uit die geskiedenis van 'n interpretasieprobleem. Kampen, Kok, 1971. „Calvyn”: p. 30—35. Thesis—Vrije Universiteit, Amsterdam.

FERGUSON, G. R. The body of Christ in the Reformed tradition, with special reference to the period from Calvin to the Westminister Confession. [Cambridge? 1965/66?] Thesis- Cambridge Univ.

HOOGLAND, Marvin P. Calvin's perspective on the exaltation of Christ in comparison with the post-reformation doctrine of the two states. Kampen, 1960. 221 p. Thesis-Vrije Univ., Amsterdam.

KLEMPA, William J. The obedience of Christ in the theology of John Calvin. Edinburgh, 1962, 408 1. Thesis-Edinburgh Univ.

KRATZ, W. Erniedrigung und Erhöhung Jesu Christi im Zeugnis Calvins. Bonn, 1958. Thesis- Bonn.

OGLESBY, William Barr Jr. The Christology of John Calvin and Emil Brunner. Richmond. Va., 1940. 101 1. Thesis- Union Theological Seminary Richmond, Va.

RAKOW, Mary. Christ's descent into hell: Calvin's interpretation. **Religion in life,** 43: 14—35, 1973.

ROMANE-MUSCULUS, Paul. L'image de Jésus-Christ dans les églises et la doctrine réformées. **Foi et vie,** 36: 803—817, 1935.

STAEDTKE, Joachim. Die Lehre von der Königsherrschaft Christi und den zwei Reichen bei Calvin. **Kerygma und Dogma,** 18 (3) 202—214, 1972.

SWEETING, Maurice. De l'imitation de Jesus-Christ d'après Calvin. Paris, 1939. 83 1. Thesis- Facultè libre de theologie protestante de Paris.

TYLENDA, Joseph N. Christ the mediator; Calvin versus Stancaro. **Calvin theological journal,** 8: 5—16, 1973.

WILLIS, Edward David. Calvin's catholic christology; the function of the so-called extra-Calvinisticum in Calvin's theology. Leiden, Brill, 1966. 164 p. (Studies in medieval and Reformation thought, v. 2).

Church see also State and Church.

Church: general.

ALONSO, Juan José Hernández. Pensamiento de Juan Calvino sobre la iglesia de Dios. **Ciencia Tomista,** 99: 103—133, 1972.

BAKER, Alvin L. Calvin's doctrine of the visible and invisible church. Dallas Tex., 1973. 63 1. Thesis-Dallas Theological Seminary.

BERKOUWER, Gerrit Cornelis. Calvin and the church. **Free University quarterly,** 4 (4) 247—252, 1959.

BOADEN, J. M. The church in the theology of John Calvin. [Cambridge? 1965/66?] Thesis- Cambridge Univ.

BOTHA, C. J. Wanneer mag die kerk skeur? Die antwoord van Calvyn [Samevatting van: Die noodsaaklikheid waarom die kerk hervorm moet word, vir Ryksdag van Spiers, 1543] **Kruispunte,** 5 (6) 2—5, 1970.

BURKHART, John Ernest. Kingdom, church and baptism; the significance of the doctrine of the church in the theology of John Calvin. [Los Angeles?] 1959. 260 1. Thesis-University of Southern California, Los Angeles.

COETZEE, Petrus Johannes. Calvyn sien die kerk in 'n suiwer lig. **Die Kerkblad,** 61 (1516) 6—8, 1959.

CONGAR, Yves Marie Joseph. Vraie et fause réforme dans l'église. 2 éd. rev et corrigée. Paris, Du Cerf, 1950. "Calvin": p. 388—396.

DE JONG, Jerome. Calvin and church unity. **Church herald,** 26: 18, 30, 1969.

DE KOSTER, Lester Roland. Keep the church out of what? **Christian century,** 84: 404—407, 1967.

DE VRIES, W. G. Centrum en grenzen der kerk [Re: Calvin and discipline in the church; influence of Bucer and Baptists] **De Reformatie,** 46: 25—44, 1971.

DUVENAGE, Schalk Carel Willem. Die wese van die kerk volgens Calvyn. **Koers,** 26 (11) 377—384, 1959.

DIJK, Klaas. Calvyn en die diens van die kerk. **Die Kerkblad,** 62 (1555) 7—8; 10, 1960.

GANOCZY, Alexandre. Calvin, théologien de l'église et du ministère. Paris, du Cerf, 1964. 447 p. (Unam sanctam. 48).

GANOCZY, Alexandre. Ecclesia ministrans; dienende Kirche und kirchlicher Dienste bei Calvin (Deutsch von Hans Sayer) Freiburg, Herder (1968) 438 p. (Ökumenische Forschungen. 1. Ekklesiologische Abteilung, Bd. 3) Original title: Thèologien de l'église et du ministère.

GUELFUCCI, Pierre. Calvin, pasteur et homme d'église. **Revue de theologie et d'action évangéliques,** 3: 328—350, 1943. **(Also in:** Bourilly, E., ed. Calvin et la Réformée en France. Ed. rev. (No. spècial de la revue "Etudes evangeliques," 1964) p. 60—82).

HANEKOM, Tobias Nicolaas. Kerk en kerkbegrip by Calvyn. **Nederduitse Gereformeerde teologiese tydskrif,** 5 (3) 149—159 1964.

HULSE, John M. The doctrine of the church in the theology of John Calvin. Pittsburgh, Pa., Pittsburgh Theological Seminary, 1965. 104 1. Thesis-Pittsburgh Theological Seminary.

HURLEY, Michael. The church in Protestant theology; some reflections on the fourth book of Calvin's Institutes **(In:** Flanagan, Donal, ed. The meaning of the church. Dublin, Gill, 1966. p. 110—143).

KNOX, E. A. Historical importance of the difference between Luther's doctrine of the church and Calvin's. **Churchman,** 50 (10) 274—282, 1930.

KÖNIG, Adrio. Gedagtes oor die kerk by Calvyn. **Nederduitse Gereformeerde teologiese tydskrif,** 7 (2) 104—110, 1966.

KUIPER, Rienk Bouke. Calvin's conception of the church. **Torch and trumpet,** 9 (6) 7—12, 1959.

MCDONNELL, Kilian, Ecclesiology of John Calvin and Vatican II. **Religion in life,** 36: 542—556, 1967.

MACGREGOR, Geddes. Corpus Christi; the nature of the church according to the Reformed tradition. London, Macmillan, 1959. "Calvin": p. 43—65. Thesis-Oxford Univ.

MACLEOD, John. Calvin's idea of the church in its bearing on our history. Paper read before the General Assembly, Free Church of Scotland, 22nd May, 1909. [n.p., 1909?] 12 p.

MCNEILL, John Thomas. John Calvin; doctor ecclesiae **(In:** The heritage of John Calvin, ed. by John H. Bratt. Grand Rapids, Eerdmans, 1973. p. 9—22). (Heritage Hall Lectures, 1960—1970) (Heritage Hall publications, no 2).

MANSSON, Nicolaas. Calvin och gudstjänsten. En historisk översikt och en skiss av Calvin syn pá församlingens gemensamma andakt. Stockholm, Verbum, 1970. 144 p.

METCALFE, G. Calvin's doctrine of the church. [Bangor? 1963/64?] Thesis-Wales.

MILNER, Benjamin Charles. Calvin's doctrine of the church. Leiden, Brill, 1970. 210 p. (Studies in the history of Christian thought, v. 5) Thesis-Harvard Univ.

MOOI, Remko Jan. Het kerk- en dogmahistorisch element in de werken van Johannes Calvijn. The church, and dogmahistorical aspect of the works of John Calvin. Wageningen Veenman, 1965. 406 p. Thesis-Utrecht.

NAUTA, Doede. Calvijns afkeer van een schisma **(In:** Ex auditu verbi. Theologische opstellen aangeboden aan Prof. Gerrit C. Berkouwer ter gelegenheid van zijn vijfentwintigjarige ambtsjubileum als hoogleraar in de Fakulteit der Godgeleerdheid van de Vrije Universiteit te Amsterdam. Kampen, 1965. p. 131—156).

PATTERSON, Robert Glasgow. The church as vehicle of grace in the theology of John Calvin. New Haven, Conn., 1958. 333 p. Thesis-Yale Univ.

PEDERSEN, P. L. Luthersk og reformert kyrksyn. **Norsk teologisk tidsskrift,** 49: 65—76, 1948.

PETER, James Fletcher. The ministry in the early church, as seen by John Calvin. **Evangelical quarterly,** 35: 68—78, 133—143, 1963.

PEW, J. Howard. Calvin's influence in church affairs. **Christianity today,** 6 (16) 9—11, 1962.

RIDDLE, Franklin Ray, Calvin's doctrine of the church. Richmond. Va., 1959. 101 l. Thesis-Union Theological Seminary, Richmond, Va.

ROGGE. Joachim. Anmerkungen zum Kirchenbergriff Calvins. Zum 400. Todestag des Genfer Reformators. **Zeichen der Zeit.** 18: 180—186, 1964.

RÜCKERT, Hanns. Volkskirche und Bekenntniskirche bei Calvin. **Deutsche Theologie,** 2: 242—255, 1935. **(Also in:** Vorträge und Aufsätze zur historischen Theologie. Tübingen, Mohr (Siebeck) 1972).

SENARCLENS, Jacques de. De la vraie église selon Jean Calvin. Genève, Labor et Fides, 1965. 54 p. (Les cahiers du renouveau, 27).

TONKIN, John Maxwell. The church and the secular order in Reformation thought. New York, Columbia Univ. Press, 1971. "Calvin": p. 93—130.

TONKIN, John Maxwell. The Protestant Reformation and the institutional church. Madison, N. J., 1968. Calvin: p. 143—200. Thesis-Drew Univ., Madison.

TRIMP, Cornelis. Calvijn over de kerk. **De Reformatie,** 39 (34) 263—265, 1964.

VINAY, Valdo. Ecclesiologia di Giovanni Calvino con particolare riguarda alla indagine catholica e protestante più recente. Roma, Facoltà Valdese di Teologia, 1971. 116 l.

VINAY, Valdo. Ecclesiologia ed etica politica in Giovanni Calvino. **Protestantesimo,** 26 (3) 129—149, 1971.

WALKER, George Stuart Murdoch. Calvin and the church. **Scottish journal of theology,** 16: 371—389, 1963.

WEBER, Otto. Die Treue Gottes in der Geschichte der Kirche. Neukirchen, Neukirchener Verl. des Erziehungsvereins, 1968. "Calvin": p. 19—104. (Beiträge zur Geschichte und Lehre der reformierten Kirche, Bd. 29).

WEBER, Otto. L'unité de l'église chez Calvin. **Revue de theologie et de philosophie, N.S.,** 9 (2) 153—165, 1959.

Church: discipline and policy.

BABUT, Jacques. La notion calvinienne dans l'église et du gouvernement spirituel. Paris [1925?] 72 l. Thesis-Faculté libre de th.ologie protestante de Paris.

BRUSTON, H. La discipline ecclésiastique réformée dans la pensée de Calvin. Lézau 1936.

CASWELL. R. N. Calvin's view of ecclesiastical discipline **(In:** Duffield, G. E. ed., John Calvin. Appleford, Courtenay (1966) p. 210—226) (Courtenay studies in Reformation theology, 1).

CASWELL, R. N. The theory and practice of Calvinistic church discipline. Belfast 1960. 435 l. Thesis-Queen's Univ. Belfast.

COURVOISIER, Jaques. La dialectique dans l'ecclésiologie de Calvin. **Revue d'histoire et de philosophie religieuses,** 44 (4) 348—363, 1964. **(Also in:** Regards contemporains sur Jean Calvin. Actes du colloque Calvin, Strasbourg, 1964. Paris, Presses Universitaires de France, 1965, p. 86—101) (Cahiers, RHP, 39).

DAHN, Karl. Calvin und die Kirchenzucht. **Der Evangelist,** 110: 318—319, 1958.

JOHNSON. Thomas Cary. Calvin's contribution to church polity **(In:** Calvin memorial addresses; delivered before the General Assembly at Savannah, May 1909, in observance of the birth of John Calvin. Richmond, Va., Presbyterian Committee of Publication [n.d.] p. 57—88).

JONKER, Willem Daniël. Volkskerk of belydende gemeente; enkele gedagtes oor die verskil tussen Luther en Calvyn met betrekking tot die vraag na die regering van die kerk. **Nederduitse Gereformeerde teologiese tydskrif,** 8 (4) 202—211, 1967.

JOOSTE, Josef Petrus. Die regering van die kerk volgens Calvyn. **Koers,** 26 (12) 410—420, 1959.

JORDAAN, J. T. Die tweede sleutel: kerklike tug [includes: Calvin] **Die Kerkbode,** 98 (10) 335—339, 1966.

NAGY, S. Kálvin egyházkormányzati alapelvei a gyakorlatban [Principles of Calvin in matter of church discipline] **Theológiai szemle,** 2: 327—341, 1959.

PLOMP, Johannes. De kerkelijke tucht bij Calvijn. Kampen, Kok.

1969. 400 p. Thesis-Vrije Univ., Amsterdam.

REDALIE, Raymond. Les fondements de la discipline ecclésiastique d'après Calvin (Genève?) 1939. 200 p. Thesis-Genève.

VAN DE POLL, Gerrit Jan. De kerkelijke tucht in de Reformatie. **Hervormd weekblad- de Geref. Kerk,** 71: 126; 140, 1959/60.

VAN DER WALT, Jan Jacobus. Christus as hoof van die kerk en die presbiteriale kerkregering. [Potchefstroom?] 1974. 207 1. "Die presbiteriale kerkregeringstelsel: die Calvinisme 'n reformasie" [Calvin and Bucer] p. 126—173.

WEERDA, Jan. Nach Gottes Wort reformierte Kirche; Beiträge zu ihrer Geschichte und ihrem Recht (von) Jan Remmers Weerda. Mit einem Geleitwort von Rudolf Smend. Aus dem Nachlass hrsg. von Anneliese Sprengler-Ruppenthal. München, Kaiser, 1964. "Ordnung zur Lehre, zur Theologie der Kirchenordnung bei Calvin": p. 132—161; "Die Gemeinde als Gestalt und Problem in frühen reformierten Kirchenrecht": p. 190—203. (Theologische Bücherei, Bd. 23: Historische Theologie).

YATSECK, Lois F. The basis of church order in Calvin's theology. Chicago. 1958. 72 1. Thesis-University of Chicago.

Church: liturgical matters.

CYPRIS, Ottomar Frederick. Public worship in Calvin. New York, 1953. 134 1. Thesis-Union Theological Seminary, New York.

DU PLESSIS, Hugo. Calvyn en die erediens. **Die Kerkblad,** 69 (1964) 11, 1966.

ENGELBRECHT, Barend Jacobus. Calvyn as liturg. **Die Hervormer,** 50 (2) 26—27; 30, 1959.

GUELFUCCI, Pierre. L'oeuvre catéchètique de Calvin. **Revue de théologie et d'action evangéliques,** 5 (1/2) 10—31, 1945.

HAMERSMA, John Edward. John Calvin on Christian worship. [New York] 1952. 45 1. Thesis-Union Theological Seminary, New York.

JANSEN, John Frederick. Calvin on a fixed form of worship; a note in textual criticism. **Scottish journal of theology,** 15: 282—287, 1962.

LEKKERKERKER, Arie Frederik Nelis. Calvijn en de eredienst. **In de waagschaal.** 9/5/1959.

LEKKERKERKER, Arie Frederik Nelis. Gereformeerde liturgiek in de XVIe eeuw. **Nederlands theologisch tijdschrift,** 6: 72—89, 1951/52.

McDONNELL, Kilian. Calvins Liturgieverständnis und die Zukunft der römisch-katholischen Liturgie. **Concilium,** 5 (2) 112—117, 1969.

McDONNELL, Kilian. Conception en la liturgie selon Calvin. **Concilium** [French] 42: 75—84, 1969; **Concilium** [American] 42: 87—97, 1969; **Concilium** [German] 5 (2) 112—117, 1969.

MAXWELL, William Delbert. An outline of Christian worship; its developments and forms (9th impression) London, Oxford Univ. Press (1963) "Calvin": p. 112—119.

MOREL, Bernard. Les origines liturgiques du culte réformé de langue française **Foi et vie,** 52: 1—17, 1954.

NAUTA, Doede. Calvijn en het vieren van feestdagen. **Centraal weekblad voor de Gereformeerde kerken in Nederland,** 9 (50) 467, 1961.

NICHOLS, James Hastings. Corporate worship in the Reformed tradition. Philadelphia, Westminster, 1968. 190 p.

NICHOLS, James Hastings. The intent of the Calvinistic liturgy **(In:** The heritage of John Calvin, ed. by John H. Bratt. Grand Rapids, Eerdmans, 1973. p. 87—109) (Heritage Hall Lectures, 1960—1970) (Heritage Hall publications, no. 2) **(Also in:** Corporate worship in the reformed tradition. Philadelphia, Westminster Press, 1968. p. 29—51).

NICHOLS, James Hastings. The liturgical tradition of the Reformed churches. **Theology Today,** 11: 210—224, 1954/55.

OOSTENDORP, Elcott. Calvin's liturgical legacy. **Reformed journal,** 9: 14—16, 5/1959.

REULOS, Helena. La teologia del culto en Calvino. **Guidernos teologicos,** 10 (3) 201—208, 7-9/1961.

SCHÜTZEICHEL, Heribert. Calvins Kritik an der Firmung **(In:** Zeichen des Glaubens; Studien zu Taufe und Firmung. Balthasar Fischer zum 60. Geburtstag, hrsg. v. Hansjörg Auf der Mur und Bruno Kleinheyer. Zurich, etc., 1972. p. 123—135).

SMOLIK, J. Závislost Calvinovy liturgie ve páne na Bucerovi [The church liturgy of Calvin compared with that of Bucer] **Theologia evangelica,** 3: 102, 1950.

WILL, R. La première liturgie française. **Societé de l'histoire du protestantisme français. Bulletin,** 87: 367—370, 1938.

Church: ministry, offices, pastoral care.

ALONSO, Juan José Hernández. Ministerios en la iglesia en la teologia de Calvino. **Dialogo ecumenico,** 7: 143—166, 1972.

BÉKÉSI, A. De ministerio. **Kálvin tanítása az ige szolgáirol. Református egyház,** 15: 173—175, 1963.

BLASER, Klauspeter. Calvins Lehre von den drei Ämtern Christi. (Zürich) EVZ (c1970) 54 p. (Theologische Studien, 105).

BOLT, Robert Gillis. The conception of the ministry and the nature of ordination in the writings of John Calvin. Pittsburgh, 1961. 64 1. Thesis-Pittsburgh Theological Seminary.

BOON, Rudoîf. Apostolisch ambt en Reformatie. Primair probleem der oecumene. Nijkerk, Callenbach, 1965. 227 p.

CRAWFORD, John Richard. Calvin and the priesthood of all believers. **Scottish journal of theology,** 21 (2) 145—156, 1968.

DANKBAAR, Willem Frederik. L'apostolat chez Calvin. **Revue d' histoire et de philosophie religieuses,** 41 (4) 345—354, 1961.

DANKBAAR, Willem Frederik. Het doctorenambt bij Calvijn. **Nederlands theologisch tijdschrift,** 19: 135—176, 1964/65.

DANKBAAR, Willem Frederik. L'office des docteurs chez Calvin. **Revue d'histoire et de philosophie religieuses,** 44 (4) 364—388, 1964. **(Also in:** Regards contemporains sur Jean Calvin. Actes du colloque Calvin, Strasbourg, 1964. Paris, Presses Universitaires de France, 1965. p. 102—126) (Cahiers RHP, 39).

DEDDENS, K. Calvijn en het pastoraat. **De Reformatie,** 35 (8) 60—61; (9) 68; (10) 77—78; (11) 84—85; (12) 92—93; (14) 113—114, 1959-'60.

EASTWOOD, Charles Cyril. The priesthood of all believers; an examination of the doctrine from the Reformation to the present day. London, Epworth Press, 1960. "Calvin": p. 66—90.

FABER, Jelle. De dienst der barmhartigheid in de reformatietijd, IV: Calvijn. **De Reformatie,** 35 (46) 368—370, 1960.

FARRIS, A. L. Calvin and the laity. **Canadian journal of the theology,** 11: 54—67, 1965.

GOUMAZ, Louis. Het ambt bij Calvijn; een samenvatting naar zijn commentaren op het Nieuwe Testament. Vert. en ingeleid door K. Deddens. Franeker, Wever (pref. 1964) 170 p. Orininal title: Timothèe, ou le ministère évangélique d'après Calvin et ses commentaires sur le Nouveau Testament.

HENDERSON, Robert Waugh. The doctoral ministry in the Reformed tradition; a study of the history of the second of the four ministries recognized by J. Calvin. [Cambridge?] 1959. 370 1. Thesis-Harvard Univ.

HENDERSON, Robert Waugh. The teaching office in the Reformed tradition. Philadelphia, Westminster Press, 1962. 227 p.

HUH, Soon Gil. Presbyter in volle rechten; het debat tussen Charles Hodge en James H. Thornwell over het ambt van ouderling. Groningen, "De Vuurbaak", 1972. "Calvijn en het ambt van presbyter": p 121—131. Thesis—Kampen.

KARRES, D. J. De gemeente en haar diakonaat. 's-Gravenhage, Boekencentrum, 1969. "De visie van Luther en Calvijn": p. 170—173 (Praktische theologische handboekjes, no. 32).

LEKKERKERKER, Arie Frederik Nelis. Oorsprong en funktie van het ambt. 's-Gravenhage, Boekencentrum, 1971. "Het ambt bij de reformatoren": p. 128—149.

LESTRINGANT, P. La cure d'ame évangélique dans l'énseignement des Reformateurs Calvin. **Les cahiers calvinistes,** 18 (12) 6—9, 1963.

MILLS, Liston Oury. Pastoral care in John Calvin. Louisville, 1956. 98 1. (Psychology of religion) Thesis-Southern Baptist Theological Seminary, Louisville.

NAUTA, Doede. De ambtsopvatting der Reformatie onder kritiek [re: Boon: Apostolisch ambt en Reformatie; primair probleem der oecumene. Nijkerk, Callenbach, 1965] **Gereformeerd theologisch tijdschrift,** 66: 129—138, 1966.

PFISTERER, E. Wie Calvin die Seelsorge an die Seelsorgern ordnete. **Deutsches Pfarrerblatt,** 43: 377—, 1939.

TRINTERUD, Leonard J. The ministry in the thought of John Calvin. **MacCormick speaking,** 4, April 1951: Alumni supplement.

VAN GENDEREN, J. Calvijn en de ambtsdragers. **Ambtelijk contact,** 26: 252—254, 1964.

VAN 'T SPIJKER, Willem. Ambt en gemeente aan het begin van de Gereformeerde traditie. **Theologia reformata,** 16: 8—31, 1973.

VAN'T SPIJKER, Willem. De leer van het kerkelijk ambt bij de kerkreformatoren. **Ambtelijk contact,** 1962—'65: 353—356; 459—463; 468—472; 529—532.

WATKIN, R. N. Jr. The forming of the Southern Presbyterian minister; from Calvin to the American Civil War. Nashville, Tenn., 1969.

"Calvin": p. 1—78. Thesis-Vanderbilt Univ., Nashville.

WEERDA, Jan. Nach Gottes Wort reformierte Kirche; Beiträge zu ihrer Geschichte und ihrem Recht (von) Jan Remmers Weerda. Mit einem Geleitwort von Rudolf Smend. Aus dem Nachlass hrsg. von Anneliese Sprengler-Ruppenthal. München, Kaiser, 1964. "Kirche und Diakonie in der Theologie Calvins": p. 118—131 **(Also in: Die innere Mission,** 49: 129—139, 1959).

Commentaries on Bible Books
see Bible and Calvin: Own Works.

Community.

HAGE, L. J. M. Calvijn en het maatschappelijk leven **(In:** Zicht op Calvijn [door] J. van Genderen [e.a.] Amsterdam, Buijten & Schipperhijn, 1965. p. 148—182).

HENDERSON, Robert Waugh. Sixteenth century community benevolence; an attempt to resacralize the secular. **Church history,** 38: 421—428, 1969.

HOYER, Ferdinand. Der Unterschied in der Gesellschafts- und Wirtschaftsauffassung zwischen Luther und Calvin. Wien, 1961. "Calvin": p. 54—104. Dissertation-Wien.

LITTLE, David. Religion, order and law; a study in pre-revolutionary England. New York, Harper & Row, 1970. "The new order of John Calvin": p. 33—80. (Harper torchbooks. The library of religion and culture). Also published by Fitzhenry & Whiteside, Toronto, 1970.

SANCHEZ, Rafael Jr. The concept of community in Calvin's theology. (Madison?) 1965. 96 1. Thesis-University of Wisconsin.

SHARRATT, P. The **institutio Christiana** in Calvin and his contemporaries. [Durham? 1963/64?] Thesis-St. Cuthbert's, Durham.

Confessions and ecclesiastical discussions.

AUGUSTIJN, Cornelis. Kerk en belijdenis. Kampen, Kok, 1969. "Calvin": p. 29—36. (Cahiers voor de gemeente, 7).

BARTH, Karl. The faith of the church; a commentary on the Apostle's Creed according to Calvin's Catechism. Ed. by Jean-Louis Leuba; tr. [from the German] by Gabriel Vahanian. London, Collins, 1960. 160 p. (Fontana books, 464). Also published by Meridian Books, New York, 1958.

BARTH, Karl. Das Glaubensbekenntnis der Kirche; Erklärung des Symbolum Apostolicum nach dem Katechismus Calvins. Aus dem Französischen übers. von Helmut Goes. Zürich, E.V.Z.-Verl. (c1967) 160 p. Original title: La confession de foi de l'église.

BAVAUD, Georges, La dispute de Lausanne (1536) Une étappe de l'évolution doctrinale des Réformateurs Romands. Fribourg, Editiones Universitaires, 1956. "Calvin": p. 143—209. Thesis-Fribourg.

BUNTING, Ian David. The Consensus Tigurinus and John Calvin. Princeton, N. J., 1960. 134 1. Thesis-Princeton Theological Seminary.

CADIER, Jean. La confession chez Calvin. **Les cahiers calvinistes,** 15 (3) 1—7, 1963.

DIERMANSE, Johan Murk Riënts. De fundamentele en nietfundamentele geloofsartikelen in de theologische discussie. Franeker, Wever, 1974. Thesis. "Calvijn", p. 38—43.

DUFOUR, Théophile André. Notice bibliographique sur le Catéchisme et la Confession de foi de Calvin, 1537, et sur les autres livres imprimés à Genève et à Neuchâtel dans les premiers temps de la réforme, 1533—1540. Genève, Slatkine Repr., 1970 (1878) 191 p.

LABARTHE, Olivier. La relation entre le premier catéchisme de Calvin et la première confession de foi de Genève. Recherche historique à partir d'une comparaison de textes catéchètiques et de particularitès typographiques. Genève, 1967. 129 p. Thesis-Universitè de Genève.

NAUTA, Doede. Een geloofsbelijdenis van Calvijn; Mei 1537. **(In:** Schrift en uitleg; studies van oudleerlingen, collega's en vrienden aangeboden aan Prof. Dr. W. H. Gispen, ter gelegenheid van zijn vijfentwintigjarig ambtsjubileum als hoogleraar aan de Vrije Universiteit te Amsterdam, en ter gelegenheid van het bereiken van de zeventigjarige leeftijd. Kampen, Kok, 1970. p. 141—166).

NEUSER, Wilhelm Heinrich. Calvins Beitrag zu den Religionsgesprächen von Hagenau, Worms und Regensburg (1540-'41) **(In:** Studien zur Geschichte und Theologie der Reformation. Festschrift: Ernst Bizer. Hrsg. von Luise Abramoski und J. F. Gerhard Goeters. Neukirchen-Vluyn, Neukirchener Verl., 1969. p. 213—238).

NEUSER, Wilhelm Heinrich. Calvins Urteil über den Rechtfertigungsartikel des Regensburger Buches **(In:** Reformation und Humanismus. Robert Stupperich zum 65. Geburtstag. Hrsg. von M. Greschat und J. F. G. Goeters. Witten, Luther, 1969. p. 176—194).

NIJENHUIS, Willem. Calvijn en de Augsburgse Confessie. **Nederlands theologisch tijdschrift,** 15 (6) 416—433, 1961.

NIJENHUIS, Willem. Calvin's attitude towards the symbols of the early church during the conflict with Caroli **(In:** Ecclesia reformata; studies on the Reformation. Leiden, Brill, 1972. p. 73—96) (Kerkhistorische Bijdragen, dl. 3).

NIJENHUIS, Willem. Calvijns houding ten aanzien van de oudkerkelijke symbolen tydens het conflict met Caroli. **Nederlands theologisch tijdschrift,** 15 (1) 24—47, 1960.

PETER, Rodolphe, L'abécédaire genevois ou catéchisme élémentaire de Calvin. **Revue d'histoire et de philosophie religieuses,** 45 (1) 11—45, 1965. **(Also in:** Regards contemporains sur Jean Calvin; actes du colloque Calvin, Strasbourg, 1964. Paris, Presses Universitaires de France, 1965. p. 171—205) (Cahiers, R.H.P., 39).

POLMAN, Andries Derk Rietema. Calvijn en de Oude Kerk [Re: Luchesius Smits, Saint Augustin dans l'oevre de Jean Calvijn] **Vox theologica,** 30: 72—79, 1960.

PRAAMSMA, Louis. Met de kerk van alle eeuwen; over confessionele trouw en ontrouw. Amsterdam; Buijten & Schipperheijn, 1971. "Calvijn en de belijdenis:" p. 42—51. (Ichthusreeks, nr. 1).

REVEILLAUD, Michel. L'autorité de la tradition chez Calvin. **La revue reformée,** 9 (2) 25—45, 1958.

REYNOLDS, S. M. Calvin's view of the Athanasian and Nicene creeds. **Westminister theological journal,** 23: 33—37, 1960.

STUPPERICH, Robert. Calvin und die Konfession des Paul Volz. **Revue d'histoire et de philosophie religieuses,** 44 (4) 279—289, 1964.

(Also in: Regards contemporains sur Jean Calvin; actes du colloque Calvin, Strasbourg, 1964. Paris, Presses universitaires de France, 1965. p. 17—27) (Cahiers R.H.P., 39).

TORRANCE, Thomas Forsyth, **ed,** The school of faith; the catechisms of the Reformed Church. London, Clarke, 1959. "Calvin": p. 3—65.

VAN DER LINDE, Simon. 400 jaar Confessio Helvetica Posterior. **Theologia reformata,** 9: 132—149, 1966.

VAN GENDEREN, J. De reformatorische belijdenis in discussie. 's-Gravenhage, Willem de Zwijger-stichting, 1971. "Calvijn en de belijdenis": p. 28—38.

WILKINS, Lewis. Das Zweite Helvetische Bekenntnis; 400 jähriges Zeugnis des reformierten Glaubens. **Reformierte Kirchenzeitung,** 107: 83—84, 1966.

Conversion see Redemption

Covenant of Grace.

BROUWER, Arie R. Calvin's doctrine of children in the covenant; foundation for Christian education. **Reformed review,** 18: 17—29, 1965.

BRUGGINK, Donald J. Calvin and federal theology. **Reformed review,** 13: 15—22, 1959.

DILLISTONE, Frederick William. The structure of the divine society. Philadelphia, Westminster, 1951. "The covenant conception in Calvin": p. 117—129.

EDWARDS, Charles Eugene. Calvin on infant salvation. **Bibliotheca sacra.** 88: 316—328, 1931.

EENIGENBURG, Elton M. The place of the covenant in Calvin's thinking. **Reformation review,** 10: 1—22, 1957.

HOEKEMA, Anthony A. Calvin's doctrine of the covenant of grace. **Reformation review,** 15: 1—12, 5/ 1962.

HOEKEMA, Anthony A. The covenant of grace in Calvin's teaching. **Calvin theological journal,** 2 (2) 133—161, 1967.

STAGG, John Weldon. Calvin, Twisse and Edwards on the universal salvation of those dying in infancy. Richmond, Va., Presbyterian Committee of Publication [c1902] "Calvin": p. 66—116.

WEBB, R. A. Calvin's doctrine of infant salvation **(In:** Calvin memorial addresses, delivered before the General Assembly at Savannah May 1909, in observance of the birth of John Calvin. Richmond, Va., Presbyterian Committee of Publication [n.d.] p. 107—126).

Creation.

CONTAMIN, André-Dieudonné. Calvin et la creation. Genève, 1950. 70 1. Thesis-Université de Genève.

CONTAMIN, André-Dieudonné. Calvin et le monde créé (Suite de Calvin et la creation(Genève [n.d.] 89 1.

CREMER, J. Doctrine de Calvin sur la creation. Paris, 1939. 66 1. Thesis-Faculté libre de théologie protestante de Paris.

DEMOUGEOT, Marcel. Notes relatives à la notion trinitaire de Dieu et de son acte créatur, chez Calvin, d'après les chaptires XIII & XIV du livre I de l'Institution de 1559. Paris, 1947. 65 1. Thesis-Faculté libre de théologie protestante de Paris.

OSMAN, John. The sources of thought in John Calvin; Calvin and cosmology. Richmond, Va., 1942, 228 l. Thesis-Union Theological Seminary, Richmond, Va.

SMITH, Samuel David. A study of the relation between the doctrine of creation and the doctrine of revelation through the created universe in the thought of John Calvin, Friedrich Schleiermacher and Paul Tillich. Nashville, Tenn., 1965. Calvin: p. 15—99. Thesis-Vanderbilt Univ., Nashville.

Ecclesiastical discussions see Confessions.

Economics; social philosophy.

BALDWIN, Walter Paul. The economic implications of Calvin's ethics. Princeton, N. J., 1947. 142 l. Thesis-Princeton Theological Seminary.

BEAUPÈRE, René. Calvin et l'argent. **Lumière et vie,** 8: 80—89, 1959.

BÉKÉSI, A. Kálvin szociáletikája. **Theologiai szemle,** 7: 356—363, 1964.

BERGIER, Jean Francois. La pensée économique et sociale de Calvin [re: Biéler, André. La pensée économique et sociale de Calvin. Genève, 1959] **Annales-economies, sociétès, civilisations,** 17 (2) 348—355, 1962.

BIELER, André. Calvin and capitalism. **Reformed and Presbyterian world,** 26: 151—162, 1960.

BIELER, André. Calvin; das Gelt und der Kapitalismus. **Der deutsche Hugenott,** 25: 34—45, 1961.

BIELER, André. Calvin; prophète de l'ere industrielle; fondaments et methode de l'éthique calvinienne de la sociéte. En appendice; une suggestion aux églises chrétiennes. Genève, Labor et Fides, 1964. 72 p. (Debats, 3).

BIELER, André. Gottes Gebot und der Hunger der Welt; Calvin, Prophet des industriellen Zeitalters. Grundlage und Methode der Sozialethik Calvins (Übers- aus dem Französischen: A. Döbeli) Zürich, EVZ-Verl. (c1966) 87 p. (Polis, 24).

BIELER, André. L'humanisme social de Calvin. **Les cahiers protestants,** 44: 193—241, 1960.

BIELER, André. La pensée économique et sociale de Calvin. Pref. de Antony Babel. Genève, Librairie de l'Université, 1961 (c1959) 562 p. (Publications de la Faculté des sciences Économiques et Sociales de l'Université de Genève, v. 13).

BIELER, André. The social humanism of Calvin [Tr. by] P. T. Fuhrmann. Richmond, Knox, 1964. 79 p.

BIELER, André. L'umanesimo sociale di Calvino. Pref. W. A. Visser 't Hooft [Tr.: G. Conte] Torino, Claudiana, 1964. 107 p. (Piccòla collana moderna, 5).

BLANC, Adolphe. Calvin; législateur, économiste et politique. **Revue du christianisme social,** 15 (6) 329—341, 1902.

BROPHY, Liam. Calvin; father of finance capitalism. **Apostle,** 42: 19—21, 1964.

BROPHY, Liam. The consequences of Calvinism. **Social justice review,** 56 (11) 364—368, 3/1964.

BUSINO, Giovanni. Intorno al pensiero economico e sociale di Calvino. **Schweizerische Zeitschrift für Geschichte,** 10: 418—421, 1960.

BUSINO, Giovanni. Intorno al pensiero economico e sociale di Calvino; note critique. **Schweizerische Zeitschrift für Geschichte,** 11: 287—290, 1961.

CALVYN spreek ook nog mee oor

rentekoerse. **Woord en daad,** 9 (60) 3: 11, 1967.

DELMONTE, Carlos. Revision del pensamiento social de Calvino. **Cristianismo y sociedad,** 3 (8) 96—114, 1965.

DEMPSEY, B. W. Calvin and 'big business'. **Month,** 69: 321—327, 1932.

DOWLEY, Tim. Calvin and usury in Geneva. **Christian graduate,** 25: 88—90, 1972.

GANOCZY, Alexandre. Ist Calvin der "Vater des Kapitalismus"? **Reformatio,** 23: 416—425, 1974.

GEIGER, Max. Calvin, Calvinismus, Kapitalismus **(In:** Gottesreich und Menschenreich. Ernst Staehelin zum 80. Geburtstag [Hrsg. von M. Geiger] Basel, Helbing & Lichtenhahn (1969) p. 229—286).

GOLAY, J. La pensée économique et sociale de Calvin. **Revue de théologie et de philosophie,** N.S., 9: 371—375, 1959.

GOUDZWAARD, B. Calvijns ethiek van het sociaal-economische leven. **Antirevolutionaire staatkunde,** 30: 137—152, 1960.

GRAHAM, William Fred. The constructive revolutionary; John Calvin and his socio-economic impact. Richmond, Va., Knox [1971]. 251 p.

GRAHAM, William Fred. The permeation of Calvin's social and economic thought into Genevan life: 1536—1564. (Iowa City) 1965. 304 l. Thesis-University of Iowa.

GRIN, E. De Calvin à Charles Secrétan. **Theologische Zeitschrift,** 16: 195—215, 1960.

HESSEL, R. A. E. Calvin versus Confucius; a sociological inquiry. **Japan Christian quarterly,** 26: 175—179, 1960.

JOHN Calvin and the Scottish bankers (Editorial) **Canadian banker,** 77: 2—3, 1970.

JOHN Calvin as a rationalist or John Calvin versus John Maynard Keynes. **Progressive Calvinism,** 4 (5) 135—136, 1958.

KITCH, M. J. Capitalism and the Reformation. London, Longmans, 1967. 218 p. (Problems and perspectives in history) Calvin and Calvinism; passim. Also pub. by Barnes & Noble, New York, 1968.

LEITCH, Addison Hardie. Calvin and capitalism. Pittsburgh, 1938. 80 l. Thesis-Xenia Theological Seminary, Pittsburgh.

LE ROUX, Jurie Hendrik. 'n Godsdienssosiologiese ontleding van Max Weber se stelling dat Protestantisme verantwoordelik is vir Kapitalisme. Pretoria, 1971. Thesis-Univ. of Pretoria.

LÜTHY, Herbert. Calvinisme et capitalisme. Après soixante ans de débat. **Cahiers vilfredo pareto,** 2: 5—35, 1963.

LÜTHY, Herbert. La république de Calvin et l'essor de la Banque protestante en France de la révocation de L'Edit de Nantes à la revolution. **Schweizer Beiträge zur allgemeinen Geschichte,** 11: 73—107, 1953.

MARTIN, Paul Edmond. Les ministres de Genève et le taux de l' intérêt 1565. **Les cahiers protestants,** 43: 220—226, 1959.

MEYLAN, Henri. Calvin et les hommes d'affaires. **Revue d'histoire et de philosophie religieuses,** 45 (1) 1—10, 1965. **(Also in:** Regards contemporains sur Jean Calvin; actes du colloque Calvin, Strasbourg, 1964. Paris, Presses Universitaires de France, 1965. p. 161—170) (Cahiers R. H. P., 39).

MIHÁLY, Bucsay. ökumenikus szempontok a Kálvin-kutatásban; új összefoglalás Kálvin életéröl és teológiájárol. **Református egyház,** 23: 49—50, 1971.

MITCHELL, Robert M. The Weber thesis as tested by the writings of John Calvin and the English puritans of the sixteenth and seventeenth centuries. East Lansing, Mich., 1969. Thesis—Michigan State Univ. **(Excerpts in: Fides et historia,** 4: 55—72, 1972).

NEDERBRAGT, John Alexander. Kalvinismus; Studien und Skizzen. Budapest, Sylvester, 1938. "Kalvinismus und Oekonomie:" p. 131—168.

NYMEYER, Frederick. John Calvin on interest. **Progressive Calvinism,** 3 (2) 55—62, 1957.

POSSELT, Alfred Maria. Calvin und der Kapitalismus. Wien 1947. 182 1. Thesis-Hochschüle für Welthandel.

RAMP, Ernst. Die Stellung von Luther, Zwingli und Calvin zur Zinsfrage. Zürich, Zwingli, 1949. Calvin: p. 81—97; Calvin und Calvinismus: p. 106—110. (Quellen und Abhandlungen zur Geschichte des schweizerischen Protestantismus, Bd. 4) Thesis-Universität, Zürich.

ROSSIER, Georges. Calvin prophète de l'ère industrielle. **Jeunesse socialiste,** no 10 (1/5/1965) 5.

SAINT-JEAN, Claude. Calvin économiste. **Revue des deux mondes,** 1/9/64: 65—73.

SEBESTYÉN, J. Kálvin és a kapitalizmus. Maros, Vásárhely, 1911.

STARK, Werner. Capitalism, Calvinism and the rise of modern science **(In:** Wiener, Philip P., ed. Readings in philosophy of science; introduction to the foundations and cultural aspects of the sciences. New York, Scribner [c 1953] p. 340—348).

TANIS, E. J. Social teachings of Calvin's Institutes. **Calvin forum,** 2: 53—56, 1936/37.

TEMPLIN John Alton. Implications for a social concern in the theology of Calvin. **Iliff review,** 26: 33—44, 1969.

TRANDA, Bogdan. Mezczyzna i kobieta w etyce Kalwina. **Jednota,** 8: 9—11, 1964.

WIESENMÜLLER. Die Wirtschaftsethik Thomas von Aquinas, Luthers und Calvins, und das deutsche Unternehmertun desVor- und Frühkapitalismus. [Neurenberg.] c1968. "Die calvinistische Wirtschaftsethik": p. 253—322. Thesis-Erlangen.

Economics; social philosophy see **also State and church.**

Ecumenical relations.

ALMEIDA, D. Manuel d'. Calvinismo e ecumenismo. **Broteria,** 81 (5) 439—450, 1965.

BERSMA, S. C. Het oecumenisch streven bij Calvijn. **Gereformeerd weekblad,** 15 (36) 287, 1959/60.

BLANKE, Fritz. Calvins oekumenische Bedeutung. **Reformatio,** 13 (10) 590—600, 1964.

BOON, Rudolf, Apostolisch ambt en Reformatie; primair probleem der oecumene. Nijkerk, Callenbach, 1965. 227 p.

BRATT, John Harold. Calvin and ecumenicity. **Reformed journal,** 9: 8—10; 17—18, 1959.

CADIER, Jean. Calvin and the union of the churches **(In:** Duffield, G. E., ed. John Calvin. Appleford, Courtenay (1966) p. 118—130) (Courtenay studies in Reformation theology).

CADIER, Jean. Calvin, l'homme de l'union des églises. **La revue reformée,** 13 (4) 11—20, 1962.

DE VILLIERS, David Willem. Calvinia Oecumenicus. **Die Kerkbode,** 83 (13) 522—523, 1959.

DE VRIES, W. G. Calvijns oecumenische betekenis. Goes, Oosterbaan & Le Cointre, 1959. 40 p.

DOEZEMA, Lambert. Calvin and the unity of the church. **Reformation guardian,** 3: 166, 1957.

DURAND, Johannes Jacobus Fourie. Calvyn as ekumeniese gees. **Nederduitse Gereformeerde teologiese tydskrif,** 5 (3) 167—182, 1964.

DUVENAGE, Benonie. Calvyn en die ekumeniese roeping van die kerk; 'n oriëntering. **In die Skriflig,** 1 (2) 16—21, 1967.

EMONET, Pierre. Un problème du dialogue oecuménique avec les protestants; la Mariologie. **Esprit et vie,** 81: 225—236, 1971.

GLOEDE. Günter. Calvinus oecumenicus. Weg und Werk des Reformators (**In:** Rogge, J. Johannes Calvin; 1509—1564; eine Gabe zu seinem 400. Todestag. Berlin, Evangelische Verlagsantstalt [1963] p. 9—26).

KORTZFLEISCH, Siegfried von. Ökumene im Geiste Calvins; der reformierte Weltbund in Frankfurt. **Christ und Welt,** 17 (33) 10, 1964.

KROMMINGA, John H. The great brotherhood; John Calvin and the unity of the church. **Young Calvinist,** 48: 10—12, 1/1967.

LOCHER, Gottfried Wilhelm. Calvin Anwalt der Ökumene. Zollikon, Evangelischer Verl. (1960) 28 p. (Theologische Studien, Hft. 60).

McNEILL, John Thomas. Calvin as an ecumenical churchman. **Church history,** 32: 379—391, 1963 (**Also in:** Calvin anniversary lectures. Grand Rapids, Mich., Calvin College, 1959. 10 1.).

MEINHOLD, Peter. Calvins ökumenische Bedeutung für die Einheit des Protestantismus. **Christ und Welt,** 17 (21) 10, 1964.

NIJENHUIS, Willem. Calvijn en de oecumene. **In de waagschaal,** 30/5/59.

PRAAMSMA, Louis. John Calvin as an ecumenical figure. **The Banner,** 94 (50) 7, 1959.

PRAAMSMA, Louis. John Calvin as an ecumenical figure [Synopsis of address at Westminister Seminary, by John H. Skilton] **Torch and trumpet,** 9 (7) 164, 1959; **Reformation review,** 1 (1) 13—18, 1953.

RANKIN, Lynn Boyd. The ecumenical spirit of John Calvin. Ann Arbor, University Microfilms, 1967. 256 1. Thesis-Temple Univ.

RASKER, Albert Jan. Calvinus oecumenicus. **In de waagschaal,** 15 (1) 11—13, 1959.

SMIDT, Udo. Johannes Calvin in seiner ökumenischen Bedeutung (**In:** Gott ist am Werk. Festschrift für Hanns Lilje zum 60. Geburtstag. Hamburg, 1959. p. 37—44).

SNYMAN, W. J. Ekumenisiteit van die kerk by Calvyn. **Die Kerkblad,** 61 (1520) 6—9, 1959.

STAUFFER, Richard. Calvin, pionnier de l'unité chrétienne. **La revue reformée,** 21 (81) 1—17, 1970.

STRASSER, Otto Erich. Calviniana Oecumenica. **Kirchenblatt für die**

reformierte Schweiz, 118: 101—103, 1962.

STUTTERHEIM, J. F. Calvyn en die eenheid van die kerk. **Die Hervormer,** 50 (12) 6—7; 19, 1960.

STUTTERHEIM, J. F. Calvyn en kerkeenheid. **Die Brug,** 12 (3) 4—6, 1963.

VORHIS, James Thompson. Some permanent contributions of John Calvin to ecumenical Christianity. Pittsburgh, 1936. 68 1. Thesis-Xenia Theological Seminary, Pittsburgh.

WEBER, Otto. Die Treue Gottes in der Geschichte der Kirche. Neukirchen, Neukirchener Verl. des Erziehungsvereins, 1968. „Die Einheit der Kirche bei Calvin": p. 105—118. (Beiträge zur Geschichte und Lehre der reformierten Kirche, 29).

Education.

ALEXANDER, Robert C. The influence of the Protestant Reformation on Protestant religious education in the 16th century. Nashville, Tenn., 1926. "Calvin": p. 75—84. Thesis-Vanderbilt Univ., Nashville.

ANDERSON, William Henry. The educational relevance of Calvin's eschatology; an examination of the eschatological doctrines of John Calvin to discover the behaviour-modifying concepts directly implied by these doctrines. [New York?] 1960. 210 1. Thesis-New York Univ.

BAINTON, Roland Herbert. Methods of great religious teachers; Calvin and his circle. **International journal of religious education,** 9: 6—7, 1932.

BERKHOF, William. Calvin's influence upon educational progress. **The Banner,** 62: 440—441, 1927.

BILLICA, Willard C. Calvin and education. Pittsburgh, 1950. 83 1. Thesis-Xenia Theological Seminary, Pittsburgh.

BOCKWOLDT, Gerd. Das Verständnis der Erziehung bei Calvin. Kiel, 1966. 214 1. Thesis-Kiel.

BRATT, John Harold. Calvin and the Genevan schools. **Christian home & school,** 37 (3) 12—15, 1959.

BREEN, Quirinus. The church as the mother of learning. **Encounter,** 22 (4) 363—419, 1961.

BROUWER, Arie R. Calvin's doctrine of children in the covenant; foundation for Christian education. **Reformation review,** 18: 17—29, 1965.

CADIER, Jean. Calvin éducateur (Calvin à Malaga) **Foi education,** 25 (73) 116—127, 1965.

COETZEE, Johannes Christiaan. Die Geneefse Akademie van Calvyn. **Koers,** 27 (2), 45—49, 1959.

DEDDENS, K. Parentaal pastoraat [Catechism, De Brès, Calvin] **De Reformatie,** 41 (1) 4—6, 1965.

DE JONG, Peter Ymen. Calvin's contribution to Christian education. **Calvin theological journal,** 2 (2) 162—201, 1967.

DENDY, Marshall C. Changing patterns in Christian education. Richmond, Va., John Knox Press, 1964. "Calvin and Christian education": p. 15—34.

DENNY, George H. Calvin's influence on educational progress (**In:** Calvin memorial addresses, delivered before the General Assembly at Savannah, May 1909, in observance of the birth of John Calvin. Richmond, Va., Presbyterian Committee of Publications (n.d.) p. 147—174).

DEVAUX, Jeanne. La pédagogie selon Calvin. **Centre Protestant d'études & de documentation. Bulletin,** 9 (1) 1957.

EBY, Frederick. Early Protestant educators; the educational writings of Martin Luther, John Calvin, and other leaders of Protestant thought [Repr.] New York, 1971 (1931) "Calvin": p. 231—270.

FURCK, Carl Ludwig. Die Erziehung zu einem bewusst aktiven Leben in der calvinistischen Pädagogik. **Zeitschrift für Pädagogik,** 10 (4) 340—360, 1964.

GASSER, Adolf. Calvin als Erzieher. **Reformatio,** 13: 203—216, 1964.

GEIGER, Max. Schickt uns Holz, und wir machen Pfeile daraus [Jean Calvin] **Kirchenblatt für die reformierte Schweiz,** 116: 2—5, 1960.

HARPER, Norman Edmond. A comparative study of the educational implications of the thought of John Calvin and Soren Kierkegaard [Missouri] 1966. 237 p. Thesis—University of Mississipi.

HEDTKE, Reinhold. Erziehung durch die Kirche bei Calvin, der Unterweisungs-und Erziehungsauftrag der Kirche und seine antropologischen und theologischen Grundlagen. Heidelberg, Quelle & Meyer, 1969. 230 p. (Pädagogische Forschungen, 39. Reihe: Editionen und Monographien) Thesis-Göttingen.

JAARSMA, Cornelius Richard. John Calvin and education. **The Banner** 94 (24) 6; 19, 1959.

MEHL, Roger. Calvin professeur à la Haute-Ecole de Strasbourg. **Foi et vie,** 39: 396—403, 1938.

NIXON, Leroy. John Calvin's teaching and their implications for the theory of reformed Protestant Christian education. [New York? 196-?] Thesis-New York Univ.

NORDMANN, W. Calvin; der Mensch, das Werk, die pädogogische Bedeutung. **Der evangelische Religionslehrer an der Berufsschule,** 12 (4) 113—122, 1964.

OECHSLI, W. Die Akademie Calvins. **Schweizerische pädagogische Zeitschrift,** 11: 1—23, 1902.

PAASCH, H. J. Sturms und Calvins Schulwesen; ein Vergleich. Münster, 1915. Thesis-Münster.

PIXBERG, Hermann. Der deutsche Calvinismus und die Pädagogik. Gladbeck, Heilmann, 1952. "Calvin": p. 13—16; "Calvinismus in der Pfalz": p. 20—28.

PRUDEN, Edward H. John Calvin and religious education. **Union Seminary quarterly review,** 47 (1) 6—22; (4) 199—217, 1935/36; 48 (1) 1—14, 1936/37.

PIJPER, Fredrik. De invloed van de Broeders des gemeenen levens op de schoolstichting van Calvijn. **(In:** Kerkhistorische opstellen, van het gezelschap S.S.S. Nieuwe bundel. 's-Gravenhage, Nijhoff, 1914. p. 115—129)

RÜSCH, Ernst Gerhard. Calvin als Erzieher. **Reformatio,** 13: 203—216, 1964.

SAPP, Charles Leon. John Calvin, humanist educator; the history of ideas and their relationship to social change. Ann Arbor, University Microfilms, 1970. 264 p. Thesis-North Carolina State Univ. Raleigh.

VAN DER LINDE, Simon. Calvijn als paedagoog. **Theologia reformata,** 8: 69—79, 1964.

VAN WYK, Jan Hendrik & SMIT, P. J. Calvyn en die onderwys. **Onderwysblad vir Christelike en na-**

sionale onderwys en opvoeding; orgaan van die Transvaalse Onderwysersvereniging, 71: 179—182; 225—228, 1964.

WHITE, Robert. The school in Calvin's thought and practice. **Journal of Christian education,** 12: 5—26, 1969.

Ethical matters.

ABEL, Jean. The ethical implications of the doctrine of the Holy Spirit in John Calvin. Richmond, Va., 1948. 144 1. Thesis-Union Theological Seminary, Richmond, Va.

ANDERSON, Raymond Kemp. Love and order; the life-structuring dynamics of grace and virtue in Calvin's ethical thought: an interpretation. (Chambersburg, Wilson College, 1973) 418 p. Formerly published as the author's thesis by Basel Univ., 1964.

BEACH, Waldo & NIEBUHR, Helmut Richard, **editors.** Christian ethics; sources of the living tradition. New York, Ronald, 1955. "Calvin": p. 267—297.

BÉKÉSI, A. Kálvin etikája — halálának negyszazadik évfordulójan. **Theologiai szemle,** 7: 226—236, 1964.

BIÉLER, André. L'homme et la femme dans la morale calviniste; la doctrine réformée sur l'amour, le mariage, le célibat, le divorce, l' adultère et la prostitution, considérée dans son cadre historique. Préf. de Madeleine Barot. Genève, Labor et Fides (c1963) 160 p. (Nouvelle série théologique, no. 15).

BIÉLER, André. Mann und Frau in Calvins Ethik. **Der deutsche Hugenott,** 28: 69—76, 1964; **Reformed and Presbyterian world,** 27: 357—363, 1963.

BIÉLER, André. Der universale Humanismus Calvins. **Kirchenblatt für reformierte Schweiz,** 117: 130—133, 1961.

BCCKWOLDT, Gerd. Das Menschenbild Calvins. **Neue Zeitschrift für systematische Theologie und Religionsphilosophie,** 19 (2) 170—189, 1968.

BRONKHORST, Alexander Johannes. De reformatie en de (on) ontbindbaarheid van het huwelijk **(In:** (On) ontbindbaarheid van het huwelijk. Red.: Th. A. G. van Eupen. Utrecht, Brand, 1970. p. 166—183) (Annalen van het Thijmgenootschap, 581).

BROZ, L. Calvin a humanismus. **Kostnické jiskry,** 49, 1964.

BRYAN, George McLeod. John Calvin and the new morality. **Foundations,** 9 (3) 197-204, 1966.

BURNOTTE, M. La pensée mariale de Jean Calvin. **La revue réformée** 23 (4) 185—191, 1972.

BÜSSER, Fritz. Calvins Wirtschafts- und Sozialethik. **Zwingliana,** 11 (6) 395-409, 1961.

CADIER, Jean. Calvin's view of the Christian life. **International reformed bulletin,** 7 (18) 2—5, 1964.

CADIER, Jean. La vie de l'homme chretien après J. Calvin. **Les cahiers calvinistes,** 21 (9) 11—14, 1964.

CLIVE, H. P. The Calvinists and the question of dancing in the 16th century. **Bibliotheque d'humanisme et renaissance,** 23: 296—323, 1961.

CONDITT, Marion W. More acceptable than sacrifice; ethics and election in the theology of John Calvin. Basel, Reinhardt, 1973. 146 p. (Theologische Dissertation, 10).

COWPER, Macknight Crawford. Calvin's doctrine of predestination and its ethical consequences. New

York, 1942. 90 l. Thesis—Union Theological Seminary, New York.

DANCY, North Barry. The transformed individual and his social responsibility in the thought of John Calvin. Philadelphia, 1972. 231 l. Thesis- Temple Univ., Philidaelphia.

DU PLESSIS, Lodewicus Johannes. Die etiek van Calvyn. **Anti-revolutionaire staatkunde,** 5: 245—265, 1931.

DUVENAGE, Benonie. Beroepsarbeid in die lig van die Christelike etiek. (Odendaalsrus, pref. 1956) Calvin: p. 42—48. Thesis-P.U. vir C.H.O., Potchefstroom.

DUVENAGE, Benonie. Die dinamiek van Calvyn se roepingsgedagte spreek skerp. **Woord en daad,** 9 (64) 1: 6, 1967.

DUVENAGE, Benonie. Roeping en arbeid by Calvyn. **Die Kerkblad,** 62 (1555) 4—6, 1960.

FABER, Jelle. Imago Dei bij Calvijn; Calvijns leer over de mens als beeld Gods krachtens de schepping. **Lucerna,** 1: 5—32, 1960.

FARRIS Allan L. John Calvin, social revolutionary. **Presbyterian record,** 98: 10—11, 5/1974.

FEINBERG, John Samuel. The doctrine of human freedom in the writings of John Calvin. Deerfield, Ill., 1972. Thesis-Trinity Evangelical Divinity School.

GENTRY, C. Jr. A study of John Calvin's understanding of moral obligation and moral norms in Christian ethics. Ann Arbor, Mich., 1970. 169 1. Thesis-Southern Methodist Univ., Dallas, Tex.

GOUDZWAARD, B. Sociale ethiek van Calvijn. **Belijden en beleven,** 17 (43) 7, 1960.

HALL, Basil. Calvin and Biblical humanism. **Huguenot Society of London. Proceedings,** 20: 195—209, 1961.

HALL, Robert Gaston. The social ethics of John Calvin. Richmond, Va., 1947. 112 1. Thesis-Union Theological Seminary, Richmond, Va.

HALL, Thomas Cuming. Was John Calvin a Reformer or a reactionary? **Hibbert journal,** 6: 171—185, 1908.

HARRIS, Thomas Cecil. John Calvin's contribution to the principle of religious liberty. Nashville, Kent., 1929. 164 1. Thesis-Vanderbilt Univ., Nashville.

HEERING, Gerrit Jan. The fall of Christianity; a study of Christianity, the state, and war (Repr.) **Tr.** [**of:** De zondeval van het christendom] by J. W. Thompson, with a foreword by E. Stanley Jones. With a new introd. by Walter F. Bense. New York, Garland, 1972 (1930): "The Calvinist synthesis; Calvin and war": p. 56—64.

HIEMSTRA, William L. Calvin's doctrine of Christian liberty. **Reformation review,** 13: 10—14, 1959.

HOOYKAAS, J. C. Calvijn's leer van het huwelijk (Doctrina Calvini de matrimonia) Benevens de oratio aperturae en de peroratio; rede. Sliedrecht, Curatorium der Academia Theologiae Reformatae, 1959. 22 p.

JONKER, Willem Daniël. Heilige Skrif en sosiale etiek by Calvyn. **Suid-Afrikaanse vereniging vir die bevordering van Christelike wetenskap. Bulletin,** 39 (12) 31—37, 1973.

KEHM, George H. Christ and man in Calvin's theology. **Perspective,** 12 (3) 197—216, 1971.

KINGDON, Robert M. The control of morals in Calvin's Geneva **(In:**

The social history of the Reformation, ed. by Lawrence P. Buck and Jonathan W. Zophy. Columbus, Ohio State Univ., Press (c-1972). "In honour of Harold J. Grimm", p. 3—16).

KOLTERMANN, Johannes. Aussatz ist kein Ehescheidungsgrund nach Kalvin. **Verein für hessische Geschichte und Landeskunde. Zeitschrift,** 67: 222—223, 1956.

LEAHY, F. S. John Calvin's social consciousness. **Christianity today,** 3: 7—9, 1959.

LEBEAU, J. Calvin, maître d'énergie morale. Nessonvaux [1911] 22 p.

LIARD, Philippe. L'anthropologie de Calvin; recherche des thèmes, de leurs sources et essai de critique. Montpellier 1963. 181 1. Thesis-Faculté libre de théologie protestante.

LYON, David Henry Scott. The intramundane ascetism of Calvin. (New York) 1949. 95 1. Thesis-Union Theological Seminary, New York.

MCALPINE, John Robert. The anthropology of Calvin and Brunner; a comparison. Richmond, Va., 1940. 89 1. Thesis-Union Theological Seminary, Richmond, Va.

MARCEL, Pierre. L'humilité d'après Calvin. **La revue reformée,** 9: 1—38, 1961.

MELAN, E. F. The Stoic doctrine of indifferent things and the conception of Christian liberty in Calvin's Institutio religionis Christianae. **Romanic review,** 28, 1937.

OLSEN, Viggo. Norskov. The New Testament logia on divorce; a study of their interpretation from Erasmus to Milton. Tübingen, Mohr (Siebeck) 1971. "John Calvin": p. 94—103. (Beiträge zur Geschichte der biblischen Exegese, 10). Thesis—Basel.

PRINS, Richard. The image of God in Adam and the restoration of man in Jesus Christ; a study in Calvin. **Scottish journal of theology,** 25: 32—44, 1972.

PRUYSER, Paul W. Calvin's view of man; a psychological commentary. **Theology today,** 26 (1) 51—68, 1969/70.

RAE, S. H. Calvin, natural law and contemporary ethics; a brief note. **Reformed theological review,** 30 (1) 14—21, 1971.

RICHGELS, Robert William. Calvin and Bellarmine on man; a comparative study of the anthropology of the Institutes and the Disputations. Madison, Wisc., 1968. 123 1. Thesis-University of Wisconsin.

RIOUX, Etienne. La piété chretienne selon Calvin. Paris, 1947. 112 1. Thesis-Faculté libre de théologie protestante de Paris.

ROACH, Dewey R. Ethical implications of John Calvin's theology. Fort Worth, Tex., 1951. 264 1. Thesis-Southwestern Baptist Theological Seminary, Fort Worth.

ROBERTS, William Henry. Calvin in human relations. **The Interior,** 40 (2030) 515—517, 1909.

ROTHUIZEN, Gerard Theodoor. Tweërlei ethiek by Calvijn? Kampen, Kok, 1964. 31 p.

SCHMIDT, John L. A comparative study of the doctrine of man in Sigmund Freud and John Calvin. Pittsburgh, 1959. 119 1. Thesis—Xenia Theological Seminary Pittsburgh.

SCHWARZ, R. Johannes Calvin und die Toleranz. **Garbe,** 20 [25?]: 724—729; 753—760, 1941/42.

SEE, Ruth Douglas. The Protestant doctrine of vocation in the Presbyterian thought of nineteenth-century America. Ann Arbor, Mich., 1967 (1953) "Calvin" p. 56—97. Thesis-New York Univ.

SMITH, William Kyle. Calvin's ethics of war; a documentary study. Annapolis [Published for Westminster Foundation of Annapolis by] Academic Fellowship, 1972. 166 p.

SNYMAN, W. J. Calvyn oor die lewe. **Die Kerkblad,** 67 (1750) 13; 15—16, 1964.

STOKER, Hendrik Gerhardus. Oorsprong en rigting. Kaapstad, Tafelberg, 1967. "Calvin and ethics": v. 1, p. 284—304.

THURIAN, Fr Max. L'Anthropologie réformée. **Irenikon,** 25: 20—52, 1952.

TWISS, Sumner B. Jr. Evaluation, prescription, and justification in the ethical discourse of John Calvin; a conceptual analysis and reconstruction of an ethical system. (New Haven, Conn.) Yale Divinity School, 1968. 118 1.

VAHANIAN, Gabriel Antoine. An eschatalogical consideration of Calvin's conception of responsibility. Princeton, N. J. 1950. 87 1. Thesis-Princeton Theological Seminary.

VAN DELLEN, Idzerd. De Gereformeerde vroomheid volgens Calvijn. **De Wachter,** 92 (2) 10—11; (3) 10—11, 1959.

VAN DER HAAR, J. Het geestelijke leven bij Calvijn; de onbekende Calvijn. 2e dr. Utrecht, De Banier, 1960. 263 p.

VAN DER LINDE, Simon. Het christenleven in kerk en staat bij Calvijn, volgens boek IV van de Institutie. **Theologia reformata,** 15: 102—118, 1972.

VAN ZYL, A. H. Calvyn oor die Christelike lewe. **Nederduitse Gereformeerde teologiese tydskrif,** 5 (3) 182—200, 1964.

VERLOOP, C. De Christelijke arbeidswaardeering in haar historische ontwikkeling tot Calvijn. Heusden, Veerman [s.j.] 206 p.

VINAY, Valdo. La parabola dei talenti e l'etica di Giovanni Calvino. **Protestantesimo,** 26 (2) 79—87, 1971.

WALLACE, Ronald S. Calvin's doctrine of the Christian life (repr.) Grand Rapids, Mich., Eerdmans (1961) 349 p.

WOOLLEY, Paul. Calvin and toleration **(In:** Calvin anniversary lectures. Grand Rapids, Mich., Calvin College, 1959. 21 1).

ZICKGRAF, Thomas. Die Sexualethik Calvins. München, 1970. 43 p. Thesis-München.

ZIMMERMAN, J. A. K. Christian life in Luther and Calvin. **Lutheran quarterly,** 16: 222—230, 1964.

ZUIDEMA, Sytse Ulbe. Calvijn had een diepe afkeer van revolusie. Interview by Piet Koenes. **Patrimonium,** 82: 41—59, 1971.

Eucharist see Sacraments.

Faith see Redemption.

Free will see Redemption.

Geneva and Switzerland.

AUBERT, H. V. Nicolas Colladon et la Compagnie des pasteurs et professeurs de Genève. **Societé d'histoire et d' archéologie de Genève. Bulletin,** 2: 138—163, 1900.

BARROIS, Georges A. Calvin and the Genevans. **Theology today,** 21: 458—465, 1965.

BATTLES, Ford Lewis. Against luxury and license in Geneva; a forgotten fragment of Calvin. **Interpretation,** 19 (2) 182—202, 1965.

BORGEAUD, Charles, Calvin et Genève. Genève, 1909. (Extrait du Numéro des Jubilés par le **Journal de Genève,** 5/7/1909).

BOULITROP, Eugène. Histoire de la Réforme en Savoie. Aix-les-Bains, 1964. "Calvin": p. 73—107.

BRATT, John Harold. Calvin and the Genevan schools. **Christian home & school,** 37 (3) 12—15, 1959.

CASTIGLIONE, Tommaso Riccardo. La "Impietas Valentini Gentilis" e il corrucio di Calvino **(In:** Roma, Facolta Valdesi di Teologica. Ginevra et l'Italia; recolta di studi promossa dalla Facolta Valdesi di Teologica di Roma a cura Delio Cantimori [et al] Firenze, Sansoni [1959] p 149—176) (Bibliotheca Storica Sansoni, 34).

CHOISY, Eugène. Calvin à Genève avant Strasbourg. **Societè de l'histoire du protestantisme français. Bulletin,** 87: 349—354, 1938.

COMPAGNIE DES PASTEURS DE GENÈVE. Registres de la Compagnie des Pasteurs de Genève au temps de Calvin, publiés sous la direction des Archives d'État de Genève, par R. M. Kingdon et J. G. Bergier. Genève, Droz, 1962-'69 [v. 1: 1964] 3 v.

COMPAGNIE DES PASTEURS DE GENÈVE. The register of the company of pastors of Geneva in the time of Calvin. Grand Rapids, Mich., Eerdmans (c1966) 380 p.

COUDY, Julien. **ed.** The Huguenot wars. Tr. by Julie Kernan. Philadelphia, Chilton, 1969. "Calvin organizes the reform at Geneva": p. 47—55.

COURVOISIER, Jaques. Le sens de la discipline dans la Genève de Calvin. **(In:** Hommage et reconnaisance. Recuiel de travaux publiés a l'occasion du soixantième anniversaire de K. Barth Neuchatel [1946] p. 19—31).

d'ASSONVILLE, Victor Edouard. Calvyn verdedig sy stad; sy antwoord aan kardinaal Sadoletus. Potchefstroom, Pro Rege, 1974. 16 p.

DECRUE DE STOUTZ, Francis. L'action politique de Calvin hors de Genève, d'après sa correspondance. Genève, Georg, 1909. 76 p. (Memoire publié à l'occasion du jubilé de l'Université de Genève).

DICKENS, Arthur Geoffrey. Reformation and society in sixteenth-century Europe. London, Thames & Hudson (1966) "Calvin and Geneva": p. 151—164. [Library of European civilization].

DUFOUR, Alain. Le mythe de Genève au temps de Calvin. **Revue Suisse d'histoire,** 8: 489—518, 1959.

GRAHAM, William Fred. Calvin and the city council. **Presbyterian life,** 18 (10) 6—8, 1965.

GREENE, Theodore A. Ecclesiastical organization of Geneva in the time of Calvin. **Journal of presbyterian history,** 11 (8) 305—367, 1923.

GRIER, William James. Calvin's Geneva **(In:** Puritan and Reformed studies. Conference, 15th, London, 1964. Able ministers of the New Testament; papers read at the conference. [London, 1965] p. 66—74).

GUERDAN, René. La vie quotidienne à Genève au temps de Calvin. Paris, Hachette, 1973.

GUGGISBERG, Kurt. Calvin und Bern **(In:** Festgabe Leonhard von Muralt zum 70. Geburtstag. 17 Mai

1970. Zurich, Berichthaus (1970) p. 266—285).

HALL, Basil. The Reformation city. **John Rylands Library, Bulletin,** 54: 102—148, 1971/72.

HENRY, Carl Ferdinand Howard. Calvin and politics in Geneva [With reference to The register of the company of pastors of Geneva] **Christianity today,** 10 (23) 1204—1205, 1966.

HEXTER, Jack H. Utopia and Geneve [Comparing the ideas of Moore and Calvin's influence in Geneva] **(In:** Action and conviction in early modern Europe; essays in memory of E. H. Harbison. Editors: Theodore K. Robb & Herrold E. Siegel. Princeton, University Press, 1969. p. 77—89).

HILLERBRAND, Hans Joachim. Brennpunkte der Reformation; zeitgenössische Texte und Bilder. Göttingen, Vandenhoeck & Ruprecht (c1967) „Johannes Calvin und die Reformation in Genf": p. 191—229. Original title: The Reformation; a narrative history related by contemporary observers and participants.

HOPKINS, Henry Charles, Calvyn in Genève. **Die Kerkbode, 95** (43) 1358—1360, 1965.

HUGHES, Philip Edgecumbe. Geneva of John Calvin. **Churchman,** 78:254—275, 1964.

KAPPSTEIN, Th. Wie Genf eine moralische Stadt wurde. **Christliche Welt,** 48: 928—932, 1934.

KINGDON, Robert Mc Cune. The control of morals in Calvin's Geneva. **(In:** The social history of the Reformation, ed. by Lawrence P. Buck & Jonathan W. Zophy. Columbus State Univ. Press (c1972). "In honor of Harold J. Grimm." p. 3—16).

KINGDON, Robert McCune. The deacons of the Reformed church in Calvin's Geneva **(In:** Mélanges d'histoire du XVIe siècle, offerts à Henri Meylan. Genève, Droz, 1970. p. 81—90) (Travaux d'humanisme et renaissance, 60).

KINGDON, Robert McCune. Social welfare in Calvin's Geneva. **American historical review,** 76 (1) 50—69, 1971.

KRAMER, Neilie. Calvin as organizer and systematizer of the church and state in Geneva. **The Banner,** 62: 473—474, 1927.

KUYPER, H. H. Calvijn en het Meer van Genève. [n.p.] Garrago [n.d.] 8 p.

LANG, August. Genfer Liturgie des J. Knox. **Reformierte Kirchenzeitung,** 81: 315—,1931.

MARINI, Lino. La libertà politica di Ginevra agli inizi del seicento **(In:** Roma, Facolta Valdesi di Teologica. Ginevra et l'Italia; recolta di studi promossa dalla Facolta Valdesi di Teologica di Roma a cura Delio Cantimori [et al]. Firenze, Sansoni (1959) p. 413—450) (Bibliotheca Storica Sansoni, 34).

MARTIN, Charles. La famille Stafford à Genève; son conflit avec Calvin, 1556. Genève, 1918.

MERZ, Hans. Die Differenzen swischen Bern und Calvin **(In:** Universität Bern. Johannes Calvin. Akademische Feier der Universität Bern zu seinem 400. Todestag. Bern, Haupt, 1965. p. 7—9) (Berner Universitätsschriften, Hft. 13).

MONTER, E. William. Crime and punishment in Calvin's Geneva, 1562. **Archiv für Reformationsgeschichte,** 64: 281—287, 1973.

NAUTA, Doede. Calvijn en zijn gemeente **(In: Zicht op Calvijn**

[door] J. van Genderen (e.a). Amsterdam, Buyten & Schipperheyn, 1965. p. 105—141).

NEDERBRAGT, Johan Alexander. Kalvinismus; Studien und Skizzen. Budapest, Sylvester, 1938. „Aus der Stadt Kalvins". p. 97—130.

NICOLINI, B. Bernardino Ochino esule a Ginevra; 1542—1545 **(In:** Roma, Facolta Valdesi di Teologica. Ginevra et l'Italia; recolta di studi promossa dalle Facolta Valdesi di Teologica di Roma a cura Delio Cantimore [et al] Firenze, Sansoni [1959] p. 135—148) (Bibliotheca Storica Sansoni, 34).

OLIVET A. La Compagnie des pasteurs de l'église protestante de Genève de 1543 à 1800. **Revue de theologie et de philosophie, N.S.,** 3: 114—139, 1915.

OLIVIERI, Achille. La Ginevra di Calvino in un libro recente [re: Monter, E. W. Calvin's Geneva] **Critica storica,** 6: 574—581, 1967.

PASCAL, Arturo. La colonia piemontese a Ginevra nel sec. XVI **(In:** Roma, Facolta Vadesi di Teologica. Ginevra et l'Italia; recolta di studi promossa dalla Facolta Valdesi di Teologica di Roma a cura Delio Cantimore [et al] Firenze, Sansoni [1959] p. 65—135) (Bibliotheca Storica Sansoni, 34).

PITTARD, Hélène (Dufour) L'Académie de Calvin; a propos d'un quatrième centenaire [par] Noëlle Roger [pseud.] **Foi et vie,** 38: 21—33, 1937.

PLATH, Uwe. Calvin und Basel in den Jahren 1552—1556. Frankfurt, Weber 1973. 310 p. (Basler Studien zur historischen und systematischen Theologie, Bd. 22).

PONS, Emilio. L'accademia di Calvino. **Rivista Cristiana, N.S.** 3: 375—379, 1901.

ROBERTSON, Archibald. The Reformation. London, Watts, 1960. "Calvin at Geneva": p. 127—140.

RODENS, Franz. Calvin und der Geist von Genf. **Die neue Schau,** 21: 351—352, 1960.

RUSHDOONY, Rousas John. Politics of guilt and pity. Nutley, N. J., Craig Press, 1970. "Calvin in Geneva; the sociology of justification by faith": p. 263—290.

STAEDTKE, Joachim. Calvin in Zürich. **Neue zürcher Zeitung,** 59 (2230) 4; 5, 1964.

STAUFFENEGGER, Roger. A propos des "Registres de la Compagnie des pasteurs de Genève au temps de Calvin". **Schweizerische Zeitschrift für Geschichte,** 1: 95—106, 1965.

STICKELBERGER, Emanuel. Wie Calvin nach Genf kam. **Reformatio,** 8: 293—295, 1959.

TAYLOR, Benjamin Harrison. A historical study of the mission of the church in Geneva 1536—1564. Richmond, Va., 1968. 288 l. Thesis-Union Theological Seminary, Richmond, Va.

TOURN, Giorgio. Calvino e la Riforma a Ginevra. Torina, Claudiana, 1965. 113 p. (I testimoni, 2).

VANCE, James I. John Calvin, the citizen. **Union Seminary quarterly review,** 47 (1) 1—6, 1935.

VAN ITTERZON, G. P. De Universiteit van Genève. **Hervormd weekblad-de Geref. Kerk,** 70 (3529) 292—294, 1958/59.

WOOLLEY, Paul. Calvin as a reformer in Geneva. **Torch and trumpet,** 9 (2) 11—13, 1959.

YOUNGE, Leigh. A day in the city of Calvin. **The Interior,** 40 (2030) 520—521, 1909.

God.

BELLANT, Roger. De la Doctrine trinitaire; et tout specialement, des rapports entre la première et la deuzième personnes, selon l'expose de l'Institution chrètienne. Paris, 1938. 88 1. Thesis-Faculté libre de théologie protestante de Paris.

BOISSET, Jean. Calvin et la souverainité de Dieu. Paris, Seghers (1964) 189 p. (Philosophes de tous les temps, 12).

BRUN, Marcel Jean. Religious knowledge and the honor of God in Calvin's theology. New York, 1932. 194 l. Thesis-Union Theological Seminary, New York.

BULMAN, James Michael. A comparison of John Calvin's and Emil Brunner's doctrine of God. Louisville, 1949, 205 1. Thesis-Southern Baptist Theological Seminary, Louisville.

BUSCHBECK, Bernhard. Die Lehre von Gottesdienst im Werk Johannes Calvins. [Marburg] 1968. 385 p. Thesis-Marburg.

CADIER, Jean Calvin, un homme passioné de la gloire de Dieu. **Societé de l'histoire du protestantisme français Bulletin** 110: 148—149, 1964.

CADIER, Jean. Rachetés pour glorifier Dieu [Festive sermon] **La revue réformée,** 15 (60) 31—37, 1964.

CHALKER, William Houston. Calvin and some seventeenth century English Calvinists; a comparison of their thought through an examination of their doctrines of the knowledge of God, faith and assurance. Durham, N.C., 1961. Calvin: p. 10—86. Thesis-Duke Univ., Durham, N.C.

DEMOUGEOT, Marcel. Notes relative à la notion trinitaire de Dieu et de son acte créateur, chez Calvin, d'après les chapitres XIII & XIV du livre I de l'Institution de 1559. Paris, 1947. 65 1 Thesis-Faculté libre de théologie protestante de Paris.

DE WOLF, Lotan Harold. Theological rejection of natural theology; an evaluation. **Journal of religious thought,** 15: 91—106, 1958.

EBELING, Gerhard. Cognito Dei et hominis **(In:** Geist und Geschichte der Reformation; Festgabe Hanns Rückert zum 65. Geburtstag. Hrsg. von H. Liebing [u.a.] Berlin, De Gruyter, 1966. p. 271—322) (Arbeiten zur Kirchengeschichte 38) **(Also in:** Lutherstudien. Tübingen, Mohr (Siebeck) 1971. v.I. p. 221—272).

FABER, Jelle. Calvijn over het beeld Gods. **Lucerna,** 5 (4) 159—189, 1964.

FILES, Leslie R. A biblical and theological study of natural theology. Westminster, 1964. "Calvin": p. 49—81. Thesis-Westmινister Theological Seminary.

FINLAYSON, R. A. Calvin's doctrine of God **(In:** Puritan and Reformed studies, Conference 15th, London, 1964. Able ministers of the New Testament. Papers read at Conference. [London, 1965] p. 3—18).

GERRISH, Brian Albert. To the unknown God; Luther and Calvin on the hiddenness of God. **Journal of religion,** 53: 263—292, 1973.

HARMAN, Allan M. Speech about the Trinity: with special reference to Novatian, Hilary and Calvin. **Scottish journal of theology,** 26 (4) 385—400, 1973.

HOUGH, Robert Spencer. A study of the Presbyterian doctrine of the will of God. Richmond, Va., 1949. "Calvin": p. 71—212. Thesis-Union

Theological Seminary, Richmond, Va.

KUIZENGA, Henry Bernard. The relation of God's grace to his glory in John Calvin (**In:** Littel, Franklin Hamlin, ed. Reformation studies; essays in honor of R. H. Bainton. Richmond, Knox [c1962] p. 95—105).

LECERF, Auguste. Études calvinistes recueillies et introduites par André Schlemmer. Neuchâtel, Delachaux et Niestlé [c1949] „La souverainitè de Dieu d'après le calvinisme; étude de quelques objections": p. 19—24. (Série théologique de l'actualité protestante).

MAILLART, Claude. Evolution de la doctrine de la connaissance de Dieu. De Calvin à l'orthodoxie protestante du XVIIe siècle. Paris, 1959. 118 1. Thesis-Faculté libre de théologie protestante de Paris.

OSTERHAVEN, Maurice Eugene. Our knowledge of God according to John Calvin. Princeton, N.J., 1948. 243 1. Thesis-Princeton Theological Seminary.

PARKER, Thomas Henry Louis. Calvin's doctrine of the knowledge of God (rev. ed.) Grand Rapids, Mich, Eerdmans (1959) 128 p. Original title: The doctrine of the knowledge of God; a study in the theology of John Calvin. 2nd ed. published by Oliver and Boyd, Edinburgh. 1969.

POSTEMA, Gerald J. Calvin's alleged rejection of natural theology. **Scottish journal of theology,** 24 (4) 423—434, 1971.

PULLIAM, Paul R. The Trinity in the teachings of John Calvin and Karl Barth. Pittsburgh, 1960. 117 1. Thesis-Xenia Theological Seminary, Pittsburgh.

RIEMENS, Johannes, Jr. De kenbronnen der goddelijke waarheid volgens Calvijn. **Troffel en zwaard,** 11: 39—61, 1908.

RIST, Gilbert. Objet et méthode de la théologie d'après saint Anselme, Abèlard, saint Bernard, saint Thomas, Calvin et Karl Barth. Genève, 1964. „La connaissance existentiélle de Dieu; le type calvinien de théologie:" p. 115—138. Thesis-Genève Université.

SMITH Samuel David. A study of the relation between the doctrine of creation and the doctrine of revelation through the created universe in the thought of John Calvin, Friedrich Schleiermacher and Paul Tillich. Nashville, Tenn., 1965. "Calvin": p. 15—99. Thesis-Vanderbilt Univ., Nashville.

THOMAS, Ivor Bishton. The problem of natural theology in the theology of John Calvin; a study of Calvin's doctrine of the knowledge of God the Creator. (New York) 1962. 85 1. Thesis-Union Theological Seminary, New York.

THOMAS, John Newton. The place of natural theology in the thought of John Calvin. **Journal of religious thought,** 15 (2) 107—136, 1958.

TORRANCE, Thomas Forsyth. Calvin and the knowledge of God. **Christian century,** 81: 696—699,1964.

TORRANCE, Thomas Forsyth. Knowledge of God and speech about Him, according to John Calvin. **Revue d'histoire et de philosophie religieuses,** 44 (4) 402—422, 1964/65. **Also in:** Regards contemporains sur Jean Calvin. Actes du colloque Calvin, Strasbourg, 1964. Paris, Presses Universitaires de France, 1965. p. 140—160. (Cahiers R.H.P., 39).

VAN DER LINDE, Simon. Calvijn

over het kennen van God. **Theologia reformata.** 13 (1) 3—14, 1970.

WISKERKE, J. R. De geestelijkheid van God [Calvijns beschouwingen] **De Reformatie,** 42 (5—19) 1966/67.

ZIGMUND, H. A. Calvin's concept of the Trinity [Poem] **Hartford quarterly,** 5: 58—64, 1965.

Grace see Redemption.

Historiography see Philosophy.

Holy communion see Sacraments.

Holy Spirit.

ABEL, Jean. The ethical implications of the doctrine of the Holy Spirit in John Calvin. Richmond, Va., 1948. 144 1. Thesis- Union Theological Seminary, Richmond, Va.

BÉKÉSI, A. Kálvin, a Szentlélek theologusa [Calvin, theologian of the Holy Spirit] **Theológiai szemle,** 2: 50—52, 1952.

BOYLE, Robert Martin. The doctrine of the witness of the Holy Spirit in John Calvin's theology considered against a historical background. Abilene, Tex., 1967. Thesis—Abilene Christian College.

BRUNET, Simone. La spiritualité calvinienne. Montpellier, 1973. 502 1. Thesis-Université Paul Valéry.

CUBINE, Margaret Virginia. John Calvin's doctrine of the work of the Holy Spirit examined in the light of some contemporary theories of interpersonal psychotherapy. Ann Arbor Mich., University Microfilms, 1955. 375 1. Thesis-Northwestern Univ., Illinois.

FARRIS, Allan Leonard. The place of the Holy Spirit in the thought of John Calvin. [Edinburgh? 195-?] Thesis.

GREIJDANUS, Seakle. Karakter van het Testimonium Spiritus Sancti volgens Calvijn. **Gereformeerd theologisch tijdschrift,** 14 (12) 519—554, 1914.

KIEVIT, I. Leven van de hoop. Kampen, Kok, 1970. 187 p.

KOOLE, J. Testimonium spiritus sancti bij Calvijn. **Stromata,** 4 (14) 2—5, 2/1959.

KRAUS, Hans-Joachim. Charisma prophetikon; eine Studie zum Verständnis in neutestamentlichen Geistesgabe bei Zwingli und Calvin **(In:** Wort und Gemeinde; Probleme und Aufgaben der praktischen Theologie. Eduard Thurneysen zum 80. Geburtstag. Hrsg. von Rudolf Bohren und Max Geiger. Zürich, EVZ-Verl., 1968. p. 80—103).

LOCHER, Gottfried Wilhelm. Testimonium internum; Calvins Lehre vom Heiligen Geist und das hermeneutische Problem. Rede an der Gedächtnisfeier der Universität Basel zum 400. Todestage Johannes Calvins am 27. Mai 1964. Zürich, EVZ-Verl. (c1964) 30 p. (Theologische Studien, Hft. 81).

LOCHER, Gottfried Wilhelm. Zu Calvins Lehre vom Heiligen Geist; Gedanken zum hermeneutischen Problem. **Basler Nachrichten. Sonntagsblatt** 58 (223) 23, 1964.

LÖSCHHORN, Albert. Christus in uns; die Lehre von der Einwohnung Christi. Gütersloh, Rufer-Verl., 1954. 133 p. (Sammlung lebendige Gemeinde).

LOUWERENS, Guilielmus S. J. L'habitation de l'Esprit Saint dans l'âme du fidèle d'après la doctrine de Jean Calvin. Romae, 1952. 32 1. Thesis-Pontificia Universitas Gregoriana.

PARRATT J. K. The witness of the Holy Spirit; Calvin, the Puritans and St. Paul. **Evangelical quarterly,** 41 (3) 161—168, 1969.

PIN, Jean-Pierre. La présence de Jésus-Christ aux hommes d'après l'Institution de 1560 de Jean Calvin. Strasbourg, 1971. 265 1. Thesis-Université Strasbourg.

QUISTORP, H. J. J. Th. Calvins Lehre vom Heiligen Geist **(In:** De Spiritu Sancto; bijdragen tot de leer van de Heilige Geest by gelegenheid van het 2e eeuwfeest van het Stipendium Bernardinum. Utrecht, Kemink, 1964. p. 109—150).

RAY, R. Witness and Word. **Canadian journal of theology,** 15: 14—23, 1969.

RICHARD, Lucien J. The spirituality of John Calvin; its sources and originality. Cambridge, Mass., 1972. Thesis—Harvard University.

STIKTBERG, William Robert. The mystical element in the theology of John Calvin. (New York, 1951) 118 1. Thesis-Union Theological Seminary, New York.

VAN DER LINDE, Simon. Calvijns leer van de Heilige Geest. **Theologia reformata,** 14 (1) 15—31, 1971.

VAN ITTERZON, G. P. Het testimonium Spritus Sancti bij Calvijn. **Hervormd Weekblad-de Geref. Kerk,** 74: 190; 197; 206; 214, 1962/63.

WALTERS, Gwyn. The doctrine of the Holy Spirit in John Calvin. Edinburgh, 1949. 374 p. Thesis-University of Edinburgh.

ZERWAS, Jack La-Vere. The Holy Spirit in Calvin. New York, 1947. 79 1. Thesis-Union Theological Seminary, New York.

Inspiration see Bible.

Institutes.

BARTOS, F. M. Nové svetlo do osudu ceského prekladu Kalvínovy Instituce. **Kostnicke jiskry,** 51 (41) 3, 1966.

BASTIDE, Ch. La traduction anglaise de l'"Institution chretienne." **Societé de l'histoire du protestantisme français. Bu letin,** 73: 140—147, 1914.

BATTLES, Ford Lewis. An analysis of the Institutes of the Christian religion of John Calvin, by Ford Lewis Battles, assisted by John Walchenbach. Rev. ed. Pittsburgh, Pa., Pittsburgh Theological Seminary, 1970. 2 v.

BATTLES, Ford Lewis. A computerized concordance to Institutio christiance religionis 1559 of Joannes Calvinus. Based on the critical text of Petrus Barth & G. Guilelmus Niesel (Books 1—2 : 1967 [i.e. 1957] Book 3: 1959, Book 4: 1962) corrected from the original text of 1559, by F. L. Battles with the assistance of Charles Miller.
Pittsburg, Pa, Clifford E. Barbour Library, Pittsburgh Theological Seminary, 1972. 3 reels (Microfilm) — Printed introduction, lemmatic index & other aids. [1st ed.] 81 p.

BATTLES, Ford Lewis. Englishing the Institutes of John Calvin. **Babel,** 9 (1/2) 94—98, 1968.

BATTLES, Ford Lewis. New light on Calvin's Institutes; a supplement to the McNeill-Battles translation. Hartford, Conn., Hartford Seminary Press, 1966. 1 v. (unpaged).

BÉKÉFI, B. Kálvin; 400-éves Institutioja [Quatercentenary of the Institutes of Calvin] **Református egyház,** 2: 140-, 1959.

BELLANT, Roger. De la doctrine trinitaire; et tout specialement, des rapports entre la première et la deuxième personnes, selon l'exposé de l'Institution chrétienne. Paris,

1938. 88 l. Thesis-Faculté libre de théologie protestante de Paris.

BELLARMINO, Roberto Francesco Romolo. Notes marginales de Cyrille Lucar dans un exemplaire du grand catéchisme de Bellarmin [The Italian text with the Greek tr. of Leonardos Philaras and the marginal notes of Kurillos. Ed. and annotated, with special reference to the Institutio christianae religionis of Calvin and to the works of Thomas Aquino, by Keetje Rozemond] Den Haag, 1963. 75 p. (Kerkhistorische studien, dl. 11).

BENOîT, Jean Daniel. The history and development of the Institutio: how Calvin worked. **(In:** Duffield, G. E., ed. John Calvin. Appleford, Courtenay (1966) p. 102—117) (Courtenay studies in Reformation theology, 1).

BENOîT, Jean Daniel. D'une édition à l'autre de l'Institution; comment Calvin travaillait. **La revue réformée,** 11 (2) 39—51, 1960.

BLISS, Carey S. A much-travelled association copy of Calvin's Institutes. **Book collector,** 17 (4) 458—462, 1968.

BÖNHOFF, L. Die erste wissenschaftliche protestantische Glaubenslehre. Zum 400. Jubileum von Calvins Institutio religionis christianae. **Neue sächsische Kirchenblatt,** 42: 494-, 1935.

BÖTTGER, Paul Christoph. Calvins Institutio als Erbauungsbuch; Versuch einer literarischen Analyse. Göttingen, 1964. 159 1. Thesis- Göttingen.

BOZZA, Tommaso. Il beneficio di Cristo e la Istituzione della religione cristiana di Calvino. Roma, Arti Grafiche Italiane, 1961. p. 3—14.

BROMILEY, Geoffrey William. The doctrine of hope in Calvin's **Institutes. Churchman,** 67: 148—152, 1953.

BÜSSER, Fritz. Calvins Institutio; einige Gedanken über ihre Bedeutung. **Zwingliana,** 11: 93—105, 1959 [Niesel 1004] **(Also in:** Wirkungen der deutschen Reformation bis 1555. Hrsg. von Walther Hubatsch. Darmstadt, Wissenschaftliche Buchgesellschaft, 1970 (1967) p. 157—173) (Wege der Forschung, Bd. 203).

COETZEE, Carel Frederik Christoffel. Die skopus van die Skrif by Calvyn; 'n dogmatiese verkenning van sekere hoofstukke uit die Institusie van Calvyn. Potchefstroom, 1972. 139 1. Thesis-P.U. vir C.H.O., Potchefstroom.

COSTE, Henri. Le probleme de l'incarnation dans les chapitres 6 à 17 du livre II de l'Institution de la religion chrétienne. Quelques aspects de la christologie de Calvin. Genève, 1949. 125 1. Thesis-Genève.

CRAWFORD, David James. God in human history; a study of Calvin's understanding of history; with special reference to the Institutes. Toronto, 1967. 156 1. Thesis-Knox College, Toronto.

d'ASSONVILLE, Victor Edouard. Calvyn se Institusie as handboek vir John Knox. **In die Skriflig,** 3 (10) 49—52, 1969.

d'ASSONVILLE, Victor Edouard. John Knox and the Institutes of Calvin; a few points of contact in their theology (Durban, Drakensberg Press, pref. 1968) 112 p. Thesis-University of Natal, Durban.

DEAN, Albert Clarke. The Institutes of 1539 and the letter to the Romans. Richmond Va., 1953. 209 1. Thesis-Union Theological Seminary, Richmond, Va.

DE KLERK, Willem Johannes. Die Institusie van Johannes Calvyn. **Woord en daad,** 4 (6) 4, 1959.

DE KROON, M. J. J. P. De eer van God en het heil van de mens; bijdrage tot het verstaan van de theologie van Johannes Calvijn naar zijn Institutie. Roermond, Romen, 1968. 191 p. Thesis-Utrecht.

DEMOUGEOT, Marcel. Notes relatives à la notion trinitaire de Dieu et de son acte créateur, chez Calvin, d'après les chapitres XIII & XIV du livre I de l'Institution de 1559. Paris, 1947. 65 1. Thesis-Faculté libre de théologie protestante de Paris.

DIEHL, Charles E. John Calvin and the Institutes of the Christian religion. [n.p.] 1937. p. 47—64.

DREYER, Johannes Gerhardus Martinus. Calvyn dra sy Institusie op. **Die Hervormer,** 50 (2) 31, 1959.

DUFFIELD, Gervase E. The growth of Calvin's Institutio **(In:** Puritan and Reformed studies. Conference, 15th. London, 1964. Able ministers of the New Testament; papers read at Conference. (London 1965) p. 56—65).

DUVENAGE, A. Een en ander oor Calvyn se Institusie. **Koers,** 26 (9) 333—336, 1959.

FRAENKEL, Peter. Quelques observations sur le "Tu es Petrus" chez Calvin, au Colleque de Worms en 1540 et dans l'Institution de 1543. **Bibliotheque d'humanisme et renaissance,** 27: 607—628, 1965.

GRISLIS, Egil. Calvin's use of Cicero in the Institutes, I: 1—5; a case study in theological method. **Archiv für Reformationsgeshichte,** 62 (1) 5—37, 1971.

HESSE. Zur vierjahrhundert Feier des Institutio Calvins und der Reformation in Genf. **Reformierte Kirchenzeitung,** 86: 194-, 1936.

HESSELINK, I. John. Development and purpose of Calvin's Institutes. **Reformed theological review,** 24: 65—72, 1965 [Repr., tr. from Japanese, from Calvin studies, I, Tokyo, 1965] **Reformation review,** 28: 136—142, 1970.

HUNT, S. Leigh. Predestination in the "Institutes of the Christian Religion". **Evangelical quarterly,** 9: 38—45, 1937.

HURLEY, Michael. The church in Protestant theology; some reflections on the fourth book of Calvin's Institutes **(In:** Flanagan, Donal, ed. The meaning of the church. Dublin, Gill 1966. p. 110—143).

HUTTAR, Charles Adolph. The first English translator of Calvin's Institutes [John Daus] **Gordon review,** 8: 69—83, 1962.

KEENEY, William. An analysis of Calvin's treatment of the Anabaptists in the Institutes. Hartford, Conn., 1958 (Unpublished — Hartford Seminary paper).

KEMPFF, Dionysius. Die boek van die Hervorming (Institusie) **Die Kerkblad,** 72 (2023) 2—3; (2024) 2—4, 1969.

KONAR, Jan. Geneza i charakter instytucji Kalwina. **Jednota,** 8: 8—9, 1964.

LAMPRECHT, J. C. Eskatologiese gedagtes in die Institusie van Calvyn. [Stellenbosch] 1937. 67 1. Thesis-Universiteit van Stellenbosch.

LOMBARD, Jacobus Christoffel. Die betekenis en invloed van die Institusie van Calvyn. **Die Kerkbode,** 126 (14) 438—440, 1974.

LÜTHI, Jesse Leo. Divine sovereignty, law and grace in John Calvin's

Institutes. Madison, N. J., 1950. 137 l. Thesis-Drew Univ., Madison, N.J.

MARCEL, Pierre. Réédition de l'Institution chrétienne de Jean Calvin. **La revue réformée,** 5 (4) 51—56, 1954.

MARICHAL, Walter M. L'Institution de la religion chretienne de Jean Calvin. **Les cahiers calvinistes,** 2 (4) 3—14, 1960.

MELAN, E. F. The Stoic doctrine of indifferent things and the conception of Christian liberty in Calvin's Institutio religionis Christianae. **Romanic review,** 28, 1937.

MEYER, B. Sacramental theology in the Institutes of John Calvin. **American Benedictine review,** 15: 60—80, 1964.

MOLNÁR, Amedeo. Zapomenutý podnét Calvinovy Instituce [Hidden motive of the Institutes by Calvin]**Krestanska revue,** 18: 176—182, 1951.

MONTSERRAT, J. Le quatrième centenaire de L'Institution chrétienne; pèlerinage à la maison de Calvin. **I lustration,** 190: 278—279, 1935.

MURRAY, H. John Calvin and his Institutes of religion. **South African libraries/Suid-Afrikaanse biblioteke,** 10: 48—52, 1952.

MURRAY Robert H. John Calvin and his Institutes **(In:** The political consequences of the Reformation; studies in sixteenth-century political thought. New York, Russel & Russel, 1960, c1926. p. 80—128).

'n PAAR gedagtes na aanleiding van Calvyn se Institusie. **Woord en daad,** 8 (41) 8—9, 1965.

PAUCK, Wilhelm. The heritage of the Reformation; rev. and enl. ed. New York, Free Press of Glencoe, 1961. "Calvin's Institutes": p. 61—72.

PERRIER, Marc. La notion de foi dans l'Institution chrétienne. Paris, 1957. 76 l. Thesis-Faculté libre de théologie protestante de Paris.

PIN, Jean-Pierre. La présence de Jésus-Christ aux hommes d'après l'Institution de 1560 de Jean Calvin. Strasbourg, 1971. 265 l. Thesis-Université Strasbourg.

POTGIETER; Frederick Johannes Mentz. Die Institusie van Calvyn. **Die Kerkbode,** 84 (1) 13—15, 1959.

RICHGELS, Robert William. Calvin and Bellarmine on man; a comparative study of the anthropology of the Institutes and the Disputations. Madison, Wis., 1968. 123 l. Thesis-University of Wisconsin.

ROBERT, Louis C. Essai sur la notion de la foi d'après l'Institution chrétienne de Jean Calvin. Lausanne, 1918. 102 p. Thesis-Lausanne.

ROSSLEE, Diederik Daniël. Institusie aan die owerheid. **Die Kerkbode,** 84 (24) 979—980, 1959.

RUFER, Alfred. L'église protestante et son autorité d'après l'Institution chrétienne. Neuchâtel, 1931. Thesis-Neuchâtel.

RÜSCH, Ernst Gerhard. Eine private Bearbeitung der Institutio Calvins. **Theologische Zeitschrift,** 24 (6) 427—434, 1968.

SANDEN, Oscar Emanuel. Calvin's Institutes of the Christian religion. San Antonio, Tex., Sanden, 1939. 42 p.

SCHULZE, Ludolf Ferdinand. Opmerkings oor Calvyn se Institusie, III. 1. **In die Skriflig,** 1 (4) 35—43, 1967.

SCHULZE, Martin. Meditatio futurae vitae; ihr Begriff und ihre herrschende Stellung im System Calvins; ein Beitrag zum Verständnis von dessen Institutio. Aalen, Scientia, 1971 (Leipzig, 1901) 89 p. (Studien zur Geschichte der Theologie und der Kirche, Bd. 6, Hft. 4).

SCHUMMER, Leopold. Le ministère pastoral dans l'Institution chrétienne de Calvin à la lumière du troisième sacrement. Wiesbaden, Steiner, 1965. 108 p. (Veröffentlichungen des Instituts für europaïsche Geschichte, Mainz, Bd. 39. Abt. für abendländische Religionsgeschichte).

SMID, T. D. Calvijns Institutie in het Spaans. **Het Boek,** 37 (4) 207—208, 1966.

SMID, T. D. Cypriano de Valero and his Spanish translation of Calvin's Institution. **Free University quarterly,** 9 (4) 243—248, 1965.

TANIS, E. J. Social teachings of Calvin's Institutes. **Calvin forum,** 2: 53—56, 1936/37.

TIMMER, John. Calvin's Institutes; Japan. **The Banner,** 101 (5) 16, 1966.

TRAZ, Robert de. L'Institution chrétienne et Calvin. **La semaine littéraire,** 932: 529—531, 1911.

UNMACK, E. C. What is true religion? Or, The philosophy of Calvinism (Study of Calvin's 'Institutes'). **Evangelical quarterly,** 5: 180—188, 1933.

URBÁNKOVA, Emma. Nekolik poznámek k ceskému vydání kalvinovy Instituce [On the Czech ed. of Calvin's Institutio; summary in Eng,. p. 246] **Literárni archiv,** 93: 237—245, 1966.

VAN DER LINDE, Simon. Het christenleven in kerk en staat bij Calvijn, volgens boek IV van de Institutie. **Theologia reformata,** 15: 102—118, 1972.

VAN DER WALT, Sarel Petrus. Die Institusie van Calvyn. **Die Kerkblad,** 61 (1519) 13; 15; 21, 1959.

VAN HALSEMA, Emo. Calvijns Insitutie. **De Wachter,** 92 (4) 4—5; (5) 4—5; (6) 4—5; (7) 4—5; (8) 5; (9) 5, 15; (11) 5, 15; (13) 4; (14) 5, 15; (17) 4; (18) 5, 11; (19) 5, 11, 1959.

VAN ITTERZON, G. P. De Institutie van Calvijn. **Hervormd weekblad — de Geref. Kerk,** 70 (3531) 307—309, 1958/59.

WALCH, Roger. Untersuchungen über die lexikalischen und morphologischen Varianten in den vier französischen Ausgaben der "Institution de la religion chrestienne" von Jean Calvin. Dorbirn, Mayer, 1960. 104 p. Thesis—Basel.

WALCH, Roger. Versuch eines Begriffssystems des theologischen Wortschatzes der "Institution de la religion chrestienne" von Jean Calvin. [Basel] 1960. 118 1.

WILLIAMS, Ivor D. An appraisal of the doctrine of justification by faith, as developed by John Calvin in the Institutes of the Christian religion. New York, 1946. 120 1. Thesis—Union Theological Seminary, New York.

Justification see Redemption.

Law see Nature and grace.

Letters.

BENOÎT, Jean Daniel. Calvin the letter-writer **(In:** Duffield, G. E. ed. John Calvin. Appleford, Courtenay (1966) p. 67—101) (Courtenay studies in Reformation theology, 1).

CABRINI, Luigi. Dieci lettere dalla Svizzera. Cremona, "Cremona Nuova," 1940. "Calvino": p. 37—48.

CLAVIER, Henri. Coup d'oeil sur la correspondence et l'action de Calvin en Provence. **France. Ministère de l'education nationale. Comité des travaux historiques et scientifiques. Bulletin du Comité. Section de philologie et d'histoire (jusqua 1610)** 1965: p. 655—667.

d'ASSONVILLE, Victor Edouard. Uit die briewe van Calvyn. **Die Kerkblad,** 71 (1945) 8—9; (1947) 8—9; (1949) 11, 13, 14; (1950) 8—9; (1953) 12; (1956) 5—6, 1968.

DE GRAAF, B. Calvijn's brieven aan Jacques de Bourgogne. **De Antiquaar,** 3: 5—13, 1972.

DUFOUR, Alain. Deux lettres obliées de Calvin à J. Andreae (1556—1558) **Bibliotheque d'humanisme et renaissance,** 24: 375—384, 1962.

FARRIS, A. L. Calvin's letter to Luther. **Canadian journal of theology,** 10: 124—131, 1964.

GAGG, Robert P. Calvins Brief an Sadolet als Warnung an uns Protestanten. **Reformatio,** 16 (2) 75—79, 1967.

HALASKI, Karl. Auch ein Calvin-Brief [re correspondence with Edel] **Reformierte Kirchenzeitung,** 105: 116—118, 1964; 105: 141—143, 1964.

HEMARDINQUER, Jean-Jacques. Un correspondant de Calvin. **Société de l'histoire du protestantisme français. Bulletin,** 107: 166—170, 1961.

HERMINJARD, Aime Louis. Correspondance des réformateurs dans les pays de langue française. Recueillie et publiée avec d'autres lettres relatives à la Réforme et des notes historiques et biographiques. Nieuwkoop. De Graaf, 1965-'66. 9 v. Facsimile of publication by Georg, Genève, 1866-'97.

HIGMAN, Francis Montgomery. A lost letter by Charles de Jonvilliers [Secretary of Calvin] **Bibliotheque d'humanisme et renaissance,** 23: 555—566, 1961.

HOMMES, Nicolaas Jan. De laatste brief van Du Tillet aan Calvyn (1 Dec. 1538) **Gereformeerd weekblad,** 23 (26) 175—176, 1967.

HORNE, Charles Silvester. Calvin in his letters **(In:** Mansfield College Essays; presented to Rev. Andrew Martin Fairbairn, on the occasion of his seventieth birthday, Nov. 4, 1908. London, Hodder & Stoughton, 1909. p. 2—20).

JA zum Martyrium. Johannes Calvins Brief an Richard Lefèvre in Lyon, 1551 **(In:** Kantzenbach, Friedrich Wilhelm. Zeugnis und Zeichen; Reden, Briefe, Dokumente. München, Kaiser, 1964. p. 27—31).

JACCARD, Pierre. De Calvin à Charles Secrétan. **Les cahiers protestants,** 45: 33—38, 1961.

MONOD, Léopold. Le caractère de Calvin, d'après ses lettres. Lyon, Librairie Royer, 1912. 43 p.

PETER, Rodolphe & ROTT, Jean, **editors.** Les lettres a Jean Calvin de la collection Sarray, publiées avec un notice sur Claude et Isaac Sarrau. Paris, Presses Universitaires de France, 1971. 104 p. (Cahiers de la Revue d'histoire et de philosophie religieuses, 43).

PLATH, Uwe. Ein unbekannter Brief Calvins vom Vorabend der Religionskriege in Frankreich. **Archiv für Reformationsgeschichte,** 62 (2) 244—265, 1971.

RIES, Johannes. Brief [van Calvyn] aan 'n koningin [Jeanne D'Albret, Koningin van Navarre] **Naweekpos,** 7 (29) 32—33, 1960.

ROSENBOOM, Johannes. Johannes Calvins Lebenswerk in seinen Briefen. **Der evangelische Erzieher,** 16: 129—137, 1964.

SCHNEIDER, Arthur. Ein Blick in das Herz Calvins. **Reformierte Kirchenzeitung,** 105: 107—108; 120—121; 129—133; 143—145; 156—157, 1964.

UIT Calvijns brieven. **Belijden en beleven,** 16(42/43) 6; (45) 6; (46) 7, 1959.

ZEEDEN, Ernst Walter. Aufgaben der Staatsgewalt im Dienste der Reformation. Untersuchungen über die Briefe Calvins an Fürsten und Obrigkeiten. **Saeculum,** 15: 132—152, 1964.

ZEEDEN, Ernst Walter. Calvins Verhalten zum Luthertum; nach seinem Briefen **(In:** Festschrift Karl Eder zum siebzigsten Geburtstag. Hrsg. von Helmut J. Mezier-Andelberg. Innsbruck, 1959. p. 83—100).

Liturgy see **Church.**

Luther and other Reformers.

BAVAUD, Georges. La dispute de Lausanne, 1536. Une étappe de l'évolution doctrinale des Réformateurs Romands. Fribourg, 1956. "De Lefèvre d'Etaples à Calvin": p. 143—209. Thesis-Univ. Fribourg.

BENOÎT, Jean Daniel. Calvin et Viret. **Revue d'histoire et de philosophie religieuses,** 45 (1) 109—127, 1965. **(Also in:** Regards contemporains sur Jean Calvin. Actes du colloque Calvin, Strasbourg, 1964. Paris, Presses Universitaires de France, 1965. p. 269—287) (Cahiers R.H.P., 39).

BLANKE, Fritz. Aus der Welt der Reformation; fünf Aufsätze. Zürich, Zwingli (c1960) "Calvins Urteile über Zwingli": p. 18—47.

BLANKE, Fritz. Calvins Urteile über Zwingli. **Zwingliana,** 11 (2) 66—92, 1959.

BOUVIER, André. Calvin et Zwingli. **Foi et vérité,** 38 (10/2) 25—41, 1959.

BOYER, Charles, **S.J.** Calvin et Luther; accords et différences. Roma, Università Gregoriana, 1973. 242 p.

CLAASEN, Johannes Petrus. Die vriendskap van Calvyn, Farel en Viret. **Die Kerkbode,** 92 (17) 554—556, 1963.

CORNITESCU, Emilian. Canonul Sfîntei Scripturi la cei doi reformatori: Martin Luther si Jean Calvin. **Studii teologice,** 21: 199—209, 1969.

D'ESZLARY, Charles. Jean Calvin, Théodore de Bèze et leurs amis hongrois. **Societé de l'histoire du protestantisme francais. Bulletin,** 110: 74—99, 1964.

EEKHOF, A. Hoe heeft Calvijn over Luther gedach? **Nederlands archief voor kerkgeschiedenis,** 14: 273—296, 1918.

1550—1552: Bucer and Calvin urge further reformation in England **(In:** Puritanism in Tudor England. Ed. by H. C. Porter. London, Macmillan, 1970. p. 53—73).

FORRESTER, Duncan B. Martin Luther and John Calvin **(In:** History of political philosophy. Ed. by Leo Strauss and Joseph Cropsey. Chicago, Rand McNally, 1963.. p. 277—313).

GERRISH, Brian Albert. John Calvin on Luther **(In:** Interpreters of Luther; essays in honour of Wilhelm Pauck. Ed.: Jaroslav Pelikan. Philadelphia, Fortress Press, 1968. p. 67—96).

HOEKSTRA, P. Calvin versus Luther. **The Banner,** 42: 509—510, 1907.

HOLL, Karl. Kleine Schriften. Hrsg. von Robert Stupperich. Tübingen,

Mohr (Siebeck) 1966. "Luther und Calvin": p. 67—81.

HOVY, W. Huldreich Zwingli; John Knox en Johannes Calvyn. **Die Gereformeerde vroueblad,** 19 (3) 17—18, 1964.

JOOSTE, Josef Petrus. Calvyn se plek onder die Hervormers. **Die Kerkblad,** 62 (1570) 8; 13, 1960.

JOOSTE, Josef Petrus. Le Febre en Farel en hulle verband met Calvyn. **Die Kerkblad,** 66 (1722) 6—8, 1963.

KIM, Young Ik. Luther and Calvin on human reason. St. Louis, 1971. 95 1. Thesis-Concordia Seminary, St. Louis.

KLINGENBURG, Georg. Das Verhältniss Calvins zu Butzer untersucht auf Grund der wirtschaftethischen Bedeutung beider Reformatoren. Bonn, Georgi, 1912. 110 p. Thesis-Rheinische Friedrich-Wilhelms-Universität, Bonn.

LANDOR, Walter Savage. Melanchton and Calvin; excerpt from Imaginary conversations **(In:** Miles, Josephine, ed. Classic essays in English. Boston, Little, Brown [1965, c1961] p. 136—145).

LEMAÎTRE, Auguste. Calvin et Luther. **Foi et vérité,** 38 (10/2) 3—24 1959.

LOCHER, Gotfried Wilhelm. The shape of Zwingli's theology; a comparison with Luther and Calvin. Tr. by J. A. Morrison, rev. by J. Adams. **Pittsburgh perspective,** 8 (2) 5—26 1967.

MARCUSE, Herbert. Studies in critical philosophy **(In:** A study on authority, Boston, Beacon, 1973. "Luther and Calvin", p. 56—78).

MEINHOLD, Peter. Calvin und Luther. **Lutherische Monatshefte,** 3: 264—269, 1964.

MÜLHAUPT, Erwin Friedrich. Luther und Calvin. **Luther,** 30: 97—113, 1959.

NAUTA, Doede. Opera minora; kerk-historische verhandelingen over Calvijn en de geschiedenis van de kerk in Nederland. Kampen, Kok, 1961. "Calvyn en Erasmus": p. 1—12; "Calvyn en Luther": p. 12—29.

OVERDUIN, Jacobus. Gaat Calvyn dieper dan Luther? **Centraal weekblad voor de Gereformeerde kerken in Nederland,** 13 (19) 1, 1965.

PAUCK, Wilhelm. The heritage of the Reformation, rev. and enl. ed. New York, Free Press of Glencoe, 1961. "Calvin and Butzer": p. 85—100.

PONT, A. D. Renata van Frankryk, hertogin van Ferreira. **Die Hervormer,** 52 (7) 9, 12—13, 20; (8) 16—17, 1961.

POTTER, George Reuben. Zwingli and Calvin **(In:** Hurstfield, Joël, ed. The Reformation crisis. London, Arnold, 1965. p. 32—43).

ROGGE, Joachim. Kritik Calvins an Luthers Zwei-Reiche-Lehre? **(In:** Theologie in Geschichte und Kunst. Walter Elliger zum 65. Geburtstag. Hrsg. von Siegfried Hermann und Oskar Söhngen. Witten, Luther, 1968. p. 152—168).

SANTO, J. Luther, Calvin, Henri VIII, et les autres chefs de la Réformé. Paris, Santo [n.d.] 72 p.

SCHAFF, D. S. Martin Luther and John Calvin, church reformers. **Princeton theological review,** 5: 530—552, 1917.

SCHALK, A. Catching up with Calvin and Zwingli. **U.S. catholic & jubilee,** 35: 19—26, 1970.

SCHEIBE, M. Calvin und Luther. **Protestantenblatt,** 97: 124, 1918.

SCHETZLER, Ch. Zwingli et Calvin. **Revue de theologie et de philosophie,** N.S., 1: 384—391, 1913.

VAN DER VYVER, Gert Christoffel Petrus. Luther en Calvyn. **Die Kerkblad,** 77 (2274) 10—11, 1974.

VAN ROOY, A. J. Calvyn en Somerset. **Die Kerkblad,** 72 (2023) 10—11, 1969.

VENTER, E. S. Van Johannes Calvyn aan die Hertogin van Ferrara. **Die Gereformeerde vroueblad.** 14 (7, 8) 28—30, 1959.

WIEDEBURG, Andrea. Calvins Verhalten zu Luther, Melanchton und dem Lutherthum. Tübingen, 1961. 2 v. Thesis—Tübingen.

WIEDEBURG, Andrea. Die Freundschaft zwischen Butzer und Calvin nach ihren Briefen. **Historisches Jahrbuch der Görrer- Gesellschaft,** 83: 69—83, 1963.

WILLIAMS, George Huntston. The radical reformation. Philadelphia, Westminister, 1962. "Calvin and the radical reformation": p. 580—614.

ZEEDEN, Ernst Walter. Calvins Verhalten zum Luthertum; nach seinen Briefen **(In:** Festschrift Karl Eder; zum siebzigsten Geburtstag. Innsbruck, Wagner, 1959. p. 83—100).

ZEEDEN, Ernst Walter. Martin Luther, Johannes Calvin und zeitgenössische katholische Stimmen zur Reformation. Düsseldorf, Schwann, 1959. 80 p. (Geschichtliche Quellenschriften).

Man see Ethical matters.

Methodology see Philosophy.

Mission.

AVIS, P. D. L. The reformers and mission. **International reformed bulletin,** 17 (56/57) 2—15, 1974.

BEAVER, Robert Pierce. The Genevan mission to Brazil. **Reformed journal,** 17: 14—20, 1967 **(Also in:** The heritage of John Calvin. Ed. by John H. Bratt. Grand Rapids, Eerdmans, 1973. p. 55—73). (Heritage Hall Lectures, 1960—1970) (Heritage Hall publications, no. 2).

CHANEY, C. Missionary dynamic in the theology of John Calvin. **Reformation review,** 17: 24—38, 1964.

DEVARANNE. Calvin sendet dem ersten protestantischen Missionare aus. **Zeitschrift für Missionskunde und Religionswissenschaft,** 49: 247-, 1934.

DEVARANNE.Calvin und die Heidenmission. **Zeitschrift für Missionskunde und Religionswissenschaft,** 47: 152-, 1931.

DU PLESSIS, Hugo. Die betekenis van Calvyn vir die sending en die sendingwetenskap. **Die Kerkblad,** 62 (1569) 11—12, 1960.

HUGHES, Philip Edgecumbe. John Calvin; director of missions. **Columbia theological seminary bulletin,** 59: 17—25, 1966 **(Also in:** The heritage of John Calvin, ed. by John H. Bratt. Grand Rapids, Eerdmans, 1973. p. 40—54) Heritage Hall Lectures, 1960—1970) (Heritage Hall publications, no. 2).

HUIZENGA, Lee S. Calvin and missions. **Young Calvinist,** 20: 3—4, 1939.

KLOOSTER, Fred H. Missions; the Heidelberg Catechism and Calvin. **Calvin theological journal,** 7 (2) 181—208, 1972.

LECERF, Auguste. Calvin et les missions **(In:** Les précurseurs de l'idée missionaire en France aux XVIe et XVIIe siècles [Cf. Les cahiers missionaires, no. 6. Paris, 1923] p. V-XV).

MORRIS, S. L. The relation of Calvin and Calvinism to missions **(In:** Calvin memorial addresses; delivered before the General Assembly at Savannah, May 1909, in observance of the birth of John Calvin. Richmond, Va., Presbyterian Committee of Publications [n.d.] p. 127—146).

OLIVIERI, Achille. Due studi riguardanti l' 'emigrazione calvinista' vicentia a Ginevra nel cinquecento. **Rivista di storia della Chiesa in Italia,** 26: 125—129, 1972.

REVERDIN, Olivier. Quatorze Calvinistes chez les Topinambous; histoire d'une mission genèvoise au Brazil, 1556—1558. Genève, Droz, 1957. 110 p. Also pub. by Minard, Paris.

RULLMANN, J. A. C. Calvijn als zendingsman. **Gereformeerd weekblad,** 14: 155—156, 1958/59.

SCHUTTE, Jan Albert. Calvyn en die sending. **Die Kerkblad,** 65 (1663) 9, 1962.

VAN DELLEN, Idzerd. De betekenis van Calvijn voor de zending en de missiologie. **De Wachter,** 92 (4) 10—11, 1959.

VAN DEN BERG, J Calvin's missionary message; some remarks about the relation between Calvinism and missions. **Evangelical quarterly,** 22: 174—187, 1950.

ZÜGER, Anton. Zur calvinistischen Mission in Brasilien im 16 Jahrhundert; eine Richtigstellung. **Neue Zeitschrift für Missionswissenschaft,** 14: 28—29, 1958.

Music and Psalter.

BENSON, Louis Fitz Gerald. John Calvin and the Psalmody of the Reformed Churches. **Journal of presbyterian history,** 5 (1) 1—21; (2) 55—87; (3) 107—118, 1909.

BISGROVE, Mildred E. Sacred choral music in the Calvinistic tradition of the Protestant Reformation in Switzerland and France from 1541 to 1600. New York, 1969. Calvin: p. 18—86. Thesis—New York Univ.

BÜSSER, Fritz. Calvin und die Kirchenmusik. **Musik und Gottesdienst,** 3 (4) 1949.

CILLIE, G. G. Invloed van die Geneefse Psalmboek van 1562 op die kerklied in Suid-Afrika. **Die Kerkbode,** 90 (17) 579—582, 1962.

DEDDENS, K. De contrafacten-theorie en recenter onderzoek naar de herkomst van de melodieën van het Geneefste Psalter. **Lucerna,** 7 (3) 99—140, 1968.

DE JONGE James. Calvin's Psalter; 400 years. **The Banner,** 97 (44) 4—5; (45) 4—5, 1962.

DE KOSTER, Lester Roland. Calvin and church music. **The Banner,** 104 (37) 10—11, 1969.

DU TOIT, John Henry Howard. Calvyn en die sing van gesange in die erediens. **Nederduitse Gereformeerde teologiese tydskrif,** 8 (4) 212—218, 1967.

GARSIDE, Charles J. Calvin and music; a study of the relationship between religious and artistic expression in the sixteenth century. [Princeton] 1950. 2 v. Unpublished thesis—Princeton Univ.

GARSIDE, Charles J. Calvin's preface to the Psalter; a reappraisal. **Musical quarterly,** 37 (10) 566—577, 1951.

GARSIDE, Charles J. Some attitudes of the major reformers toward the role of music in the liturgy. **Maccormick quarterly,** 21: 151—168, 1967.

GEROLD, Théodore. Le premier psautier. **Societé de l'histoire du protestantisme français. Bulletin,** 87: 370—375, 1938.

GILLIES, John. Calvin and the psalms. **Calvin forum,** 8: 135—136, 1943.

HEINZ, Wilhelm. Zwingli, Calvin und die sakrale Musik; die Rolle der Tonkunst in der Reformierten Kirche. **Deutscher Forschungsdienst,** 7 (50) 4—5, 1960.

HUGO, André Malan. Straatsburg; die betekenis wat dit vir die Gereformeerde kerksang gehad het. **Die Kerkbode,** 90 (17) 574—578, 1962.

KRAAN, Karel Johan. Calvin and hymn-singing, **Evangelical quarterly,** 26 (7) 167—170, 1954.

LESLIE, Robert Homer. Music and the arts in Calvin's Geneva; a study of the relation between Calvinistic theology and music and the arts, with special reference to the Cent cinquante pseaumes (1583) of Pascal de l'Estocart. Montreal, McGill Univ., 1969. 395, 415 1. Thesis—McGill University, Montreal.

MARTIN-ACHARD, Robert. Calvin et les psaumes. **Les cahiers protestants,** 40: 102—112, 1960.

MILLER, Ross James. John Calvin and the reformation of the church music in the sixteenth century. Ann Arbor, Mich., 1971. 414 1. Thesis—Claremont Graduate School and Univ., Centre, Claremont, Calif.

NEDERDUITSCH HERVORMDE KERK VAN AFRIKA. Raad vir Kerkmusiek. Vierhonderd jaar Psalmgesang; 1562—1962. **Die Hervormer,** 53 (12) 2; 4; 20; 22—24, 1963.

PETER, Rodolphe. Calvin et la traduction des psaumes de Louis Budé. **Revue d'histoire et de philosophie religieuses,** 42 (2—3) 175—192, 1962.

PIDOUX, Pierre. Die Autoren der Genfer Melodien. **Jahrbuch für Liturgiek und Hymnologie,** 5: 141—146, 1960.

PONT, A. D. Herdenking van die vierhonderdjarige bestaan van die Geneefse Psalmberyming van 1562. **Nederduitsch Hervormde Kerk van Afrika Almanak** 1964: 42—57.

POTGIETER, J. H. L. S. Calvyn en die musiek. **Standpunte,** 13 (2) 30—36, 1959; 13 (3) 54—59, 1960.

REID, William Stanford. The battle hymns of the Lord; Calvinist psalmody of the sixteenth century **(In:** Sixteenth century essays and studies. Ed. by Carl S. Meyer. St. Louis Foundation for Reformation Research, 1971. v. 2, p. 36—54).

SCHEPS, Nicolaas. Calvijn en de zang in de eredienst. **Kerknieuws,** 30 (1484) 353—355, 1972.

SCHIPPERS, Reinier. Calvijn en het psalter. **Belijden en beleven,** 16 (35) 3, 1959.

SCHOLES, P. A. The Puritans and music in England and New England; a contribution to the cultural history of two nations. London, Oxford University Press, 1934. "Calvin and music": p. 332—.

TERRY, Richard R. **ed.** Calvin's first psalter; ed., with critical notes and modal harmonies to the melodies. London, Benn, 1932. 112 p.

VAN DER WALT, J. J. A. Die Geneefse Psalmmelodieë. **Die Kerkblad,** 65 (1675) 13—16, 1962.

WENDT, Gradus. Calvyn en die Geneefse Psalter. **Die Kerkbode,** 94 (23) 744, 1964.

WENDT, Gradus. Calvyn en ritmiese kerksang. **Die Kerkbode, 95 (49)** 1585, 1965.

Natural Theology see God.

Nature and Grace; law.

ALLISON, Leon McDill. Grace and nature in the theology of John Calvin. Richmond, Va., 1960. 411 1. Thesis—Union Theological Seminary, Richmond, Va.

BÉKÉSI, A. Törvény és evangélium. Kálvin tanulmány. **Református egyház,** 15: 34—36, 1963.

BUCSAY, Mihály. Kálvin egyházkormányzó és közeleti tevékenysége. **Református egyház,** 13: 272—275, 1961.

CARBONNIER, Marianne. Le droit de punir chez Calvin. **Mémoire dact. Faculté des Lettres et Sciences Humaines,** Paris, 1970.

CARBONNIER, Marianne. Le droit de punir et le sens de la peine chez Calvin. **Revue d'histoire et de philosophie religieuses,** 54: 187—201, 1974.

COCHRANE, Arthur C. Natural law in the teachings of John Calvin (**In:** Church — state relations in ecumenical perspective. Ed.: Elwyn A. Smith. Pittsburgh, Duquesne Univ. Press, 1966. p. 176—217).

ENGELS, Wolfgang. Das Gesetzeverständnis Calvins, vornehmlich nach seinen Kommentaren zu den Briefen des Paulus. Göttingen, 1967. 2 v. Thesis—Göttingen.

GENTLE, Stanley W. The significance of the law for John Calvin. Toronto, Knox College, 1964. 75 1. Thesis—Knox College, Toronto.

GESSERT, Robert A. The integrity of faith; an inquiry into the meaning of law in the thought of John Calvin. **Scottish journal of theology,** 13: 247—261, 1960.

GROSS, Julius. Geschichte der Erbsündendogmas; ein Beitrag zur Geschichte des Problems vom Ursprung des Übels. München, Reinhardt, 1972. "Die Erbsündenlehre Calvins": p. 59—72. (Entwicklungsgeschichte des Erbsündendogmas seit der Reformation, Bd. 4).

HERNDL, George C. The high design; English renaissance tragedy and the natural law. Lexington, University Press of Kentucky, 1970. "The decline of natural law beliefs": p. 110—133.

LEITH, John Haddon. Creation and redemption; law and gospel in the theology of John Calvin (**In:** A reexamination of Lutheran and Reformed traditions. New York, Published jointly by representatives of the North American Area of the World Alliance of Reformed Churches holding the Presbyterian Order and the U.S.A. National Committee of the Lutheran World Federation, 1965. v. 3, p. 43—53) (**Also in:** Marburg revisited; a re-examination of Lutheran and Reformed tradition. Editors: C. Empie and James I. McCord. Minneapolis, 1966. p. 141—150).

LITTLE, David. Calvin and the prospects for a Christian theory of natural law. (**In:** Norm and context in Christian ethics, ed. by Gene Outka [and] Paul Ramsey. New York, Scribner [1968] p. 175—197).

LÜTHI, Jesse Leo. Divine sovereignty, law and grace in John Calvin's Institutes. Madison, N.J., 1950. 137 1. Thesis—Drew Univ., Madison.

NICOLAS, Albert. L'ordre de Jesus-Christ et l'ordre de la loi; etude critique de l'usus normativus d'après Calvin. Paris, 1943. 65 p. Thesis—Faculté libre de théologie protestante de Paris.

REIF, Walter Frank. The relation of grace to law in Luther and Calvin. New York, 1946. 93 1. Thesis—Union Theological Seminary, New York.

RÖTHLISBERGER, Hugo. Kirche am Sinai; die Zehn Gebote in der christlichen Unterweisung. Zürich, Zwingli Verl., 1965. "Calvin und der Dekalog" p. 89—102. (Studien zur Dogmengeschichte und systematischen Theologie, Bd. 19).

SCHELLONG, Dieter. Das evangelische Gesetz in der Auslegung Calvins. München, Kaiser (c1968) 81 p. (Theologische Existenz heute, Nr. 152).

STELANDRE, Jacques. Le grâce commune et la loi naturelle dans la théologie de Calvin. Paris, 1957. 117 1. Thesis—Faculté libre de théologie protestante de Paris.

SUNDQUIST, Ralph Roger. The third use of the law in the thought of John Calvin; an interpretation and evaluation. [New York] 1970. 335 1. Thesis—Columbia Univ.

TWISS, Sumner B. Jr. The concepts of nature and grace in Calvin's theological discourse; a conceptual analysis and reconstruction [New Haven, Conn.] Yale Divinity School, 1968. 141 p.

Nature and grace see also Ethical matters.

Opponents.

AUTIN, Albert. Un episode de la vie de Calvin; la crise du Nicodémisme, 1535—1545. Toulon, Tissot, 1917. 81 p. Thesis—Montpellier.

BAINTON, Roland Herbert. Hunted heretic: the life and death of Michael Servetus, 1511—1553. With a new foreword by the author (2nd print.) Boston, Beacon Press (1964, c1953) 270 p. (Beacon series in liberal religion, no. 2).

BAINTON, Roland Herbert. Michael Servetus and the pulmonary transit of the blood. **Bulletin of the history of medicine,** 25: 1—7, 1951.

BAINTON, Roland Herbert. Michel Servet; heretique et martyr, 1553—1953. Genève, Droz, 1953. 147 p.

BAINTON, Roland Herbert. Sebastian Castellio and the toleration controversy of the sixteenth century (**In:** Persecution and liberty; essays in honor of George Lincoln Burr. New York, Century, 1931. p. 183—209).

BAINTON, Roland Herbert. Servetus and Genevan Libertines. **Church history,** 5: 141—149, 1936.

BAINTON, Roland Herbert. The travail of religious liberty; nine biographical studies. London, Lutterworth, 1953. "Servetus": p. 70—92.

BAINTON, Roland Herbert. La lotta per la libertà religiosa. (Bologna, Società Editrice il Mulino, 1963) 262 p. Original title: The travail of religious liberty.

BALDENSPERGER, F. Calvin et Servet d'après Alfred de Vigny. **Revue de Paris,** 41: 77—88, 1933.

BALKE, W. Calvijn en de Doperse radikalen. Amsterdam, Bolland, 1973. 400 p. Thesis—Rijksuniversiteit, Utrecht.

BAYON, H. P. Calvin, Servet and Rabelais. **Isis,** 38 (1/2) 22—88, 1947.

BECKER, Bruno. Autour de Michel Servet et de Sébestien Castellion; recuiel. Haarlem, Tjeenk Willink, 1953. 302 p.

BECKER, Bruno. Een onbekend werk van Sebastiaan Castellio; de apostel der verdraagzaamheid. **Dietsche warande en belfort,** 49: 640—645, 1949.

BECKER, Bruno. Quelques remarques à propos du De haeriticis non puniendis de Sébastian Castellion. **Esprit et vie,** 4 (1) 35—, 1939.

BERGIER, Jean Francois. Accusation et procès de Michel Servet, 1553. Genève, Droz, 1962.

BERTIN, Claude. Les procès d'intolérance religieuse; Savonarole, Michel Servet. [Boulogne] Beauval, 1970. 320 p. (Les grands procès de l'histoire, 20).

BERTRAND, P. Das Problem der Toleranz; Castellio gegen Calvin; eder: Der Fanatismus Calvins. **Die Sammlung,** 2:598—600, 1947.

BEUMER, Johannes. Das Kirchenverständnis bei einem Humanisten der Reformationszeit: Jacopo Sadoleto. **Catholica,** 16: 196—209, 1962.

BIETENHOLZ, Peter G. Mino Celsi and the toleration controversy of the sixteenth century. **Bibliothèque d'humanisme et renaissance,** 34: 31—47, 1972.

BLANKE, Fritz. Was wollte Servet? **(In:** Alles Lebendige meinet den Menschen; Gedenkbuch für Max Niehans, hrsg. von I. Buck und G. K. Schauer. München, Francke, 1972. p. 271—276).

BOST, Charles. Sébastien Castellion et l'opposition protestante contre Calvin **Revue de theologie et de philosophie,** 2: 301—321, 1914.

BRANDSMA, J. A. Johannes Calvijn en de Dopers. **De Christen.** 76 (3477), (3479), (3480), 1959.

BUDÉ und Calvin; Studien zur Gedankenwelt des französischen Fruhhumanismus. **English historical review,** 66 (261) 619—620, 1951.

CADIER, Jean. Renan and Calvin; two religious attitudes. **Reformed and presbyterian world,** 27: 21—26, 1962; **Guidernos teologicos,** 8 (1) 27—32, 1959.

CADIER, Jean. Sadolet et Calvin. **Revue d'histoire et de philosophie religieuses,** 45 (1) 79—92, 1965. **(Also in:** Regards contemporains sur Jean Calvin. Actes du colloque Calvin, Strasbourg, 1964. Paris, Presses Universitaires de France, 1965. p. 239—252) (Cahiers R.H.P., 39).

CANTIMORI, Delio. Castellioniana (et Servetiana) **Rivista storica italiana,** 67: 81—92, 1955.

CANTIMORI Delio. Spigolature per la storia del nicodemismo italiano **(In:** Roma, Facolta Valdesi di Teologica. Ginevra et l'Italia; recolta di studi promossa dalla Facolta Valdesi di Teologica di Roma a cura Delio Cantimori [et al] Firenze, Sansoni [1959] p. 177—190) (Bibliotheca storica Sansoni, 34).

CASTIGLIONE, Thommaso Riccardo. La "Impietas Valentini Gentilis" et il corrucio di Calvino **(In:** Roma, Facolta Valdesi di Teologica. Ginevra et l'Italia; recolta di studi promossa dalla Facolta Valdesi di Teologica di Roma a cura Delio Cantimori [et al] Firenze Sansoni [1959] p. 149—176) (Bibliotheca storica Sansoni, 34).

CASTIGLIONE, Tommaso Riccardo. Valentino contro Calvino; il processo del "secondo Serveto" nel 1558, a Ginevra **(In:** Studia nad Arianizmem. Ed.: Ludwika Chmaja. Varsovie, 1959. p. 49—71).

CAVARD, Pierre. Le procès de Michel Servet à Vienne. Vienne, Syndicate d'initiative, 1953. 173 p.

CHÂTEILLON, Sébastien. Concerning heretics; whether they are to be persecuted and how they are to be treated; a collection of the opinions of learned men both ancient and modern. An anonymous work attributed to Sebastian Castellio, now first done into English, together with excerpts from other works of Sebastian Castellio and David Joris on religious liberty, by Roland H. Bainton. New York, Octagon, 1965 (c1935) 346 p. (Record of civilization: sources and studies, no. 22) Also published by Irish Univ. Press, Shannon, 1968.

CHÂTEILLON, Sébastien. Fede, Dubbio e Tolleranza [di] Sebastiano Castellione. Pagine Scelte e tr. da Giorgio Radelti. 164 p. (Filosofio e comunità mondiàle, 2).

COLLINS, Ross William. Calvin and the libertines of Geneva; ed. by F D. Blackly. Toronto, Clarke, Irwin [1968] 210 p.

d'ASSONVILLE, Victor Edouard. Calvyn verdedig sy stad; sy antwoord aan kardinaal Sadoletus. Potchefstroom, Pro Rege, 1974. 16 p.

DELORMEAU, Charles Émile. Sebastien Castellion; apôtre de la Tolérance et de la Liberté de Conscience, 1515—1563 (Préf. d'Henry Babel) Neuchâtel, Messeiler, 1964. 164 p.

DE WOLFF, I. Het tolerantievraagstuk, IV: Calvijn en de terechtstelling van Servet; V: Samenvattende bespreking van de tolerantiestrijd in Genève. **De Reformatie,** 40 (45) 357—358; (46) 365—366, 1965.

DOBY, Tibor. Discoverers of blood circulation, from Aristotle to the times of da Vinci and Harvey. Pref. by John F. Fulton. London, Abelard, Schuman [1963] "Michael Servetus and John Calvin": p. 134—153.

DOUGLAS, Richard M. Jacobo Sadoleto 1477—1547; humanist and reformer. Cambridge, Mass., Harvard Univ. Press, 1959. 307 p.

DOUMERGUE, Emile. Longue histoire d'une petite phrase. **Foi et vie,** 8: 653—658, 1905.

DROZ, Eugénie. Chemins l'heresie; textes et documents I. Genève, Slatkine Repr., 1970. "Calvin et les Nicodémites": p. 131—172.

DUFOUR, Alain. Vers latins pour Servet et contre Calvin et contre Genève **(In:** Mélanges d'histoire du XVIe siècle, offerts à Paul-E. Martin, par ses amis, ses collégues, ses élèves. Genève, 1961. p. 483—496) (Mémoirs et documents publiés par la Société d' histoire et d'archéologie de Genève, t. 40). **(Also in:** Histoire politique et psychologie historique. Genève, Droz, 1966. p 97—115).

FEBVRE, Lucien Paul Victor. Le probleme de l'incroyance au 16e siècle; la religion de Rabelais. Paris, Michel, 1962 [c1942] 552 p. (L'évolution de l'humanité, 53).

FRIEDMAN, Jerome. Servetus and antitrinitarianism: a propos Antonio Rotondo. **Bibliotheque d'humanisme et renaissance** 35: 543—545, 1973.

FRIEDMAN, Jerome. Michael Servetus; the case for a Jewish Christianity, **The sixteenth century journal,** 4: 86—110, 1973.

FULTON, John F. Michael Servetus; humanist and martyr. With a bibliography of his works and census of known copies, by M. F. Stanton. New York, Reichner, 1953. 98 p.

GAUSS, Julia. Der junge Michael Servet. **Zwingliana,** 12 (6) 410—459, 1966.

GINZBURG, Carlo. Il nicodemismo; simulazione e dissimulazione religiosa nell' Europa del' 500. Torino, Einandi, 1970. "Nicodemiti e antinicodemiti: da Lefèvre d'Etaples a Calvino": p. 85—124. (Collectio Biblioteca di cultura storica,, 107).

GIRAN, Étienne. Sébastien Castellion et la réforme calviniste; les deux réformes. Réimpr. de l'ed. de Paris, 1914, Genève, Slatkine, 1970. 584 p.

GORDON, Alexander. Addresses, biographical and historical. London, Lindsey, 1922. "Michael Servetus": p. 1—64).

GROSSE & DRESSELHAUS. Zu "Unvergessen" und "Calvin und Servet." **Deutsches Pfarrerblatt,** 59: 130, 1959.

GUGGISBERG, Hans Rudolf. Sebastian Castellio on the power of the Christian prince **(In:** The responsibility of power; historical essays in honor of H. Holborn. New York, Doubleday, 1966. Chapter 4).

GUGGISBERG, Hans Rudolf. Sebastian Castellio und seine Stellung in der Geistesgeschichte. **Basler Nachrichten. Sonntagsblatt,** 57 (4) 11—12, 1964.

GÜLDNER, Gerhard. Das Toleranz-Problem in den Niederlanden im Ausgang des. 16. Jahrhunderts. Lübeck, Matthiesen, 1968. "Die Toleranzidee Sebastian Castellios": p. 16—31 (Historische Studien, Hft. 403).

HORST, Irvin B. The Radical Brethren, Anabaptism and English reformation to 1558. Nieuwkoop, De Graaff, 1972. "Was Calvin's **Briève Instruction** a reply to the **Book of Anabaptist Confession?"** p. 185—189.

ITALIAN Reformation; studies in honor of Laelius Socinus. Ed. by John A. Tedeschi. Firenze, Le Monniere, 1965. 331 p.

JASPERSE, P. Een "Monument expiatoire" [re: Servet] **De Reformatie:** 40 (49) 393, 1965.

JONES, Rufus Matthew. Spiritual reformers in the 16th and 17th centuries, Boston, Beacon Press, 1959 (c1914) "Sebastian Castellio; a forgotten prophet": p. 88—103.

KAEGI, Werner. Castellio und die Anfänge der Toleranz. Basel, 1953. 30 p. (Basler Universitätsreden, 32).

KALSBEEK, L. Castellio's eenzaam protest. **Hervormd weekblad — de Geref. Kerk,** 84: 161—162; 169—170, 1972/73.

KALSBEEK, L. Servet op de brandstapel. **Hervormd weekblad — de Geref. Kerk,** 84: 122—123, 1972/73.

KNOTT, J. Calvin and Servetus; an episode in the history of religious persecution and scientific suppression. **American medicine, 9:** 475—485; 552—561, 1912.

LAZARRO, R. Four letters from the Socinus- Calvin correspondence, 1549 **(In:** Italian Reformation. Studies in honor of Laelius Socinus; ed. by John A. Tedeschi. Firenze, Le Monniere, 1965. p. 215—230).

LECLER, Joseph. Geschichte der Religionsfreiheit im Zeitalter der Reformation [übers. von E. Schneider] Stuttgart, Schwaben [1965] Calvin [re: Servet and Castellio] v. 1. Original title: Histoire de la tolérance au siècle de la réforme.

LEE, Hannah Farnham. Servetus and Calvin. **(In:** The Huguenots in France and America. Baltimore, Md., Genealogical Pub. Co., **1973.** v. 1: 26—33. Reprint of 1843 — edition).

LINGLE, Walter L. The burning of

Servetus. **Union Seminary quarterly review,** 21 (2) 97—107, 1909.

LUCK, G. Coleman. Calvin and Servetus. **Bibliotheca sacra, 104 (4) 236 —241,** 1947.

MELLES, Gerard. Albertus Pighius en zijn strijd met Calvijn over het liberum arbitrium. Kampen, Kok, 1973. 223p. Thesis.

MEYLAN, Henri. Sebastien Castellion, 1515—1563 **(In:** Silhouettes du XVI. siècle. [Lausanne] Editions de l'èglise nationale vaudoise [1943] p. 78—89).

NEWMAN, Louis Israel. Michael Servetus, the anti-trinitarian Judaizer **(In:** Jewish influence on Christian reform movements. New York, 1925. (Columbia Univ. oriental studies, 23) p. 511—609).

OZMENT, Steven E. Mysticism and dissent; religious ideology and social protest in the sixteenth century. New Haven, Yale Univ. Press, 1973. "Sebastian Castellio": p. 168—202.

PAULUS, N. Calvin als Verfechter der Ketzerbestraffung. **Germania. Beilage,** 29, 1910.

PERILLARD, André. Les traités de Calvin contre les anabaptistes et les libertins. Essai sur l'hérésie spiritualiste. Lausanne, 1947. 99 1. Thesis—Lausanne.

PIDOUX, Pierre. Albert Pighuis de Kampen; adversaire de Calvin, 1490 —1542. Contribution à l'histoire de leur controverse sur les doctrines du libre arbitre et de la prédestination. [Lausanne] 1932. 207 p. Thesis —Lausanne.

PLATH, Uwe. Nocheinmal "Lyncurius"; einige Gedanken zu Gribaldi, Curione, Calvin und Servet. **Bibliotheque d'humanisme et renaissance,** 31: 583—610, 1969.

PLATH, Uwe. Nikolaus Blesdijks Teilnahme an der Toleranzkontroverse gegen Calvin. **Bibliothèque d'humanisme et renaissance,** 34: 461—469, 1972.

PRIME, Ralph Earl. John Calvin and the case of Servetus; a paper read June 17, 1909, in New York city, before the Ninth Council of the Reformed churches throughout the world holding the Presbyterian system. [n.p.] 1909. 20 p.

PRINS, Pieter. Uitverkoren werktuig des satans, of voorvechter der gewetensvrijheid? [re: Châteillon] **Gereformeerd weekblad,** 10: 309—310, 1954/55.

QUATRE études sur Sébastien Castellion et l'idée de la tolérance, par Roland H. Bainton [et al] Leiden, Brill, 1951. 111 p.

RENATO, Camillo. Carmen: against John Calvin on the unjust burning of Michael Servetus **(In:** Italian Reformation. Studies in honor of Laelius Socinus; ed. by John A. Tedeschi. Firenze, Le Monniere, 1965: p. 185—195) **(Also in:** Ioannem Calvinum de iniusto Michaelis Serveti incendio, 1554. Firenze, Sansoni, 1968. p. 117—131) **(His** Opere).

RENTING, G. Calvijn en Servet in Nederland. **Gereformeerd theologisch tjdschrift,** 10: 137—146; 169—179; 201—212, 1909.

ROTONDÒ, Antonio. Calvin and the Italian anti-Trinitarians. Tr. by John and Anne Tedeschi. St. Louis, Mo., Foundation for Reformation Research, 1968. 28 p. (Reformation essays and studies, 2).

ROTONDÒ, Antonio. Calvino e gli antitrinitari italiani. **Rivista storica Italiana,** 80: 759—784, 1968.

SCHULZE, Ludolf Ferdinand. Calvin's reply to Pighuis. (Potchefstroom, Pro Rege, 1971) 177 p.

(Human Sciences Research Council. Publication series, no. 9) Thesis —University of Strasbourg.

SCHULZE, Ludolf Ferdinand. Enkele aspekte van die kontrovers tussen Calvyn en Pighuis. **Suid-Afrikaanse Vereniging vir Christelike Wetenskap. Bulletin,** 16: 240—249, 1968.

SERVETUS, Michael. Michael Servetus; a translation of his geographical, medical and astrological writings. With introductions and notes, by Charles Donald O'Malley. Philadelphia, American Philosophical Society, 1953. 208 p.

SERVETUS, Michael. The two treatises of Servetus on the Trinity. Tr. by Earl Morse Wilbur. Cambridge, Harvard Univ. Press, 1932. 264 p.

STAEHELIN, Ernst. Dichtung und Wahrheit um das Grab Sebastian Castellios. **Basler Nachrichten. Sonntagsblatt,** 58 (37) 25—26, 1964.

TEISSONNIERE, Paul. Castellion contre Calvin. Brussels, Les conférences du Foyer [193-?] 22 p.

THILO. Calvin und Servet. **Deutsches Pfarrerblatt,** 59: 82, 1959.

TYLENDA, Joseph N. The Calvin-Westphal exchange; the genesis of Calvin's treatises against Westphal. **Calvin theological journal,** 9 (2) 182—209, 1974.

VALKHOFF, M. Sebastiaan Castello and his "De Haereticis a civilo magistratu non puniendis . . . libellus" **Acta classica,** 3—4, 1960/61.

VAN DER WOUDE, Sape. Verguisd geloof; de lotgevallen van Michael Servet, martelaar van protestantse onverdraagzaamheid, en Sebastiaan Castellio, apostel der godsdienstvrijheid. Delft, Gaade [195-?] 224 p. (Vrije geluiden serie. 4e reeks).

VAN DER ZIJPP, N. Calvijn en de doopsgezinden. **Doopsgezind jaarboek,** 1960: 42—67.

VAN STOCKUM, Theodorus Cornelius. Johannes Calvijn en Ignatius van Loyola; polaire tegenstelling of omgekeerde symmetrie. **Nederlands theologisch tijdschrift,** 14: 430—439, 1959/60.

VINAY, Valdo. La chiesa nella polemica fra il card. Sadoleto e Giovanni Calvino alle luce del movimento ecumenico dei nostri giorni. **Protestantesimo,** 19: 193—213, 1964.

VOISÉ, Waldemar. Sebastian Castellion et les prémisses de la tolérance. **Revue de synthèse,** 85: 31—44, 1964.

VOISÉ, Waldemar. Sebastian Castellion, 1515—1563; problem wolnosci sumienia i tolerancji w epoce humanizmu i reformacji. Warszawa, Ksiazka i Wiedza, 1963. 175 p.

WEISS, N. Calvin et Marie Stuart, 1554. **Societé de l'histoire du protestantisme français. Bulletin,** 58: 415—416, 1909.

WELTI, Albert Jakob. Servet in Genf; 5 Akte. (Genf) Rogneux, 1930. 109 p.

WENDT, Gradus. Calvyn en Servet. **Die Kerkbode,** 94 (11) 343, 1964.

WILLIS, Edward David. The influence of Laelius Socinus on Calvin's doctrines of the merits of Christ and the assurance of faith (**In:** Italian Reformation. Studies in honor of Laelius Socinus; ed. by John A. Tedeschi. Firenze, Le Monniere, 1965. p. 231—242).

WILLIS, Edward David. Miszelle; Calvin and the Anti-Trinitarians. **Archiv für Reformationsgeschichte,** 62 (2) 279—282, 1971.

WISKERKE, J. R. Calvijns worsteling met de doperse geestesstroming. **De Reformatie,** 36 (9) 65—66; (10) 73—74, 1961.

WOOLLEY, Paul. Calvin and toleration **(In:** The heritage of John Calvin. Ed. by John H. Bratt. Grand Rapids, Eerdmans, 1973. p. 137—157). (Heritage Hall Lectures, 1960—1970) (Heritage Hall publications, no. 2).

WOUDSTRA, Marten H. Calvijn's "Boecxken" tegen den botten Hollander. **Church and nation,** 3: 69—70, 1958.

WIJNAENDTS FRANCKEN, Cornelius Johannes. Michael Servet en zijn marteldood. Calvin — Servet — Castellion. Een bladzijde uit de geschiedenis der Hervorming. Haarlem, Tjeenk Willink, 1937. 117 p.

WYNEKEN, K. H. Calvin and Anabaptism. **Concordia theological monthly,** 36: 18—29, 1965.

ZWEIG, Stefan. Svedomic proti násiliu. Castellio proti Kalvinovi. (Prelozila Jana Simulciková. Bratislava. Vydalo nakladatelstovo Epocha, 1970) 192 p. Original title: Ein Gewissen gegen die Gewalt.

Philosophy; science; methodology; historiography.

ARANGUREN, José Luis. Calvino y la filosofia [re: Calvetti] **Revista de filosofia,** 14: 397—399, 1955.

BATTLES, Ford Lewis. The sources of Calvin's Seneca commentary **(In:** Duffield, G. E., ed. John Calvin. Appleford, Courtenay [1966] p. 38—66) (Courtenay studies in Reformation theology, 1).

BENDISCIOLI, Mario. L'agostinismo dei riformatori protestanti. **Augustiniana,** 1955: 227—257; **Revue des etudes Augustiniennes,** 1: 203—224, 1955.

BERKHOUT, Peter G. Calvin and Copernicus [re: Edward Rosen] **The Banner,** 98 (3) 20—21, 1963.

BOSCH, Dieter. Calvin im Urteil der französischen Historiographie vor 1789. Köln, 1971. 236 p. Thesis—Köln.

BREEN, Quirinus. Christianity and humanism; studies in the history of ideas. Collected and published in his honor, with a foreword by Paul Oskar Kristeller and a pref. by Heiko A. Oberman. Ed. by Nelson Peter Ross. Grand Rapids, Mich., Eerdmans (c1968) "John Calvin and the rhetorical tradition": p. 107—130.

BREEN, Quirinus. John Calvin; a study in French humanism. With a foreword by John T. McNeill, 2nd ed. [Hamden, Conn.] Archon Books, 1968. 193 p. Thesis—Univ. of Chicago, 1931.

BREEN. Quirinus. Some aspects of humanistic rhetoric and the Reformation. **Nederlands archief voor kerkgeschiedenis,** 43: 1—14, 1959.

BRUNETIÈRE, Ferdinand. Discours de combat; nouvelle série. Paris, Perrin, 1903. "L'oeuvre de Calvin." p. 121—160.

CADIER, Jean. Le prétendu stoicisme de Calvin. **Etudes théologiques et réligieuses,** 41 (4) 217—226, 1966.

COCHRANE, Arthur C. A preliminary aspect of Calvin's epistemology. **University of Toronto quarterly,** 14: 382—393, 1944.

CONN, Harvie Maitland. The concept of the reason in the theology of John Calvin. Westminister, 1958. 172 l. Thesis—Westminster Theological Seminary.

CRAWFORD, David James. God in human history; a study of Calvin's understanding of history with special reference to the Institutes. Toronto, Knox College, 1967. 156 l. Thesis—Knox College, Toronto.

EDWARDS, F. The relation between Biblical hermeneutics and the formulation of dogmatic theology; an investigation in the methodology of John Calvin. Oxford [1967/68] Thesis—Oxford Univ.

GALLICET CALVETTI, Carla. La filosofia di Giovanni Calvino. **Grande antologia filosofica,** VIII: 1235—1338.

GALLICET CALVETTI, Carla. I presupposti filosofici della dottrina calvinistica del "Servo arbitrio." **Rivista di filosofia neo-scolastica,** 44: 301—333, 1952.

GOOLD, Arthur Taylor. The providential interpretation of history in John Calvin. [New York] 1944. 86 l. Thesis—Union Theological Seminary, New York.

HARBISON, Elmore Harris. Christianity and history. Princeton, University Press, 1964. "The idea of utility in the thought of John Calvin": p. 249—269; "Calvin's sense of history": p. 270—288.

HENRY, Carl Ferdinand Howard. Was Calvin a philosopher? **Calvin forum,** 14 (3) 158—160, 1949.

HOITENGA, Dewey J. Calvin and the philosophers. **Reformed journal,** 8 (2) 11—13, 1958.

L'HUMANISME européen et les civilisations d'Extrême-Orient. L'Université de Paris au temps de Calvin et de S. François-Xavier [par] R. Lebègue [et al] **Association Guillaume Bude, Bulletin,** 3 (2) 20—85, 1953.

KIM, Young Ik. Luther and Calvin on human reason. St. Louis, Concordia Seminary, 1971. 95 l. Thesis—Concordia Seminary, St. Louis.

KLAPWIJK, J. Calvijn over de filosofie. **Vereniging voor Calvinistische Wijsbegeerte. Correspondentiebladen,** 36: 13—20, 1972.

LA VALLEE, Armand Aime. Calvin's criticism of scholastic theology. Cambridge, Mass., 1967. 319 l. Thesis—Harvard University.

LE COG, John P. Was Calvin a philosopher? **Calvin forum,** 14 (3) 155—158, 1949.

LEE, Francis Nigel. Calvin on the sciences, by Nigel Lee. [London] (Sovereign Grace Union, 1969) 48 p.

LEITH, John Haddon. Calvin's theological method and the ambiguity in his theology **(In:** Littell, Franklin Hamlin, ed. Reformation studies; essays in honour of R. H. Bainton. Richmond, Va., Knox [c1962] p. 106—116).

LEON, W. Le classicisme de Calvin. **Bibliotheque d'humanisme et renaissance,** 5: 231—246, 1938.

LITTLE, Lester K. Calvin's appreciation of Gregory the Great. **Harvard theological review,** 56: 145—158, 1963.

MCLELLAND, Joseph C. Calvin and philosophy. **Canadian journal of theology,** 11: 42—53, 1965.

MARCEL, Pierre. Calvin et la science; comment on fait l'histoire. **La revue réformée,** 17: 50, 1966.

MASON, S. F. The scientific revolution and the Protestant Reformation, I: Calvin and Servetus in relation to the new astronomy and the theory of the circulation of the blood. **Annals of science,** 9 (1) 64—87, 1953.

MOLNAR, Amedeo. Calvin a humanismus. **Krestanska revue,** 19: 147—152, 1952.

NIXON, Leroy. John Calvin's teaching on human reason; a synthesis from Calvin's writings. Foreword by Lee A. Belford. New York, Exposition Press, 1963. 276 p. Revision of thesis under title: John Calvin's teaching and their implications for theory of reformed protestant Christian education.

PARTEE, Charles. Calvin and experience. **Scottish journal of theology,** 26 (2) 169—181, 1973.

PARTEE, Charles Brooks, Jr. Calvin and classical philosophy; a study in the doctrine of providence. Princeton, N. J., 1971. 224 1. Thesis — Princeton, Theological Seminary.

PRÉCHAC, François. Des morceaux choisis de Sénèque, par un humaniste protestant du XVIe siècle. **Sèvriennes d'hier et d'aujourd'hui,** 12 (53) 3—15, 1968.

RATNER, J. Calvin's attitude toward Copernicus; reply with rejoinder. **Journal of the history of ideas,** 22: 382—388, 1961.

REID, William Stanford. Calvinism in sixteenth century historiography. **Philosophia reformata,** 30: 178—197, 1965.

REID, William Stanford. Christianity and scholarship. Nutley, N. J., Craig Press, 1966. "Natural science in sixteenth-century Calvinistic thought": p. 55—77.

REID, William Stanford. The present significance of Calvin's view of tradition. Redhill, Surrey, Sovereign Grace Union [1966] 22 p. Cover-title: Calvin and tradition.

REID, William Stanford. Was Calvin a philosopher? **Calvin forum,** 14: 187—191, 1949.

RICHARDS, Waldo Sumner. The religion of Calvin and the philosophy of Whitehead. Chicago, 1930. 56 1. Thesis—Univ. of Chicago.

ROSEN, Edwald. Calvin n'a pas lu Copernic; réponse à l'article de R. Stauffer: Calvin et Copernic. **Revue de l'histoire des religions,** 82: 183—185, 1972.

ROSEN, Edwald Calvin's attitude toward Copernicus. **Journal of the history of ideas,** 21: 431—441, 1960.

ROUGEMONT, Denis de. Dramatic personages. Tr. from the French, by Richard Howard. New York, Holt, 1964. "John Calvin as 'engaged' writer": p. 112—120.

STAUFFER, Richard. Calvin et Copernic. **Revue de l'histoire des religions,** 179: 31—40, 1971.

STAUFFER, Richard. Réponse: Calvin n'a pas lu Copernic, par Edward Rosen. **Revue de l'histoire des religions,** 82: 185—186, 1972.

STINSON, Charles Herbert. Reason and sin according to Calvin and Aquinas; the effects of the fall of man. Washington, D. C., 1966. 148 p. Thesis—Catholic Univ. of America, Washington, D. C.

TAYLOR, E. L. Hebden. Reformation and the development of modern science. **Churchman,** 82: 87—103, 1968.

TODD, William Newton. The function of the patristic writings in the thought of John Calvin. New York, 1964. 272 1. Thesis—Union Theological Seminary, New York.

TORRANCE, Thomas Forsyth. Infinitive and abstractive knowledge; from Duns Scotus to John Calvin. **(In:** De doctrina Ioannis Duns Scoti [Acta Congresses Scotistici Internationalis Oxonii et Edingburgi 11—17

Sept. 1966 celebrati. Romae, 1968?] p. 291—305)

TRINKAUS, Charles Edward. Renaissance problems in Calvin's theology. **Studies in the Renaissance,** 1: 59—80, 1954.

VAN ANDEL, Henry. Calvijn als wijsgeer. **De Wachter,** 92 (15) 4—5; (16) 4—5, 1959.

VANDERMOLEN, Ronald Jay. Interpretation of the secular influence of John Calvin by British and American historians. Chicago, 1965. 109 l. Thesis—De Paul Univ., Chicago.

VAN DER WATT, P. B. Die geskiedbeskouing van Calvyn. **Nederduitse Gereformeerde teologiese tydskrif,** 11 (1) 28—30, 1970.

VAN TIL, Henry R. Calvin on culture. **Torch and trumpet,** 9 (7) 7—9; 19—20, 1959.

VENTER, Erasmus Albertus. Die ontwikkeling van die Westerse denke; 'n oorsig van die geskiedenis van die filosofie gedurende 26 eeue. Bloemfontein, Sacum [n.d.] "Johannes Calvyn": p. 84—91.

VERDUIN, Leonard. Was Calvin a philosopher? **Calvin forum,** 14 (5) 211—215, 1949.

WAS Calvin a philosopher? A symposium. **Calvin forum,** 14 (10) 211 215, 1949.

WATSON, Ph. S. Calvins Geschichtsauffassung. **Erasmus,** 10: 270—272, 1957.

ZANTA, Leontine. Le Renaissance du Stoicisme au XVIe siècle. Paris, Champion, 1914. "Le stoicisme et la réformé": p. 47—73. Thesis—Univ. de Paris.

Prayers.

BUYS, Pieter Willem. Johannes Calvyn; bidder om die ewige lewe. **Die Kerkblad,** 67 (1750) 9; 11; 13, 1964.

CADIER, Jean. La prière eucharistique de Calvin **(In:** Eucharisties d'orient et d'occident; semaine liturgique de l'Institut Sainte-Serge. Introd. par Bernard Botte. Paris, Les Éditions du Cerf, 1970. V. 1, p. 171—180) (Lex orandi, no. 46—47).

DAHM, W. Gebete Calvins. **Reformierte Kirchenzeitung,** 82: 353; 390; 405, 1932.

LOGGIE, R. D. Chief exercise of faith; an exposition of Calvin's doctrine of prayer. **Hartford quarterly,** 5: 65—81, 1965.

MAURER, H. W. An examination of form and content in John Calvin's prayers. Edinburgh [1959/60?] Thesis—Edinburgh.

MAURER, Hans. Der missionarische Aspekte der Gebete Calvins. **Evangelisches Missions-Magazin, N.F.,** 105: 64—68, 1961.

REESKAMP, W. Het gebed van schuldbelijdenis. **Centraal weekblad voor de Gereformeerde Kerken in Nederland,** 9 (35) 287, 1961.

SCHOLL, Hans. Der Dienst des Gebetes nach Johannes Calvin. Zurich, Zwingli (c1968) 316 p. (Studien zur Dogmengeschichte und systematischen Theologie, Bd. 22).

Preacher and sermons.

BÉKÉSI, A. Kálvin, mint igehirdetö [Calvin, the preacher] **Theologiai szemle,** 2: 131—134, 1959.

BYTWERK, Randall. Preaching-adventure. **The Banner,** 106 (31) 4—5, 1971.

CALDESAIGNES, E. Calvin, prédicateur. **Revue de théologie et d'action evangeliques** 3: 351—368, 1943.

(**Also in:** Bourilly, E. Calvin et la réforme en France [No. spécial de la revue "Etudes evangeliques"] Aix-en-Provence, 1964. p. 83—100).

d'ASSONVILLE, Victor Edouard. Calvyn as prediker. **Die Kerkblad,** 66 (1716) 3—4; (1717) 7—9; (1718) 5—6; (1721) 5—7; (1722) 4—6, 1963.

DEDDENS, K. Johannes Calvijn; Verbi Divini Minister. **De Reformatie.** 39: 272—273; 285—286; 293—294, 1964.

DEKKER, Harold. The preacher of Geneva; Calvin's sermons, their structure and style. The theological accent of Calvin's preaching. **Calvin forum,** 16: 184—186; 205—207; 225—226, 1951.

DU TOIT, Hendrik Daniël Alphonso. Calvyn en die prediking. **Nederduitse Gereformeerde teologiese tydskrif,** 5 (3) 142—149, 1964.

GAGNEBIN, Bernard. L'histoire des manuscrits des sermons de Calvin (**In:** Calvin, Jean. Supplementa Calviniana; sermons inédits. Iussu Corporis Presbyterianorum Universalis [World Presbyterian Alliance] Moderante: James I. McCord, ed. Erwin Mülhaupt, adiuvantibus George A. Barrois [et al] Neukirchen, Neukirchener Verl. 1961- t. 2: XIV-XXVIII).

HALASKI, Karl. **ed.** Der Prediger Johannes Calvin; Beiträge und Nachrichten zur Ausgabe der Supplementa Calviniana. (Neukirchen-Vluyn) Neukirchener Verl. (c1966) 95 p. (Nach Gottes Wort reformiert, Hft. 17).

HUGHES, Philip Edgecumbe. Publication of sermons by John Calvin. **International reformed bulletin,** 10 (30) 35—36, 1967.

HUNTER, A. M. Calvin as a preacher. **Expository times,** 30: 562—564, 1918/19.

KROMMINGA, Carl Gerhard. Man before God's face in Calvin's preaching. Grand Rapids, Mich., Calvin Theological Seminary (pref. 1961) 47 p. (Calvin Theological Seminary. Monograph Series, 2).

MCGRAW, James. Great evangelical preachers of yesterday. New York, Abingdon [1961] "Calvin": p. 45—49.

NAUTA, Doede. Een Kerstpreek van Calvijn. **Centraal weekblad voor de Gereformeerde Kerken in Nederland,** 8 (50/51) 400, 1960.

NIESEL, Wilhelm. Der theologische Gehalt der jüngst veröffentlichen Predigten Calvins. **Revue d'histoire et de philosophie religieuses,** 44 (4) 270—278, 1964. (**Also in:** Regards contemporains sur Jean Calvin; actes du colloque Calvin, Strasbourg, 1964. Paris, Presses Universitaires de France, 1965. p. 8—16) (Cahiers R.H.P., 39).

NOLTENSMEIER, Hermann. Calvin als Prediger. **Kirchenblatt für die reformierte Schweiz,** 100: 56, 1954.

NOLTENSMEIER, Hermann. Der Prediger Calvin. **Deutsches Pfarrerblatt,** 64: 256—258, 1964.

NYENHUIS, Eraldo. Un ejemplo de la predicacion de Juan Calvino. **Revista teologica,** 2 (6) 21—36, 1970.

OVERDUIN, Jacobus. Calvijn en de prediking. **Centraal weekblad voor de Gereformeerde Kerken in Nederland,** 12 (19) 3, 1964.

PARKER, Thomas Henry Louis. Great preachers: Calvin. **Theology.** 54: 93—97, 1951.

PARKER, Thomas Henry Louis. Supplementa Calviniana; an account of the manuscripts of Calvin's sermons now in course of preparation. London, Tyndale Press, 1962. 23 p. (Tyndale historical theology lecture, 1962).

PIERREDON, A. Etude de quelques principes homilétiques d'après une étude des sermons de Calvin, Saurin et Bersier. Genève, 1953. 154 1. Thesis—Genève.

RÜCKERT, Hanns. Vorträge und Aufsätze zur historischen Theologie. Tübingen, Mohr (Siebeck) 1972. "Die Überlieferung der Predigten Calvins": p. 188—222.

STAUFFER, Richard. Les discours a la première personne dans les sermons de Calvin. **Revue d'histoire et de philosophie religieuses,** 45 (1) 46—78, 1965. **(Also in:** Regards contemporains sur Jean Calvin. Actes du colloque Calvin, Strasbourg, 1964. Paris, Presses Universitaires de France, 1965. p. 206—238) (Cahiers R.H.P., 39).

STAUFFER, Richard. L'homilétique de Calvin. New York, 1953. 121 1. Thesis—Union Theological Seminary, New York.

STAUFFER, Richard. Les sermons inédits de Calvin sur le livre de la Genèse. **Revue de theologie et de philosophie N.S.,** 98 (1) 26—36, 1965.

STAUFFER, Richard. Un texte de Calvin inconnu en français; le sermon sur le Psaume 46/1—6. **La revue reformée** 15 (59) 1—15, 1964.

TYLENDA, Joseph N. Calvin and the Avignon sermans of John 22. **Irish theological quarterly,** 41: 37—52, 1974.

VAN TIL, Henry R. Calvin as preacher. **Calvin forum,** 16 (8—9) 30—31, 1950.

VEENHOF, C. Calvijn en de prediking **(In:** Zicht op Calvijn [door] J. van Genderen [e.a.] Amsterdam, Buyten & Schipperheyn, 1965. p. 49—101) (Christelijk perspectief, dl. 7).

WISMAR, Don Roy. A sacramental view of preaching as seen in the writings of John Calvin and P. T. Forsyth and applied to the mid-seventeenth century. (Berkley, Calif.) 1963. 251 1. Thesis—Pacific School of Religion.

ZYLSTRA, Paul C. The well-meant offer of the Gospel preacher to sinners. **Reformed journal,** 11 (4) 17—19; (6) 18—21, 1961.

Predestination.

ADAMS, Gary B. The sovereignty of God in Calvin's doctrine of election. Abilene, Tex., 1968. Thesis—Abilene Christian College.

ALEXIS, Gerhard T. Wigglesworth's 'easiest room'. **New England quarterly,** 42: 573—583, 1969.

BAVAUD, Georges. La doctrine de la predéstination et de la reprobation d'après s. Augustin et Calvin. **Revue des études Augustiniennes,** 5: 431—438, 1959.

BERKOUWER, Gerrit Cornelis. Het hart van de zaak. **Gereformeerd weekblad,** 10 (12) 89: 1954.

BERKOUWER, Gerrit Cornelis. De spiegel der verkiezing. **Gereformeerd weekblad,** 10 (11) 81, 1954.

BOIS, Henri. La prédestination d'après Calvin **(In:** Etudes sur la Réforme; a propos du quatrième centenaire de la Réforme. Paris, Colin, 1919. p. 669—705).

BÜSSER, Fritz. Calvins Erwählungslehre. **Reformatio,** 8: 319—328, 1959.

CAMPBELL, W. S. A study of the doctrine of predestination of Calvin and Barth in the light of the scriptural statements on the subject. [Dublin, 1963/64?] Thesis—Trinity College, Dublin.

CANNON, C. K. As in a theater; "Hamlet" in the light of Calvin's doctrine of predestination. **Studies**

in English literature, 11 (2) 203—222, 1971.

CONDITT, Marion W. More accep-able than sacrifice; ethics and election in the theology of John Calvin. Basel, Reinhardt. 1973. 146 p. (Theologische Dissertationen, 10).

COWPER, Macknight Crawford. Calvin's doctrine of predestination and its ethical consequences. New York, 1942. 90 1. Thesis—Union Theological Seminary, New York.

CRISIS in the Reformed churches; essays in commemoration of the great Synod of Dort, 1618—'19. Ed. by Peter Ymen de Jong. Grand Rapids, Mich., Reformed Fellowship, 1968. "Calvin on predestination": Chapter 8.

CRISTIANI, Leon. Il sistema predestinazionista di Calvino **(In:** **Piolanti**, A., ed. Il protestantesimo ieri e oggi. Roma, Ferrari [1958] p. 710—714).

DANTINE, Johannes. Die Prädestinationslehre bei Calvin und Beza. Göttingen, 1965. 260 p. Thesis—Georg August-Univ., Göttingen.

DE HORITY, George Hupp. Calvin's doctrine of predestination; criticisms and reinterpretations. New York, 1948. 224 1. Thesis—Union Theological Seminary, New York.

EMMEN, Egbert. Een reactie op Calvijns praedestinatiegedachte. **Vox theologica,** 4 (33) 25—31, 1932.

ERMISCH, K. Predestination; an historical sketch. Sumner, Iowa, Vierth, 1937. "Calvin and Calvinism": p. 33—59.

The FIVE points of Calvinism, in a series of letters by H. Bonar [a.o.] with a foreword, Calvinism today, by Jay Green. Grand Rapids, Sovereign Grace, 1971. "Calvin, John: Unconditional election": p. 97—106.

JACOBS, Paul. Prädestination und Verantwortlichkeit bei Calvin (2., unveränd. Aufl.) Darmstadt, Wissenschaftliche Buchgesellschaft, 1968. 159 p. (Beiträge zur Geschichte und Lehre der Reformierten Kirche, 1 Bd).

KLOOSTER, Fred H. Calvin's doctrine of predestination. Grand Rapids, Mich., 1961. 77 p. (Calvin Theological Seminary. Monograph series, 3).

LECERF, Auguste. Études calvinistes, recueillies et introduites par André Schlemmer. Neuchâtel, Delachaux et Niestlé [c1949] "La predestination d'après Calvin": p. 25—32. (Série théologique de l'actualité protestante).

MCNEUR, Ronald William. Calvin's doctrine of providence. [New York, 1951] 62 1. Thesis—Union Theological Seminary, New York.

MELE, Maria Floriana. Il concetto di predestinazione in Giovanni Calvino. Bari, 1968. 171 p. Thesis—Univ. di Bari.

MOLTMANN, Jürgen. Erwählung und Beharrung der Gläubigen nach Johannes Calvin. **Kirche in der Zeit,** 14: 329—332, 1959.

MOLTMANN, Jürgen. Prädestination und Perseveranz; Geschichte und Bedeutung der reformierten Lehre "de perseverantia sanctorum." Neukirchen, Verlag der Buchhandlung des Erziehungsvereins, 1961. 188 p. (Beiträge zur Geschichte und Lehre der Reformierten Kirche, 12 Bd.).

MOREAU, William Edward. Divine foreordination and human responsibility in the theology of John Calvin. Westminister, Penn., 1962. 102

1. Thesis—Westminister Theological Seminary.

NAMYSLOWSKA, Alina. Jak pojmule predestynacje? **Jednota,** 8: 12, 1964.

NICKERSON, Hoffman. The loss of unity. London, Sidgwick & Jackson, 1961. "Devil-worshipping genius" (Calvin) p. 186—212.

OMAN, John B. The doctrines of predestination and freedom of will in the light of individual psychology. **Pastoral psychology,** 23: 63—66, 1972.

OTTEN, Heinz. Prädestination in Calvins theologischer Lehre. Mit einem Geleitwort von Ernst Wolf. (Neukirchen) Neukirchener Verl. des Erziehungvereins, 1968. 139 p. "Unveränderte fotomechanischer Nachdruck der 1. Auflage von 1938: Calvins theologische Anschauung von der Prädestination."

PARTEE, Charles Brooks, Jr. Calvin and classical philosophy; study in the doctrine of providence. Princeton. N. J. 1971. 224 1. Thesis —Princeton Theological Seminary.

PIOLANTI, Antonio. **ed.** Il protestantesimo ieri e oggi. Roma, Ferrari (1958) 1385 p.

ROULIN, S. Bible et prédestination d'après J. Calvin. **Les cahiers calvinistes,** 21 (9) 11—14, 1964.

SAVARY, Arthur. La prédestination chez Calvin; étude comparative et critique. Paris, 1901. 46 p. Thesis—Faculté libre de théologie protestante de Paris.

STARK, Carl Herman. Predestination. Richmond, Va., 1950. "Calvin's doctrine": p. 1—72. Thesis—Union Theological Seminary, Richmond, Va.

VISSCHER, H. Van de leer der praedestinatie bij Calvijn. Zeist, Van Lonkhuyzen, 1931. 32 p.

WEEKS, John Stafford. A comparison of Calvin and Edwards on the doctrine of election. Chicago, 1963. "Calvin on election": p. 58—136. Thesis—Univ. of Chicago.

WELLS, David F. Decretum dei speciale; an analysis of the content and significance of Calvin's doctrine of soteriological predestination. Deerfield, Ill., 1967. Thesis—Trinity Evangelical Divinity School.

WIESER, Gottlob. Zu Calvins Erwählungslehre. **Kirchenblatt für die reformierte Schweiz,** 115: 371—372, 1959.

WILEY, David Neeld. Calvin's doctrine of predestination; his principal soteriological and polemical doctrine. Durham, N.C., Duke Univ. 1971. 351 1. Thesis—Duke University, Durham.

Psalter see Music.

Redemption.

ANDERSON, Arthur Lloyd. Calvin's conception of sin and guilt. [New York] 1947. 123 1. Thesis—Union Theological Seminary, New York.

ANDERSON, Orvis Tse. A comparison of John Calvin's conception of salvation with that of John Wesley. Chicago, 1915. 27 p. Thesis—Univ. of Chicago.

ARENS, Jack & KUIPER, Rienk Bouke. Calvin and the sincere offer of salvation. **Torch and trumpet,** 13 (9) 9—11, 1963.

BAVAUD, Georges. La doctrine de la justification d'après Calvin et le concile de Trente. **Verbum caro,** 22 (87) 83—92, 1968.

BAVAUD, Georges. La doctrine de la justification d'après Saint Augustin et la Réforme. **Revue des études Augustiniennes,** 5: 21—32, 1959.

BAVAUD, Georges. Les rapports de la grâce et du libre arbitre; un dialogue entre saint Bernard, saint Thomas et Calvin. **Verbum caro,** 14 (56) 328—338, 1960.

BÉKÉSI, A. Keresztyénség a mindennapi gyakorlatban. Kalvin tanítasa a megszentelödesröl. **Református egyház,** 16: 85—87, 1964.

BÉKÉSI, A. A perfekció parancsa és a perfekcionizmus veszedelme. **Református egyház,** 16: 224—226, 1964.

BELTING, Natalia Maree. Calvin and the justification by faith. **The christian scholar,** 45 (3) 198—205, 1962.

BERKELEY, David. A vulgar error touching Calvin's doctrine of total. depravity. **Notes and queries for readers, writers, collectors and librarians,** 196 (14) 293—295, 1951.

BRAY, John S. The value of works in the theology of Calvin and Beza. **The sixteenth century journal,** 4: 77—86, 1973.

BULMAN, James M. The place of knowledge in Calvin's view of faith. **Review and expositor,** 50: 207—215; 323—329, 1953.

BUSCHBECK, Bernhard. Der Lebensgottesdienst des Christen nach Johannes Calvin **(In:** Solidarität und Spiritualität gleich Diakonie. Gottesdienst als Menschendienst; ein ökumen. Symposion Herbert Krimm zum 65. Geburtstag. Hrsg. von Hans Christoph von Hase, Ansgar Heuer und Paul Philippi. Stuttgart, Evangelisches Verlagswerk, 1971. p. 61—69).

CASTRÉN, Olavi. Juhàna Calvinin Pyhitysoppi [Calvin's doctrine of sanctification] **Teologisk tidskrift,** 49: 314—322, 1944.

CHALKER, William Houston. Calvin and some seventeenth century English Calvinists; a comparison of their thought through an examination of their doctrines of the knowledge of God, faith and assurance. Durham, N.C., 1961. "Calvin": p. 10—86. Thesis—Duke Univ., Durham, N.C.

CITRON, Bernhard. The evangelical doctrine of conversion; Lutheran and Reformed. Edinburgh, 1946. 258 p. Thesis—Edinburgh Univ.

COATES, Thomas. Calvin's doctrine of justification. **Concordia theological monthly,** 34: 325—334, 1963.

DANKBAAR, Willem Frederik. Calvijns oordeel over het Concilie van Trente, bepaaldelijk inzake het rechtvaardigingsdecreet. **Nederlands archief voor kerkgeschiedenis,** 45 (2) 79—112, 1962/63.

DE RU, Gerrit. De rechtvaardiging bij Augustinus; vergeleken met de leer der iustificatio bij Luther en Calvijn. Wageningen, Veenman (1966) 152 p.

DISERENS, Gaston. Esquisse des variations du dogme de la justification par la foi, dans le Pays de Vaud, de Calvin à Vinet. [Lausanne] 1946. Thesis—Lausanne.

DOUMA, Jochem. Algemene genade; uiteenzetting, vergelijking en beoordeling van de opvattingen van A. Kuyper, K. Schilder en Joh. Calvijn over algemene genade. Goes, Oosterbaan & Le Cointre, 1966. 383 p. Thesis—Theologische Hogeschool van de Gereformeerde Kerken in Nederland, Kampen.

FLASCHE, Hans. Die Erfahrung des Herzens bei Calvin und Pascal. **Orbis litterarum,** 6: 273—296, 1948.

GORDH, G. Calvin's conception of faith. **Review and expositor,** 51: 207—215, 1954.

GOSSETT, Earl Fowler. The doctrine of justification in the theology of John Calvin, Albrecht Ritschl, and Reinhold Niebuhr. Nashville, Tenn., 1961. "Calvin": p. 3—131. Thesis—Vanderbilt Univ. Nashville.

GRAAFLAND, Cornelis. De zekerheid van het geloof; een onderzoek naar de geloofsbeschouwing van enige vertegenwoordigers van reformatie en nadere reformatie. Wageningen, Veenman, 1961 "Calvijn": p. 13—60. Thesis—Utrecht.

GRIFFIS, Richard B. The renewal of man; a study of John Calvin's theology. Chicago, 1960. 73 1. Thesis—Federal Theological Faculty, Chicago.

HAZEN, Harry Booth. Calvin's doctrine of faith. Chicago, 1903. 15 p. Thesis—Univ. of Chicago.

HOOPES, Robert. Right reason in the English Renaissance. Cambridge, Mass., Harvard Univ. Press, 1962. „Calvin": p. 96—122.

KOHLER, J. Calvin und die Willensfreiheit. **Archiv für Rechts- und Wirtschaftsphilosophie,** 7: 233—246, 1914.

KUIZENGA, Henry Bernard. The idea of grace in John Calvin. New Haven, Conn., 1952. 198 p. Thesis—Yale Univ., New Haven, Conn.

LEITH, John Haddon. Creation and redemption; law and Gospel in the theology of John Calvin (**In:** Marburg revisited; a re-examination of Lutheran and Reformed tradition. Editors: C. Empie and James I. McCord. Minneapolis, 1966. p. 141—150).

LOBSTEIN, Paul. La doctrine du salut d'après les commentaires de J. Calvin sur le Nouveau Testament. **Revue de theologie et de philosophie**, 8: 28—90, 1920.

LONCKE, J. Sanctus Augustinus patronus reformatum in doctrina de peccato originali. **Collationes Brugensis,** 44: 288—293, 1948.

LUMANAUW, Th Sac. De salutis oeconomia Calvini doctrina. Excerptum ex thesi ad lauream in Facultate theol. Pontifical Univ. Urbanianae de propoganda fide. Tilburgi, 1951. 44 p.

MARCEL, Pierre. Les rapports entre la justification et la sanctification dans la pensée de Calvin. **La revue reformée,** 5 (4) 7—18, 1954.

MARCEL, Pierre. Relation between justification and sanctification in Calvin's thought. **Evangelical quarterly,** 27: 132—145, 1955.

MARSHALL, I. Howard. Sanctification in the teaching of J. Wesley and J. Calvin. **Evangelical quarterly,** 34: 75—162, 1962.

MOLTMANN, Jürgen. Prädestination und Perseveranz; Geschichte und Bedeutung der reformierten Lehre "de perseverantia sanctorum." Neukirchen, Verlag der Buchhandlung des Erziehungsvereins, 1961. 188 p. (Beiträge zur Geschichte und Lehre der Reformierten Kirche, 12 Bd.).

NEEFJES, G. De genadeleer volgens s. Thomas en Calvijn. Warmundae, 1937. 64 p. Thesis—Roma.

NÖSGEN. Bei der Entstehung der Theologie mitwirkende Momente [Calvin]. **Neue kirchliche Zeitschrift,** 22: 550—575, 577—591, 1911.

PERRIER, Marc. La notion de foi dans l'Institution chrétienne. Paris, 1957. 76 1. Thesis—Faculté libre de théologie protestante de Paris.

PIN, Jean-Pierre. La promesse et l'ésperance selon Jean Calvin. **Bulletin de litterature ecclesiastique,** 74: 14—35, 1973.

PRINS, Richard. The image of God in Adam and the restoration of man in Jesus Christ; a study in Calvin. **Scottish journal of theology,** 25: 32—44, 1972.

RÄCKE, G. Gesetz und Evangelium bei Calvin. **Theologische Literaturzeitung,** 80 (3) 179, 1955.

RICHARDS, Waldo Sumner, The nature and place of faith in the religion of John Calvin. Chicago, 1930. 39 1. Thesis—Chicago Theological Seminary.

RIOUX, Etienne. La piété chretienne selon Calvin. Paris, 1947. 112 1. Thesis—Faculté libre de théologie protestante de Paris.

ROBERT, Louis C. Essai sur la notion de la foi d'après l'Institution chrétienne de Jean Calvin. Lausanne, 1918. 102 p. Thesis—Lausanne.

RUSHDOONY, Rousas John. Politics of guilt and pity. Nutley, N. J., Craig Press, 1970. "Calvin in Geneva; the sociology of justification by faith": p. 263—290.

SANTMIRE, Harold Paul. Justification in Calvin's 1540 Romans commentary. **Church history,** 33: 294—313, 1964.

SCHAEFER, Harry. Doctrine of the atonement in the writings of Luther and Calvin. [Chicago] 1920. "Calvin": p. 22—45. Thesis—Univ. of Chicago.

SCHILDER, Klaas. Tusschen "ja" en "neen"; verzamelde opstellen. Kampen, Kok, 1929. "Calvijn over de geloofsparadox": p. 235—308.

SCHÜTZEICHEL, Heribert. Die Glaubenstheologie Calvins. [München] Hueber [1972] 276 p. (Beiträge zur ökumenischen theologie, Bd. 9).

SEBESTYÉN, Paul. The object of faith in the theology of Calvin. [Chicago] 1963. 476 1. Thesis—Univ. of Chicago.

SNELL, Farley Walter. The place of Augustine in Calvin's concept of righteousness. [New York] 1968. 245 1. Thesis—Union Theological Seminary, New York.

SPYKMAN, Gordon J. Calvijn en de zekerheid des geloofs. **De Wachter,** 93 (10) 5; 13, 1960.

STADTLAND, Tjarko. Rechtfertigung und Heiligung bei Calvin (Neukirchen) Neukirchener Verl. (c1972) 224 p. (Beiträge zur Geschichte und Lehre der Reformierten Kirche, Bd. 32).

SWITZER, Gerald Breen. The background and permanent significance of Calvin's conception of sin. New York, 1928. 67 1. Thesis—Union Theological Seminary, New York.

TOUTLEMONDE, Pierre. L'assurance du salut chez Calvin. Paris, 1948. 130 1. Thesis—Faculté libre de théologie protestante de Paris.

VAN DER LINDE, Simon. De rechtvaardiging by Luther en Calvijn. **Theologia reformata,** 8 (7) 4—15, 1965.

VAN DETH, J. P. La spiritualité de Jean Calvin. **Pages documentaires,** 15 (8) 6—13, 1969.

WEIS, J. Calvin versus Osiander on justification. **The Springfielder,** 29: 31—47, 1965.

WILLIAMS, Ivor D. An appraisal of the doctrine of justification by faith, as developed by John Calvin in the Institutes of the Christian religion. New York, 1946. 120 1. Thesis—Union Theological Seminary, New York.

WILLIAMS, Norman Powell. The ideas of the fall and of original sin; a historical and critical study.

Being eight lectures delivered befor the University of Oxford, in the year 1924, on the foundation of the Rev. John Bampton, canon of Salisbury. London, Longmans, Green, 1927. "Calvin": p. 423-.

Reformers see Luther and other Reformers.

Relations to countries; excluding Geneva and Switzerland.

ALLEN, J. F. John Calvin and the Reformation in England. **Woord en daad,** 4 (6) 2, 1959.

BALMAS, Enea Henri. Un libraire italien éditeur de Calvin **(In:** Genève et l'Italie; études publiées à l'occasion du 50e anniversaire de la Societé genevoise d'études italiennes, par Luc. Monnier. Genève, Droz, 1969. p. 79—112).

BARTEL, Oskar. Calvin und Polen. **Revue d'histoire et de philosophie** religieuses, 45: 93—108, 1965. **(Also in:** Regards contemporains sur Jean Calvin. Actes du colloque, Strasbourg, 1964. Paris, Presses Universitaires de France, 1965. p. 253—268) (Cahiers R.H.P., 39).

BARTEL, Oskar. Zwingli i Kalwin a Polska. **Przeglad historyczny,** 56: 644—650, 1965.

BASTIDE, Louis. Gérard Roussel, abbé de Clairac, sa maison des champs et son entrevue avec Calvin. **Societé de l'histoire du protestantisme francais. Bulletin,** 61: 546—550, 1912.

BOURILLY, E. Calvin et la Réforme en France. (No. spécial de la revue "Etudes evangeliques") Aix-en-Provence, 1964. "Humanisme et Réforme; la formation de Calvin": p. 6—22. **(Also in: Revue de théologie et d'action évangeliques,** 3: 274—294, 1943).

BOZZA, Tommaso, Calvino in Italia. Roma [Arti grafiche italiane] 1966. 22 p.

DANKBAAR, Willem Frederik. Calvijn en Nederland. **In die waagschaal,** 13/6/59.

d'ASSONVILLE, Victor Edouard. Dordt en die stem van Calvyn. **Die Kerkblad,** 71 (1972) 18—21, 1968.

DOUMERGUE, Emile. Calvin et Pologne. **Revue de théologie et de philosophie,** 6: 107—117, 1918.

GONNET, Giovanni. Calvino e i riformati italiani. **Societá di studi valdesi. Bolletino,** 84: 25—29, 1945.

GOOD, James I. Calvin's influence on the Reformed Church of Germany. **Christian world,** 60 (24) 4; (25) 3; (26) 4; (27) 4, 1917.

HOE, Yung Chi. The origin of parliamentary sovereignty or "mixed" monarchy; being a study of the political implications of Calvinism and Bodinism, from the mid-sixteenth to the mid-seventeenth century, chiefly in France and England. Shangai, Commercial Press, 1935. "Calvin in France": p. 58—123; "Calvin in Britain": p. 124—177.

KUYPER, H. H. Kerkgeschiedenis van de reformatietijd; dictaat. Cursus 1933—'34. Calvijn en zijn invloed in Frankrijk. [n.p., 1943?] 34 1.

LECOULTRE, H. Le séjour de Calvin en Italie d'après de documents récents. [Lausanne, Bridel, n.d.] 27 p.

MOLNAR, Amedeo. Bol Calvin Valdensky. **Kalvinske hlosy,** 15, 1950.

MONTER, E. William. Calvinists in turbans. **Bibliotheque d'humanisme et renaissance,** 29: 443—445, 1967.

NAUTA, Doede. Calvijn en de reformatie in Nederland. **Belijden en beleven,** 16 (29) 1—2; (30) 1—2, 1959.

PANNIER, Jacques. Calvin et la Hongrie **(In:** Rapports entre protestants français et protestants hongrois, 1935—1946. [Prèf. d'Albert Finet] Paris, Editions de la Calanque [n.d.] p. 75—79).

PETER, Rodolphe. Jean Calvin; avocat du comte Guillaume de Furstenberg. **Revue d'histoire et de philosophie religieuses,** 51 (1) 63—78, 1971.

REID, John Kelman Sutherland. Calvin's influence in Scotland and England. **Christian century,** 81: 699—701, 1964.

REULOS, Michel. Les attaches de Calvins dans la région de Noyon. **Societé de l'histoire du protestantisme français. Bulletin,** 110: 193—200, 1964.

RÉVÉSZ, Imre. Kálvin az 1564-i nagyengedi [Calvin and the Synod of Engedi, 1564] Cluy, 1934.

RICHTER, Mario. Attività et problemi du un poeta italiano nella Ginevra di Calvino et di Beza. **Rivista di storia e letteratura religiosa,** 2: 228—257, 1965.

ROTT, Jean. Documents strasbourgeois concernant Calvin. **Revue d' histoire et de philosophie religieuses,** 44 (4) 290—331, 1964. **(Also in:** Regards contemporains sur Jean Calvin. Actes du colloque Calvin, Strasbourg, 1964. Paris, Presses Universitaires de France, 1965. p. 28—73) (Cahiers R.H.P., 39).

RUFFINI, Francesco. Il gùereconsulto chierese Matteo Gribaldi Mofa e Calvino. **Rivista di storia del diritto italiano,** 1 (1/2) 205—269; (1/3) 417—432, 1928.

RÜSCH, Ernst Gerhard. Die Beziehungen der St. Galler Reformatoren zu Calvin. **Zwingliana,** 11(2) 106—116, 1959.

THADDEN, Rudolf von. Calvin und der Fortgang der Reformation im Reich. **Historische Zeitschrift,** 208 (1) 1—23, 1969; **La revue reformée,** 20 (80) 1—19, 1969 [In French].

TRUC, Gonzague. Calvin et les cinq prisonniers de Lyon. **Institut Historique. Revue des etudes historiques,** 86: 43—54, 1920.

VAN DER LINDE, Simon. Calvijn en Nederland **(In:** Zicht op Calvijn [door] J. van Genderen [e.a.] Amsterdam, Buijten en Schipperheijn, 1965. p. 185—219).

VINAY, Valdo. Die Schrift "Il Beneficio di Giesu Christo" und ihre Verbreitung in Europa nach der neueren Forschung. **Archiv für Reformationsgeschichte,** 58 (1) 29—72, 1967.

WEISS, N. Calvin en Angleterre; un portrait inèdit du Réformateur. **Societé de l'histoire du protestantisme français. Bulletin,** 73: 140—147, 1914.

Revelation see Bible.

Roman Catholic Church.

BAHMANN, M. K. Calvin's controversy with certain half-Papists. **Hartford quarterly,** 5: 27—41, 1965.

BAVAUD, Georges. Le jugement de Calvin sur l'église catholique. **Civitas,** 25 (4) 341—342, 1969.

BERNARD, Henri. Calvin et Loyola. **Association Guillaume Budé. Bulletin,** 6: 74—85, 1953.

BOSC, Jean. What would Calvin say to present-day Catholics? **Concilium,** 4 (2) 16—19, 1966. [In French:] 14: 31—36, 1966.

BOYER, Charles. S. J. Jean Calvin et saint Augustin. **Augustinian studies,** 3: 15—34, 1972.

BREEN, Quirinus. St. Thomas and Calvin as theologians; a comparison **(In:** The heritage of John Calvin, ed. by John H. Bratt. Grand Rapids, Eerdmans, 1973. p. 23—39) (Heritage Hall Lectures, 1960—1970) (Heritage Hall publications, no. 2).

BROPHY, Liam. Calvin; cold opposite of Saint Francis. **Friar,** 22: 58—61, 1964.

CALOREN, W. H. The virgin Mary in a Reformation theology; a reply [to James A. Shuel] **Canadian journal of theology,** 7: 176—181, 1961.

CALVIJN en Concilie. 's-Gravenhage. Stichting Uitzicht, 1964. 13 p. (Reformatorischen brochurenreeks, no. 1).

CASTEEL, Theodore W. Calvin and Trent; Calvin's reaction to the Council of Trent in the context of his conciliar thought. **Harvard theological review,** 63 (1) 91—117, 1970.

DANKBAAR, Willem Frederik. Augustinus en de Reformatie **(In:** Augustinusvoordrachten by de viering in de Rijksuniversiteit te Groningen. Groningen, 1954, p. 33—42).

DANKBAAR, Willem Frederik. Calvijns oordeel over het Concilie van Trente, bepaaldelijk in zake het rechtvaardigingsdecreet. **Nederlands archief voor kerkgeschiedenis, N.S.,** 45 (2) 79—112, 1962/63.

DOUGLAS, Richard M. Jacobo Sadoleto, 1477—1547; humanist and reformer. Cambridge, Mass., Harvard Univ. Press, 1959. 307 p.

DRISCOLL, George F. The Presbyterian Confession of 1967: historical origins and ecumenical reflections. Washington, D.C., 1969. Thesis-Catholic University of America. (Studies in sacred theology, Series II, 196) "Calvin on authority", p. 107—127.

DUPUY, B. D. La mariologie de Calvin. **Istina,** 5: 479—490, 1958.

EMONET, Pierre. Un problème du dialogue oecuménique avec les protestants: la Mariologie. **Esprit et vie,** 81: 225—236, 1971.

FISER, Zdenek. Marianska Chvala in Reformatoru. **Krestanska revue,** 37: 163—168, 1970.

GANOCZY, Alexandre. Calvin et Vaticanum II: L'église servante. Paris, Du-Cerf, 1968. 163 p.

GANOCZY, Alexandre. Calvin in present-day Catholic thought. **Concilium, 4 (2) 20—23, 1966;** [In French] **Concilium,** 14: 37—44, 1966; [In German] **Theologisches Jahrbuch,** 68: 394—400, 1968.

GANOCZY, Alexandre. Calvin und Vaticanum II; das Problem der Kollegialität (Aus dem Französischen übertragen von Karl Pellens) Wiesbaden, Steiner, 1965. 52 p. (Institut für Europäische Geschichte, Mainz. Vorträge, Nr. 37).

GANOCZY Alexandre. Points de rencontre ecclésiologiques entre Calvin et Vatican II. **Istina,** 12 (3/4) 439—482, 1967.

GANOCZY, Alexandre. La structure collégiale de l'église chez Calvin et au IIe Concile du Vatican. **Irénikon,** 38 (1) 6—32, 1965. **(Also in:** La collégialité épiscopale; histoire et théologie. Introd. de Yves M. J. Congar. Paris, Du Cerf, 1965. p. 345—369) (Unam sanctam, 52).

GARZA, M. G. El pensamiento teológico de Lutero y Calvino a la luz del Decreto de Ecumenismo. **Dialogo ecumenico,** 1 (1) 13—25, 1966.

GOETERS, J. F. Gerhard. Thomas

von Kempen und Johannes Calvin (**In:** Thomas von Kempen. Beiträge zum 500. Todesjahr. Kempen/Niederrhein, Thomas Verlag, 1971. p. 87—92).

HAAS, Albert. Calvin und Rome. **Reformierte Kirchenzeitung,** 100: 332—338, 1959; 101: 281—284, 1960; 102: 124—130, 1961.

KNUST, Romanus. Ein Beitrag zu Calvin als Reformator der Ecclesia Catholica. **Catholica,** 22 (2) 136—146, 1968.

KRETZ, Gerhard. Calvins Auseinandersetzung mit der katholischen Kirche. Tübingen, 1937. 2 v. (460 1) Thesis—Eberhard-Karls-Univ., Tübingen.

LEENHART, Franz J. La présence eucharistique. **Irenikon,** 33: 146—172, 1960.

MCDONNELL, Kilian. Calvins Liturgieverständnis und die Zukunft der römisch-katholischen Liturgie. **Concilium** 5 (2) 112—117, 1969.

MCDONNELL, Kilian. Ecclesiology of John Calvin and Vatican II. **Religion in life,** 36: 542—556, 1967.

MCDONNELL, Kilian. Roman Catholicism and Calvin's ecclesiological transcendentalism. **Reformed and Presbyterian world,** 29: 150—162, 1966.

MCLELLAND, Joseph C. Reformation and its significance today. Philadelphia, Westminster Press (1962) "John Calvin and Mother Church": p. 38—52.

MCNEILL, John Thomas. Calvin and episcopacy. **The Presbyterian tribune,** 58 (16) 14—16, 1942.

MOOS, R. W. von. Begegnung mit Calvin, Calvinismus und Katholizismus. **Zofingia,** 1936: 652—659.

NAUTA, Doede. Augustine and the Reformation. **Free University quarterly,** 3: 237—247, 1954/55.

NIESEL, Wilhelm. The gospel and the churches; a comparison of Catholicism, Orthodoxy and Protestantism. Tr. by David Lewis. Philadelphia, Westminister Press, 1962. 384 p. Original title: Das Evangelium und die Kirchen; ein Lehrbuch der Symbolik.

SCHNEIDER, Manfred. Calvins Lehre von den Konzilien und seine Stellungnahme zu dem Konzil von Trient. Dargestellt an Hand der Institutio Christianae Religionis I, 7—9, und IV, 7—9 und unter Berücksichtigung der Adnotationes zu dem Mahnschreiben Papst Paul III an Kaiser Karl V, vom 24. 8. 1544, und der "Acta Synodi Tridentinae cum antidoto" von 1547. Zulassungsarb. Lehrambt an Gymnasien.[Freiburg] 1966. 97 p.

SHUEL, J. A. The Virgin Mary in a reformation theology. **Canadian journal of theology,** 6: 275—283, 1960; 7: 176—281, 1961.

STAKEMEIER, Eduard. Doctrine mariale des orthodoxes et des réformés. Les réformateurs, Luther, Zwingli, Calvin (**In:** De mariologia et oecumenismo, 4e partic. Roma, 1962).

STOB, Henry. Calvin and Aquinas. **The Reformed journal,** 24: 17—20, 5—6/1974.

SWIERENGA, Robert P. Calvin and the Council of Trent; a reappraisal. **Reformed journal,** 16 (3) 35—37; (4) 16—20; (5—6) 20—23, 1966.

TAPPOLET, Walter. **ed.** Das Marienlob der Reformatoren; Martin Luther, Johannes Calvin, Huldrych Zwingli, Heinrich Bullinger. Hrsg. von Walter Tappolet unter mitarb. von Albert Ebneter. Tübingen, Katzmann, 1962. „Calvin": p. 221—260.

THOMAS, Ivor Bishton. John Calvin's rejection of Roman Catholic Christianity. (New York, 1966) 418 l. Thesis—Union Theological Seminary, New York.

TWO centenaries; Calvin and Newman. **Tablet,** 218: 599—600; 644—645, 1964.

VAN ALLEN, R. Calvin on clerical celibacy. **American Benedictine review,** 22: 232—244, 1971.

VAN DER LINDE, Simon. Over rooms-katholieke Calvijn-waardering. **Theologia reformata,** 1: 44—52, 1958.

VAN TUINEN, Peter. Priest wants Calvin's image corrected. **The Banner,** 100 (32) 10, 1965.

Sacraments: General.

BROUWER, Arie R. A study of Calvin's concept of sacrament. **Reformed review,** 11 (6) 1—15, 1958.

DEAN, Eric Thomas. Calvin and Barth on Scripture and tradition. Chicago, 1959. 165 l. Thesis—Univ., of Chicago.

KELLER-HÜBSCHEMENGER, Max. Der Symbolcharakter in Calvins Lehre von den Sakramenten. **Evangelisch-lutherische Kirchenzeitung,** 2: 269—273, 1948.

KIRK, Cecil J. Calvin's doctrine of the sacraments. Toronto, 1969. 88 l. Thesis—Emmanuel College of Victoria University, Toronto.

MARSHALL, W. H. Calvin, Spenser and the major sacraments. **Modern language notes,** 74 (2) 97—101, 1959.

MOORE, Michael. The doctrine of the dominical sacraments in St. Thomas Aquinas, John Calvin and the early Scottish reformers. Grahamstown, 1957. 103 l. Thesis—Rhodes Univ., Grahamstown.

ORR, Robert. An exposition and evaluation of John Calvin's teaching on the sacraments, with particular reference to the sacrament of the Lord's Supper in its liturgical context. [Grahamstown] 1953. Thesis—Rhodes Univ., Grahamstown.

RAKOTOVAO, Prevost F. La doctrine des sacraments en général chez Calvin. Paris, 1961. 38 l. Thesis—Faculté libre de théologie protestante de Paris.

VILLETTE, Louis. Foi et sacrament, T. II: De Saint Thomas à Karl Barth. Paris, Bloud & Gay, 1964. "Calvin" p. 157—205.

Sacraments: Baptism.

ALTING VON GEUSAU, Leo George Marie. Die Lehre von der Kindertaufe bei Calvin; gesehen im Rahmen seiner Sakraments- und Tauftheologie. Synthese oder Ordnungsfehler? Mit einem Anhang über die Kindertaufe auf dem tridentinischen Konzil. Bilthoven, Nelissen (1963) 335 p.

BAUR, Hermann. Calvin über die Nottaufe. **Schweizerisches Protestantenblatt,** 32 (15) 118, 1909.

CASALIS, Georges. Exposé critique de la doctrine du baptême des enfants d'après Luther et Calvin. Paris, 1939. Thesis—Faculté libre de théologie protestante de Paris.

GRISLIS, Egil. Calvin's doctrine of baptism. **Church history,** 31: 46—65, 1962.

HAUTER, Françoise. Le baptême d'après Calvin. Paris, 1948. 54 l. Thesis—Faculté libre de théologie protestante de Paris.

KRABBENDAM, H. Luc. Calvin and the ground of baptism. **Lucerna,** 4: 277—280, 1963.

MIEGGE, Giovanni. Calvino e il battesimo dei fanciulli. **Gioventu cristina,** 2: 131—138, 1933.

MONTGOMERY, Hugh Reid. Baptism in the teaching of John Calvin. New York, 1965. 136 1. Thesis-The Biblical Seminary in New York.

SCHLÜTER, Richard. Karl Barths Tauflehre. Ein interkonfessionelles Gespräch. Paderborn, Verlag Bonifacius — Druckerei, 1973 (Konfessionskundliche und Kontroverstheologische Studien, Bd. 33). "Das sakramentale Taufverständnis bei Calvin", p. 141—156.

TROMP, Sebastianus Petrus Cornelis. Sacra congregatio concilii die 19 junii de baptismo Calvinistarum seu de intentione ministri **Divinitas,** 3: 15—42, 1959.

Sacraments: Lord's Supper.

BARBER, James Frederick. The basis for a theological dialogue between the contemporary disciples of Christ and the Reformation thinker John Calvin on the subject of the Lord's Supper. Nashville, Tenn., 1971. 130 1. Thesis—Vanderbilt University, Nashville, Tenn.

BEYER, Ulrich. Abendmahl und Messe; Sinn und Recht der 80. Frage des Heidelberger Katechismus. Neukirchen, Neukirchener Verl., 1965. "Calvin"; p. 60—77. (Beiträge zur Geschichte und Lehre der reformierten Kirche, 19).

BEZEMER, C. Calvijn over het avondmaal. **Hervormd weekblad — de Geref. Kerk,** 84: 200—201, 217, 1972/73.

BICHON, Jean. La doctrine de la sainte cène chez Luther, Zwingli et Calvin. **Foi et vie,** 44: 404—409, 1946.

BIZER, Ernst. Studien zum Geschichte des Abendmahlstreits im 16. Jahrhundert (3. unveränd. Aufl.) Darmstadt, Wissenschaftliche Buchgesellschaft, 1972 (c1940) 364 p.

BOELENS, Wim L. Die Arnoldshainer Abendmahlsthesen; die Suche nach einem Abendmahlskonsens in der Evangelischen Kirche in Deutschland, 1947—1957, und eine Würdigung aus katholischer Sicht. Assen, Van Gorcum, 1964. "Calvin": p. 254—295.

BOUDRIOT, W. Neue Beiträge zur Calvins Lehre von dem Gnadenmahl. **Reformierte Kirchenzeitung,** 89: 41—45, 1939.

BURKHART, John Ernest. Thinking from the table. **Mccormick quarterly,** 23: 3—16, 1969.

CADIER, Jean. La présence réelle dans le calvinisme. **Etudes théologiques et réligieuses,** 13: 293—309, 1938.

COURVOISIER, Jaques. Réflexions à propos de la doctrine eucharistique de Zwingli et de Calvin **(In:** Festgabe Leonhard von Muralt, zum siebzigsten Geburtstag, 17 Mai 1970, überreicht von Freunden und Schülern. Herausgeber: Martin Haas [und] René Hauswirth. Zürich, Berichthaus, 1970. p. 258—265).

DOLL, Charles E. Jr. The Reformed Church doctrine of the Lord's Supper. Lancaster, Pa., 1966. 109 1. Thesis—Lancaster Theological Seminary.

DU TOIT, John Henry Howard. Nagmaal; hoe dikwels? Die standpunt van Johannes Calvyn. **Die Kerkbode,** 103 (26) 886—888, 1969.

EMERY, Pierre Yves. The teaching of Calvin on the sacrificial element in the eucharist. **Reformed and**

Presbyterian world, 26: 109—114, 1960.

GERRISH, Brian Albert. John Calvin and the reformed doctrine of the Lord's Supper. **Maccormick quarterly,** 22: 85—98, 1969; **Una Sancta,** 25 (2) 27—39, 1968.

GERRISH, Brian Albert. The Lord's Supper in the Reformed Confessions. **Theology today,** 23: 224—243, 1966/67.

GOLLWITZER, Helmut. Coena Domini; die altlutherische Abendmahlslehre in ihrer Auseinandersetzung mit dem Calvinismus dargestelt an der lutherischen Frühortodoxie. München, Kaiser (1937) 327 p. Thesis—München.

GOTTSCHALK, Johannes. Die Gegenwart Christi im Abendmahl; eine dogmatische Abhandlung über die vierte und fünfte Arnoldshainer Abendmahlsthese von 1957. Essen, Ludgerus-Verl. Hubert Wingen, 1966. "Die Lehre von der Realpräsenz bei Luther und Calvin": p. 37—64 (Koinonia-Beiträge zur ökumenischen Spiritualität und Theologie, Bd. 8).

GREINER, Albert. La doctrine des sainte cene chez Calvin et Luther. **Foi et vie,** 46: 22—34, 1948.

HARTVELT, Gerrit Pieter. Verum corpus; een studie over een centraal hoofdstuk uit de avondmaalsleer van Calvijn. Delft, Meinema, 1960. 238 p.

HEIDLER, Fritz. Christi Gegenwart beim Abenmahl; eine Frage an die Evangelisch-Lutherische Kirche (2. überarb. Aufl.) Berlin, Evangelische Verlagsantalt, 1949. "Die verschiedenen Voraussetzungen der Abendmahlsdeutung bei Luther und Calvin": p. 29—48.

HEMAN Richard. Mysterium sanctum magnum; um die Auslegung des Abendsmahls. Zwingli? Calvin? Luther? Rom? Historisch-philosophische Studie. Luzern, Räber, 1937. 169 p.

HOFFMAN, J. G. H. Den kalvinska läran om nattvarden [Lord's Supper] i fransk teologie före 1700-talet. **Norsk teologisk tidsskrift** 59: 129—142, 1958.

JACOBS, Paul. Pneumatische Realpräsenz bei Calvin. **Revue d'histoire et de philosophie religieuses,** 44 (4) 389—401, 1964/65. **(Also in:** Regards contemporains sur Jean Calvin. Actes du colloque Calvin, Strasbourg, 1964. Paris, Presses Universitaires de France, 1965. p. 127—139) (Cahiers R.H.P., 39).

JANSSEN, Heinrich. Die Abendmahlslehre Johannes Calvins. **Una sancta,** 15 (2) 125—128, 1960. **(Also in:** Die Eucharistie, im verständnis der Konfessionen. Hrsg. von Thomas Sartory. Recklinghausen, 1961. p. 204—220).

JENNY, Markus. Die Einheit des Abendmahlsgottesdienstes bei den elsässischen und schweizerischen Reformatoren. Zürich, Zwingli [n. d.] "Calvin": p. 103—142. (Studien zur Dogmengeschichte und systematischen Theologie, Bd. 23).

KIM, Chin Kon. The doctrine of the Lord's Supper in John Calvin's writings. Abilene, Tex., 1970. Thesis—Abilene Christian College.

LABRUNIE, Claude Emmanuel. The discourse on the bread of life as foundation for Calvin's doctrine of the Eucharist. Princeton, N. J., 1966. 207 1. Thesis—Princeton Theological Seminary.

LEASOR, Teresa Jane. The communion service in the Reformed churches in Switzerland, France, and Scotland in the sixteenth century. New York, N.Y., 1968. 198 l. Thesis—New York University.

LECERF, Auguste. Études calvinistes, recueillies et introduites par André Schlemmer. Neuchâtel, Delachaux et Niestlé (1949) "L'élection et le sacrament": p. 33—44; "La liturgie de la sainte-cène a Genève en 1542": p. 45—54. (Serie théologique de l'actualité protestante).

LEENHART, Franz J. La présence eucharistique. **Irenikon,** 33: 146—172, 1960.

MCDONNELL, Kilian. The eucharistic doctrine of John Calvin in the light of his anticatholic polemic. Trier, 1964. 2 v. Thesis—Trier.

MCDONNELL, Kilian. John Calvin, the church, and the Eucharist. Princeton, N. J., Princeton Univ. Press, 1967. 410 p.

MEYER, Boniface John. Calvin's eucharistic doctrine, 1536—1539. **Journal of ecumenical studies,** 4 (1) 47—65, 1967.

MEYER, Boniface John. John Calvin's doctrine of the Lord's supper; an essay in historical development. (Iowa City) 1967. 226 l. Thesis—Univ. of Iowa.

MEYER, John R. Mysterium fidei and the later Calvin. **Scottish journal of theology,** 25 (4) 392—412, 1972.

NEVIN, John Williamson. The mystical presence, and other writings on the eucharist. Editors: Bard Thompson and George H. Bricker (repr.) Philadelphia, United Church Press, 1966 (1846) 431 p. (Lancaster series on the Mercersburg Theology, v. 4).

O'KEEFE, B. J. Casel and Calvin on the eucharist. **Canadian journal of theology,** 11: 8—24, 1965.

PETERS, Albrecht. Die Gegenwart Gottes im Sakrament des Altars. Luthers Abendmahlszeugnis in seinem Verhältnis zur römisch-katholischen Abendmahlslehre, zur Lehre Calvins wie zum Zeugnis des Neuen Testaments. [n.p., n.d.] "Luthers Abendmahlszeugnis im Gegensatz zur Abendmahlslehre Calvins": p. 79—85.

PRUETT, Gordon Earl. Thomas Cranmer and the eucharistic controversy in the Reformation. Princeton, N.J., 1968. "Calvin": p. 129—173, Thesis—Princeton Theological Seminary.

ROGGE, Joachim. Virtus und res; um die Abendmahlswirklichkeit bei Calvin. Stuttgart, Calwer (1965) 70 p. (Arbeiten zur Theologie, 1. Reihe, Hft. 18).

SCHALINSKE, Theodore Fred. Calvin and Luther; their doctrines of the Lord's Supper. Princeton, 1940. 77 l. Thesis—Princeton Theological Seminary.

TYLENDA, Joseph N. Calvin and Christ's presence in the supper — true or real. **Scottish journal of theology,** 27 (1) 65—75, 1974.

TYLENDA, Joseph N. Calvin on Christ's true presence in the Lord's Supper. **American ecclesiastical review,** 155: 321—333, 1966.

TYLENDA, Joseph N. A study in the eucharistic theologies of John Calvin, reformer of Geneva, and of Max Thurian, monk of Taize. Rome, 1964. Thesis—Gregorian Univ., Rome.

WALKER, George Stuart Murdoch. The Lord's Supper in the theology and practice of Calvin **(In:** Duffield, G. E., ed. John Calvin. Appleford, Courtenay [1966] p. 131—148) (Courtenay studies in Reformation theology, 1).

YAZAKI, Kunihiko. Calvin's doctrine of the Lord's Supper. Holland, Mich., 1966. 91 1. Thesis—Western Theological Seminary, Holland, Mich.

School see **Education.**

Science see **Philosophy.**

Sermons see **Preacher and sermons.**

Social philosophy see **Economics.**

State and church.

AALDERS, Willem Jan. Calvijn was tegen vermenging van geloof en politiek. **Kerknieuws,** 30 (1484) 356, 1972.

ARÉNILLA, L. Le calvinisme et le droit de résistance à l'état. **Annales-economies, sociétés, civilisations:** 22 (2) 350—369, 1967.

BAUR, Jürgen. Gott, Recht und weltliches Regiment im Werke Calvins. Bonn, Bouvier, 1965. 300 p. (Schriften zur Rechtslehre und Politik. Bd. 44) Thesis-Köln 1964.

BEAUDON, Jacques Valentin Marcel. Le developpement de la notion de souverainité politique chez les calvinistes français de Jean Calvin à la révolution française. New York, 1939. 99 1. Thesis—Union Theological Seminary, New York.

BÉKÉSI, A. Kálvin mint politikus [Calvin, political man] **Theologiai szemle,** 2: 414—423, 1959.

BEYERHAUS, Gisbert. Studien zur Staatsanschauung Calvins mit besonderer Berücksichtigung seines Souveränitätsbegriffs. Neudr. der Ausgabe 1910. Aalen, Scientia, 1971. 162 p. (Neue Studien zur Geschichte der Theologie und der Kirche, 7. Stück).

BOHATEC, Josef. Calvin und das Recht (Neudr.) Aalen, Scientia, 1971 (1934) 286 p.

BOHATEC, Josef. Calvins Lehre von Staat und Kirche, mit besonderer Berücksichtigung des Organismusgedankens (Neudr.) Aalen, Scientia, 1968 (1937) 754 p. (Untersuchungen zur deutschen Staats- und Rechtgeschichte, 147 Hft.)

BOHATEC, Josef. Calvins Staatslehre. **Protestantische Rundschau,** 19: 151—155, 1942.

BROWN, Dennis McCall. The political teachings of John Calvin. Richmond, Va., 1943. 67 1. Thesis—Union Theological Seminary, Richmond, Va.

CADIX, M. L'État, sa notion et ses rapports avec l'église d'après Calvin; essai historique. Paris, 1970. 73 1. Thesis—Faculté libre de théologie protestante de Paris.

CALVIN und die Theokratie. **Kirchenblatt für die reformierte Schweiz,** 115: 201—202, 1959.

CALVYN oor kerk en volk. **Woord en daad,** 8 (41) 3—4, 1965.

CHENEVIÈRE, Marc Édouard. La pensée politique de Calvin (Réimpr. de l'éd de Genève et Paris, 1937) Genève, Slatkine, 1970. 384 p. Thesis—Genève, 1936.

CURIE, Pierre. Etude des relations entre: la notion calvinienne de l'église et la notion calvinienne de l'état. Paris, 1950. 123 1. Thesis—Faculté libre théologie protestante de Paris.

DE GROOT, Douwe Johannes. De reformatie en de staatkunde. Franeker. Uitg. in opdracht van de Christelijke Nationale Bibliotheek, door Wever, 1955. 311 p.

DEKKER, Ralph. John Calvin and Christian citizenship. **Church observer,** 71 (1) 6, 1964.

DOOYEWEERD, Herman. Compte rendu critique: J. Bohatec: Calvin und das Recht, 1934. **Tijdschrift voor rechtsgeschiedenis/Revue d'histoire du droit,** 15: 243—258, 1937.

DU PLESSIS, Lodewicus Johannes. Die staatsteorie van Jean Calvin in verband met die wetenskap en staatspraktyk van sy tyd. Kampen, Kok [s.j.] 136 p. **(Also in: Antirevolutionaire staatkunde,** 6: 160—214, 277—302; 413—467, 1932).

FARRELL, John Thomas. The political theory of John Calvin. Chicago, 1949. 71 1. Thesis—Univ. of Chicago.

FOSTER, Herbert Darling. The political theories of Calvinists before the Puritan exodus to America. New York, MacMillan, 1916. "Calvin": p. 481—503. **(Also in: American historical review,** 20, 1916).

FUHRMANN, A. Il pensiero politico di Giovanni Calvino. Turino, 1933. Thesis—Univ. Turino.

HALL, Basil. John Calvin, the jurisconsults and the "Ius civile" **(In:** Studies in church history, ed. by G. J. Cuming. Papers: Ecclesiastical History Society, Leiden, Brill, 1966: v. 3, p. 202—216).

HERBERS-BILTHOVEN, Hein. Luthers und Calvins Verhältnis zu Macht und Staat. **Das andere Deutschland** 15 (10) 3, 1953.

HERZOG, Paul Max, Jr. John Calvin, political pragmatist; his theory of the right of resistance with particular reference to his relations with the protestants of France. Submitted for the Bowdoin prize. [Harvard?] 1927. 76 1.

HOE, Yung Chi. The origin of parliamentary sovereignty or "mixed" monarchy; being a study of the political implications of Calvinism and Bodenism, from the mid-sixteenth to the mid-seventeenth century, chiefly in France and England. Shangai, Commercial Press, 1935. "Calvin": p. 47—57.

KENNEDY, Richard K. The relevance of Calvin's doctrine in the present problem of church and state. Pittsburgh, 1952. 58 1. Thesis—Xenia Theological Seminary, Pittsburgh.

KINGDON, Robert McCune, **ed.** Calvin and Calvinism; sources of democracy? Ed. with an introd. by Robert M. Kingdon and Robert D. Linder. Lexington, Mass, Heath (c1970) 83 p. (Problems in European civilization).

KNOLL, Getrude. Calvin as a statesman. **The Banner,** 62: 506—507, 1927.

KOOPS, Hugh A. More government or less? A study in the thought of John Calvin. **Reformed journal,** 14 (7/8) 4—7, 1964; 14 (9) 17—20, 1964.

LAHR, Horst. Calvin als Politiker. **Deutsches Pfarrerblatt,** 51: 6—7, 1951.

LECERF, Auguste. Études calvinistes, recueillies et introduites par André Schlemmer. Neuchâtel, Delachaux et Niestlé (c1949) "Essai d'une détermination des rapports entre l'église et l'état d'après le calvinisme": p. 91—97. (Série théologique de l'actualité protestante).

LENZ, Georg. Luthers und Calvins Verhältnis zum Staat. **Evangelisch-lutherische Kirchenzeitung,** 5: 268—270, 1951.

LEW, Paul. La theologie politique de Calvin et le Nouveau Testament. Montpellier, 1945. Thesis—Montpellier.

LUBBE, W. J. G. Calvyn en die staat. **Nederduitse Gereformeerde**

teologiese tydskrif, 5 (3) 200—208, 1964.

MCNEILL, John Thomas. John Calvin on civil government. **Journal of Presbyterian history,** 42: 71—91, 1964. **(Also in:** Hunt, George Laird, ed. Calvinism and the political order; essays prepared for the Woodrow Wilson lectureship of the National Presbyterian Center, Washington, D. C. John T. McNeill, consulting ed. Philadelphia, Westminister Press [c1965] p. 23—45).

MACWILLIAM, Stuart Wilson. A comparison between Barth's idea of the relation between church and state with that of Luther and Calvin. New York, 1940. 81 l. Thesis—Union Theological Seminary, New York.

MEYER, Roelf. Die evangelie en die politiek volgens Calvyn. **Pro veritate,** 13 (1) 16—20, 1974.

MUELLER, William A. Church and state in Luther and Calvin; a comparative study. Nashville, Broadman, c1954. 187 p. (Anchor Book, A 454) Also published by Doubleday, Garden City, N. Y., 1965.

NAGY, Barnabas. Kálvin politikai theológiájának krisztológiai alapvetése [Christological foundation of Calvin's political theology] **Theologiai szemle,** 17: 13—30, 1941.

NAUTA, Doede. Calvijn en de monarchie. **Centraal weekblad voor de Gereformeerde Kerken in Nederland,** 20 (49) 8, 1972.

OMODEO, A. Giovanni Calvino progenitore della libertà. **Acropoli,** 2: 76—85, 1946.

RAINES, John Curtis. The cosmic kingdom in the rise of the Christian interpretation of the state; a study of the interaction of religious and political mythology from Hebraic prophetism through John Calvin. New York, 1967. "John Calvin and the order of Christian living": p. 323—394. Thesis—Union Theological Seminary, New York.

RICE, J. J. Calvin the founder of republics. **The Banner,** 63: 499, 1928.

RO, Bong Rin. The church and state in Calvin. St. Louis, 1967. 133 l. Thesis—Concordia Seminary, St. Louis.

ROSSLEE, Diederik Daniël. Die verhouding staat en kerk in die Westerse staatsfilosofiese denke [Bloemfontein? 1958?] „Calvin": p. 144—158. Thesis—U.O.V.S., Bloemfontein.

RÜCKERT, Hanns. Christentum und Staat bei Calvin **(In:** Berichte über die 15. Versammlung deutscher Historiker vom 3. bis 9.10.1926. Breslau, Priebatsch (1926) p. 27—).

SCHOLL, Hans. Fürbitte für das weltliche Regiment und Ermahnung der Obrigkeit bei Calvin **(In:** Freude am Evangelium. Alfred de Quervain zum 70. Geburtstag am 28. September 1966. Hrsg. von Johan Jakob Stamm und Ernst Wolf. München, 1966. p. 107—119) (Beiträge zur evangelische Theologie, Bd. 44).

SEYNES, François de. Introduction à une étude de l'état quant à sa place dans une dogmatique réformée. Paris, 1947. "Les magistrats chez Calvin:" p. 23—44. Thesis—Faculté de théologie protestante de Paris.

SMITH, Elwyn Allen. Calvin's theory of the relation of church and state. **Union Seminary quarterly review,** 57 (1) 25—39, 1945/46.

SMITH, Elwyn Allen. The realization of Calvin's state-church theory in Geneva. Cambridge, Mass., 1942, 256 l. Thesis—Harvard Univ., Cambridge, Mass.

SMITH, George L. Religion and trade in New Netherland; Dutch origins and American development. Ithaca, Cornell University Press, 1973. "Church and state in Calvin's theology", p. 23—39.

STAEDTKE, Joachim. Calvins Genf und die Entstehung politischer Freiheit (**In:** Staat und Kirchen in der Bundesrepublik. Staatskirchenrechtliche Aufsätze, 1950—1967. Hrsg. von Helmut Quaritsch und Hermann Weber. Bad Hamburg, 1967. p. 100—114).

STEVENSON, Richard Taylor. John Calvin, the statesman. New York, Abingdon, 1907. 203 p. (Men of the kingdom).

STOFFEL, Ernest Lee. An outline of the political philosophy of John Calvin. [Richmond, Va., 1946] 22 l.

VAN DER WATT, Louis. Die reg van verset: 'n staatsfilosofiese studie. Bloemfontein, 1963. "Calvyn" p. 51—58. Thesis—U.O.V.S., Bloemfontein.

VENTER, Erasmus Albertus. Gesagsbeskouing by Calvyn, met verwysing na die moderne parlementêre staat. (Kaapstad?) 1947. 373 l. Thesis—Univ. of Cape Town.

VENTER, Erasmus Albertus. 'n Kritiese beoordeling van Calvyn se soewereiniteitsleer in die lig van die Thomistiese en Cartesiaanse toerieë. (Pretoria) 1948. 309 l. Thesis—UNISA, Pretoria.

VERCIER, M. J. Les principes politiques de Calvin. **Revue de theologie et d'action evangéliques,** 3: 369—381, 1943. (**Also in:** Bourilly, E. Calvin et la Réforme en France [No. special de la revue "Etudes evangeliques, 1964] Aix-en-Provence (1967) p. 101—113).

WALKER, Williston. Calvin and civil liberty. **The Interior,** 40 (2030) 513—515, 1909.

WALZER, Michael. The revolution of the saints; a study in the origins of radical politics. Cambridge, Mass., Harvard Univ. Press, 1965. "Calvin": p. 22—65.

WEBER, Otto. Compétence de l'église et compétence de l'état d'après les ordonnances ecclésiastiques. **Revue d'histoire et de philosophie religieuses,** 44: 336—347, 1964. (**Also in:** Regards contemporains sur Jean Calvin. Actes du colloque Calvin, Strasbourg, 1964. Paris, Presses Universitaires de France, 1965. p. 74—85) (Cahiers R.H.P., 39).

WEBER, Otto. Die Treue Gottes in der Geschichte der Kirche. Neukirchen, Neukirchener Verl. des Erziehungsvereins. 1968. "Kirchliche und staatliche Kompetenz in den ordonnances ecclésiatiques von 1561": p. 119—130. (Beiträge zur Geschichte und Lehre der reformierten Kirche, 29).

WESSELS, Francois Jacobus Hendrik. Die owerheidstaak. [Bloemfontein, 1957] "Die owerheidstaak by Calvyn": p. 323—335. Thesis—U.O.V.S., Bloemfontein.

WINTERS, Peter Jochen. An der Wiege des modernen Staates; Johannes Calvin als politischer Denker. **Christ und Welt,** 17 (21) 11, 1964.

WINTERS, Peter Jochen. Die "Politik" des Johannes Althusius und ihre zeitgenossischen Quellen. Freiburg, Rombach, 1963. "Die Sozialtheologie Calvins": p. 37—60.

WOLIN, Sh. S. Calvin and the Reformation; the political education of Protestantism. **American political science review**, 51 (2) 428—454, 1957.

ZAMPETTI, Pier Luigi. Profilo unitario del pensiero politico di Calvino. Milana, Giuffrè, 1959. 81 p.

Switzerland see **Geneva and Switzerland.**

Vocation see **Ethical matters.**

2. CALVINISM.

2.1 CALVINISM - GENERAL:

Calvin's influence through the ages.

AALDERS, W. Calvijn en het Gereformeerd protestantisme. **Theologia reformata,** 15: 258—269, 1972.

AMAKER, David M. Calvin's influence in the development of democracy **(In:** A symposium: John Calvin. On the occasion of the 450th anniversary of his birth and the 400th anniversary of the final edition of the Institutes. Three addresses delivered to the Memphis Presbytery. Memphis, Tenn., 1959. p. 4—7).

ANET, Daniel. Calvin et la cité. **Connaître**, 1/8/1937: 25—31.

BAUKE, Hermann. Calvin und die Theologie der Gegenwart. **Theologische Blätter,** 5: 173—, 1926.

BEARD, Charles. The Reformation of the 16th century in its relation to modern thought and knowledge. Foreword by Joseph Dorfman. Introd. by Ernest Barker. [Ann Arbor] University of Michigan Press (1962) "Calvin": p. 242—261. (Ann Arbor paperbooks, AA 61).

BECANUS, Martinus. A controversy, in which Calvin is overthrowne **(Bound with:** Boaistuau, Pierre. Gorsedd y byd, 1615. Tr. by Rosier Smyth [Repr. of 1615 ed.] Menston, Scolar Press, 1970) (English recusant literature, 1558—1640, v. 46).

BERGUER, Henry. Calvin aujourd'hui. Genève, Wyss et Duchêne, 1910. 11 p.

BOERKOEL, J. D. De Afscheiding en Calvijn. **De Bazuin,** 104 (27) 1—2; (28) 1—2; (29) 1—2; (30) 1—2; 1961.

BOUYER, Louis. Die Theologien Luthers und Calvins; protestantistische Religiosität in der 2. Hälfte unseres Jahrhunderts **(In:** Getauft auf einem Namen; Christus und die Kirchen, von Roger Aubert [u.a.] Nürnberg, 1963. p. 118—144).

BRASELMANN, Werner. Zum Calvinbild Reinhold Schneiders. **Reformierte Kirchenzeitung,** 104: 114—116, 1963.

BRATT John Harold, **comp.** The heritage of John Calvin, ed. by J. H. Bratt. Grand Rapids, Eerdmans [1973] 222p. (Heritage Hall lectures, 1960—1970) (Heritage Hall publications, no. 2).

BRILLENBURG WURTH, Gerrit. Is de boodschap van Calvijn in de wereld van vandaag nog actueel? **Horizon,** 22 (11) 267—272, 1959.

BROWN, William Adams. Calvin's influence upon theology **(In:** Union Theological Seminary, New York. Three addresses delivered at a service in commemoration of the four hundredth anniversiary of the birth of John Calvin. New York, 1909. p. 20—35).

BROYER, F. G. M. Calvijn en de kerkgeschiedenis. **Hervormd weekblad — de Geref. Kerk,** 77: 133—135, 1965/66.

CADIER, Donald J. Calvin in Japan. **Reformed review,** 13: 51—52, 1959.

CADIER, Jean. Actualité de Calvin. **Revue de théologie et de philosophie, N.S.,** 9 (2) 105—113, 1958.

CADIER, Jean. Aspects actuels de la pensée de Calvin. **La revue réformée,** 20 (80) 35—42, 1969.

CALVIN considered as a moral force. **Homiletic review,** 58: 8—13, 7—12/1909.

CALVYN en sy betekenis vir ons. **Woord en daad,** 9 (64) 3; 9, 1967.

CHOISY, Eugène. Calvin et la conférence de Stockholm. **Protestantische Rundschau,** 3: 17, 1927.

CLIPSHAM, E. F. Andrew Fuller and Fullerism; a study in evangelical Calvinism, 2: Fuller and John Calvin. **Baptist quarterly,** 2 (4) 146—154, 1963.

COLLINS, George Norman MacLeod. Calvinisme; vandag in Groot-Brittanje. **Die Kerkblad,** 67 (1772) 8—9, 1964.

COURTHIAL, Pierre. Calvins toujours vivant. **Societé de l'histoire du protestantisme français. Bulletin,** 110: 201—206, 1964.

DARBY, W. J. Calvin and the 20th century. **Cumberland Presbyterian,** 77 (5) 136; (6) 168; (7) 200; (8) 232; (9) 264, 1906.

d'ASSONVILLE, Victor Edouard. Calvyn se invloed op die Griekse kerk. **In die Skriflig,** 6 (23) 39—44, 1972.

DAVIS, C. Grier. John Calvin and current thought. **Union Seminary quarterly review,** 50 (4) 336—350, 1938/39.

DE KOSTER, Lester Roland. Calvin and revolution. **Reformed journal,** 17 (1) 20—22, 1967.

DE KOSTER, Lester Roland. John Calvin comes to town. **Young Calvinist,** 48: 6—8, 1967.

DE VILLIERS, David Willem. Calvyn en Suid-Afrika. **Die Kerkbode,** 84 (1) 16—19, 1959.

DICKENS, Arthur Geoffrey. The age of humanism and reformation; Europe in the fourteenth, fifteenth and sixteenth centuries. Englewood Cliffs, N.J. Prentice-Hall, 1972. "Calvin and the reformed churches": p. 164—172.

DOUMERGUE, Emile. Calvin et l'Entente. **Revue de metaphysique et de morale,** 1918: 807—840.

DOUMERGUE, Emile. Calvin et l'Entente. De Wilson à Calvin. **Foi et vie,** 22: 12—22, 1919. **(Also in:** Etudes sur la Réforme; a propos du quatrième centenaire de la Réforme. Paris, Colin, 1919. p. 807—840).

DOUMERGUE, Emile. Jean Calvin, prédecesseur de Blaise Pascal. **Foi et vie,** 26: 810—820, 1923.

DU PLESSIS, Lodewicus Johannes. Calvyn se betekenis vir die Westerse kultuurontwikkeling in die algemeen. **Koers,** 27 (1) 6—10, 1959.

DU TOIT, Stefanus. Calvyn in Japan. **Die Kerkblad,** 67 (1751) 8—9, 1964.

EBELING, Gerhard. Calvins Vermächtnis. **Reformatio,** 13: 588—590, 1964.

EBNETER, Albert. Calvin gestern und heute. **Orientierung,** 23: 99—103, 1959.

EDEL, Gottfried. Calvin; eine Entgegung. **Reformierte Kirchenzeitung,** 105: 127—128, 1964.

EGGERS-LECOUR, Conrado E. Calvino y Rousseau, o la ambivalencia ginebrino. **Razon y fe,** 772 (5) 481—494, 1962.

EVENHOUSE, Henry J. Calvin speaks in Japan. **The Banner,** 103 (43) 6, 1968.

GERSTNER, John H. Calvin's political influence in the United States **(In:** Calvin anniversary lectures at Calvin College. Grand Rapids, Mich., 1959. 11 1).

GEYL, P. Calvijn en zijn apologeten. **Vrij Nederland,** 13/2/1960.

GILG Peter. Oliver Cromwells Staatsauffassung und ihre Beziehung zur Lehre Calvins. **Schweizer Beiträge zur allgemeinen Geschichte,** 6: 50—90, 1948.

GLASGOW, Frank T. Calvin's influence upon the political development of the world **(In:** Calvin memorial addresses; delivered before the General Assembly at Savannah, May 1909, in observance of the birth of John Calvin. Richmond, Va., Presbyterian Committee of Publication [n.d.] p.175—195).

HALL, Basil. Calvin against the Calvinists. **Huguenot Society of London. Proceedings,** 20: 284—301, 1962 **(Also in:** Duffield, G. E., ed. John Calvin. Appleford, Courtenay [1966] p. 19—37) (Courtenay studies in Reformation theology, 1).

HALL, Basil. The Calvin legend **(In:** Duffield, G. E., ed. John Calvin. Appleford, Courtenay [1966] p. 1—18) (Courtenary studies in Reformation theology, 1).

HALL, T. Christian's life; Wesley's alternative to Luther and Calvin. **Duke Divinity School bulletin,** 28: 111—126, 1963.

HALL, Thomas Cuming. The inner spirit of the Calvinistic Puritan state **(In:** Union Theological Seminary, New York. Three addresses delivered at a service in commemoration of the four hundredth anniversary of the birth of John Calvin, May 1909. New York (1909) p. 36—47).

HARMS, Klaus. Calvins Einfluss auf den Osten. **Deutsches Pfarrerblatt,** 64: 258—260, 1964.

HAUGAARD, William P. John Calvin and the catechism of Alexander Nowell. **Archiv für Reformationsgeschichte,** 61 (1) 50—66, 1970.

HEES, G. Barth, Calvin und Luther. **Volkstum,** 15: 670—680, 1933.

HENRY, Carl Ferdinand Howard. The legacy of John Calvin. **Christianity today,** 8 (7) 794—795, 1964.

HESSELINK, John. Calvin's popularity in Japan **(In:** Takemori, Masaichi. Calvin's influence in the Japanese church. Tokyo, Japan Calvin Translation Society, 1963. p. 3—6) (Calvin in Japan, 1).

HEYNS, Johan Adam. Is Calvyn nog tuis in Suid-Afrika? **Die Huisgenoot,** 42 (2458) 16—17, 1969.

HOEKSEMA, Herman. Calvin, Berkhof and H. J. Kuiper; a comparison. Grand Rapids [n.d.] 60 p.

HONDERICH, Pauline. John Calvin and Doctor Faustus. **Modern language review,** 68 (1) 1—13, 1973.

HUGHES, Philip Edgecumbe. Calvinism in Great Britain today. **Christianity today,** 3: 11—13, 1959.

The INFLUENCE of John Calvin down the centuries on the religious and political development of the Protestant nations. **Journal of the transactions of the Victoria Institute,** 56: 156—182, 1924.

JACOBS, Paul. Johann Calvin in Geschichte und Gegenwart. **Zeichen der Zeit,** 18: 274—277, 1964.

JANSMA, Theodore J. Psychologizing Luther and Calvin. **Torch and trumpet,** 12 (3) 7—10, 1962.

KENNEDY, Edwin O. Calvin speaks to our age. **The Presbyterian tribune,** 58 (2) 9—10, 1942.

KIRBY, Linnie Sue. The influence of John Calvin and his circle on present-day hymnody. Louisville, 1955. 118 1. Thesis—Southern Baptist Theological Seminary, Louisville.

KLOOSTER, Fred H. Karl Barth and John Calvin. **Stromata,** 2 (6) 4—6, 3/1957.

KORTZFLEISCH, Siegfried von. Ökumene im Geiste Calvins; der reformierte Weltbund in Frankfurt. **Christ und Welt,** 17 (33) 10, 1964.

KROMMINGA, John H. Lessons from Calvin. **Reformed journal,** 9 (9) 7—10, 1959.

KUWADA, H. Calvin and the Japanese church. **Reformed and presbyterian world,** 28: 258—265, 1965.

LADY, D. B. America's indebtedness to Calvin. **Christian world,** 60 (22) 5; (23) 2, 1917.

LAU, Franz. Die Bedeutung Calvins für die evangelische Diaspora. **Die evangelische Diaspora,** 30: 133—143, 1959/60.

LEUBE, Hans. Calvin im französischen Geistesleben. **Deutschland — Frankreich,** 2 (7) 57—91, 1944.

LLOYD-JONES, David Martyn. John Calvin and George Whitfield **(In:** Puritan and Reformed Studies. Conference, 15th, London, 1964. Able ministers of the New Testament; papers read at conference. [London, 1965] p. 75—96).

LOMBARD, Jacobus Christoffel. Calvyn; moderne evangelis spreek in moderne Frans en Rome se vrees. **Roeping,** 9 (3) 10—13, 1961.

LOMBARDI, Franco. Calvin und sein Beitrag zur Gestaltung der modernen Welt **(In:** Militanter Humanismus; von den Aufgaben der modernen Soziologie. Hrsg. van Alphons Silbermann. Frankfurt a.M., 1966, p. 141—171).

LOMBARDI, Franco. Calvino e il suo contributo alla formazione del mondo moderno. **De Homine,** 2: 19—20, 101—142, 1966.

MCDONNELL, Kilian. Calvin without myths. **Commonweal,** 81: 163—166, 1964.

MACFARLAND, Charles S. The permanent contributions of Geneva and John Calvin to church and state in America. **Union Seminary quarterly review,** 37 (2) 99—114, 1925/26; **Reformed Church review,** 4 (10) 439—455, 1925.

MADSEN, Erik Munch. Er Calvin Niels Hemmingens eksegetische Forbillede. **Dansk teologisk tidsskrift,** 9: 1—10, 1946.

MALAN, D. G. Calvinism in South Africa. **Evangelical quarterly,** 8: 167—174, 1936.

MARKARIAN, John Jacob. The Calvinistic concept of the Biblical revelation in the theology of B. B. Warfield. Madison, N. J., 1963, 261 l. Thesis—Drew Univ., Madison.

MARQUESS, Hoge. Calvin and the modern world **(In:** Calvin celebration by the Presbytery of Louisville. Addresses delivered at the celebration of the 400th anniversary of the birth of John Calvin. Louisville, Kent., 1909. p. 35—46).

MEAD, Edwin D. John Calvin after four centuries. **The Standard,** 11: 272—277, 1925.

MEHL, Roger. Calvin et notre temps. **Revue de théologie et de philosophie,** 14 (4) 205—216, 1964.

MIEGGE, Giovanni. Calvino all' Accademia d'Italia. **Gioventu cristina,** 5: 100—108, 1936.

MOFFAT, James D. The influence of Calvin on religious thought. **Auburn seminary record,** 5: 157—166, 1909.

MOORE, Walter Lane. Schleiermacher as a Calvinist; a comparison of Calvin and Schleiermacher on providence and predestination. **Scottish journal of theology,** 24 (2) 167—183, 1971.

MOUSSEAUX, M. Treue zu Jean Calvin. **Der deutsche Hugenott,** 29 (2) 47—49, 1965.

MURRAY, John. Calvin, Dort and Westminister, a comparative study (**In:** De Jong, Peter Ymen, ed. Crisis in the Reformed Churches; essays in commemoration of the great Synod of Dort, 1618—1619. Grand Rapids, Reformed Fellowship, 1968. Chapter 8).

NAUTA, Doede. Calvijns erfenis. **Gereformeerd theologisch tijdschrift,** 64: 81—94, 1964.

NIESEL, Wilhelm. Calvins Bedeutung für die Kirche. **Deutsches Pfarrerblatt,** 60: 2—4; 27—29, 1960.

OVERHOLSER, James. Calvin's continuing influence in theological developments of our day (**In:** A symposium: John Calvin. On the occasion of the 450th anniversary of his birth and the 400th anniversary of the final edition of the Institutes. Three addresses delivered to the Memphis Presbytery. Memphis, Tenn., 1959. p. 8—14).

PACKER, James Innell. Calvinism in Britain; its status and prospects. **Torch and trumpet,** 9 (7) 21—22, 1959.

PEW, J. Howard. Calvin's influence in church affairs. **Christianity today,** 6 (16) 769—771, 1962.

PINOMAA, Lennart. Tro, lag helgelse hos Luther, Calvin och John Wesley. **Norsk teologisk tidsskrift,** 69 (1/2) 107—118, 1968.

QUERVAIN, Alfred de. Kohlbrügge und das Erbe Calvins. **Evangelische Theologie,** 25 (4/5) 263—273, 1965.

QUERVAIN, Alfred de. Das Lob Gottes bei Calvin und seine Bedeutung für die Welt heute. **Kirchenblatt für die reformierte Schweiz,** 120: 162—166, 1964; **Kirche in der Zeit,** 19 (5) 201—204, 1964.

QUISTORP, Heinrich. Calvin und Robespierre. **Reformierte Kirchenzeitung,** 106: 218—219, 1965.

RIVIERE, William T. Karl Barth and John Calvin. **Calvin forum,** 2 (9) 37—39, 1936.

ROBERT, Daniel. Le rôle historique de Calvin. **La revue réformée,** 15 (60) 42—48, 1964.

ROCKWELL, W. W. Calvin and the reformation. (**In:** Union Theological Seminary, New York. Three addresses delivered at a service in commemoration of the four hundreth anniversary of the birth of John Calvin, May 1909. New York (1909) p. 5—19).

ROLSTON, Holmes. Departure from Geneva. **The Presbyterian outlook,** 154: 5—6, 1972.

ROLSTON, Holmes. John Calvin versus the Westminister Confession. Richmond, Va., John Knox, 1972. 124 p.

ROLSTON, Holmes. Responsible man in reformed theology; Calvin versus the Westminister Confession. **Scottish journal of theology,** 23 (2) 129—156, 1970.

RUNIA, Klaas. Calvijns betekenis in onze tijd. Potchefstroom, Instituut vir Bevordering van Calvinisme, P.U. vir C.H.O., 1969. 20 p.

RUNIA, Klaas. Spurgeon en het Calvinisme. **Centraal weekblad voor de Gereformeerde Kerken in Nederland,** 11 (21) 2, 1963.

SAVAGE, Theodore F. Back to Calvin. **Religion in life,** 17 (1) 63—69, winter 1947/48.

SCHALKWIJK, Francisco L. Calvijn en Zuid-Amerika. **Die Kerk-**

blad, 67 (1772) 15; 17, 1964. **Gereformeerd weekblad,** 20 (43) 310, 1965.

SCHRÖTER, F. Calvins Bedeutung für Kirche und Theologie der Gegenwart **(In:** Rogge, J. Johannes Calvin, 1509—1564; eine Gabe zu seinem 400. Todestag. Berlin, Evangelische Verlagsanstalt (1963) p. 72—97).

SCHWEITZER, Eduard. Gruss Calvins (und eines Neutestamentlers) an Gottfield W. Locher. **Zwingliana,** 13 (6) 370—374, 1971.

SINGER, Charles Gregg. John Calvin; America's first founding father. **Eternity,** 10 (7) 5—7, 1959.

SPITZ, Lewis W. The Renaissance and Reformation movements. Chicago, McNally, 1971. "Calvin and Calvinism": p. 411—440. (Rand McNally history series).

STEVENSON, J. Ross. Calvin's influence on civic and social life. **Auburn seminary record,** 5: 167—176, 1909.

STUERMANN, Walter Earl & GEOCARIS, Konstantin. The image of man; the perspectives of Calvin and Freud. **Interpretation,** 14: 28—42, 1960.

SZEKERES, Attila. Die Bedeutung Calvins für unsere Welt zwischen Materialismus und Existentialismus. **Nederlands theologisch tijdschrift,** 19 (3) 213—224, 1965.

TAKEMORI, Masaichi. Calvin's influence in the Japanese church. Tokyo, Japan Calvin Translation Society, 1963. 11 p. (Calvin in Japan, 1).

TIMMER, John. Calvin in Japan. **The Banner,** 98 (18) 6, 1963.

TIMMER, John. Grote belangstelling in Japan voor werken van Calvijn. **Centraal weekblad voor de Gereformeerde Kerken in Nederland,** 11 (26) 5; (27) 3, 1963.

TOON, Peter. The emergence of hyper-Calvinism in English nonconformity, 1689—1765. London, Olive Tree, 1967. "Calvin and Calvinism": p. 11—30.

UNGER, Hermann. Calvin im zwanzigsten Jahrhundert. [Schmetzingen, Schmetzinger Verlagsdruckerei, 1950] 93 p.

VAN BAAK, Edward A. Calvyn; sy voortgesette invloed in Japan. **Die Kerkblad,** 67 (1772) 11; 13, 1964.

VAN DEN BERG, J. Calvijn en de vrijzinnigheid. **Gereformeerd weekblad,** 15 (2) 14, 1959.

VAN DER LINDE, Simon, Calvijn en Coornhert. **Theologia reformata,** 2: 176—187, 1959.

VAN DER WALT, T. Calvyn en die jeug. **Die Kerkblad,** 67 (1672) 6—7, 1964.

VAN DER WOUDE, Cornelis. Confrontatie met de drie John's [Calvin, Knox, Wesley] **Gereformeerd weekblad,** 22 (1) 608, 1966.

VAN DER ZIJPP, N. Calvijn en wij. **Algemeen doopsgezind weekblad,** 14: 13, 1959.

VANNOY, J. R. Calvin and the Confession of 1967. **Reformation review,** 15 (2) 76—97, 1967/68.

VAN TIL, Cornelius. Calvin and modern subjectivism. **Torch and trumpet,** 9 (4) 14—16, 1959.

VAN TIL, Cornelius. John Calvin and John Dewey. **Christian opinion,** 3 (7) 107—108, 1946.

WALTY, J. N. Bulletin d'histoire des doctrines modernes; Calvin et la Calvinisme. **Revue des sciences philosophiques et theologiques,** 49 (2) 245—287, 1965.

WAMELINCK, J. H. H. Calvijn contra Colijn. Apeldoorn, Apeldoornsche Drukkers [1929] 93 p.

Reformation.

AALDERS, Willem Jan. De reformatie en de kultuur. **Stemmen des tijds,** Reformatie-nummer: 78—116, 1917.

ALLMEN, J. J. von. Ministry and ordination according to Reformed theology [i.e. Second Helvetic Confession] **Scottish journal of theology,** 25 (1) 75—88, 1972.

ALLMEN, Jean Jacques von. Le saint ministère selon la conviction et la volonté des Réformés de XVIe siècle. Neuchâtel, Delachaux et Niestlé, 1968. 225 p. (Bibliothèque théologique).

AUGUSTIJN, Cornelis. De godsdienstgesprekken tussen Rooms-Katholieken en Protestanten van 1538 tot 1541. Haarlem, Bohn, 1967. 149 p.

BABINGTON, John Albert. The Reformation; a religious and historical sketch (Repr.) Port Washington, N. Y., Kennikat Press (1971, 1901) 362 p.

BAINTON, Roland Herbert. Interpretations of the Reformation. **American historical review,** 66: 74—84, 1960/61.

BAINTON, Roland Herbert. The role of women in the Reformation; introduction to the following three papers. **Archiv für Reformationsgeschichte,** 63: 141—142, 1972.

BAINTON, Roland Herbert. Studies on the Reformation. Boston, Beacon Press (1963) 289 p. **(His** Collected papers in church history, ser. 2).

BAKELANTS, Louis. Les rapports de l'humanisme et de la réforme. **Revue de l'Université de Bruxelles,** 18: 264—282, 1965/66.

BARTH, Karl. Das Vaterunser nach den Katechismen der Reformation [La prière] Übers. Helmut Goes. Zürich, EVZ-Verl. (1965) 114 p.

BAUMER, Remigius. Die Auseinandersetzung über die römische Petrustradition in den ersten Jahrzehnten der Reformationszeit. **Römische Quartalschrift,** 54: 20—57, 1962.

BEARD, Charles. The Reformation of the 16th century in its relation to modern thought and knowledge. Foreword by Joseph Dorfman. Introd. by Ernst Barker. [Ann Arbor] University of Michigan Press (1962) 450 p. (Ann Arbor paperbooks, AA 61).

BECKMANN, Joachim. 450 Jahre Reformation. **Luther,** 39 (1) 1—13, 1968.

BIZER, Ernst. The problem of inter-communion in the Reformation **(In:** Inter-communion; the report of the Theological Committee appointed by the Continuation Commission of the World Council on Faith and Order, together with a selection from the material presented to the Commission. London, S.C.M. Press, 1952. p. 58—83).

BLOCKX, Karel. "Si quae culpa..." [L'église catholique et la Réformation] **Ephemerides theologicae lovaniensis,** 40 (3) 474—490, 1964.

BOHLMAN, Ralph Arthur. The criteria of Biblical canonicity in sixteenth century Lutheran, Roman Catholic, and Reformed theology. New Haven, 1968. 308 l. Thesis—Yale Univ.

BOISSET, Jean. Erasme de Rotterdam et la Réforme. **Societé de l'histoire du protestantisme français. Bulletin,** 116 (1/3) 22/40, 1970.

BREEN, Quirinus. Humanism and the Reformation. **Archiv,** 62 (1) 5, 1971. **(Also in:** The impact of the church upon its culture, ed. by Jerald C. Brauer. Chicago, 1968. p. 145—171) (Essays in Divinity, v. 2).

BROMILEY, G. W. The authority of the Bible; the attitude of the reformers. **Evangelical quarterly,** 19: 110—136, 1947.

CADIER, Jean. La Réforme et les spirituels. **Foi et vie,** 36: 762—779, 1935.

CADIER, Jean & SCHLEMMER, André. Le culte réforme. **Études théologiques et réligieuses,** 22: 3—10, 1947.

CANTIMORI, Delio. Au coeur religieux du XVIe siècle. **Annales-economies, sociétes, civilisations,** 15 (3) 556—568, 1960.

CARTER, C. Sydney. The Reformation; its unity and solidarity. **Churchman,** 50: 87—99, 1936.

CARTER, C. Sydney. The Reformer's doctrine of the Holy communion. **Churchman,** 66: 92—99, 1952.

CHEVALIER, J. Les deux réformes: Le Luthéranisme en Allemagne; Le Calvinisme dans les pays de langue anglaise **(In:** Etudes sur la Réforme; a propos du quatrième centenaire de la Réforme. Paris, Armand Colin, 1919. p. 841—891).

CLARK, Francis. Eucharistic sacrifice and the Reformation. Westminster, Mad., Newman, 1960. 582 p. Also published by Darton, Longman, London.

COCHRANE, Arthur C. **ed.** Reformed confessions of the 16th century. Philadelphia, Westminster Press (c1966) 336 p. Also published by SCM Press, London.

COURTHIAL, Pierre. Actualité et catholicité de la Réformation. **Les cahiers protestants,** 43: 115—124, 1959.

COURVOISIER, Jaques. Eugène Choisy; historien de la Réforme Calvinienne. **Genava, N.S.,** 7 (1—2) 89—102, 1959.

COURVOISIER, Jaques. Reformation and politics. Tr. by Grace A. Gibson. [Newcastle on Tyne, Univ. of Newcastle on Tyne, 1971] 20 p. (Earl Grey memorial lecture, 50).

CUNNINGHAM, William. The reformers and the theology of the reformation [Ed. by James Buchanan and James Bannerman] London, Banner of Truth Trust (1967, 1862) 616 p. (Students' reformed theological library).

DAMBORIENA, Prudencio. Fe catolica e iglesias y sectas de la Reforma. Madrid, Razon y Fe, 1961. "Balance final de la Reforma protestante": p. 193—214.

DANIEL-ROPS, Henry. The Protestant Reformation; tr. from the French by A. Butler. London, Dent (1961) 560 p. (History of the Church of Christ, 4) Original title: Une révolution religieuse.

DELUMEAU, Jean. Naissance et affirmation de la Réforme. 3 éd. Paris, Presses Universitaires de France, 1973. 416 p.

DE MOLEN, Richard L. **ed.** The meaning of the Renaissance and Reformation; essays, by Richard L. De Molen [a.o.] Boston, Houghton Mifflin [1973, c1974] 385 p.

DEMURA, Akira. [History of the Swiss Reformation] Tokyo, Protestant Pub. Co., 1971. [In Japanese]

D'ESPINE, H. Le vrai sens de la Réformation. **Centrallblatt,** 76: 637—643, 1936.

DICKENS, Arthur Geoffrey. Reformation and society in sixteenth-century Europe. London, Thames & Hudson (1966) 216 p. ([Library of European civilization]).

DICKENS, Arthur Geoffrey. La Réforme et le protestantisme. Genève, Crémille [1969] 216 p. Translation of: Reformation and society in sixteenth-century Europe. Also published by Flammarion, Paris, 1969.

DOUMERGUE, Emile. La démocratie et la Réforme. **Foi et vie,** 21: 93—101, 1918.

DOUMERGUE, Emile. La Réformation et la Révolution. Paris, **Foi et vie,** 1910. "La Réforme et le Moyen-Age": p. 5—38; "La Réforme et les Temps modernes": p. 41—69

DRESS, W. Die Zehn Gebote und der Dekalog; ein Beitrag zu der Frage nach den Unterschieden zwischen lutherischem und calvinistischem Denken. **Theologische Literaturzeitung,** 79 (7/8) 415—422, 1954.

DUGMORE, Clifford William. Some recent aids to Reformation studies. **Journal of ecclesiastical history,** 18: 59—64, 1967.

DU TOIT, Jacob Daniël, HAMERSMA, T. & LOS, Siete Oene. De Hervorming; een gedenkschrift. [Potchefstroom] Calvijn Jubileum Fonds [n.d] 45 p.

EASTER, B. R. Missionary thought and practice within the reformed tradition **(In:** Press toward the mark; papers read at the Puritan and Reformed studies conference, December 1961. Chizwick, Evangelical Magazine, 1962. p. 31—45).

ELLUL, Jacques. Actualité de le Réforme, **Foi et vie,** 58: 39—64, 1959.

FRAENKEL, Peter. Einigungsbestrebungen in der Reformationszeit [zwei Wege, zwei Motive] Wiesbaden, Steiner, 1965. 70 p. (Institut für Europäische Geschichte, Mainz. Vorträge, Nr. 41).

FRAENKEL, Peter. Institut d'histoire de la réformation; rapport d' activité 1969—'71. **Revue de theologie et de philosophie,** 105: 42—47, 1972.

GASSMANN, Benno. Ecclesia Reformata; die Kirche in den Reformierten Bekenntnisschriften. Freiburg, Herder, 1968. 479 p.

GILMONT, Jean François. Les martyrologes protestants du XVIe siècle; essai de présentation générale [Louvain] 1966. 385 1. Thesis—Univ. Catholique, Louvain.

GRESCHAT, Martin. Renaissance und Reformation. **Evangelische Theologie,** 29 (12) 645, 1969.

GRIMM, Harold John. The Reformation. Washington, D. C., American Historical Association (c1972) 34 p. (AHA-pamphlets, no. 403).

GRIMM, Harold John. The Reformation in recent historical thought. New York, Macmillan, 1964. 28 p. (American Historical Association. Service Center for Teachers of History. Publications, no. 54) Also published by Collier-Macmillan, London.

HAGEMAN, Howard G. The liturgical origins of the reformed churches **(In:** The heritage of John Calvin, ed. by John H. Bratt. Grand Rapids, Eerdmans, 1973, p. 110—136) (Heritage Hall Lectures, 1960—1970) (Heritage Hall publications, no. 2).

HARMS, Klaus. Die Bedeutung des gedruckten Wortes im Jahrhundert der Reformation. **Pastoralblätter,** 103: 401—414, 1963.

HAUSAMMANN, Susi. 'Leben aus Glauben' in Reformation, Reformorthodoxie und Pietismus. **Theologische Zeitschrift,** 27: 263—289, 1971.

HENDERSON, Robert Waugh. Problems of the Reformed eldership in its early history. **Journal of Prebyterian history,** 45: 227—242, 1967.

HENRY, Stuart Clark, True and lively heritage. **Journal of Presbyterian history,** 45: 1—7, 1967.

HILLERBRAND, Hans Joachim. Spread of the Protestant Reformation of the sixteenth century; a historical case study in the transfer of ideas. **South Atlantic quarterly,** 67: 265—286, 1968.

HILLERBRAND, Hans Joachim. The world of the Reformation. New York, Scribner [1973], 229 p.

HOEKEMA, Anthony A. The sovereignty of God principle. **The Banner,** 94 (22) 9; 21, 1959.

HOLSTEN, W. Reformation und Mission. **Archiv für Reformationsgeschichte,** 44: 1—32, 1953.

HUDSON, W. S. Democratic freedom and religious faith in the Reformed tradition. **Church history,** 15: 177—194, 1946.

JACOBS, Paul. Reformierte Theologie und Ökumene. **Reformierte Kirchenzeitung,** 103: 245—247, 1962.

KINDT, Karl. Die Reformation im Urteil der Reformation **(In:** Begegnung der Christen; Studien evangelischer und katholischer Christen. Otto Karrer gewidmet zum 70. Geburtstag. Hrsg. von M. Roesle und O. Cullmann. Stuttgart, 1959. p. 601—618).

KINGDON, Robert Mc Cune, **ed.** Transition and revolution; problems and issues of European Renaissance and Reformation history, ed. R. M. Kingdon. Minneapolis, Burgess [1974] 274 p.

KJOLLERSTRÖM, Sven. Striden kring kalvinismen i Sverige under Erik XIV. En kyrkohistorisk studie. Lund, 1935. 280 p.

KÖHLER, Walther. Reformation und Ketzerprozess. Tübingen, Mohr, 1901. 48 p (Sammlung gemeinverständlicher Vorträge und Schriften aus dem Gebiet der Theologie und Religionsgeschichte, N. 22).

KUYPER, H. H. Het zedelijk karakter der Reformatie gehandhaaf tegenover Rome. Kampen, Kok, 1912. 180 p.

LANG, August. Zur Geschichte der Protestantismus. Eine Liebesgeschichte aus den Tagen Butzers und Calvin **(In:** Cohn, G. Universitätsfragen und Erinnerungen. Stuttgart, Enke, 1918. p. 136—155).

LECLER, Joseph. Protestantisme et "libre examen"; les étapes et le vocabulaire d'une controverse. **Recherches de science religieuse,** 57: 321—374, 1969.

LEHMANN, Paul L. The servant image in Reformed theology. **Theology today,** 15 (3) 333—351, 1958.

LEUBA, J. L. La réforme, une pierre d'achoppement. **Centrallblatt,** 76: 648—657, 1936.

LUCAS, Henry Stephen. The Renaissance and the Reformation; 2nd ed. New York, Harper [c1960] "The Calvinist revolt": p. 559—620. (Historical series).

MCLELLAND, Joseph C. The Reformed doctrine of predestination. **Scottish journal of theology,** 8 (3) 255—271, 1955.

MACEK, Josef. La ríforma popolare. Firenze, Sansoni, 1973. 104 p.

(Scuola aperta, 29. Storia).

MANSCHRECK, Clyde Leonard. Prayers of the reformers. Philadelphia, Muhlenberg (1958) 183 p.

MASCALL, Eric Lionel. Eucharistic sacrifice and the Reformation. **Theology,** 64: 310—316, 1961.

MAURER, Wilhelm. Der Laie in der Reformationszeit. **Die neue Furche Zeitwende,** 33: 21—29, 1962.

MERLE d'AUBIGNE, Jean-Henri. Histoire de la réformation en Europe au temps de Calvin. Réimpr. [n.p.] 1968. 8 v.

MERLE D'AUBIGNE, Jean Henri. Histoire de la réformation du seizième siècle. Réimpr. de led. 1847-1853. [n.p.] 1968. 5 v.

MILLER, Charles. How Calvinism spread in Switzerland, Germany and France. **The Banner,** 94 (9) 9; 21; (12) 9; 29, 1959.

MOURS, Samuel. Essai sommaire de géographie du protestantisme réformé français au XVII siècle. Paris, Librairie protestante, 1966. 48 p.

NAUTA, Doede. Augustine and the Reformation. **Free University quarterly,** 3: 237—247, 1954/55.

NAUTA, Doede. De geschiedbeschouwing der Reformatie **(In:** Gezelschap van Christelijke historici in Nederland. De zin der geschiedenis; lustrumbundel. Wageningen, Zomer en Keuning, 1944. p. 140—160).

NEUBIG, Karl Heinz. Renaissance und Reformation, 1350—1648. Ebenhausen bei München, Langewiesche, Brandt, 1962. 288 p. (Lesewerk zur Geschichte).

NEUSER, Wilhelm Heinrich. Kirche und Staat in der Reformationszeit **(In:** Kirche und Staat. Festschrift für Bischof D. Herman Kunst, zum 60. Geburtstag am 21. Januar 1967. Hrsg. von Kurt Aland und Wilhelm Schneemelcher. Berlin, 1967. p. 50—78).

NICOLE, Roger. Divine sovereignty; cornerstone of the Reformation [Contains parts of unpublished lecture by Emile Doumergue] **Christianity today,** 9 (2) 72—75, 1964.

NIESEL, Wilhelm. Reformed symbolics; a comparison of Catholicism, Orthodoxy, and Protestantism. Tr. by D. Lewis. Edinburgh, Oliver and Boyd [1962] 384 p.

PEW, J. Howard. Our Reformed heritage. **Christian economics,** 14 (19) 1; 3, 1962; 16 (19) 1; 3 1964.

PONT, A. D. Die kerkhervorming van die sestiende eeu. **Die Hervormer,** 55 (7) 7—10, 1964; 59 (7) 5—8, 1968.

POST, Regnerus Richardus. Twee reformaties in de zestiende eeuw? **Studia Catholica,** 3: 196—208, 1963.

RAWLINS, A. J. B. Gereformeerde simbole. **Die Voorligter,** 24 (8) 12—13, 1961.

REFORMATION and election. **Christian century,** 77: 1235—1236, 1960.

La RÉFORME; 36 diapositives. Introd. et commentaire de Henri Dubief. Lausanne, Recontre, 1965. 96 p. (Images des grandes civilizations, 19) (Bibliovision Rencontre).

REFORMIERT-PRESBYTERIANISCHES Jubiläum.. **Der deutsche Hugenott,** 22: 103—105, 1958.

REID, John Kelman Sutherland. Gospel and eucharist; a reformed exposition **(In:** Oecumenica [Annales de recherche oecuménique, Strasbourg] Paris, Du Cerf, 1970. p. 212—239).

RIGG, W. H. Positive message of the Reformation. **Churchman,** 48 (?) 94—107, 1934.

RITCHEY, George Arch. A study of the clergy on the continent of Europe during the Reformation period. Louisville, Ky., 1935. Thesis—Southern Baptist Theological Seminary, Louisville.

ROBERT, Daniel. Histoire du protestantisme. Bulletin historique. **Revue historique,** 89 (234) 159—172, 1965.

ROYAL, R. Fletcher. The contribution of Christian education to the Reformation. Fort Worth, Tex., 1949. Thesis—Southern Baptist Theological Seminary, Fort Worth.

RUPP, Ernest Gordon. Patterns of salvation in the first age of the Reformation. **Archiv für Reformationsgeschichte,** 57 (1/2) 52—66, 1966.

RUPP, Ernest Gordon. The reform of reformation? **Time and tide,** 43: 30—31, 1962.

SCHMIDT, Rainer, **ed.** Die Bedeutung der Reformation für die Welt von Morgen; 22 Beiträge aus 9 Ländern. Frankfurt a.M., Lembeck, 1967. 309 p.

SCHULZE, Ludolf Ferdinand. Perspektiewe vanuit die Reformasie [re: ethics and predestination] **In die Skriflig,** 2 (6) 1—17, 1968.

SESTON, William. Simples remarques sur la culture biblique des protestantisme du XVIe au XVIIIe siècle. **Societé de l'histoire du protestantisme français. Bulletin,** 115: 301—306, 1969.

SKILES, Elwyn Lloyd. A study of some of the lesser known heroes of the Reformation. Louisville, Ky., 1941. Thesis—Southern Baptist Theological Seminary, Louisville.

SPITZ, Lewis W. Humanism in the Reformation **(In:** Renaissance; studies in honor of Hans Baron. Ed. by Anthony Molho and John A. Tedeschi. Dekalb, Ill, Northern Illinois University Press, 1971. p. 641—662).

STAUFFER, Richard. La Réforme, 1517—1564. Paris, Presses Universitaires de France, 1970. "La réforme calvinienne": p. 79—102. (Que saisje? no. 1376).

STEK, John H. The modern problem of the Old Testament in the light of Reformation perspective. **Calvin theological journal,** 2 (2) 202—225, 1967.

STROHL, Henri. La pensée de la Réforme. Neuchatel, Torre Pellice, 1951. 264 p. (Manuals et précis de théologie, 32).

STUPPERICH, Robert. Übereinstimmungen und Unterschiede in der Theologie der Reformatoren. **Kyrko-historiska föreningen, Upsala. Skrifter, ser. 1. Kyrkohistorisk arsskrift,** 62: 46—67, 1962.

SYKES, Norman. The legacy of the Reformation. **Modern churchman,** 46: 9—24, 1956.

TAVARD, George Henri. Reformed piety. **Worship,** 37: 400—411, 1963.

TILLICH, Paul. Gesammelte Werke, Bd. 7: Der Protestantismus als Kritik und Gestaltung. Hrsg. von Renate Albrecht. Stuttgart, Evangelisches Verlagswerk, 1961. "Die Wiederentdeckung der prophetischen Tradition in der Reformation": p. 171—225.

TODD, John Murray. Reformation. London, Darton, Longman & Tod, 1972. 377 p.

TORRANCE, Thomas Forsyth. History and reformation. **Scottish journal of theology,** 4: 279—291, 1951.

TSCHACKERT, Paul. Die Entstehung der lutherischen und der reformierten Kirchenlehre, samt ihren innerprotestantischen Gegensätzen. Göttingen, Vanderhoek & Ruprecht, 1910. "Den Calvinismus und der Lehrgehalt der calvinistischen Bekenntnisschriften der reformierte Kirche": p. 381—445.

VAN DER LINDE, Simon. Verschillen tussen de wereld van de Reformatie en het heden, beoordeeld in het licht van de apostolaire taak der kerk (**In:** Zending in Nederland; bundel opstellen over de missionaire roeping van de gemeente. Uitg. ter gelegenheid van het 35-jarig jubileum van de Hervormde Bond voor Inwendige Zending op Gereformeerde Grondslag. 's-Gravenhage, Boekencentrum, 1970. p. 61—73).

VAN DER WALT, Barend Johannes. Interpretasie van die reformasie. **Woord en daad,** 15 (146) 10; 12, 1974.

VAN DER WOUDE, Cornelis. Réforme et scolastique. **Etudes evangeliques,** 25: 77—97, 1965.

VINAY, Valdo. La Riforma protestante. Brescia, Paideia, 1970. 479 p. (Biblioteca di cultura religiosa, 20).

VISSER, J. Th. De Reformatie en de staatkunde. **Stemmen des tijds,** Reformatie-nummer: 117—146, 1917.

VOGLER, Bernard. La réforme et le concept de miracle au XVIe siècle. **Revue d'histoire de la spiritualité,** 48: 145—149, 1972.

WAGNER, A. Reformatorium sacculi XVI. de necessitate baptismi doctrina. **Divus Thomas,** 45: 5—34; 157—185, 1942.

WALLAU, R. Gemeinschaft, Reich Gottes und Kirche und die Calvinische Reformation. **Furche-Almanach,** 1925: 18—27.

WARFIELD, Benjamin Breckinridge. Predestination in the Reformed confessions. **Presbyterian and Reformed review,** 12: 49—128, 1901.

WEBER, Hans Emil. Reformation, Orthodoxie und Rationalismus (2. Aufl.) Gütersloh, Mohn [1967?] 2 v. in 3. (Beiträge zur Förderung christlicher Theologie. 2. Reihe, Bd. 35, 45, 51) Unveränderter reprografischer Nachdruck der 1. Auflage, Gütersloh, 1935—'51.

WENDEL, Francois & ROUSSEL, Bernard. L'église à l'époque de l'humanisme et de la Réforme. **Revue d'histoire et de philosophie religieuses,** 51: 342—360, 1971.

WHALE, John Seldon. Christian reunion; historic divisions reconsidered. Grand Rapids, Eerdmans, 1971; London, Lutterworth, 1971. "Lutheran and reformed; the dissension of first cousins": p. 75—96.

WHITLOCK, Glenn E. The call to the ministry in the reformed tradition. **Theology today,** 17 (3) 311—321, 1960.

WILLIAMS, George Huntston. The radical reformation. Philadelphia, Westminster, 1962. 924 p.

WILLIAMS, John Rodman. The covenant in Reformed theology. **Austin Seminary bulletin,** 78 (6) 24—38, 1963.

WOLF, Horst. Dokumente zur Reformationszeit. **Börsenblatt für den deutschen Buchhandel,** 134 (43) 833—834, 1967.

WOLLGAST, Siegfried. Literatur zur Reformation. **Die Bibliothekar,** 21 (4) 1185—1191, 1967.

WORKMAN, H. B. The political issues of the Reformation. **London quarterly review,** 160: 433—428, 1936.

ZEEDEN, Ernst Walter. Die Enstehung der Konfessionen; Grundlagen and Forschungen der Konfessionsbildung im Zeitalter der Glaubenskämpfe. München, Oldenburg, 1965 [c1964] 213 p.

ZEEDEN, Ernst Walter. Probleme und Aufgaben der Reformationsgeschichts-schreibung. **Geschichte in Wissenschaft und Unterrich,** 6: 201—217; 278—300, 1955.

ZELLER, Gaston. La Réforme. Paris, S.E.D.E.S., 1973. 430 p. (Regards sur l'histoire, 13. Historie générale, 2).

ZIEGLER, Donald Jenks. **ed.** Great debates of the Reformation. New York, Random House [1969] 358 p.

Calvinism: General.

ATHERTON, L. Calvinism; its personal application **(In:** International Conference of Calvinists. 1st, London, 1932. The reformed faith commonly called Calvinism. Report of the International Conference held in May, 1932. London, Sovereign Grace Union [1932] p. 99—107).

ATTEMA, Dirk Sijbolt. A remarkable testimony on Calvinism of the year 1671. **Free university quarterly,** 4: 99—132, 1955/57.

BAINTON, Roland Herbert. What is Calvinism? **Christian century,** 42: 351—352, 1925.

BOISSET, Jean. Histoire du protestantisme. Paris, Presses Universitaires de France, 1970. "Le calvinisme en Europe": p. 60—71. (Que sais-je? 427).

BRATT, John Harold **ed.** The rise and development of Calvinism; a concise history (2nd ed., 3rd print.) Grand Rapids, Mich., Eerdmans (1968, c1964) 136 p.

BRILLENBURG WURTH, Gerrit. Het Calvinisme vandaag. Wageningen, Zomer en Keuning [195-?] 86 p.

Die CALVINISME het 'n eie weg; verwarring oor liberaal en konserwatief. **Woord en daad,** 10 (66) 1; 7—8, 1968.

CHALMERS, Randolph Carleton. The active character of Calvinism. **Canadian journal of theology,** 2: 27—34, 1956.

CORREVON, Ch. Weltmarkt der Calvinismus. **Reformierte Kirchenzeitung,** 75: 126-, 1925.

DAKIN, Arthur. Calvinism. Port Washington, N.Y., Kennikat Press, 1971 (1940) 252 p.

d'ASSONVILLE, Victor Edouard. Is die benaming „Calvinisme", „Calvinis", „Calvinisties" verantwoord? **Die goue kandelaar,** 9: 70, 1970.

DE KLERK, Willem Johannes. Die Calvinisme in 'n neutedop. **Potchefstroomse Universiteit vir Christelike Hoër Onderwys. Instituut vir bevordering van Calvinisme. Studiestuk,** 36, 1969.

DE VRIES, W. G. De Internationale federasie van Calvinisten en haar invloed op de onderlinge verhoudingen in de Gereformeerde kerken in Nederland in de dertiger jaren van de twintigste eeuw. Kampen, 1974. Thesis—Theologische Hoogeschool, Kampen [Broederweg].

DOOYEWEERD, Herman. Het Calvinistisch beginsel der souvereiniteit in eigen kring als staatkundig beginsel. **Nederland en Oranje,** 4: 98—99; 185—189, 1923; 5; 5—15; 27—31; 71—76, 1924.

DOOYEWEERD, Herman. Leugen en waarheid over het Calvinisme. **Nederland en Oranje,** 6: 81—90, 1925.

DUMAS, André. Sous le signe de Jonas ou signification du Calvinisme. **Foi et vie,** 49: 548—553, 1951.

DU TOIT, Jacob Daniël. Enkele grondbeginsels van die Calvinisme **(In:** Koers in die krisis; artikels versamel deur die Federasie van die Calvinistiese Studenteverenigings in Suid-Afrika. Met 'n erewoord van H. Colijn en 'n voorw. van J. D. Kestell. Stellenbosch, Pro Ecclesia, 1935-'41. v. 1, p. 36—47).

ENGELSMA, David. A defense of Calvinism as the gospel. **The standard bearer,** 49: 15—16; 68—69; 138—140; 164—166, 1972/73.

FAZZO, Vittorio. Protestanti e cattolici. Roma, Paoline [1962?] "Il Calminismo": p. 130—147.

FEENSTRA, C. A. Calvinism in the light of God's Word; or God's Word versus man's words. Sioux Center, Iowa., 1968.

FOUQUET, R. Internationaler Calvinisten-Kongress, Montpellier, 23 —31 Aug. 1953. **Der deutsche Hugenott,** 17 (4) 105—108, 1953.

FRASER, A. M. How may the principles of Calvinism be rendered most effective under modern conditions? **(In:** Calvin memorial addresses; delivered before the General Assembly at Savannah, May, 1909, in observance of the birth of John Calvin. Richmond, Va., Presbyterian Committee of Publication [n.d.] 241—260).

GORING, Jeremy. Calvinism in decline. **Hibbert journal,** 60: 204—211, 1960.

GROSHEIDE, Frederik Willem. The individuality of Calvinism **(In:** International conference of Calvinists. 1st, London, 1932. The reformed faith commonly called Calvinism. Report of the International Conference held in May, 1932. London, Sovereign Grace Union [1932] p. 67—82) **Also in: Evangelical quarterly,** 5: 379—390, 1933.

HAMILTON, Floyd Eugene. The reformed faith in the modern world (reimpression) London, Sovereign Grace Union (1949) 36 p. (S.G.U. publication, no. 239).

HANKO, H., HOEKSTRA, H. C. & VAN BAREN, G. J. The five points of Calvinism. Grand Rapids, Published by the Protestant Reformed Churches in America, 1967.

HEPP, Valentin. The distinctive doctrines of Calvinism **(In:** International Conference of Calvinists. 1st, London, 1932. The reformed faith commonly called Calvinism. Report of the International Conference held in May, 1932, London, Sovereign Grace Union [1932] p. 83—98). **Also in: Evangelical quarterly,** 4: 337—348, 1932.

HEYNS, Johan Adam. Calvinisme. **Handhaaf,** 4 (2) 22—23, 1966.

HOBSBAUM, P. Calvinism in action; the super-ego triumphant. **Hudson review,** 25: 23—50, 1972.

HOWE, D. W. Decline of Calvinism; an approach to its study. **Comparative studies in society and history,** 14: 306—327, 1972.

JONKER, Willem Daniël. Die aktualiteit van die Calvinisme. **Woord en daad,** 4 (3) 9, 1959.

KEVAN, E. F. The re-emergence of Calvinism. **Evangelical quarterly,** 15: 216—223, 1943.

KING, Samuel A. How far has original Calvinism been modified by time? **(In:** Calvin memorial addresses; delivered before the General Assembly at Savannah, May 1909, in observance of the birth of John Calvin. Richmond, Va., Presbyterian Committee of Publication [n.d.] p. 195—222).

KROMMINGA, John H. Calvinism in the light of its current revival. **The Banner,** 94 (35) 9, 1959.

KROMMINGA, John H. Why we speak. **Calvin theological journal,** 1 (1) 5 — 10, 1966.

KUYPER, Abraham. Lectures on Calvinism; six lectures delivered at Princeton Univ. under auspices of the C. P. Stone Foundation. Grand Rapids, Eerdmans, 1961. 199 p. (Stone lectures).

LAMA, D. Universele Calvinisme; Calviniste en Calvinisme in ander lande. **Woord en daad,** 8 (39) 9—11; (40) 2—4, 1965.

LANE, George Eric. What is this Calvinism? (2nd ed.) Redhill, Surrey, Sovereign Grace Union (1968) 18 p.

LINDEQUE, J. G. Die Calvinisme in ons tyd. **Die Kerkbode,** 95 (50) 1619—1620, 1965.

LUBBE, W. J. G. Calvinisme. **Die Kerkbode,** 103 (19) 652; (20) 684; (21) 716; (23) 788; (24) 820; (26) 884—885, 1969.

MCNEILL, John Thomas. The history and character of Calvinism. New York, Oxford Univ. Press, 1967 (c1954) 470 p. (Galaxy book, 190).

MEER as 'n kerklike godsdienstige rigting; Calvinisme nie goed verstaan. **Woord en daad,** 11 (83) 1; 11, 1969.

MEETER, H. Henry. The basic ideas of Calvinism; 5th ed., rev. Grand Rapids, Mich., Grand Rapids International Publications, 1967 (c1956) 253 p.

MEETER, H. Henry. Calvinism as a vital force. **(In:** National Union of Christian schools. Educational convention papers. Our faith put to the test. Chicago, 1932, p. 72—91).

MOLTMANN, Jürgen. Zur Bedeutung des Petrus Ramus für Philosophie und Theologie im Calvinismus. **Zeitschrift für Kirchengeschichte,** 68 (6) 295—318, 1957.

PERRIRAZ, Louis. Histoire de la théologie réformée française. Neuchâtel, Messeiler, 1961. "Calvinisme": t. 4 p. 36—68.

POULAIN, André. Le principe d'activité du Calvinisme. New York [n.d.] 83 p. Thesis—Union Theological Seminary, New York.

REEVE, James Josiah. Calvinism; a brief historical sketch and estimate. Louisville, 1905. 54 1. Thesis—Southern Baptist Theological Seminary, Louisville.

RICE, John R. Some serious, popular false doctrines answered from the Scriptures. Murfreesboro, Tenn., Sword of the Lord Publishers, 1970. "Hyper-Calvinism; a false doctrine": p. 273—289.

RITSCHL, Albrecht. Three essays: Prolegomena (to) The history of pietism. Tr. and with an introd. by Philip Hefner. Philadelphia, Fortress Press, 1972. "Lutheranism and Calvinism": p. 105—122.

RUNIA, Klaas. De praktijk (toepassing) van het Calvinisme in een geseculariseerde wereld **(In:** Potchefstroomse Universiteit vir Christelike Hoër Onderwys. Besinning en uitsig; 'n keur uit die referate gelewer tydens die eeufeesjaar van die P.U. vir C.H.O. en die Teologiese Skool, 1969. [Potchefstroom, 1971] p. 175—194).

SCHOMERUS, H. Der calvinischer Mensch. **Volkstum,** 15: 93—98, 1932.

SIMPSON, P.Carnegie. Three elements in essential Calvinism. **Congregational quarterly,** 20: 209—219, 1942.

SMITH, J. W. D. Calvinism. **Year book of education,** 1951: 168—181.

STEELE, David N. & THOMAS, Curtis C. The five points of Calvinism; defined, defended (and) documented. Pref. by Roger Nicole. Philadelphia, Pa., Presbyterian and Reformed Pub. Co., 1967. 95 p. (International library of philosophy and theology: Biblical and theological studies).

STOKER, Hendrik Gerhardus. Praktiese Calvinisme. Praatjies gelewer oor die Afrikaanse sender van die S.A.U.K., 23 Oktober — 20 November 1955. Potchefstroom, Pro Rege, 1956. 32 p.

STOKER, Hendrik Gerhardus. Die wese van die Calvinisme. **Die Huisgenoot,** 16 (521) 25; 61, 1932.

VAN DER PLOEG, John. Calvinism and 1959. **The Banner,** 94 (1) 4—5, 1959.

VAN DER WALT, Barend Johannes. Calvinisme in neutedop. **Bond van Jongeliedeverenigings op Gereformeerde Grondslag in Transvaal. Perspektief in ons J.V.-werk; instruksieblad,** 3 (3) 11—62; 137—150, 1965.

VAN DER WALT, Jan Jacobus. Die Calvinisme. **Die Gereformeerde vroueblad,** 22 (5) 9—11, 1967.

VAN SCHELVEN, Aart Arnout. Het Calvinisme in historisch perspectief **(In:** Koers in die krisis, dl. 1. Stellenbosch, Pro Ecclesia, 1935. p. p. 48—55).

VAN TIL, Cornelius. The case for Calvinism. Philadelphia, Presbyterian and Reformed Pub. Co., 1964. 153 p. (International library of philosophy and theology).

VICTOR, J. The revival of Calvinism. **Evangelical quarterly,** 8: 36—46, 1936.

WALLER, G. F. The popularization of Calvinism: Thomas Beard's The theater of God's judgments. **Theology,** 75: 176—187, 1972.

WARFIELD, Benjamin Breckinridge. Present day attitude to Calvinism **(In:** Calvin memorial addresses; delivered before the General Assembly at Savannah, May 1909, in observance of the birth of John Calvin. Richmond, Va., Presbyterian Committee of Publication [n.d.] p. 223—240).

WHITE, John H. The need for Calvinism today. **The Presbyterian guardian,** 42: 67, 1973.

WILSON, R. M. Calvinism. **The Churchman,** 27: 112—, 1913.

WILTERDINK, Garrett. Calvinism and other isms. **Reformed review,** 13: 41—50, 1959.

Calvinism and the church.

ELERT, Werner. Law and Gospel. Tr. by Edward H. Schroeder. Philadelphia, Fortress Press [c1967] "A critique of Calvinism": Chapter 9. (Facet books. Social ethics series, 16).

HAAN, B. J. Calvinism and the contemporary crisis in the church. **Torch and trumpet,** 19 (2) 20—23, 1969.

HAITJEMA, Theodorus Lambertus. Calvinisme en Barthianisme. **Nederlands theologisch tijdschrift,** 10: 76—95, 1955.

HEIDEMAN, Eugene. Calvinism and church government. **Reformed review,** 13: 1—9, 1959.

KLOOSTER, Fred H. Calvinism and orthodoxy. **The Banner,** 94 (40) 9, 1959.

KNIEPER, Barbara. Die Naturrechtslehre des Hugo Grotius als Einigungsprinzip der Christenheit, dargestellt an seiner Stellung zum Calvinismus. Frankfurt a.M., 1971. 190 p. Thesis—Frankfurt a.M.

KOCHER, D. R. Calvinism and confirmation. **Princeton Seminary bulletin,** 54 (2) 28—31, 1960.

MACCAFFREY, James. History of the Catholic Church from the Renaissance to the French Revolution [Repr. of 1915 ed.] Freeport, N.Y., Books for Libraries Press, 1970. "Progress of Calvinism": v. 1, p. 140—177.

NUTTALL, Geoffrey Fillingham. Calvinism in free church history. **Baptist quarterly,** 22: 418—428, 1969.

OSTERHAVEN, Maurice Eugene. Calvinism and the ecumenical movement. **Reformed review,** 13: 30—40, 1959.

PALM, Franklin Charles. Calvinism and the religious wars. New York, Fertig, 1971 (c1932) 117 p. "Calvinism, an international religion", p. 65—102.

PARKER, Thomas Henry Louis. The reformation and the church today. **Churchman,** 87: 29—35, 1973.

REED, Frank Otheman. Public worship in sixteenth century calvinism. [Oxford] 1934. Thesis—Oxford Univ.

RIDDERBOS, Herman Nicolaas. Reformierte Grundsätze; ein Vortrag. Nordhorn, Selbstverlag des Bundes altreformierten Jünglingsvereine, 1950. 15 p.

SCHULZE, Ludolf Ferdinand. Straatsburg en artikel 2 van die Dordtse Kerkorde. **Koers,** 33 (4) 310—313, 1966.

SCHUMM, Karl. Zerstörung kirchlicher kunst in Hohenlohe durch calvinistische Einflüsse. **Blätter für wurttenbergische Kirchengeschichte,** 64: 113—124, 1964.

STONE, Arthur. Evangelical Calvinism. Newcastle on Tyne, Bealls [1962] 60 p.

STREET, T. Watson. Recovering the Calvinistic heritage of Christian worship. **Austin Seminary bulletin,** 75 (8) 39—47, 6/1960.

TIGCHELAAR, J. J. Vormt de Rematorische verkiezingsleer een hindernis voor de roeping van de kerk in de wereld? (**In:** Zending in Nederland; bundel opstellen over de missionaire roeping van de gemeente. Uitg. ter gelegenheid van het 35-jarig jubileum van de Hervormde Bond voor Inwendige Zending op Gereformeerde Grondslag. 's-Gravenhage, Boekencentrum, 1970. p. 74—88).

TRIMP, Cornelis. De dienst van de mondige kerk; een confrontatie met het appèl van de 'mondige' wereld. Goes, Oosterbaan & le Cointre, 1971. "Het patroon van het Calvinisme": p. 9—48.

YOUNG, William. Historic Calvinism and Neo-Calvinism. **Westminster theological journal,** 36 (1) 48—64; (2) 156—173, 1973/74.

Calvinism: Special subjects.

ALEXANDER, Robert C. The influence of the Protestant Reformation on Protestant religious education in the 16th century. Nashville, Tenn., 1926. "Calvinistic education": p. 112—154. Thesis—Vanderbilt Univ., Nashville, Tenn.

ARÉNILLA, L. Le calvinisme et le droit de résistance à l'état. **Annales-economies, societes, civilisations,** 22 (2) 350—369, 1967.

BARON, Hans. Calvinist republicanism and its historical roots. **Church history,** 8: 30—42, 1939.

BARTH, P. Die Entwicklung zur sittlichen Persönlichkeit im Calvinismus **(In:** Die Entwicklung zur sittlichen Persönlichkeit [hrsg. von] J. Neumann. Gütersloh, Bertelsmann, 1931. p. 164—181).

BARTH, P. Sozialethik des Calvinismus. **Kirche und Welt,** 1: 80—92, 1932.

BORKENAU, Franz. Drei Abhandlungen zur deutschen Geschichte. Frankfurt am Main, Klostermann [1947] "Luther: Ost oder West": p. 76—110.

CALVINISM and Darwinism. **Bibliotheca sacra,** 66 (264) 685—691, 1909.

CALVINISM and democracy. **Review of religion,** 12: 124—127, 1948.

CHENEVIÈRE, Marc Édouard. Essai sur le Calvinisme et l'état moderne. **Centralblatt,** 78: 149—154, 1938.

COETZEE, Johannes Hendrik. Die Calvinisme en volkereverhoudinge. **Potchefstroomse Universiteit vir Christelike Hoër Onderwys. Instituut vir Bevordering van Calvinisme. Studiestuk, no. 47.**

COETZEE, Johannes Hendrik. Die Calvinisme in politieke geding. **Woord en daad,** 11 (82) 2—3; 8, 1969.

DAEHNE VAN VARICK, August von. Diplomatie calviniste; discours pronouncé à l'occasion de fêtes du monument de la Réformation [Par] A. de Daehne de Varick. Genève, 1909.

DEMARCHI, Franco. Calvinismo e capitalismo. **Protestantesimo,** 14: 225—230, 1959.

DOUMERGUE, Emile. L'origine calviniste de la déclaration des droits de l'homme. **Foi et vie, 7:** 215—219, 1964.

DU PLESSIS, Lodewicus Johannes. Calvinisme en Marxisme. **Koers,** 33 (6) 442—445, 1966.

EISENSTADT, Shmuel N. The protestant ethic thesis in an analytical and comparative framework **(In:** The protestant ethic and modernization; a comparative view. Ed. by S.N. Eisenstadt. New York, Basic Books, 1968. p. 3—45) **(Also in: Diogenes,** 59: 25—46, 1967) **(Also in:** Sociology of religion; selected readings. Ed. by Roland Robertson. Baltimore, Penguin Books, 1969. p. 297—317) (Penguin modern sociology readings).

FRANCÈS, Madeleine. La morale de Spinoza et la doctrine calvinienne de la prédestination. [Strasbourg, 1933] 8 p. Extract from: **Revue d'histoire et de philosophie religieuses.**

FREDERICQ, Paul. Self-government and Calvinism. **Presbyterian historical society. Journal,** 5: 270—273, **1909/10.**

FUETER, E. Der Calvinismus und die Naturwissenschaft. **Schweizerische naturforschende Gesellschaft. Verhandlungen,** 118: 193—, **1937.**

FURSTENBERG, Jakob Petrus du Toit. Kultuurideaal van die Calvinisme. **Die Stellenbosse student,** 23 —26, 1958.

GERBRANDY, Pieter Sjoerds. Calvinisme en maatschappelijke orde. **Reünisten Organisatie van N.D.D.D. Publicaties,** 9, 1939.

GOUMAZ, Louis. Calvinisme et liberté. **Foi et verite,** 22, 1951.

HART, Hendrik. Calvinism as a cosmoscope **(In:** Potchefstroomse Universiteit vir Christelike Hoër Onderwys. Instituut vir Bevordering van Calvinisme. Die atoomeeu; in

U lig. Potchefstroom, 1969. p. 52—61).

HIRSCH, E. Staat und Kirche im Calvinismus. **Deutsches Volkstum,** 18: 865—, 1936.

HUIZINGA, A.V.C.P. The Calvinistic view of church and state. **Bibliotheca sacra,** 83: 174—189, 1926.

KINGDON, Robert McCune. Calvinism and democracy (**Also in:** The heritage of John Calvin, ed. by John H. Bratt. Grand Rapids, Eerdmans, 1973. p. 177—192) (Heritage Hall Lectures, 1960—1970) (Heritage Hall publications, no. 2).

KINGDON, Robert McCune. Calvinism and democracy; some political implications of debates on French Reformed church government, 1562—1572. **American historical review,** 69 (2) 393—401, 1964.

KLÜSENER, P.A.A. National-socialisme of Calvinisme als nationale kracht. Voordracht uitgesproken op den Bondsdag van Ned. Hervormde Jongelingsvereenigingen op Gereformeerde grondslag, 10 Mei 1934. Utrecht, Bondsboekhandel [1934] 32 p.

KNIGHT, J. A. Calvinism and psychoanalysis; a comparative study. **Pastoral psychology,** 14: 10—17, 1963.

LANGFORD, Norman F. Christians and politics; the Calvinist background. **Church and society,** 62: 12—16, 1972.

LECERF, Auguste. Thesen zur christlichen Staatsverständnis des Calvinismus. **Kirche und Welt,** 3: 82—90, 1934.

LITTLE, David. Calvinism and law (**In:** The protestant ethic and modernization; a comparative view. Ed. by Shmuel Noah Eisenstadt. New York, Basic Books, 1968. p. 177—183). (**Also in:** The new order and old England. New York, Harper & Row, 1967).

LOUBSER, Jan J. Calvinism, equality, and inclusion; the case of Afrikaner Calvinism (**In:** The protestant ethic and modernization; a comparitive view. Ed. by Shmuel Noah Eisenstadt. New York, Basic Books, 1968. p. 367—383).

MEETER, H. Henry. Calvinism and society. **The Banner,** 94 (37) 9; (39) 9, 1959.

MEETER, H. Henry. Het Calvinisme; zijn theologische en staatkundige grondgedachten. Vert. door P. Prins. Kampen, Kok, 1957. 173 p.

MEETER, H. Henry. Calvinist view on the relations of grace to nature. **The Banner,** 94 (42) 9; 29, 1959.

MOLNÁR, Amedeo. Rok 1559 v kalvinske reformace [The year 1559 in the Calvinistic reformation] **Krestanska revue,** 26: 144—149, 1959.

MOSSE, George Lachmann. Calvinism; authoritarian or democratic. New York, Holt, Rinehart and Winston (1965, c1957) 25 p. (Source problems in world civilization).

MÜLLER-ARMACK, Alfred. Religion und Wirtschaft-Geistesgeschichtliche Hintergründe unserer europäischen Lebensform. Stuttgart, Kohlhammer, 1959. "Der Calvinismus und der neuzeitliche Wirtschaftsstil": p. 107—120.

NOBBS, Douglas. Theocracy and toleration; a study of the disputes in Dutch calvinism from 1600 to 1650, by Douglas Nobbs. Cambridge, University Press, 1938. 280 p.

PAMP, F. E. jr. Communism and Calvinism; an historical analogy. **Journal of general education;** 7: 133—145, 1953.

REID, William Stanford. The impact of Calvinism on sixteenth century culture. **International reformed bulletin,** 10 (31) 3—10, 1967.

RITSCH, H. Calvinismus und Luthertum in ihrem Einfluss auf der modernen Staats- und Gesellschaftsbildung. **Schweizer Monatshefte für Politik und Kultur,** 18: 296—311, 1938.

ROTHUIZEN, Gerard Theodoor. Het Calvinisme en de vrije tijd. **Gereformeerd theologisch tijdschrift,** 69 (1) 32—57, 1969.

RUNIA, Klaas. Calvinism in Australia. **Free university quarterly,** 7: 222—231, 1960/61.

RIJNSDORP, Cornelis. In de greep van het reus-achtige; een literator over Calvinisme. Kampen, Kok [1966] 119 p.

SCHOUTEN, Willem Johannes Adriaan. Calvinisme en natuurphilosophie; een beoordeling van Prof. Hepp's Stone-lectures. [n.p., 1931?] 31 p. „Overdruk uit het Orgaan der Chr. Vereeniging van Natuur- en Geneeskundigen in Nederland".

STARK, W. Capitalism, Calvinism and the rise of modern science. **Sociological review,** 43 (5) 95—104, 1951.

STARK, Werner. The sociology of religion; a study of Christendom. v. 5, Types of religious culture. New York, Fordham Univ. Press, 1972. "Excursus, the Calvinist attitude of symbolism and art": p. 155—212. "The self-interpretation of Calvinism as a covenant-society": p. 247—274.

The STATUS of Calvinism in Australia and its prospects [by] Klaas Runia [a.o.] **Torch and trumpet,** 9 (9) 21—23, 1960.

THOMAS, Helen. Jacob and Esau; "rigidly Calvinistic?" **Studies in English literature,** 9: 199—213, 1969.

TIMMERMAN, John. Calvinism and literary criticism. **The Banner,** 94 (26) 9; 29, 1959.

TOTH, Kálman Dezsó. The dialectic in the political ethics of Calvinism. [New York] 1938. 314 1. Thesis—Union Theological Seminary, New York.

TYLER, Glenn Edward. The influence of Calvinism on the development of early modern science in England and America. Minnesota [n.d.] 411 1. Thesis—Univ. of Minnesota.

UNMACK, E. C. The philosophy of Calvinism **(In:** International conference of Calvinists. 1st. London, 1932. The reformed faith commonly called Calvinism. Report of the International Conference held in May, 1932. London, Sovereign Grace Union [1932] p. 54—66).

VAN DER MOLEN, R. Political Calvinism. **Journal of church and state,** 11: 457—463, 1969.

WEBER, Hellmuth von. Calvinismus und Strafrecht **(In:** Festschrift für Eberhard Schmidt zum 70. Geburtstag. Hrsg. von Paul Böskelmann und Wilhelm Gallas. Göttingen, 1961. p. 39—53).

WEINSTOCK, Heinrich. Arbeit und Bildung; die Rolle der Arbeit im Prosess um unsere Menschwerdung. Heidelberg, Quelle & Meyer, 1954. "Calvinistische Arbeitsaskese": p. 22—25.

WHARTON, J. Calvinism; its statesmanship **(In:** International Conference of Calvinists. 1st, London, 1932. The reformed faith commonly called Calvinism. Report of the International Conference held in May, 1932. London, Sovereign Grace Union [1932] p. 108—134).

ZWEMER, S. M. Calvinism and the missionary enterprise. **Theology today,** 7: 206—216, 1950/51.

2.2 VARIOUS REFORMERS:

Beze, Theodore de

ARENS, J. C. Latijnse gedichten van Th. Beza; vert. door J. de Decker [e.a.] **Spiegel der Lettern,** 7 (3) 213—215, 1963/64.

AUBERT, Fernand & BOISONNAS, Henri. Note sur un portrait de Théodore de Bèze jeune. **Genava, N.S.,** 1 (2) 61—68, 1953.

AUBERT, Fernand, BOSSARD, J. & MEYLAN, Henri. Un premier recueil de poésies latines de Theodore de Bèze. **Bibliotheque d'humanisme et renaissance,** 15 (2) 190—191; (3) 257—294, 1953.

BERNUS, Auguste. Théodore de Bèze à Lausanne. Lausanne, Bridel, 1900. 112 p.

BÈZE, Théodore de. Chréstiennes méditations; texte établi et introd. par Mario Richter. Genève, 1964. 99 p. (Textes littéraires français, 113).

BÈZE, Théodore de. Correspondence. Recueillie par. H. Aubert, publiée par Fernand Aubert et Henri Meylan. Genève, Droz, 1960—68 5v.

BÈZE, Théodore de. Histoire ecclésiastique des églises réformées au Royaume de France. Ed. nouvelle, avec commentaire, notice bibliographique et table des Faits et des noms propers par G. Baum et E. Cunitz [Repr.] Nieuwkoop, De Graaf, 1970. (1883—1889) 3 v.

BÈZE, Théodore de. De iure magistratuum [von] Theodor Beza. Hrsg. von Klaus Sturm. Neukirchen, Neukirchener Verl., 1965. 93 p. (Texte zur Geschichte der evangelischen Theologie, Hft. 1).

BÈZE, Théodore de. Théodore de Bèze. Pro domo. **Les cahiers protestants,** 46: 121—128, 1962.

CHAUNU, Pierre. La correspondence de Bèze, 1539—1561. **Revue suisse d'histoire,** 15 (1) 107—116, 1965.

DANTINE, Johannes. Das christologische Problem im Rahmen der Prädestinationslehre von Theodor Beza. **Zeitschrift für Kirchengeschichte,** 77 (F.4, Bd. 15, H. 1/2) 81—96, 1966.

DROZ, Eugénie. Chemins de l'hérésie; textes et documents I. Genève, Slatkine Repr., 1970. "Bèze, apôtre de la non-vengeance": p. 395—430.

DROZ, Eugènie. Les débuts de Théodore de Bèze à Genève. **Genava, N.S.,** 13: 59—71, 1965.

DROZ, Eugénie. L'ecclesiaste de Théodore de Bèze et ses éditions allemandes, 1599 et 1605. **Revue d'histoire et de philosophie religieuses,** (4) 338—346, 1967.

DROZ, Eugénie. L'imprimeur de l'histoire ecclesiastique, 1580. **Bibliotheque d'humanisme et renaissance,** 22: 371—376, 1960.

DROZ, Eugénie. Notes sur Théodore de Bèze. **Bibliotheque d' humanisme et renaissance,** 24 (2) 392—412„ 1962.

DROZ, Eugénie. L'original des Chréstiennes méditations de Bèze, 1581. **Societé de l'histoire du protestantisme français. Bulletin,** 112: 236—249, 1966.

DUFOUR, Alain. Une oeuvre inconnue de Bèze? **Bibliotheque d'humanisme et renaissance,** 22 (2) 403—405, 1960.

GARDY, Frédéric Louis. Bibliographie des oeuvres théologiques littéraires, historiques et juridiques de Théodore de Bèze. Publiée avec la collaboration d'Alain Dufour. Genève, 1960. 243 p. (Travaux d'humanisme et renaissance, 41).

GEISENDORF, Paul Frédérik. Théodore de Bèze. Genève, Jullien, 1967. 457 p.

GIESEY, Ralph E. The monarchomach triumvirs: Hotman, Beza and Mornay. **Bibliotheque d'humanisme et renaissance,** 32 (1) 41—56, 1970.

GRAAFLAND, Cornelis. De zekerheid van het geloof; een onderzoek naar de geloofsbeschouwing van enige vertegenwoordigers van reformatie en nadere reformatie. Wageningen, Veenman, 1961. „Beza": p. 61—74. Thesis—Utrecht.

HÖSS, I. Zur Genesis der Widerstandslehre Bezas; Karl Griewank zum Gedächtnis. **Archiv für Reformationsgeschichte,** 54 (2) 198—214, 1963.

HUGHES, Philip Edgecumbe. Beza as correspondent and poet. **Churchman,** 86 (1) 16—26, 1972.

KICKEL, Walter. Vernunft und Offenbarung bei Theodor Beza; zum Problem des Verhältnisses von Theologie, Philosophie und Staat. (Neukirchen) Neukirchener Verl. des Erzichungsvereins, 1967, 292 p. (Beiträge zur Geschichte und Lehre der Reformierten Kirche, 25: Bd.).

KINGDON, Robert McCune. The first expression of Theodor Beza's political ideas. **Archiv für Reformationsgeschichte,** 46: 88—99, 1955.

KINGDON, Robert McCune. Les idées politiques de Bèze d'après son Traite de l'authorité du magistrat et la punction des hèrétiques. **Bibliotheque d'humanisme et renaissance,** 22: 566—569, 1960.

KINGDON, Robert McCune. Political resistance of the Calvinists in France and the Low Countries. **Church history,** 27: 220—233, 1958.

KWEKKEBOOM, J. Supplément à la bibliographie des éditions hollandaises de Bèze. **Bibliotheque d'humanisme et renaissance,** 23: 567—571, 1961.

LINDEBOOM, Johannes. De "Satyres chrestiennes de la cuisine papale" en hun auteur. Amsterdam, N.H.U.M., 1955. 16 p.

LINSE, E. Beza and Melanchton on political obligation. **Concordia theological monthly,** 41 (1) 27—35, 1970.

LOHMEYER, W. Zwei unbekannte. Bezabriefe aus dem Jahre 1588 und 1589 **(In:** Aus Theologie und Geschichte der Reformierten Kirche; Festgabe für E. F. K. Müller zu dessen 70. Gebürtstag. Neukirchen, Erziehungsverein, 1933. p. 305—320).

MARABUTO, M. Lettre adressée en 1594 à Théodore de Bèze par les fidèles de la région rochelaise. **Societé de l'histoire du protestantisme français. Bulletin,** 113: 481—483, 1967.

MARUYAMA, Tadataka. The reform of the true church: the ecclesiology of Theodore Beza. Princeton, N. J., 1973. 461 1. Thesis-Princeton Theological Seminary.

MEYLAN, Henri. Bèze et les Italiens de Lyon, 1566. **Bibliotheque d'humanisme et renaissance,** 14 (1) 235—249, 1952.

MEYLAN, Henri. La conversion de Bèze ou les longues hésitation d'un humaniste chrétien. **Genava, N.S.,** 7 (1/2) 103—125, 1959.

MEYLAN, Henri. Les deux "mains" de Théodore de Bèze. Paris, 1955. 274—279 p. (Extrait du Recuiel de Travaux offert à m. Clovis Brunel, 1955).

MEYLAN, Henri. En marge de la correspondance de Théodore de Bèze; un hérétique onblié. **Revue de theologie et de philosophie, N.S.** 9 (2) 177—181, 1959.

NEWMEYER, Edna, Beza and Milton; new light on the temptation of learning. **New York Public Library. Bulletin,** 66: 485—498, 1962.

RAITT, Jill. The conversion of the elements in reformed eucharistic theology, with special reference to Theodore Beza. Chicago, 1970. 249 l. Thesis—University of Chicago.

RAITT, Jill. The eucharistic theology of Theodore Beza; development of the reformed doctrine. Chambersburg, Pa., American Academy of Religion, 1972 (AAR studies in religion, no. 4).

RAITT, Jill. Roman Catholic new wine in reformed old bottles? The conversion of the elements in the eucharistic doctrines of Theodore Beza and Edward Schillebeeckx. **Journal of ecumenical studies,** 8: 581—604, 1971.

SCADUTO, Mario. La ginevra di Teodoro Beza nei ricordi di un gesuita Lucano Luca Pinelli [1542—1607] **Archivum historicum sicietatis Jesu,** 20: 117—142, 1951.

SMID, T. D. Beza en Nederland. **Nederlands archief voor kerkgeschiedenis, N.S.,** 46 (3) 169—191, 1963/64.

STAEDTKE, Joachim. Theodor von Beza. Zum Gedenken seines 450. Geburtstages. **Deutches Pfarrerblatt,** 69: 372—374, 1969.

STEINMETZ, David Curtis. Reformers in the wings. Philadelphia, Fortress Press (1971) "Theodore Beza; eternal predestination and divine sovereignty": p. 162—171.

TROCME, Etienne. L'ascension de Théodore de Bèze, 1549- 1561; au miroir de sa correspondance. **Journal des savants,** 607—624, 1965.

VAN SCHELVEN, Aart Arnout. Beza's De iure magistratuum in subditos. **Archiv für Reformationsgeschichte,** 45: 62—81, 1954.

VOLMAR, Melchior. Théodore de Bèze de Vezelay. **Almanach Jean Calvin,** 1935.

Brès, Guy de

BRAEKMAN, Emile M. Connaissance de Guy de Brès. **Les cahiers calvinistes,** 1: 1—15, 1957.

BRAEKMAN, Emile M. Les fondaments de la vie de Guy de Brès. **Les cahiers calvinistes,** 4 (12) 12—19, 1961.

BRAEKMAN, Emile M. Guy de Brès. Bruxelles, Librairie des Éclaireurs Unionistes, 1960. 2 v. (Histoire du protestantisme en Belgique et en Congo Belge, t. 6, 7).

BRAEKMAN, Emile M. Guy de Brès; pages choisies. **Les cahiers calvinistes,** 8 (31/3) 3—72, 1967.

BRAEKMAN, Emile M. La pensée politique de Guy Brès. **Societé de l'histoire du protestantisme français. Bulletin,** 115 (4) 1—28, 1969.

BRÈS, Guy de. Guido de Brès speaks from his death cell [From letters by De Brès] **The Banner,** 96 (22) 6—7, 1961.

BUYS, Pieter Willem. Guido de Brès; geloofsheld sonder doodsvrees. **Die Kerkblad,** 64 (1622 [not 1922]) 11; 13, 1961.

DEDDENS, D. Rondom het eerste geschrift van Guido de Brès: Le baston de la Foy. **Lucerna,** 3 (6) 817—831, 1962.

"ETAT et église" chez Guy de Brès. **Les cahiers calvinistes,** 7 (27/3) 13—20, 1966.

MARICHAL, Walter M. La doctrine de Guy de Brès. **Les cahiers calvinistes,** 4 (12) 20—23, 1961.

NAUTA, Doede. Guido de Brès; terechtgesteld op 31 Mei 1567. **Centraal weekblad voor de Gereformeerde Kerken in Nederland,** 15 (21) 2, 1967.

NAUTA, Doede. De opsteller van de N.G.B.: Guido de Brès. **Centraal weekblad voor de Gereformeerde Kerken in Nederland,** 9 (42) 372, 1961.

PONT, A. D. Guido de Bray. **Die Hervormer,** 52 (7) 21—23, 1961.

PRAAMSMA, Louis. Guido de Brès; the man of the Confession — the Confession of the man. **Torch and trumpet,** 11 (6) 9—11; (7) 13—15, 1961.

VAN DER VYVER, Gert Christoffel Petrus. 'n Eer om vir God te ly; marteldood van Guido de Brès. **Die Kerkblad,** 70 (1905) 5—6, 1967.

VAN DER WALT, Stephanus Johannes. Guido de Brès, opsteller van die Nederlandse Geloofsbelydenis. **Die Kerkblad,** 64 (1621 [not 1921]) 7—9, 1961.

VAN HALSEMA, Emo. Guido de Brès. **De Wachter,** 94 (3) 5; (4) 4; (5) 5, 9; (6) 4—5; (8) 4—5, 1961.

VAN HALSEMA, Thea (Bouma) Glorius heretic; the story of Guido de Brès. Grand Rapids, Eerdmans, 1961. 38 p.

Bullinger, Heinrich

BLANKE, Fritz. Der junge Bullinger, 1504—1531. Mit Bilderbeilage bearb. von Leo Weisz. Zürich, Zwingli-Verl. (c1942) 179 p. (Zwingli-Bücherei, 22).

BÜSSER, Fritz. De prophetae officio; eine Gedenkrede Bullingers auf Zwingli (**In:** Festgabe Leonhard von Muralt, zum siebzigsten Geburtstag, 17. Mai 1970, überreicht von Freunden und Schülern. Herausgeber: Martin Haas [und] René Hauswirth. Zürich, Berichthaus, 1970. p. 245—257).

DALBERT, Peter. Die Reformation in den italienischen Talschaften Graubündens nach dem Briefwechsel Bullingers. Zürich, 1948. 149 p. Thesis—Zürich.

EGLI, Emil. Bullingers Beziehungen zu Zwingli. **Zwingliana,** 1 (16) 439—443, 1904.

FAST, Heinold. Heinrich Bullinger und die Täufer; ein Beitrag zur Historiographie und Theologie im 16. Jahrhundert. Meierhof, Pfalz, 1959. 214 p. (Schriftenreihe des Mennonit Geschichtsvereins, 7).

HEIN, L. Heinrich Bullinger und seine Einfluss auf die reformierten Gemeinden in Kleinpolen. **Kyrios,** 4: 91—107, 1964.

KEEP, D. J. Henry Bullinger, 1504—'75; a sketch of his life and work, with special reference to recent literature. **London quarterly & Holborn review,** 191: 135—146, 1966.

KOCH, Ernst. Die Grundzüge der Liturgik Heinrich Bullingers. **Jahrbuch für Liturgik und Hymnologie,** 10: 22—34, 1965.

Der NACHLASS Heinrich Bullingers. **Kirchenblatt für die reformierte Schweiz,** 119: 393—394, 1963.

PRUETT, Gordon Earl. Thomas Cranmer and the eucharistic controversy in the Reformation. Princeton, N. J., 1968. „Bullinger": p 173—194. Thesis—Princeton Univ.

REINERTH, K. Zum Bullinger-Brief an Johannes Honterus. **Zwingliana,** 12 (4/2) 287—292, 1966.

RüSCH, Ernst Gerhard. Die Theologie des reifen Bullinger. **Zwingliana,** 12 (4/2) 293—295, 1966.

SCHLÉGL, J. Die Beziehungen Heinrich Bullingers zu Ungarn. **Zwingliana,** 12 (5) 330—370, 1966.

SCHULZE, W. A. Die Lehre Bullingers vom Zins. **Archiv für Reformationsgeschichte,** 48: 225—229, 1957.

STAEDTKE, Joachim. Blarer und Bullinger **(In:** Der Konstanzer Reformator Ambrosius Blarer, 1492—1564. Gedenkschrift zu seinem 400. Todestag. Im Auftrag der Evangelischen Kirchengemeinde Konstanz im Gemeinschaft mit Fritz Blanke [u.a.] Hrsg. von Bernd Moeller. Konstanz, Thorbecke, 1964. p. 193—204).

STAEDTKE, Joachim. Das literarische Werk Heinrich Bullingers und die Vorbereitung zu seiner Erschliessung. **Theologische Literaturzeitung,** 80: 249—254, 1965.

STAEDTKE, Joachim. Der Nachlass Heinrich Bullingers in der Zentralbibliothek Zürich. **Librarium,** 6: 118—137, 1963.

STAEDKTE, Joachim. Die niederländischen Ausgaben der Werke H. Bullingers. **Zwingliana,** 12 (6) 407—419, 1971.

STAEDKTE, Joachim. Die Theologie des jungen Bullingers. Zurich, Zwingli, 1962. 312 p. (Studien zur Dogmengeschichte und systematischen Theologie, Bd. 16).

STEINMETZ, David Curtis. Reformers in the wings. Philadelphia, Fortress Press (1971) "Heinrich Bullinger; Covenant and the continuity of salvation history": p. 133—142.

TAPPOLET, Walter. **ed.** Das Marienlob der Reformatoren; Martin Luther, Johannes Calvin, Huldrych Zwingli, Heinrich Bullinger. Hrsg. von Walter Tappolet unter mitarb. von Albert Ebneter. Tübingen, Katzmann, 1962. „Bullinger": p. 263—334.

WALSER, Peter. Glaube und Leben nach Heinrich Bullinger. **Zwingliana,** 11 (9/1) 607—616, 1963.

WALSER, Peter. Die Prädestination bei Heinrich Bullinger im Zusammenhang mit seiner Gotteslehre. Zürich, Zwingli, 1957. 288 p. (Studien zur Dogmengeschichte und systematischen Theologie, Bd. 11).

Butzer, Martin

ANRICH, Gustav. Ein Bedacht Buccers. Leipzig. 1929.

ANRICH, Gustav. Ein Bedacht Bucers über die Einrichtung von "Christliche Gemeinschaften." **Archiv für Reformationsgeschichte. Ergängungsbd. 5: Festschrift fur H. v. Schubert,** 46—70, 1929.

ANRICH, Gustav. Martin Bucer. Strassburg, Trübner, 1914. 147 p.

ATKINSON, James. Martin Bucer, 1491—1551; ecumenical pioneer. **Churchman,** 79: 19—28, 1965.

AUGUSTIJN, Cornelis. De gesprekken tussen Bucer en Gropper tijdens het Godsdienstgesprek te Worms in December 1540. **Vaderlandsch archief voor kerkgeschiedenis, N.S.,** 47 (4) 208—230, 1965/66.

BACH, U. Martin Butzer. Strassburg, Buchhandlung der Evangelischen Gesellschaft, 1905. 36 p. (Evangelische Lebensbilder aus dem Elsass, 9).

BARNIKOL, Hermann. Bucers Lehre von der Rechtfertigung, dargestellt an seinem Römerbriefkommentar. Göttingen, 1961. Thesis—Göttingen.

BARRON, W. S. The controversy between Martin Bucer and Bartholomew Latomus (1543—1546). Washington, D. C., 1966. 290 l. Thesis, Catholic University, Washington.

BAUM, Martin. Capito und Butzer; Strassburgs Reformatoren. 2. unveränd. Ausg. Nieuwkoop, De Graaf, 1967. 611 p.

BELLARDI, Werner. Anton Engelbrecht, 1485—1558; Helfer, Mitarbeiter und Gegner Bucers. **Archiv für Reformationsgeschichte,** 64: 183—206, 1973.

BELLARDI, Werner. Die Geschichte der "Christliche Gemeinschaft" in Strassburg, 1546/1550. Der Versuch einer "zweiten Reformation." Ein Beitrag zur Reformationsgeschichte Strassburgs mit zwei Beilagen. New York, Johnson Reprint, 1971. 217 p. (Quellen und Forschungen zur Reformationsgeschichte, Bd. 18) Reprint of ed. by Heinsius, Leipzig, 1934.

BENDER. G. Die Anfänge der Irenik M. Bucers, 1523—8, Marburg, 1970. (Schriften des Instituts für Wissenschaftliche Irenik, 5).

BERNOULLI, Wilhelm. Das Diakonenamt bei Butzer. Greifensee, Schweizerisches Reformierte Diakonessenhaus, 1953. 31 p.

BIBLE. O. T. Psalms. English. 1530. Butzer. The psalter of David [by] Aretius Felinus [pseud] Tr. by George Joye. Introd. by G. E. Duffield. Appleford, Sutton Courtenay Press (Pref. 1971) 260 p. (Courtenay facsimile, 1).

BIZER, Ernst. Martin Butzer und der Abendmahlsstreit. **Archiv für Reformationsgeschichte,** 35: 203—237, 1938; 36: 68—87, 1939.

BIZER, Ernst. Die Wittenberger Konkordie in Oberdeutschland und die Schweiz; unbekannte Aktenstücke aus der Vermittlertätigkeit Martin Butzers. **Archiv für Reformationsgeschichte,** 36: 214—252, 1939.

BOON, Rudolf. De eerste drie geschriften van de Straatsburgse reformator Martin Bucer; het begin van de ontwikkeling zijner theologie. **Nederlands archief voor kerkgeschiedenis,** 39 N.S.: 193—218, 1952—53.

BORNERT, René. Martin Bucer et la liturgie strasbourgeoise de 1537—1539. **Archives de l'Église d'Alsace,** 35 (19) 105—125, 1971.

BORNKAMM, Heinrich. Das Jahrhundert der Reformation; Gestalten und Kräfte. 2., verm. Aufl. (mit einem neuen Aufsatz über die Frage der Obrigkeit) Göttingen, Vandenhoeck & Ruprecht (1966, c1961) "Martin Bucer, der dritte deutsche Reformator": p. 88—112.

BORNKAMM, Heinrich. Martin Bucers Bedeutung für die europäische Reformationsgeschichte; Bibliographia Bucerana, von Robert Stupperich. Gütersloh, Bertelsmann, 1952. 95 p. (Schriften des Vereins für Reformationsgeschichte, 169).

BORNKAMM, Heinrich. Ökumenische Reformation [re: Bucer] **Zeitwende,** 22: 759—761, 1950/51.

BUTZER, Martin. Common places of Martin Bucer. Tr. & ed. by D. F. Wright. Appleford, Sutton Courtenay Press, 1972. 520 p.

BUTZER, Martin. Martin Buceri opera omnia. Series I — Deutsche Schriften, hrsg. von Robert Stupperich. Gütersloh, Mohn, 1960- v.

BUTZER, Martin. Martini Buceri opera omnia. Series II. Opera Latina [red. Francois Wendel, et al] Paris, Presses Univ. de France, 1954- v.

BUTZER, Martin. Résumè sommaire de la doctrine chrétienne. Texte établi et traduit par François Wendel. Paris, Presses Univ. de France, 1951. 103 p. (Cahiers de la Revue d'histoire et de philosophie religieuses, 33).

COHEN, Carl. Martin Bucer and his influence on the Jewish situation. **Leo Baeck Institute. Yearbook,** 13: 93—101, 1968.

COLLINSON, Patrick. The reformer and the archbishop: Martin Bucer and an English Bucerian. **The Journal of religious history,** 6: 305—330, 1970/71.

COURVOISIER, Jaques. Bucer et la discipline ecclésiastique **(In:** Mélanges d'histoire du XVIe siècle, offerts à Henri Meylan. Genève, Droz, 1970. p. 21—30) (Travaux d'humanisme et renaissance, 60).

COURVOISIER, Jaques. Une traduction française du commentaire de Bucer sur l'Evangile selon S. Matthieu. Paris, Alcan, 1933. 51 p. (Cahiers d'histoire et de philosophie religieuses, 26) **(Also in: Revue d'histoire et de philosophie religieuses,** 13: 164—177, 1933).

DANKBAAR, Willem Frederik. Martin Bucers Beziehungen zu den Niederlanden. Den Haag, Nijhoff, 1961. 60 p. (Kerkhistorische studiën, 9).

DECLERCK, P. Martin Bucer en de Straatsburgse Hervorming, 1491—1551. **Collationes Brugensis,** 9: 98—121, 1963.

DIEHL, Wilhelm. Martin Butzers Bedeutung für das kirchliche Leben in Hessen. Halle, Haupt, 1904 **(In:** Schriften des Vereins für Reformationsgeschichte, Leipzig, Heinius. Nr. 83. p. 39—58).

DONAHUE, John Matthew. Martin Bucer, 1491—1551; a program of ecclesiastical reform for England, 1550. New York, 1969. 548 l. Thesis—Fordham Univ. New York.

DONCKEL, Emil. Martin Bucer und die "Springenden Heiligen" von Echternach. **Kurtrierisches Jahrbuch,** 8: 137—140, 1968.

DROZ, Eugénie. Claude Baduel traducteur de Bucer. **Bibliothèque d'humanisme et renaissance,** 17 (3) 347—350, 1955.

EELS, Hastings. The attitude of Martin Bucer toward the bigamy of Philip of Hesse. New Haven. Conn., Yale Univ. Press., 1924. 253 p. (Yale historical publications. Miscellany, 12).

EELS, Hastings. Bucer's plan for the Jews. **Church history,** 6: 127—135, 1937.

EELS, Hastings. The contributions of Martin Bucer to the Reformation. **Harvard theological review,** 24: 29—42, 1931.

EELS, Hastings. The correct date for a letter to Zwingli [Bucer to Zwingli, 30.4.1528] **Revue belge de philologie et d'histoire,** 1: 514—519, 1922.

EELS, Hastings. The failure of church unification efforts during the German Reformation; in memoriam M. Buceri. **Archiv für Reformationsgeschichte,** 42: 16—174, 1951.

EELS, Hastings. The genesis of Martin Bucer's doctrine of the Lord's Supper. **Princeton theological review,** 24: 225—251, 1926.

EELS, Hastings. Martin Bucer. New Haven, Yale Univ. Press., 1931. 539 p. Also published by Oxford Univ. Press, London.

EELS, Hastings. The origin of the Regensburg Book. **Princeton theological review,** 26: 355—372, 1928.

EELS, Hastings. Sacramental negotiations at the diet of Augsburg, 1530. **Princeton theological review,** 23: 213—235, 1925.

ENGELBRECHT, Anton. Abconterfeytung Martin Butzers (1546) Hrsg v. Werner Bellardi. Münster, Westf., Aschendorff, 1974. 112 p. (Corpus catholicorum, Bd. 31).

ERB, Jörg. Martin Butzer **(In:** Kosmos und Ekklesia; Festschrift für D. Wilhelm Stählin zu seinem 70. Geburtstag. Kastel, Stauda, 1953. p. 102—105).

ERBES, Jean. Martin Bucer, le réformateur alsacien inconnu et méconnu. Grasse, Libraire protestantes, 1966. 32 p.

ERBES, Jean. Martin Bucers Concordienbestrebungen und die heutige Lage der ökumene. **Kirchenblatt für die reformierte Schweiz,** 121 (13) 196—201, 1965.

ERICHSON, Alfred. Martin Bucer. Zum 400. jährigen Todestag des elsäsisschen Reformators. Neu hrsg. [Vorw.: Ch. Brandt] Strasbourg, Société Pastorale de Strasbourg, 1951. 77 p.

FABER, Jelle. De dienst der barmhartigheid in de reformatietijd, III: Bucer. **De Reformatie,** 35 (45) 360—361, 1960.

FELLMANN, Walter. Martin Bucer und Hans Denck. **Mennonitische Geschichtsblätter,** 23 (18) 29—35, 1966.

FICKER, Johannes. Bucer; ein Vortrag. Bilder zu seinem Leben und Wirken und aus der Kreise seiner Zeitgenossen. Strassburg, 1917. 63 p. (Quellen und Forschungen zur Kirchen- und Kulturgeschichte von Elsas und Lotharingen, 5).

FICKER, Johannes. Das erste Holzschnittbildnis Martin Bucers. **Elsass-Lotharingisches Jahrbuch,** 2: 49—55, 1923.

FRÖHLICH, Hugo. Ein Strassburger Wirtshausdisput über die kölner Reformation in September 1543. **Monatshefte für evangelische Kirchengeschichte des Rheinlandes,** 10: 148—154, 1961.

GARDINER, Stephen, **bp. of Winchester.** Obedience in church and state; three political tracts. Ed., with an introd., tr. and notes, by Pierre Janelle. Cambridge, University Press, 1930. "Answer to Bucer, 1541" [3rd tract].

GILBERT, A. H. Martin Bucer on education. **Journal of english and germanic philology,** 18: 321—345, 1919.

GÖTZE, Alfred. Martin Butzers Erstlingsschrift [Dialogus zwischen einem Pfarrer und einem Schultheiss] **Archiv für Reformationsgeschichte,** 13: 1—64, 1906.

GRESCHAT, Martin. Die Anfänge der reformatorischen Theologie Martin Bucers **(In:** Reformation und Humanismus. Robert Stupperich zum 65. Geburtstag. Hrsg. von M. Greschat und J. F. G. Goeters. Witten, Luther, 1969. p. 124—140).

HALL, Basil. Diakonia in Martin Butzer **(In:** Service in Christ; essays presented to Karl Barth on his 80th birthday. Ed. by J. I. McCord and T. H. L. Parker. Grand Rapids, Eerdmans (c1966) p. 89—100).

HARVEY, A. Edw. Martin Bucer in England. Marburg a.L., Bauer, 1906. 182 p. Thesis—Univ. Marburg.

HASE, Martin von. Bibliographia Bucerana. **Börsenblatt für den deutschen Buchhandel,** 9 (60) 377, 1953.

HASENCLEVER, Adolf. Martin Bucer als Verfasser eines bisher anonymen Berichtes über das Regenburger Colloquium vom Jahre 1546. **Zeitschrift für die Geschichte des Oberrheins,** N. F., 26: 491—500, 1911.

HEITZ, J. J. Étude sur la formation de la pensée ecclésiologique de Bucer d'après les traites polémiques et doctrinaux des années 1523—38. Strasbourg, 1947. Thesis.

HOFFMANN. Zum Gedächtnis Martin Bucers. **Deutsches Pfarrerblatt,** 51: 138—139, 1951.

HOLSTEN, W. Christentum und nichtchristliche Religionen nach der Auffassung Bucers. **Theologische Studien und Kritiken, N.F.** 2 (107) 105—194, 1936. **(Also in:** Das Evangelium und die Völker. Beiträge zur Geschichte und Theorie der Mission. Berlin-Friedenau, Gossnersche Mission, 1939. p. 9—72).

HOPF, Constantin. An English version of parts of Bucer's reply to the Cologue Antididagma of 1544. **Journal of theological studies,** 11: 94—110, 1960.

HOPF, Constantin. A letter of Martin Bucer. **Journal of theological studies,** 44: 67—72, 1943.

HOPF, Constantin. Martin Bucer and the English Reformation. Oxford, Blackwell, 1946. 290 p.

HOPF, Constantin. Martin Bucers Bedeutung für die Geschichte der englischen Reformation. **Deutsches Pfarrerblat,** 51 (3) 67—68; (4) 94—95, 1951.

HOPF, Constantin. Martin Bucer's letter to John à Lasco on the Eucharist. **Journal of theological studies,** 48: 64—70, 1947.

HOPF, Constantin. Martin Bucer und England; sein Betrag zur englischen Reformationsgeschichte. **Zeitschrift für Kirchengeschichte,** 71 (4/9) 82—109, 1960.

HYMA, Albert. Hoen's letter on the eucharist and its influence upon Carlstadt, Bucer and Zwingli. **Princeton theological review,** 24: 124—131, 1926.

ITTI, G. Dans quelle mesure Bucer est-il piétiste? Strasbourg, 1936. Thesis—University of Strasbourg.

JANELLE, Pierre. La controverse entre Étienne Gardiner et Martin Bucer sur la discipline ecclésiastique, 1541—1548. **Revue des science religieuses,** 7: 452—466, 1927.

JANELLE, Pierre. Le voyage de Martin Bucer et Paul Fagius de Strasbourg en Angleterre en 1549. **Revue d'histoire et de philosphie religieuses,** 8: 162—177, 1928.

KANTZENBACH, Friedrich Wilhelm. Martin Butzer, Streiter für die Einheit in der Kirche in der Reformationszeit **(In:** Ökumenische Profile; Brückenbauer der einen Kirche. Hrsg. von Günter Gloede. Stuttgart, 1961. Bd. 1, p. 42—50).

KITTELSON, James M. Martin Bucer and the sacramentarian controversy; the origins of his policy of concord. **Archiv für Reformationsgeschichte,** 64: 166—183, 1973.

KOCH, Karl. Studium pietatis; Martin Bucer als Ethiker. Neukirchen, Neukirchener Verl., 1962. 267 p. (Beiträge zur Geschichte und Lehre der Reformierten Kirche, 14 Bd.)

KÖHLER, Walther. Zu unserer Tafel [Jakob Zieglers Übersendung einer antipäpslichen Schrift und Zeichnung an Bucer] **Zwingliana,** 3: 500—503, 1913/1920.

KOHLS, Ernst-Wilhelm. Ein Abschnitt aus Martin Bucers Entwurf für die Ulmer Kirchenordnung vom Jahr 1531. **Blätter für wurttenbergische Kirchengesichite** 60/61: 177—213, 1960/61.

KOHLS, Ernst-Wilhelm. Blarer und Bucer (**In:** Der Konstanzer Reformator Ambrosius Blarer, 1492—1564. Gedenkschrift zu seinem 400. Todestag. Im Auftrag der Evangelischen Kirchengemeinde Konstanz im Gemeinschaft mit Fritz Blanke [u.a.] Hrsg. von Bernd Moeller. Konstanz, Thorbecke, 1964. p. 172—192).

KOHLS, Ernst-Wilhelm. Holzschnitvon Hans Baldung in Martin Bucers "Kürtzer Catechismus". **Theologische Zeitschrift,** 23: 267—284, 1967.

KOHLS, Ernst-Wilheim. Martin Bucer und die Neuordnung des Strassburger Schulwesens. **Theologische Zeitschrift,** 16: 379—407, 1960.

KOHLS, Ernst-Wilhelm. Die Schule bei Martin Bucer in ihrem Verhältniss zu Kirche und Obrigkeit. Heidelberg, Quelle & Meyer, 1963. 224 p. (Pädagogische Forschungen, Veröffentiichen des Comenius-Instituts, 22).

KÖHN, Mechtild. Martin Bucers Entwurf einer Reformation des Erzstiftes Köln. Untersuchung der Entstehungsgeschichte und die Theologie des "Einfaltigen Bedenckens" von 1548. Ein Beitrag zur Bucer-Forschung und zur Geschichte der Kölner Reformation. Münster, 1963. 200 p. Thesis—Münster. Also published by Luther-Verl., Witten, 1966, in the series: Untersuchungen zur Kirchengeschichte, Bd. 2.

KRONENBERG, Maria Elizabeth. Is Martinus Butzer onder het pseudoniem Hermannes Bodius de auteur van de Unio dissenditium geweest? **Het Boek,** 34 (3) 1—11, 1960/61.

KRÜGER, Friedhelm. Bucer und Erasmus; eine Untersuchung zum Einfluss des Erasmus auf die Theologie Martin Bucers, bis zum Evangelien-Kommentar von 1530. Wiesbaden, Steiner, 1970. 233 p.

LANG, August. Die Evangelienkommentar M. Butzers und die Grundzüge seiner Theologie. Leipzig, Dietrich, 1900. 471 p. (Studien zur Geschichte der Theologie und der Kirche, 2. Bd., Hft. 2). Reprint: Aalen, Scientia, 1972.

LANG, August. Martin Bucer. **Evangelical quarterly,** 1: 159—165, 1929.

LANG, August. Martin Butzer. **Reformierte Kirchenzeitung,** 79: 201-, 1929.

LANG, August. Martin Butzer; ein Gedächtniswort zu seinem 350-jährigen Sterbetag. **Reformierte Kirchenzeitung,** 24: 60—61; 67—69; 77—78, 1901.

LANG, August. Martin Bucer in England. **Archiv für Reformationsgeschichte,** 38: 230—249, 1941.

LANG, August. Puritanismus und Pietismus; Studien zu der Entwicklung von M. Butzer bis zum Methodismus. Neukirchen, Buchhandlung des Erziehungsvereins, 1941. 360 p. (Beiträge zur Geschichte und Lehre der Reformierte Kirche, 6).

LANG, August. Zwingli, Butzer, Calvin als Männer der Weltliteratur (**In:** Die religiose Entwicklung der Mensschheit im Spiegel der Weltliteratur. Hrsg. von L. Weber. Gütersloh, Bertelsman, 1901, p. 277—299) (**Also in:** Lang, August Reformation und Gegenwart. Detmold, Meyer, 1918, p. 7—38).

LESTRINGANT, P. La cure d'ame évangélique dans l'énseignement des Reformateurs Bucer. **Les cahiers calvinistes,** 18 (12) 1—4, 1963.

LIENHARD, Albert. Martin Butzer, der elsässische Reformator und

Mitarbeiter Luthers. Strassburg, Heitz, 1914. 31 p.

LINDSAY, T. M. Martin Bucer and the Reformation. **Quarterly review,** 220: 116—133, 1914.

LINN, Charles Adolphus. Butzer and the eucharistic controversy between Luther and Zwingli. Hartford Conn., 1924. Thesis.

LITTELL, Franklin Hamlin. New light on Butzer's significance **(In:** Reformation studies; essays in honor of R. H. Bainton. Ed.: F. H. Littell, Richmond, Knox [c1962] p. 145—167).

LITTELL, Franklin Hamlin. What Butzer debated with the Anabaptists at Marburg; a document of 1538. **Mennonite quarterly review,** 36: 256—276, 1962.

LOOSS, Sigrid. Butzer und Capito in ihrem Verhältnis zum Bauernkrieg und Taufertum **(In:** Weltwirkung der Reformation. Internationales Symposium anlässlich der 450. Jahr-Feier der Reformation in Wittenberg von 24. bis 26. Oktober 1967. Referate und Diskussionen. Hrsg. von Max Steinmetz und Gerhard Brendler. Berlin, VEB Deutsch-verl. der Wissenschaften, 1969. p. 226—232).

MARTIN, B. Feier in Heidelberg. **Deutsches Pfarrerblatt,** 51: 179—180, 1951.

MAURER, Wilhelm. Kirche und Geschichte; gesammelte Aufsätze. Hrsg. von Ernst-Wilhelm Kohls und Gerhard Müller. Göttingen, Vandenhoeck & Ruprecht (c1970) "Martin Butzer und die Judenfrage in Hessen": Bd. 2, p. 347—365.

MAURER, Wilhelm. Martin Butzer und die Judenfrage in Hessen. **Verein für hessische Geschichte und Landeskunde. Zeitschrift,** 64: 29—43, 1953.

MAURER, Wilhelm. Martin Butzer und Hessen. **Deutsches Pfarrerblatt,** 51 (5) 128—129; (6) 159—160, 1951.

MICHAELIS, O. Martin Bucer, der elsässiche Reformator. **Evangelisch-kirchliche Rundschau Deutschland,** 18: 39—, 1941.

MITCHELL, Charles Buell. Martin Bucer and sectarian dissent; a confrontation of the magisterial Reformation with Anabaptists and Spiritualists. New Haven, Conn. (1964) 409 l. Thesis—Yale University.

MOELLER, Bernd. J. V. Pollet: Martin Bucer. **Theologische Literaturzeitung,** 3 (3) 194—195, 1968.

MOELLER, Bernd. Reichsstadt und Reformation. [Gütersloh] Gütersloher Verlagshaus (c1962) 79 p. (Schriften des Vereins für Reformationsgeschichte, Nr. 180, Jg. 69).

MOLNÁR, Amadeo. Češti bratří a Martin Bucer. Listy kritického pratelstvi. Stud. texty Komenshéko bohoslovecké evangelické fak. 1 vyd. Praha, ÚCN, rozmn. ST 6, 1972. 95p.

MOLNÁR, Amedeo. La correspondance entre les Frères tchèques et Bucer 1540 à 1542. **Revue d'histoire et de philosophie religieuses,** 31 (1) 102—156, 1951.

MOSSE, George Lachmann. The Reformation; 3rd ed. New York, Holt, Rinehart and Winston (c1963) "Bucer" p. 52—57. (Berkshire studies in European history).

MUELLER, Johannes. Martin Bucers Hermeneutik. Gütersloh, Mohn, 1965. 278 p. (Quellen und Forschungen zur Reformationsgeschichte, Bd. 32).

NAUTA. Doede. Datering van een brief van Martin Bucer uit 1540. **Nederlands archief voor kerkgeschiedenis,** N.S., 43: 250—253, 1959/60.

NIEBERGALL, Alfred. Kirche und Seelsorge nach Bucers Schrift "Von der waren Seelsorge". **Gesellschaft für niedersächsische Kirchengeschichte. Jahrbuch,** 63: 35—75, 1965.

NOTTINGHAM, William Jesse. The social ethics of Martin Bucer. (New York) 1962. 359 1. Thesis—Columbia Univ.

NIJENHUIS, Willem. Een merkwaardige historische argumentatie in Bucers "Judenratschlag". **Nederlands theologisch tijdschrift,** 20: 401—415, 1965/66.

OBERREINER, C. Martin Bucer en Angleterre. **Revue catholique d'Alsace,** 34: 263—277; 410—419; 481—491; 536—547; 613—620; 663—670; 755—758, 1919; 35: 29—35; 98—107, 1920; 36: 393—398, 1921.

PAUCK, Wilhelm. Bucer's conception of a Christian state. **Princeton theological review,** 26 (1) 80—88, 1928.

PAUCK, Wilhelm. The heritage of the Reformation; rev. and enl. ed. New York, Free Press of Glencoe, 1961. "Luther and Butzer": p. 73—84.

PAUCK, Wilhelm. Martin Butzers "De regno Christi" und die englische Staatskirche des 16. Jahrhunderts. Berlin, 1925. Thesis.

PAUCK, Wilhelm. Melanchton and Bucer. London, S.C.M. Press (1969) 406 p. (Library of Christian classics, v. 19).

PAUCK, Wilhelm. Das Reich Gottes auf Erden. Utopie und Wirklichkeit; eine Untersuchung zu Butzers "De regno Christi" und zur englischen Staatskirche des 16. Jahrhunderts. Berlin, De Gruyter, 1928. 208 p. (Arbeiten zur Kirchengeschichte, 10).

PAULUS, Nikolaus. Butzers Stellung zur Hexenfrage. **Elsässische Monatsschrift für Geschichte und Volkskunde,** 1: 723—726, 1910.

PEREMANS, Nicole. Erasme et Bucer d'après leur correspondance. Paris, Les Belles Lettres, 1970. 162p.

POLLET, Jacques Vincent. Bucer et l'école. **Bibliothèque d'humanisme et renaissance,** 26 (3) 559—572, 1964.

POLLET, Jacques Vincent. La correspondance inédite de Martin Bucer. **Archiv für Reformationsgeschichte,** 46: 213—221, 1955.

POLLET, Jacques Vincent. Martin Bucer; études sur la correspondance avec de nombreux textes inédits. Paris, Presses Univ. de France, 1958- v.

POLLET, Jacques Vincent. Die neue Bucer-Ausgabe. **Theologische Literaturzeitung,** 87: 579—584, 1962.

PONT, A. D. Martin Bucer; 1491—1551. **Nederduitsch Hervormde Kerk van Afrika. Almanak,** 64: 63—72.

PORTER, Harry Culverwell. Bucer in Cambridge. **Cambridge review,** 74 (1800) 185—187, 1952/53.

PRUETT, Gordon Earl. Thomas Cranmer and the eucharistic controversy in the Reformation. Princeton, N.J. 1968. "Bucer": p. 195—232. Thesis—Princeton.

RAUBENHEIMER, R. Martin Bucer und seine humanistischen Speyerer Freunde. **Blätter für pfalzische Kirchengeschichte und religiöse Volkskunde,** 32 (1/2) 1—52, 1965.

ROSENSTIEHL, C. La confirmation chez Bucer et chez Spener. Strasbourg, 1930. Thesis.

ROTH, F. Zur Kirchengüterfrage in der Zeit von 1538 bis 1540; die

Gutachten Martin Bucers und der Augsburger Wolfgang Musculus und Bonifacius Wolfart über die Verwendung der Kirchengüter. **Archiv für Reformationsgeschichte,** 1: 299—336, 1903/4.

ROTSCHEIDT, W. Martin Butzers Rechtfertigung seiner Wirksamkeit in Bonn, 1543. **Monatshefte für rheinische Kirchengeschichte,** 37: 10—23, 1943.

ROTT, Jean. Bucer et les débuts de la querelle sacramentaire. **Revue d'histoire et de philosophie religieuses,** 34: 234—254, 1954.

ROTT, Jean. Documents strasbourgeois concernant Calvin. III. Une lettre inédite de Bucer concernant la doctrine eucharistique de Calvin pendant son séjour à Strasbourg. **Revue d'histoire et de philosophie religieuses,** 44 (4) 325—231, 1964. (**Also in:** Regards contemporains sur Jean Calvin. Actes du colloque Calvin, Strasbourg, 1964. Paris, Presses Universitaires de France, 1965. p. 28—73) (Cahiers R.H.P., 39).

ROTT, Jean. Le sort des papiers et de la biliothèque de Bucer en Angleterre. **Revue d'histoire et de philosophie religieuses,** 46 (4) 346—367, 1966.

ROULET, J. L. La notion de l'etat chez Bucer. Neuchâtel, 1935.

RUPP, Ernest Gordon. Martin Bucer; prophet of a new reformation (**In:** Prospect for theology. Essays in honour of Herbert Henry Farmer, ed. by F.G. Healy. Welwyn, 1966. p. 183—199).

SCHMIDT, Gerhart. Martin Butzer als protestantische Politiker. Köningsberg, 1936. 43 p. Thesis.

SCHUBERT, Hans von. Bucers Gegenbekenntnis zu den Schwabacher Artikeln vertreten durch Jacob Sturm und gegen Sams Glossen. **Zeitschrift für Kirchengeschichte,** 30: 229—257, 1911.

SCHUBERT, Hans von. Die Beteiligung der dänisch-holsteinischen Landesfürsten am hamburger Kapitelstreit und das Gutachten Martin Bucers von 1545 (**In:** Schriften des Vereins für schleswig-holsteinische Kirchengeschichte. II Reihe, Bd. 3, 1904—1905. p. 1—64; 394—396).

SCHULTZ, Rudolf. Martin Butzers Anschauung von der christlichen Oberkeit, dargestellt im Rahmen der reformatorischen Staats- und Kirchenteorien. Freiburg i. Br., 1932. 117 p. Thesis.

SCHULZE, Ludolf Ferdinand. Die vertikale en die horisontale by Bucer (**In:** Die saailand is die wêreld. Uitgegee in opdrag van die Kuratorium van die Hammanskraalse Teologiese Skool van die Gereformeerde Kerk in Suid-Afrika. L. Floor (red) [Hanmmanskraal, 1973] p. 103—118).

SCHULZE, Ludolf Ferdinand. „Das ym selbs" van Martin Bucer. **In die Skriflig,** 3 (10) 24—33, 1969.

SCHWEITZER, G. E. Der Reformator Martin Bucer. Strassburg, Heinrich, 1917. 36 p.

SHORT, H. E. Bucer and church organisation. Hartford, Conn., 1942. Thesis—Hartford Theological Seminary.

SIG, L. Martin Butzer und Luther [nach Grisar: Luther] **Strassburger Diözesanblatt,** 33 (1) 22—32, 1914.

SMYTH, C. H. Cranmer and the Reformation under Edward VI; repr. Westpost, Conn., Greenwood (1970, 1926) Chapter 5; "Cambridge and Bucer."

SPITZER, J. Zur Geschichte des

Reformationsstreites zwischen Hamburg und dem Domkapitel: das Responsum Martin Butzers. **Verein für hamburgische Geschichte. Mitteilungen,** 25: 15—21, 1905/6.

STAEHELIN, Ernst. Oekolampad und Butzer in französischer Übersetzung. **Zeitschrift für Kirchengeschichte, N.F.,** 47 (10) 57—63, 1928.

STÄHLIN, R. Martin Bucer und die Einheit der Kirche. **Evangelisch-lutherische Kirchenzeitung,** 6 (4) 55—59, 1952.

STEINMETZ, David Curtis. Reformers in the wings. Philadelphia, Fortress Press (1971) "Martin Bucer; the church and the social order:" p. 121—132.

STEPHENS, W. P. The Holy Spirit in the theology of Martin Bucer. Cambridge, University Press, 1970. 291 p.

STRASSER, Otto Erich. Die letzten Anstrengungen der Strassburger Theologen Martin Bucer und Wolfgang Capito, eine Union zwischen den deutschen Lutheranern und den schweizerischen Reformierten herzustellen. **Zwingliana,** 6: 5—15; 1934/37.

STROHL, Henri. Un aspect de l'humanisme chrétien de Bucer. **Revue d'histoire et de philosophie religieuses,** 18: 432—447, 1939.

STROHL, Henri. Bucer et son activité scientifique. **Revue d'histoire et de philosophie religieuses,** 36: 122-, 1956.

STROHL, Henri. Bucer, humaniste chrétien. Paris, Alcan, 1939. 56 p. (Cahiers de la Revue d'histoire et de philosophie religieuses, 29).

STROHL, Henri. Bucer interprète de Luther. **Revue d'histoire et de philosophie religieuses,** 19: 223—261, 1939.

STROHL, Henri. Deux études sur Bucer. **Revue d'histoire et de philosophie religieuses,** 10: 571-, 1930.

STROHL, Henri. Martin Bucer und Strasburg. **Deutsches Pfarrerblatt,** 51 (7) 193—194, 1951.

STROHL, Henri. Les précurseurs du christianisme social en Alsace au 16e siècle: Martin Bucer. **Revue du christianisme social,** p. 993—1011, 1922.

STUPPERICH, Martin. Schrifverständnis und Kirchenlehre bei Butzer und Gropper. **Verein für westfalische Kirchengeschichte. Jahrbuch.** 43: 109—128, 1950.

STUPPERICH, Robert. Bibliographia Bucerana. Unter Mitwirkung von E. Steinborn **(In:** Schriften des Vereins für Reformationsgeschichte, 169. Gütersloh, Bertelsman, 1952. p. 37).

STUPPERICH, Robert. Buceriana. **Archiv für Reformationsgeschichte,** 43: 106—107, 1952.

STUPPERICH, Robert. Bucers Anschauungen von der Kirche, **Zeitschrift für systematische Theologie,** 17: 131—148, 1940.

STUPPERICH, Robert. Die Kirche in M. Bucers theologischer Entwicklung. **Archiv für Reformationsgeschichte,** 35: 81—101, 1938.

STUPPERICH, Robert. Die kritische Ausgabe der Werke Martin Bucers. **Theologische Literaturzeitung,** 82: 91—94, 1957.

STUPPERICH, Robert. Martin Bucer **(In:** Schmidt, Wilhelm, ed. Gestalten der Reformation. **Wuppertal,** Jugenddienst-Verl. [1967] p. 67—76).

STUPPERICH, Robert. Martin Bucer; der Reformator des Elsasses und Einiger des deutschen Protestantismus. Berlin, Heliand, 1941. 16 p. (Heliand-Hefte, Nr. 70).

STUPPERICH, Robert. Martin Butzer; der Theologe und Kirchenmann. **Zeichen der Zeit,** 5 (7) 253—258, 1951.

STUPPERICH, Robert. Martin Butzers Anteil an den sozialen Aufgaben seiner Zeit. **Hessische kirchengeschichtliche Verenigung. Jahrbuch,** 5: 120—141, 1954.

STUPPERICH, Robert. Stand und Aufgabe der Butzer-Forschung; Forschungsbericht. **Archiv für Reformationsgeschichte,** 42: 244—259, 1951.

STUPPERICH, Robert. Der Ursprung des "Regensburger Buches" von 1541 und seine Rechtfertigungslehre. **Archiv für Reformationsgeschichte,** 36: 88—116, 1939.

SWEETING, William J. Martin Bucer and the reformation in Strasbourg. Oak Brook, Ill. Thesis—Northern Baptist Theol. Sem.

TEMMEL, L. Glaube und Gewissheit in der Theologie Martin Bucers, vornehmlich nach seinem Römerbriefkommentar. Wien 1950. Thesis—Wien.

THOMPSON, B. Bucer study since 1918. **Church history,** 25: 63—82, 1956.

TORRANCE, Thomas Forsyth. Kingdom and church; a study in the theology of the Reformation. Edinburgh, Oliver & Boyd, 1956. "The eschatology of love: Martin Bucer": p. 73—89.

TORRANCE, Thomas Forsyth. Kingdom and church in the thought of Bucer. **Journal of ecclesiastical history,** 6 (1) 48—59, 1955.

VAN DEN BOSCH, Johannes Willem. Bucer over de verhouding van kerkelijk ambt en zielzorg. **Gereformeerd theologisch tijdschrift,** 37: 397—407, 1936.

VAN DEN BOSCH, Johannes Willem. Martinus Bucer en de zending. **Gereformeerd theologisch tijdschrift,** 33: 492—514; 544—568, 1933.

VAN DEN BOSCH, Johannes Willem. De ontwikkeling van Bucer's praedestinatiegedachten vóór het optreden van Calvijn. Harderwijk, Mooij (1922) 125 p. Thesis—Vrije Univ., Amsterdam.

VAN DE POLL, Gerrit Jan. Martin Bucer's liturgical ideas. Assen, Van Gorcum [1954] 179 p. Thesis—Groningen.

VAN DER WALT, Jan Jacobus. Bucer en ons kerkregering. **Die Kerkblad,** 73 (2057) 10—11, 1970.

VAN DER WALT, Jan Jacobus. Christus as hoof van die kerk en die presbiteriale kerkregering [Potchefstroom] 1974. 207 1. "Die presbiteriale kerkregeringstelsel: die Calvinisme 'n reformasie" [Calvin and Bucer] p. 126—173.

VAN 'T SPIJKER, Willem. De actuateit van Martin Bucers ambtsopvatting. 's-Gravenhage, Willem de Zwijgerstichting, 1971. 58 p.

VAN 'T SPIJKER, Willem. De ambten bij Martin Bucer. Kampen, Kok, 1970. 480 p. Thesis—Vrije Univ., Amsterdam.

VAN 'T SPIJKER, Willem. Goddelijk recht en kerkelijke orde bij Martin Bucer. Kampen, Kok, 1972. 40 p. (Apeldoornse studies, no 3).

VARRENTRAPP, C. Zur Charakteristik Hermanns von Wied, Bucers und Groppers. **Zeitschrift für Kirchengeschichte,** 20 (1) 37, 1900.

VESEY, Wesley James. The sources of the idea of active resistance in the political theory of John Knox. Boston, Mass., 1961. 247 l. Thesis—Boston University Graduate School.

VOGT, Herbert. Martin Bucer und die Kirche von England. Munster, 1966. 221 l. Thesis—Westfalische Wilhelms-Univ., Munster.

WATSON, Robert Lowell. A comparison of the **Tetrapolitan Confession** of 1530 and Martin Bucer's **Summary of Christian doctrine**. Nashville, Tenn., 1969. 370 l. Thesis—Vanderbilt University.

WEBER, Wilhelm. Martin Butzer, 1491—1551 **(In:** Philipp Melanchton, 1497—1560. Gedenkschrift zum 400. Todestag des Reformators, 19 April 1560/1960. Hrsg. von George Urban. 2., erw. Aufl. Bretten, 1960. p. 117—118).

WENDEL, François. Un document inédit sur le séjour de Bucer en Angleterre. **Revue d'histoire et de philosophie religieuses,** 34 (3) 223—233, 1954.

WENDEL, François. Martin Bucer; esquisse de sa vie et de sa pensée, publiée à l'occasion du 4e centenaire de sa mort, 28 février 1551. Strasbourg, Société pastorale, 1951. 47 p. Extract from **Revue de la Quinzaine protestante,** 1932.

WILLIAMS, G. H. The radical reformation. Philadelphia, Westminster, 1962. "Bucer", p. 234—298.

ZELLER, Winfried. Zum 400. Todestag Martin Butzers. **Kirche in der Zeit,** 6 (5/6), 1951.

ZENTGRAF, R. Wer war Martin Butzer? **Weg und Wahrheit,** 5: 368, 1950/51.

ZIEGLER, Donald Jenks. Marpeck versus Butzer; a sixteenth-century debate over the uses and limits of political authority **(In:** Sixteenth century essays and studies, 1971. V.2. 95—107).

ZIPPERT, Christian. Der Gottesdienst in der Theologie des jungen Bucer. Marburg, 1969. 273 p. Thesis—Marburg Univ.

ZWANENBURG. L. G. Martin Bucer over de Heilige Geest. **Theologia reformata,** 8: 105—129, 1955.

Farel, Guillaume

BERNOULLI, Wilhelm. Das Diakonenamt bei W. Farel. Greifensee, Schweizerisches Reformierte Diakonessenhaus, 1957. 22 p.

BEVAN, Frances. La vie de Guillaume Farel. Vevey, 1932 (c1885) 388 p.

BINZ, G. Basler Ratsmandat über Farels Disputation vom Jahre 1524. **Centralblatt für Bibliothekswesen,** 47: 585—589, 1930.

BURGER, Jean Daniel. La conversion de Farel. **Societé de l'histoire du protestantisme français. Bulletin,** 111: 199—212, 1965.

BURGER, Jean Daniel. Le pasteur Guillaume Farel. **Theologische Zeitschrift,** 21: 410—426, 1965.

CARRIERE, Victor. Guillaume Farel; propogandiste de la Réformation. [Ad. 1536] Paris, Société d'histoire ecclésiastique de la France, 1934. 44 p. Extract from: **Revue d'histoire de l'Église de France,** 1934.

COURVOISIER, Jaques. Farel and Geneva; tr. by E. Hilgert. **Maccormick quarterly,** 21: 123—135, 1967.

DELATTRE, S. Guillaume Farel. Privas, Ardèche, 1931. 264 p.

DE ZEEUW, Pieter. Willem Farel, 1489—1565. **Belijden en beleven,** 18 (50) 6, 1961.

DU PASQUIER, Marc. La conversion de Guillaume Farel. **Almanach Jean Calvin,** 1936: 28—33.

FAREL, Guillaume. Guillaume Farel, 1489—1565; biographie nouvelle écrite d'après les documents originaux par un groupe d'historiens, professeurs et pasteurs de Suisse, de France et d'Italie. Neuchâtel, Delachaux & Niestlé, 1930. 781 p.

GRIER, William James. Hus and Farel; heroic pioneers of the Reformation. London, Evangelical Library, 1965, 24 p. (Evangelical Library. Annual Lectures, 1965).

MACVICAR, Donald H. William Farel, reformer of the Swiss Romand; his life, his writings and his theology. New York, 1954. Thesis—Union Theological Seminary, New York.

MEYLAN, Henri. Farel et les gens de Gap [Letter to Viret] **Musée neuchâtelois,** 4 (3) 29—33 [1968?]

MICHAELIS, O. Wilhelm Farel. **Deutsches Pfarrerblatt,** 43: 734—, 1939.

NAUTA, Doede. Guillaume Farel; 13 September 1565. **Centraal weekblad voor de Gereformeerde Kerken in Nederland,** 13 (37) 2, 1965.

PFISTER, Rudolf. Die Freundschaft zwischen Guillaume Farel und Huldrych Zwingli. **Zwingliana,** 8 (7) 372—389, 1947.

STUCKI, Alfred. Guillaume Farel. Evangelist, Kämpfer, Reformator. St. Gallen, Buchhandlung der Evangelischen Gesellschaft, 1942. 132 p.

URECH, Edouard. Guillaume Farel. La Chaux-de-Fonds, Saint-Clair, 1965. 111 p.

WEISS, N. Une plaquette inconnue de Farel. **Zeitschrift für schweizerische Geschichte,** 8: 371—377, 1929.

Knox, John

ANDERSON William James. John Knox as registrar. **Innes review,** 7: 63, 1956.

BARBÉ, Louis A. The story of John Knox. Glasgow, Wilson, 1921. 28 p. (Saint Andrew series of famous Scots, no. 3).

BORGEAUD, Charles. Le "vrai portrait" de John Knox. **Societé de l'histoire du protestantisme français. Bulletin,** 84: 11—36, 1935.

BOUWMEESTER, G. John Knox, de hervormer van Schotland. 's-Gravenhage, Willem de Zwijgerstichting, 1964. 122 p. (Reformatorische stemmen).

BOWEN, Marjorie, **pseud.** Life of John Knox; 2nd ed. London, Watts [1949] 246 p. (The thinker's library, no. 134) Also published by Jenkins, London, 1940.

BOWIE, Walter Russel. Men of fire; torch bearers of the Gospel. New York, Harper, 1961. "Knox": p. 157—168.

BROADBENT, J. B. Grey eminency; John Knox. **Cambridge review,** 74 (1816) 572—573, 1952/53.

BRUCE-WATT, Jeremy. Haddington; John Knox's town. **Scotland's magazine,** 10: 28—32, 1960.

BURNS, James Henderson. John Knox and revolution, 1558. **History today,** 8: 565—573, 1958.

BURNS, James Henderson. Knox and Bullinger. **Scottish historical review,** 34 (117) 90—91, 1955.

CHEYNE, A. C. Worship in the Kirk: Knox, Westminster and the 1940 Book **(In:** Reformation and revolution; essays presented to the very reverend principal emeritus Hugh Watt, on the sixtieth anniversary of his ordination. Ed. by

Duncan Shaw. Edinburgh, St. Andrew Press, 1967. p. 70—81).

COLLINS, George Norman MacLeod. John Knox en Skotland vandag. **Die Kerkblad,** 75 (2173) 6—7, 1972.

COLLINS, George Norman MacLeod. Knox and the Scottish Reformation **(In:** Puritan and Reformed Studies. Conference 11th, London, 1960. Increasing in the knowledge of God; Puritan papers. [London?] 1961. p. 29—39).

COWAN, Henry. John Knox; the hero of the Scottish Reformation [Repr.] New York, A. M. S. Press [1970, 1905] 404 p.

d'ASSONVILLE, Victor Edouard. Calvyn se Institusie as handboek vir John Knox. **In die Skriflig,** 3 (10) 49—52, 1969.

d'ASSONVILLE, Victor Edouard. John Knox and the Institutes of Calvin; a few points of contact in their theology. (Durban, Drakensberg Press, pref. 1968) 112 p. Thesis—University of Natal, Durban.

d'ASSONVILLE, Victor Edouard. John Knox as Calvinis. **Die Kerkblad,** 75 (2173) 8—9; 12, 1972.

d'ASSONVILLE, Victor Edouard. John Knox, die Skotse Calvinis. **Koers,** 26 (9) 308—313; (10) 344—351; (11) 397—402, 1959.

DAVIS, Robert Lee, Jr. John Knox and his contribution to modern democracy. Nashville, Tenn., 1925. 89 l. Thesis—Vanderbilt Univ., Nashville, Tenn.

EBY, Frederick. Early Protestant educators; the educational writings of Martin Luther, John Calvin, and other leaders of Protestant thought [Repr.] New York, 1971 (1931) "John Knox" p. 271—298.

ENGELBRECHT, Barend Jacobus. Die leer van John Knox oor die reg van opstand teen die burgerlike owerheid. **Die Hervormer,** 51 (2) 7—8; 25—28, 1960.

FINLAYSON, J. P. A volume associated with John Knox. **Scottish historical review,** 38 (126) 170—172, 1956.

GANNON, P. J. Martin Luther and John Knox [Comparison] **Studies,** 29: 309—320, 1930.

GREAVES, Richard L. John Knox and the covenant tradition. **Journal of ecclesiastical history,** 24 (1) 23—32, 1973.

GRIER, William James. John Knox se beginsels. **Die Kerkblad,** 75 (2173) 4—6, 1972.

HART, A. B. Knox as a man of the world. **American historical review,** 13 (2) 259—280, 1908.

HENDERSON, G. D. John Knox le réformateur de l'Ecosse. **Almanach Jean Calvin,** 1934: 22—25.

HENDERSON, Ian. Reassessments of the Reformers **(In:** Reformation and revolution; essays presented to the very reverend principal emeritus Hugh Watt, on the sixtieth anniversary of his ordination. Ed. by Duncan Shaw. Edinburgh, St. Andrew Press, 1967. p. 34—41).

HILL, David C. Messengers of the King. Illus. by Paul Konsterlie. Minneapolis (1968) "John Knox; stern saint of the Scots": p. 42—49.

HOPE, Norman V. A reminder from John Knox. **Christianity today,** 17 (2) 5—6, 1972.

HOUGHTON, S. M. John Knox **(In:** Puritan and Reformed studies. Conference, 16th, London, 1965. Approaches to Reformation of the Church. [n.p.] 1966. p. 46—56).

HURAULT, E. John Knox et ses relations avec les églises reformées du continent. Cahors, 1902.

JANTON, Pierre. John Knox, ca. 1513—1572. L'homme et l'oeuvre. Clermont, De Bussae, 1967. 548 p. Thesis—Paris.

JOHN Knox und die Reformation in Schottland. **Kirchenblatt für die reformierte Schweiz,** 116: 136—137, 1960.

KEMPFF, Dionysius. John Knox en Suid-Afrika. **Die Kerkblad,** 75 (2173) 2, 1972.

KIK, Jacob Marcellus. Church and state; the story of two kingdoms. New York, Nelson, 1963. "Knox": p. 87—101.

KNOX, John. Great thoughts from Knox; selected by Hilda Noel Schroetter. London, Collins [1968] 94 p. (Ginger Books).

KNOX, John. Scripture and the ordering of worship **(In** The Reformation of the church; a collection of Reformed and Puritan documents on church issues. Selected, with introd. notes by Iaian Murray. London, Banner of Truth Trust, 1965. p. 75—84).

LANG, Andrew. John Knox and the Reformation. London, Longmans, 1905. 281 p.

LANG, Andrew. Knox as historian. **Scottish historical review,** 2 (6) 113—130, 1905.

LEASOR, Teresa Jane. The communion service in the Reformed churches in Switzerland, France, and Scotland in the sixteenth century. New York, N.Y., 1968. 198 l. Thesis—New York University.

LEE, Maurice, Jr. John Knox and his history. **Scottish historical review,** 45: 79—88, 1966.

LITTLE, Paul M. John Knox and English social prophecy. **Journal of presbyterian history,** 14: 117—127, 1970.

LOCHER, Gottfried Wilhelm. John Knox und die schottische Reformation. **Kirchenblatt für die reformierte Schweiz,** 117: 83—85, 1961.

LOOTS, Zacharias Blomerus. John Knox; 'n man van God gestuur. **Die Kerkbode,** 108 (17) 562—562; 574, 1971.

MACDONALD, Colin M. John Major and humanism. **Scottish historical review,** 13 (50) 149—158, 1916.

McDOUGALL, David. The queen sends for Knox; the story of John Knox, the great reformer. 2nd ed. Edinburgh, Scottish Reformation Society [1968] 24 p.

McEWEN, James Stevenson. The faith of John Knox. London, Lutterworth, 1961. 116 p. (The Croall lectures for 1960).

McGRAW, James. Great evangelical preachers of yesterday. New York, Abingdon [1961] "Knox": p. 40—44.

MACGREGOR, Geddes. The thundering Scot; a portrait of John Knox. London, MacMillan, 1958. 244 p.

MCHARTY, J. The priesthood of Knox. **Innes review,** 7: 62—63, 1956.

MACKIE, John Duncan. John Knox; rev. ed. London, Historical Association, 1968. 24 p. (Historical Association. General series, G.20).

MACLEAN, Fitzroy. A concise history of Scotland. London, Thames and Hudson (c1970) "John Knox": p. 85—95.

McLELLAND, Joseph C. Reformation and its significance today. Philadelphia, Westminster Press (1962) "John Knox and the kingship of Christ": p. 67—78.

MACLEOD, George F. John Knox und wir. Genf, John Knox Haus Gesellschaft (1960) 23 p. (Vorlesung der John Knox Haus Vorlesungsreihe, 5. 30 Mai 1959).

MAIN, A. The origins of John Knox's doctrine of Just Rebellion. Aberdeen [1962/63?] Thesis—Aberdeen.

MEZGER, Adrien. John Knox et ses rapports avec Calvin. Montauban, 1905. 88 p. Thesis—Montauban.

MUIR, Edwin. John Knox [repr.] Port Washington, N.Y., Kennikat Press (1972, 1929).

MUIR, Edwin. John Knox; portrait of a Calvinist. London, Cape, 1929. 316 p.

MYRICK, Prentiss Allen. John Knox's concept of Christ. Cambridge, Mass., 1952. 98 p. Thesis—Harvard Univ., Cambridge, Mass.

NEILSON, George Alexander. Twelve Reformation heroes. London, Pickering & Inglis, 1960 "John Knox": p. 89—96.

NYGAARD, Norman Eugene. Tempest over Scotland; the story of John Knox. London, Oliphants, 1961. 183 p.

The ORDINATION of John Knox; a symposium. **Innes review,** 6: 99—106, 1955.

PAISLEY, Ian R.K. Three great reformers. (Belfast, Puritan Press) [1968] "Knox": p. 31—48.

PERCY, **Lord** Eustace Sutherland Campbell. John Knox. London, Hodder and Stoughton, 1937. 438 p.

PICHAL, E. La vie de John Knox, le réformateur. **Les cahiers calvinistes,** 2 (10) 1—12, 1961.

PONT, A. D. John Knox, 1513—1572. **Die Hervormer,** 51 (2) 11; 14—15; 18—19, 1960.

RAIT, R. S. Knox and Reformation. **Nation,** 82: 287—296, 1906.

RAIT, R. S. Strength and limitations of John Knox. **Current literature,** 39: 168—169, 1905.

RAIT, Robert Sangster. Scotland and John Knox. **The fortnightly review,** N.S. 78: 95—108, 1905 [Vol. 84 Old Series]

READ, David H. C. Great preachers, 14: John Knox. **Theology,** 55 (382) 143—146, 1952.

REID, William Stanford. John Knox in Amerika. **Die Kerkblad,** 75 (2173) 12—13, 1972.

REID, William Stanford. Knox's attitude to the English Reformation. **Westminster theological journal,** 25: 1—32, 1963/64.

RIDLEY, Jasper Godwin. John Knox. Oxford, Clarendon Press, 1968. 596 p.

ROSS, Anthony. John Knox; prophet or hypocrite? **Scotland's magazine,** 68 (11) 14—16, 1972.

RUNIA, Klaas. John Knox, the reformer of Scotland. **Trowel and sword,** 20 (3) 14—16, 1972.

STEVENSON, Robert Louis. Familiar studies of men and books; fine-paper ed. London, Chatto & Windus, 1907: "John Knox and women": p. 229—277. (St. Martin's library).

STRAUKAMP, J. Knox, Calvin, and English diplomacy. Knox's: The first blast of the trumpet against the monstrous regiment of women. **Heythrop journal,** 4: 61—63, 1963.

The THUNDERING Scot. **Christianity today,** 17 (2) 26—27, 1972.

TREVOR-ROPER, Hugh Redwald. Great confrontations; Mary, queen of Scots and John Knox. **Horizon,** 5 (5) 28—32, 1963.

UITTENBOGAARD, W. John Knox and education. **Christliches Erziehungsblatt,** 1 (4) 14—16, 1939.

VAN HALSEMA, Emo. John Knox. **De Wachter,** 5 (44) 4— 5, 1962.

VESEY, Wesley James. The sources of the idea of active resistance in the political theory of John Knox. Boston, Mass., 1961. 247 p. Thesis—Boston Univ., Graduate School.

WATT, Hugh. John Knox in controversy; being the Stone lectures delivered at Princeton theological seminary, in 1949. London, Nelson, 1950. 110 p.

WHITLEY, Elizabeth. Plain Mr. Knox. Edinburgh, Scottish Reformation Society, 1972. 223 p. Also published by Skeffington, London, 1960.

WILDBOLZ, Eduard. Die Auslegung der Bibel bei John Knox und seinen schottischen Zeitgenossen. Edinburgh, 1952, 273 1. Thesis—Edinburgh Univ.

WOLF, Ernst. John Knox, der Reformator Schottlands. **Kirchenblatt für die reformierte Schweiz,** 116: 327, 1960.

Laski, Jan

BARTEL, Oskar, Johannes à Lasco und Erasmus von Rotterdam. **Luther,** 32: 48—66, 1965.

BERNOULLI, Wilhelm. Das Diakonenamt bei J. à Lasco. Greifensee, Schweizerisches Reformierte Diakonessenhaus, 1951. 24 p.

BOUWMEESTER, G. Johannes à Lasco; een uitverkoren instrument Gods. 's-Gravenhage, Willem de Zwijgerstichting, 1956. 112 p. (Reformatorische stemmen).

DALTON, Hermann. Johannes à Lasco; Beitrag zur Reformationsgeschichte Polens, Deutschlands und Englands. Nachdr. der Ausg. 1881. Nieuwkoop, De Graaf, 1970. 605 p.

DE WILDE, Willem Johannes. Een Pools hervormer; Johannes à Lasco. **Hervormd weekblad — de Geref. Kerk,** 71: 10; 20; 28; 37; 45; 62; 70, 1959/60.

FABER, Jelle. De dienst der barmhartigheid in de reformatietijd, V. Johannes à Lasco. **De Reformatie,** 35 (47) 376—377, 1960.

HALL, Basil. John à Lasco, 1499—1560; a Pole in Reformation England. London, Dr. Williams's Trust, 1971. 36 p. (Friends of Dr. Williams's Library. 25th Lecture).

HEIN, Karl. Die Sakramentslehre des Johannes à Lasco. Bonn, 1904. 102 p. Thesis—Friedrich-Wilhelms-Univ., Bonn.

KOWALSKA, Halina, Dzialalnosc reformatorska, Jana Laskiego w Polsce, 1556—1560. Wrocıaw, Zaklad Narodowy im. Ossolinskich, 1969. 174 p.

LASKI, Jan. The abolition of vestments **(In:** The Reformation of the church; a collection of Reformed and Puritan documents on church issues. Selected, with introd. notes by Iaian Murray. London, Banner of Truth Trust, 1965. p. 63—74).

MAZIERSKI, Roman K. A. concise history of the Polish Reformed Church; its origin, past and present. [n.p.] Polish Reformed Church in Great Britain, 1966. "John à Lasco, the pillar of the Polish Reformed Church in the sixteenth century": p. 9—14.

SLADE, M. W. John à Lasco and the English Reformation. Bristol, 1953. Thesis, Bristol University.

SMITH, James Frantz. John à Lasco and the strangers' churches.

Nashville, 1964. 349 1. Thesis—Vanderbilt Univ., Nashville.

Viret, Pierre

BARNAUD, Jean. Pierre Viret, sa vie et son oeuvre. Saint-Amans, Carayol, 1911.

BARNAUD, Jean. Quelques lettres inédites de Pierre Viret. Saint-Amans, Carayol, 1911.

BERNOULLI. Wilhelm. Das Diakonenamt bei P. Viret. Greifensee, Schweizerisches Reformierte Diakonessenhaus, 1958. 24 p.

BERNOULLI, Wilhelm. P. Virets Gedanken über das Diakonenamt. Greifensee, Schweizerisches Reformierte Diakonessenhaus, 1969. 27 p.

BRIDEL, Eugene. Pierre Viret le réformateur, 1511—1571. Lausanne, Bridel, 1911.

CHAUSSON, Huguette. Pierre Viret, ce viret qui fit virer. [Lausanne] Eglise Nationale Vaudoise, 1961. 98 p.

DOUMERGUE, Émile. Lausanne au temps de le réformation avec une introduction sur Pierre Viret et Orbe, sa ville natale. Lausanne, Bridel, 1903.

FÉLICE, Philippe de & PINEAUX, Jacques. En mémoire de Pierre Viret 1511—1571. **Société de l'histoire du protestantisme français. Bulletin,** 109: 1—10, 1962.

HEUBI, William. Une lettre inédite de Pierre Viret. **Revue historique vaudoise** 24: 353—358, 1916.

KOLFHAUS, Wilhelm. Petrus Viretus. **Theologische Studien und Kritiken,** 27: 54—110; 209—246, 1914.

LATOURETTE, Louis. Des dernières annees de Pierre Viret. **Revue de théologie et de philosophie,** 2: 60—68, 1938.

LINDER, Robert Dean. The Bible and biblical authority in the literary works of Pierre Viret **(In:** Sixteenth century essays and studies, ed. by Carl S. Meyer, 1971. V. 2: 55—71).

LINDER, Robert Dean. Pierre Viret and the sixteenth-century English Protestants. **Archiv für Reformationsgeschichte,** 58 (2) 149—171, 1967.

LINDER, Robert Dean. Pierre Viret and the sixteenth-century French Protestant revolutionary tradition. **Journal of modern history,** 38: 125—137, 1966.

LINDER Robert Dean. Pierre Viret's ideas and attitudes concerning humanism and education. **Church history,** 34: 25—35, 1965.

LINDER, Robert Dean. The political ideas of Pierre Viret. (Iowa City) 1963. 461 1. Thesis—State Univ. of Iowa.

LINDER, Robert Dean. Toward a Viret bibliography; a proposal. **Foundation for Reformation Research. Bulletin of the library,** 2 (1) 3—6, 1967.

MASSIAS, F-V. Essai historique sur Pierre Viret, réformateur du Pays de Vaud. Paris, Coueslant, 1900. 102 p. Thesis—Université de Paris.

PIERRE VIRET d'après lui-même, par edts. Charles Schnetzler, Henri Vuilleumier & Alfred Schroeder. Lausanne, Bridel, 1911.

SCHNETZLER, Charles & BARNAUD, Jean. Notice bibliographique sur Pierre Viret. Lausanne, Bridel, 1905.

VUILLEUMIER, Henri. Notre Pierre Viret. Lausanne, La Concorde, 1911.

WEERDA, Jan. Nach Gottes Wort reformierte Kirche; Beiträge zu ihrer Geschichte und ihrem Recht [von] Jan Remmers Weerda. Mit einem Geleitwort von Rudolf Smend. Aus dem Nachlass hrsg. von Annelieze Sprengler-Ruppenthal. München, Kaiser, 1964. "Peter Viret, der Lausanner Reformator": p. 204—231.

Minor figures

ANDERSON, Marvin W. Word and Spirit in exile, 1542—1561; the Biblical writings of Peter Martyr Vermigli. **Journal of ecclesiastical history,** 21: 193—201, 1970.

BRUSH, John W. Lefèvre d'Etaples; three places of his life and work **(In:** Littel, Franklin Hamlin, ed. Reformation studies in honor of R. H. Bainton. Richmond, Va., Knox [c1962] p. 117—128).

DANKBAAR, W. F. Op de grens der Reformatie: de rechtvaardigingsleer van Jacques Lefèvre d'-Étaples. **Nederlands theologisch tijdschrift,** 8: 327—345; 1954.

DECORVET, Benjamin. Bref exposé, par mode de comparaison avec la pensée Thomiste, du rôle de l'analogie dans la connaissance de noms communs à Dieu et aux créatures, d'après Jérôme Zanchi, Daniel Chamier et Francois Turretin, théologiens calvinistes. (Lausanne) 1956. 110 1. Thesis—Lausanne.

DUFFIELD, Gervase E. & McLELLAND, Joseph C., **editors.** The life, early letters, and eucharistic writings of Peter Martyr, Appleford, Courtenay, 1971.

FRIELINGHAUS, Dieter. Ecclesia und Vita; eine Untersuchung zur Ekklesiologie des Andreas Hyperius. (Neukirchen) Neukirchener Verl., 1966. 177 p. (Beiträge zur Geschichte und Lehre der Reformierten Kirche, 23. Bd.).

GAGNEBIN, M. L'impression de la Bible d'Olivetan à Neuchâtel. **Almanach Jean Calvin,** 1935: 1—7.

GRAAFLAND, Cornelis. De zekerheid van het geloof; een onderzoek naar de geloofsbeschouwing van enige vertegenwoordigers van reformatie en nadere reformatie. Wageningen, Veenman, 1961. Zanchius: p. 75—84.

GRÜNDLER, Otto. Die Gotteslehre Girolami Zanchis und ihre Bedeutung für seine Lehre von der Prädestination. Neukirchen, Neukirchener Verl., 1965. 131 p. (Beiträge zur Geschichte und Lehre der Reformierten Kirche, 20).

GRÜNDLER, Otto. Thomism and Calvinism in the theology of Girolamo Zanchi, 1516—1590. Princeton, N. J., 1960. Thesis—Princeton Theological Seminary.

JENNY, Markus. Nachtrag zu Leo Juds Nythard-Lied. **Zwingliana,** 12 (6) 463, 1966; **Archiv für Reformationsgeschichte,** 57: 229, 1966.

JORDAN, James Daniel. The church reform principles in the Biblical works of Jacques Lefèvre d'Étaples. Durham, N. C., 1966. 401 1. Thesis —Duke Univ. Durham, N. C.

KITTELSON, James. Wolfgang Capito, the Council, and Reform Strasbourg. **Archiv für Reformationsgeschichte,** 63: 126—140, 1972.

LEFÈVRE, Jacques, **d'Étaples.** Epistres et evangilés pour les cinquante et deux sepmaines de l'an. Facsim. de la Ire éd. Simon du Bois. Avec introd., note bibliographique et appendices, par M. A. Screech. Genève, Droz, 1964. 52 p. (Travaux d'humanisme et renaissance, 63).

McLELLAND, Joseph C. The visible words of God; an exposition of the sacramental theology of Peter Martyr Vermigli, A. D. 1500—1562. Edinburgh, Oliver & Boyd, 1957. 291 p.

McNAIR, Philip. Peter Martyr in Italy; an anatomy of apostacy. Oxford, Clarendon, 1967. 326 p.

McNAIR, P. M. J. The life and work of Pietro Martire Vermigli in Italy. Oxford, 1963. Thesis, Oxford Univ. (Christ Church).

PAIST, Benjamin F. Peter Martyr and the Colloguy of Poissy. **Princeton theological review,** 20: 418—447, 616—646, 1922.

SANTINI, Luigi. Scisma ed eresia nel pensiero di P. M. Vermigli. **Bolletino della Società di studi Valdesi,** 90 (125) 27—43, 1969.

SHEPHERD, Norman. Zanchius on saving faith. **Westminister theological journal,** 36 (1) 31—47, 1973/74.

SPIESS, Karl. Der Gottesbegriff des J. Faber Stapulensis. Marburg, 1931. Thesis.

STAUFFER, Richard. Lefèvre d'-Étaples, artisan ou spectateur de la Réforme? **Societé de l'histoire du protestantisme français. Bulletin,** 113: 405—423, 1967.

STEINMETZ, David Curtis. Reformers in the wings. Philadelphia, Fortress Press (1971) "Peter Martyr Vermigli; the eucharistic sacrifice": p. 151—161.

STURM Klaus. Die Theologie Peter Martyr Vermiglis während seines ersten Aufenthalts in Strassburg 1542—1547; ein Reformkatholik unter den Vätern der reformierten Kirche. Neukirchen—Vluyn, Neukirchener Verlag, 1971. 292 p.

VAN PROOSDIJ, C. Jacques le Fèvre d'Étaples, voorganger van Calvijn. Eene studie. Leiden, Donner, 1900. 85 p.

VASOLI, Cesare. Jacques Lefèvre d'Étaples e le origini del fabrismo. **Rinascimento,** 10: 221—254, 1959.

WEISS, N. Réforme et Préréforme; Jacques Lefèvre d'Étaples **(In:** Études sur la Réforme; a propos du quatrième centenaire de la Réforme. Paris, Colin, 1919. p. 617—667).

2.3 COUNTRIES, MATTERS AND OPPONENTS.

America.

AKERS, Charles W. Calvinism and the American revolution **(In:** The heritage of John Calvin, ed. by John H. Bratt. Grand Rapids, Eerdmans, 1973. p. 158—176) (Heritage Hall Lectures, 1960—1970) (Heritage Hall publications, no. 2).

BAINTON, Roland Herbert. The Puritan theocracy and the Cambridge platform. **The minister's quarterly,** 5: 16—21, 1949. **(Also in:** The Cambridge platform of 1648; tercentenary commemoration. Boston, 1949. p. 76—86).

BAIRD, Charles Washington. History of the Huguenot emigration to America. Baltimore, Regional Pub. Co., 1966 (1885) 2 v. Reissued: Baltimore, Genealogical Publishing Co., 1973.

BARITZ, Loren. Our Puritan roots. **Nation,** 204: 699—700, 1967.

BEEBE, David Lewis. The seals of the covenant; the doctrine and place of the sacraments and censures in the New England Puritan theology underlying the Cambridge platform of 1648. (Berkeley, Calif.) 1966. 323 l. Thesis—Pacific School of Religion.

BRADLEY, Michael Raymond. The Puritans of Virginia; their influence on the religious life of the old dominion, 1607—1659. Nashville, Tenn., 1971 220 1. Thesis—Vanderbilt University.

BRATT, John Harold. Calvinism in America; a tragic story. **The Banner,** 94 (20) 9; 29, 1959.

BROCK, Robert Alonzo, **ed.** Documents, chiefly unpublished, relating to the Huguenot emigration to Virginia. Ed. and comp. for the Virginia Historical Society. Baltimore, Genealogical Pub. Co., 1966. 255 p.

BYINGTON, Ezra Hoyt. The Puritan in England and New England. Boston, Little, Brown, 1900. 457 p.

FULCHER, John Rodney. Puritan piety in early New England; a study in spiritual regeneration from the Antinomian controversy to the Cambridge Synod of 1648 in the Massachusetts Bay Colony. [Princeton, N. J.] 1963. 354 1. Thesis—Princeton Theological Seminary.

GOOD, James Isaac. Calvin and the new world. **Presbyterian historical society. Journal,** 5: 179—187, 1909/10.

HALL, David D. The faithful shepherd; a history of the New England ministry in the seventeenth century. Williamsburg, Va., Published for the Institute of Early American History and Culture by the Univ. of North Carolina Press, 1972. "A ministry of the word": p. 3—20.

HERTZ, Karl H. Max Weber and American puritanism. **Journal for the scientific study of religion,** 1: 189—197, 1961.

HUNT, George Laird. Our Calvinist heritage in church and state **(In:** Calvinism and the political order. Essays prepared for the Woodrow Wilson lectureship of the National Presbyterian Center, Washington, D. C. [Ed. by] G. L. Hunt. John T. McNeill, consulting ed. Philadelphia, Westminster Press [c1965] p. 175—192).

KIK, Jacob Marcellus. Church and state; the story of two kingdoms. New York, Nelson, 1963. "A free church in a free state" p. 103—116 [Puritans, North America].

KIRBY, Ethyn Williams. The lay Feoffees; a study in militant Puritanism. **Journal of modern history,** 14: 1—25, 1942.

KLEBER, L. C. Spain and France in Florida [re: Huguenot colony, 1562—1565] **History today,** 18: 487—494, 1968.

KRUGLER, John David. Puritan and Papist: politics and religion in Massachusetts and Maryland before the restoration of Charles II. Urbana, Ill., 1971. 353 l. Thesis—Univ. of Illinois at Urbana-Champaign.

KRUIZINGA, J. H. Zij vertrokken in 1620 naar Amerika. **Centraal weekblad voor de Gereformeerde Kerken in Nederland,** 18 (17) 3; 5, 1970.

LART, Charles Edmund. Huguenot pedigrees. Baltimore, Genealogical Pub. Co., 1967 (1924-'28) 2 v. in 1.

MACFARLAND, Charles S. Permanent contributions of Genéva and John Calvin to church and state in America. **Reformed church review,** 4: 439—455, 1925.

MILLER, Perry. Errand into the wilderniss. [Cambridge, Mass.] Harvard Univ. Press, c1956. 244 p.

MILLER, Perry. The New England mind; from Colony to Province. Cambridge, Mass., Harvard Univ. Press, 1962 (c1953) 513 p.

MILLER, Perry. The New England mind; the seventeenth century. Cambridge, Mass., Harvard Univ. Press, 1963 (c1939) 528 p.

MILLER, Perry. Orthodoxy in Massachusetts, 1630—1650. Gloucester, Mass., Smith, 1965. 319 p.

MORAND, Julia P. **comp.** Catalogue of bibliography of the library of the Huguenot Society of America. 2nd ed. Baltimore, 1971. 351 p.

PARKER, Henry A. The Feoffees of impropriation. **Colonial society of Massachusetts: transactions. Publications,** 11: 263—277, 1906/07.

PERRY, Ralph Barton. Puritanism and democracy. New York, Vanguard Press, 1944. 688 p.

POPE, Earl Aurel. New England Calvinism and the disruption of the Presbyterian Church. [Ann Arbor] 1971. 438 1. Thesis—Brown Univ., 1962.

REAMAN, George Elmore. The trial of the Huguenots, in Europe, the United States, South Africa and Canada. Baltimore, Genealogical Pub. Co., 1966 (c1963) 318 p.

RIEMENS, Kornelis Jacobus. Une tentative de colonisation huguenote à Rio de 1555 à 1560. **Commission de l'histoire des églises Wallone,** 5 (5) 6—9, 1955.

SCHEPS, Nicolaas. De Pilgrim Fathers verlieten 350 jaar geleden ons land. **Kerknieuws,** 28 (1380) 1—2; 1970.

SEIDMAN, Aaron B. Church and state in the early years of the Massachusetts Bay Colony. **New England quarterly,** 18: 211—233, 1945.

STOEVER, William Kenneth Bristow. The covenant of works in Puritan theology: the antinomian crisis in New England. New Haven, Conn., 1970. 278 l. Thesis—Yale University.

VOS, Johannes G. Calvinism in America today and tomorrow. **Torch and trumpet,** 9: 10—11, 1959.

WOLF, William J. Abraham Lincoln and Calvinism **(In:** Calvinism and the political order; essays prepared for the Woodrow Wilson lectureship of the National Presbyterian Center, Washington, D. C. [Ed. by] G. L. Hunt. John T. Mc Neill, consulting ed. Philadelphia, Westminster Press [c1965] p. 104—156).

Anabaptists.

BAUMAN, Clarence. Gewaltlosigkeit im Täufertum; eine Untersuchung zur theologischen Ethik des oberdeutschen Täufertums der Reformationszeit. Leiden, Brill, 1968. 410 p. (Studies in the history of Christian thought, 3) Thesis, Bonn.

BENDER, H. S. Pacifism of the sixteenth century Anabaptists. **Church history,** 24: 119—131, 1955.

BRANDSMA, J. A. Doperse leiders in de Hervormingstijd [Overzicht van belangrijke publicaties der laatste vijf jaar] **Vox theologica,** 30: 166—173, 1960.

FAST, Heinold. Der linke Flügel der Reformation; Glaubenszeugnisse der Täufer, Spiritualisten, Schwärmer und Antitrinitarier. Bremen, Schünemann [1962] 431 p. (Klassiker des Protestantismus, Bd. 4).

HILLERBRAND, Hans Joachim. The origin of 16th century Anabaptism; another look. **Archiv für Reformationsgeschichte,** 53: 152—180, 1962.

VERDUIN, Leonard. The Reformers and their stepchildren. Grand Rapids, Eerdmans (c1964) 292 p.

WALZER, Michael. The revolution of the saints; a study in the origins of radical politics. Cambridge, Mass., Harvard Univ. Press, 1965. 334 p.

YODER, John Howard. Täufertum und Reformation im Gespräch. Dogmengeschichte Untersuchung der frühen Gespräche zwischen schweizerische Täufern und Reformatoren. Zurich, EVZ, 1968. (Basler Studien zur historischen und systematischen Theologie, Bd. 13).

YODER, John Howard. Täufertum und Reformation in der Schweiz: 1. Die Gespräche zwischen Täufern und Reformatoren, 1523—1538. Hrsg. von Mennonitischen Geschichtsverein e. V. Weierhof. Karlsruhe, Schneider, 1962, 184 p. (Schriftenreihe des Mennonitischen Geschichtsvereins, Nr. 6) Thesis—Basel.

ZUCK, Lowell Hubert. Anabaptist revolution through the covenant in the sixteenth century continental Protestantism. New Haven, Conn., 1955. 295 p. Thesis—Yale Univ.

Arminius.

ARMINIUS, Jacobus. Verklaring van Jacobus Arminius afgelegd in de vergadering van de Staten van Holland op 30 Oktober 1608. Opnieuw uitg. door G. J. Hoenderdaal. Lochem, De Tijdstroom, 1960. 138 p.

ARMINIUS, Jacobus. The writings of James Arminius. Transl. by James Nichols and W. R. Bagnall. 3. v. Grand Rapids, Mich., Baker, 1956.

BAKHUIZEN VAN DEN BRINK, Jan Nicolaas. Arminius te Leiden. **Nederlands theologisch tijdschrift,** 15: 81—89, 1960/61.

BANGS, Carl Oliver. "All the best bishoprics and deaneries": the enigma of Arminian politics. **Church history,** 42 (1) 5—16, 1973.

BANGS, Carl Oliver. Arminius; a study in the Dutch Reformation. Nashville, Abingdon, 1971. 382 p.

BANGS, Carl Oliver. Arminius and reformed theology. Chicago. 1958. 285 l. Thesis—Univ. of Chicago.

BANGS, Carl Oliver. Arminius and the Reformation. **Church history,** 30: 155—170, 1961.

BANGS, Carl. Arminius as a reformed theologian **(In:** The heritage of John Calvin, ed. by John H. Bratt. Grand Rapids, Eerdmans, 1973. p. 209—222). (Heritage Hall Lectures, 1960—1970) (Heritage Hall publications, no 2).

COLIE, Rosalie L. Light and enlightenment; a study of the Cambridge Platonists and the Dutch Arminians. Cambridge, 1957. 162 p.

DE WIT, John R. The Arminian conflict and the Synod of Dordt **(In:** Puritan and Reformed Studies Conference, 1968. The manifold grace of God; papers read at the Puritan and Reformed Studies Conference, 1968. London, Evangelical Magazine [1968?] p. 5—21).

DIJKSTRA, S. Kerkelijke interruptie in 1587. **Centraal weekblad voor de Gereformeerde Kerken in Nederland,** 16 (47) 6, 1968.

GLEBE MOLLER, Jens. Arminiusherdenking; lofrede of confrontatie? **Vox theologica**, 31: 26—31, 1961.

GLEBE MOLLER, Jens. Trostbegrebet hos Jakob Arminius. **Dansk teologisk tidsskrift,** 23: 148—156, 1960.

HARRISON, Archibald Harold Walter. The beginnings of Arminianism to the Synod of Dordt. London, London Univ. Press 1926. 408 p. Thesis—Univ. of London.

HOENDERDAAL, Gerrit Jan. The life and struggle of Arminius in the Dutch republic **(In: Man's** faith and freedom; the theological influence of Jacobus Arminius. Ed. by G. O. McCullin. New York Nashville, Abingdon, c1962 p. 11—26).

HOENDERDAAL, Gerrit Jan. The life and thought of Jacobus Arminius. **Religion in life,** 29 (4) 540—547, 1960.

HOENDERDAAL, Gerrit Jan. De theologische betekenis van Arminius. **Nederlands theologisch tijdschrift,** 15: 90—98, 1960/61.

HOENDERDAAL, Gerrit Jan. Uytenbogaert in Utrecht. **Nederlands theologisch tijdschrift** 22: 3—12, 1967/68.

KOEKEMOER, J. H. Die karakteristiek van die Arminianisme. **Hervormde teologiese studies,** 25 (2) 98—105, 1969.

McCULLOH, Gerald O. **ed.** Man's faith and freedom; the theological influence of Jacobus Arminius. New York, Abingdon Press c1962. 128 p.

NAUTA, Doede, Arminius; grondlegger van het Remonstrantisme. **Centraal weekblad voor de Gereformeerde Kerken in Nederland,** 8 (39) 309, 1960.

VAN HALSEMA, Emo. Arminius en Dordt. **De Wachter,** 93 (43) 4—5, 1960.

Austria see Germany.

Belgic Confession.

BAKHUIZEN VAN DEN BRINK, Jan Nicolaas. Ecclesia II; een bundel opstellen; uitg. ter gelegenheid van zijn afscheid als hoogleraar der Rijksuniversiteit te Leiden. Leiden, Nijhoff, 1966. "Quelques notes sur l'histoire de la confession des Pays-Bas en 1561 et en 1566": p. 296—308.

BAKHUIZEN VAN DEN BRINK, Jan Nicolaas. De Nederlandsche Belijdenisgeschriften; vergelijkende teksten. Amsterdam, 1940. 287 p.

BRAEKMAN, Emile M. Les sources de la confessio Belgica. **Commission de l'histoire des églises Wallone. Bulletin,** 5 (7) 4—24, 1961.

DEDDENS, D. De Nederlandse Geloofsbelijdenis; een en ander over haar geschiedenis. **De Reformatie, 37(6)** 46—47, 1961.

ENGELBRECHT, Barend Jacobus. Die Nederlandse Geloofsbelydenis vier eeue oud. **Die Hervormer,** 52 (8) 8, 1961.

FABER, Jelle. De katholiciteit der confessie. **De Reformatie,** 37 (6) 44—45, 1961.

FRANCKE, Joh. De Nederlandse Geloofsbelijdenis in de politiek. **De Reformatie,** 37 (5) 37—38, 1961.

JOOSTE, Josef Petrus. Die ontstaan van die Nederlandse Geloofsbelydenis. **Die Kerkblad,** 64 (1621 [not 1921]) 9—15, 1961.

NAUTA, Doede. De Nederlandse Geloofsbelijdenis en de eenheid des geloofs. **Centraal weekblad voor de Gereformeerde Kerken in Nederland,** 9 (42) 369, 1961.

PEKELDER, Bernard E. The Belgic Confession. **The Banner,** 95 (36) 1960 — 97 (15) 1962.

TRIMP, Cornelis. De belijdenis omtrent de openbaring Gods. **De Reformatie,** 37 (6) 42—43, 1961.

VAN DER LINDE, Simon. Karakter en bedoeling van de Nederlandse Geloofsbelijdenis, belicht uit de geschiedenis van haar ontstaan. **Theologia reformata,** 4: 110—125, 1961.

VAN DER WAAL, Corneiis. De Nederlandse Geloofsbelijdenis en de Rijksdag te Augsburg in 1566. **De Reformatie,** 42: 201—202; 209—211; 225—226, 1967.

VAN ITTERZON, G. P. De Nederlandsche Geloofsbelijdenis. **Hervormd weekblad — de Geref. Kerk,** 73: 3; 26, 1961/62.

Belgium see **Netherlands: Southern parts.**

Eastern Europe.

ANDREAS, W. Calvinismus in Ungarn. **Zeitschrift für osteuropäische Geschichte,** 2: 331—335, 1937.

BRADOW, Charles King. The career and confession of Cyril Loukaris; the Greek Orthodox Church and its relation with Western Christians (1543—1638). Ohio, 1960. 221 1. Thesis- Ohio State University.

BROWN, Harold O. J. Polens Beitrag zur Entwicklung des Protestantismus; eine polnische Stellungnahme zur Reformation. **österreichische Osthefte,** 8 (2) 101—106, 1966.

BROWN, Harold O. J. Probleme einer polnische Reformationsgeschichte. **Österreichische Osthefte,** 8 (6) 478—482, 1966.

BUCSAY, M. Belényesi Gergely, Kálvin magyar tanitványa [G. B., hungarian disciple of Calvin] **Egyháztörténet,** 2: 1—104, 1944.

DOUMERGUE, Emile. La Hongrie calviniste. Toulouse, Société d'Édition [1912] 209 p. Also published by Fischbacher, Paris.

FERENCZY, Ch. A missziói felelösseg nyomai a magyar református keresztyénség elsö szazadában, az egykorii theologiai irodalom a lapján [Evidences of missionary responsibility in Hungarian Reformed Christianity, during its first century of existence] **(In:** Kalvin és a kálvinismus; tanulmányok. Az Institutio négyszázadik évfordulójára irták a Debreceni M. Kir. Tisza Istvan-Tudomány-eguetem Református Hitudományi Karának tanarai és doctorai. Debrecen, Debrecen Szabad Királyi város és a Tiszántúli Református Egyhazkerület Konyvnyomda-Vállalata, 1936. p. 341—362).

FOX, Paul. The Reformation in Poland; some social and economic aspects, Baltimore, Johns Hopkins Press, 1924. 153 p. (Johns Hopkins University. Studies in historical and political science, ser. 42, no 4) Also published by AMS Press, New York, 1971. Thesis, 1923.

GEISSLER, Bruno. Vom magyarischen Kalvinismus in den Abtrennungsländern Ungarns. **Die evangelische Diaspora,** 30: 57—61, 1959/60.

HARTLEB, Kazimierz. Kalwin a Polska [Calvin and Poland] Lwowie, Lozinskiego, 1912. 23 p.

JARRA, Eugeniusz. Andrew Wolan; sixteenth century Polish Calvinist writer and philosopher of law **(In:** Studies in Polish and comparative law; a symposium of twelve articles, with a foreword by H. C. Gutteridge. London, Stevens, 1945. p. 124—155).

JARRA, Eugeniusz. Skarga a Wolan rzecznik kalwinizmu polskiego w. XVI. wieku. Paris, Jarra, 1963. 23 p.

KÖVY, A. Chris van het Hongaarse Calvinisme. **Gereformeerd weekblad,** 16 (41) 321; (42) 329; (43) 337; 344, 1961.

LORENZ, Hein. Der Sandomirer Konsens von 1570. **Kyrios. N.F.,** 3 (2) 65—77, 1963.

MAZIERSKI, Roman K. A concise history of the Polish Reformed Church; its origin, past, and present. [n.p.] Polish Reformed Church in Great Britain, 1966. "Establishment of the Reformed Faith in Poland": p. 5—9.

NAGY, Géza. A belmisszió nyomai az erdélyi reformatus egyház regebbi történetében [Die Anfänge der Inneren Mission in der älteren Geschichte der reformierten Kirche Siebenbürgens] **(In:** Kalvin és a kálvinismus; tanulmányok. Az Institutio négyszázadik évfordulójára a Debrecini M. Kir. Tisza Istvan-Tudomány-egyetem Református Hiitudományi Karának tanarai és doctorai. Debrecen, Debrecen Szabad Királyi Város és a Tiszántúli Református Egyhazkerület Konyvnymda-Vállalata, 1936. p. 363—380).

NAGY, Tibor. A kálvini reformáció társadalmi mondanivalója korunkban: az októberi lelkészértekezlet anyage. **Református egyház,** 24: 196—200, 1972.

NAUTA, Doede. De Heidelbergse Catechismus in Hongarije. **Centraal weekblad voor de Gereformeerde Kerken in Nederland,** 16 (27) 1, 1968.

ODLOZILÍK, Otakar. Bohemian Protestants and the Calvinistic churches. **Church history,** 7:342—355, 1939.

PRONIEWICZ-ZALOMAY, Jadwiga. The influence of the teaching of Luther and Calvin on the literary works of Mikotaj Rej. London, 1965. 324 l. Thesis—Univ. of London.

RAPPORTS entre protestants français et protestants hongrois, 1935—1946 [Prèf. d'Albert Finet] Paris, Editions de la Calanque [n.d.] 87 p.

RÉVÉSZ, Imre. The Hungarian Reformed Church and [the influence upon it of] Calvinism. **Evangelical quarterly,** 6: 398—421, 1934.

RÉVÉSZ, Imre. Kálvin élete és a kálvinizmus; a nagy reformátor halála emlékének háromszázados for dulatára. 3. kiad. Debreczen, Hegedüs és Sándor bizománya [1909] 364 p. (Révész Imre munkai, 1).

RUMPLER, Helmut. Der Protestantismus und die magyarische Nation. **Österreichische Osthefte,** 8 (6) 512—514, 1966.

SCHLÉGL, J. Die Beziehungen Heinrich Bullingers zu Ungarn. **Zwingliana,** 12 (5) 330—370, 1966.

SCHRAMM, Gottfried. Der polnische Adel und die Reformation, 1548—1607. Wiesbaden, Steiner, 1965. 380 p. (Veröffentlichungen des Instituts für Europäische Geschichte, Mainz, Bd. 36. Abt. Universalgeschichte).

SEBESTYÉN, J. Het Calvinisme in Hongarye uit politiek oogpunt beschouwd. **Anti-revolutionaire staatkunde,** 4 (2) 1—21, 1929.

SKWARCZYNSKI, Pawel. Szkice z dziejow reformacji w Europie Srodkowo-wschodniej [Historical sketch of the Reformation in central-east Europe] London, Odnowa, 1967. 173 p.

TAZBIR, Janusz. Les échos de la persécution des hérétiques occidentaux dans les polémiques religieuses en Pologne. **Bibliothèque d'humanisme et renaissance,** 34: 125—136, 1972.

TÓTH, Endre. Papa város plébá nosa és Kálvin Institiója [Der römisch-katholische Pfarrer der Stadt Papa und Calvins Institutio] (**In:** Kalvin és a kálvinismus; tanulmányok. As institutio négyszázadik évfordulójara irták a Debrecini M. Kir. Tisza Istvan-Tudományegyetem Református Hittudományi Karának tanarai és doctorai. Debrecen, Debrecen Szabad Királyi Város és a Tiszántúli: Református Egyhazkerület Konyvnyomda-Vállalata, 1936. p. 395—402).

TWOREK, Stanislaw. Dzialalósc oswiatowo kulturalna kalwinizmu malopolskiego, polowa XVI — polowa XVIII w. [The influence of the "malopolska" type of Calvinistic culture from mid-sixteenth to mid-eighteenth century] Wydawn, Lubelskie [1970] 394 p.

TWOREK, Stanislaw. Gimnazjum kalwinskie dystryktu lubelskiego i chelmskiego w Kocku. **Ordrodzenie. i Reformacja w Polsce,** 10: 117—139, 1965. [Fragment of his thesis: Szkolnictwie Kalwinskim w Malopolsce w XVI-XVIII w.]

TWOREK, Stanislaw, Lycee calviniste de la province de Petite-Pologne à Betzyce dans la première moitié du XVIIe siècle. **Annales Universitatis Mariae Curie-Sklodowska,** 17 (65) 155—194, 1962; 18 (66) 53—93, 1963.

TWOREK, Stanislaw. Materialy do dziejów kalwinizmu w Wielkim Ksiestwie Litewskim w XVI wieku. [Collection of papers (theses etc.) dealing with the action of Calvinism in the Lithuanian principality in the 16th century] **Odrodzenie i Reformacja w Polsce,** 4: 199—215, 1969.

TWOREK, Stanislaw. Program nauczania i prawa gimnazjum kalwinskiego w Belzycach w 1653 roku. [The teaching programme (syllabus) and the laws of the Calvinistic College in Belzycach in 1653] **Odrodzenie i Reformacja w Polsce,** 12: 225—235, 1967.

TWOREK, Stanislaw. Szkolnietwo kalwinskie w Malopolsce i jego zwiazki z innymi ósrodkami w kraju i za granicą w XVI-XVII w. [The Calvinistic school of thought in the malopolska region and its connections with other centres in the country and abroad in the 16th and 17th century. Thesis] rozprawa habilitacyjna. Lublin, 1966. 500 1.

TWOREK, Stanislaw. Z zagadnien organizacji zborów kalwinskich w Malopolsce w XVI-XVII w. [The organisation of Calvinistic works (i.e. papers etc) in "Malopolska" in the 16th and 17th century] **Rocznik Lubelski,** 8: 63—75, 1965.

TWOREK, Stanislaw. Z zagadnien ruchu kalwinskiego w Malopolsce. [The movement of Calvinism in "Malopolska"] **Rocznik Lubelski,** 10: 153—170, 1967.

VAN DER WOUDE, Cornelis. Een kerk jubilerend rondom haar belijdenis [Hungary and the 4th centenary of the 2nd Helvetic confession] **Gereformeerd weekblad,** 22 (47) 340—341, 1967.

VAN SCHELVEN, Aart Arnout. Het Calvinisme gedurende zijn bloeitijd; zijn uitbreiding en cultuurhistorische betekenis. III: Polen, Bohemen, Hongarije en Zevenburgen. Amsterdam, Ten Have, 1965. 176 p.

WEGIERSKI, Andrzej. Andreae Wengerscii Libri quattuor Slavoniae reformatae. Praefatione instruxit Ianussius Tazbir (Repr.) Varsoviae [Panstwowe Wydawn, Naukowe] 1973 (1679).

ZSINDELY, Andreas. Der Calvinismus in Ungarn. **Reformatio,** 8: 342—349, 1959.

Economics.

ADAMS, J. L. Theokratie, Kapitalismus und Demokratie. Eine Kritik an Max Webers Darstellung der protestantische Ethik. **Zeitschrift zür evangelische Ethik,** 12: 247—267, 1968.

BALL, Donald W. Catholics, Calvinists, and rational control; further explorations in the Weberian thesis. **Sociological analysis,** 26: 181—188, 1965.

BEBBINGTON, D. W. The Weber-Tawney thesis. **Christian graduate,** 25: 52—56, 1972.

BEER, Gil L. Cromwell's policy in its economic aspects. **Political science quarterly,** 17 (1) 46—70, 1902.

BERGIER, Jean Francois. Taux et l'intérêt et crédit à court terme à Genève dans la seconde moitié du XVIe siècie. Milano, Giuffrè, 1962. p. 91—119. (Estratto da Studi in onore di Amintore Fanfani, IV).

BESNARD, Philippe. Protestantisme et capitalisme; la controverse post-Weberienne. Paris, Colin, 1970. 427 p.

BÜRGIN, Alfred. Kapitalismus und Calvinismus; Versuch einer wirtschaftsgeschichtlichen und religionssoziologischen Untersuchung der Verhältnisse in Genf. im 16. und beginnenden 17. Jahrhundert. Basel, 1960. 224 p. Thesis—Basel. Also published by Keller, Starnberg, 1960.

BURRELL, Sidney Alexander. Calvinism, capitalism, and the middle classes; some afterthoughts on an old problem. **Journal of modern history,** 32: 129—141, 1960. **(Also in:** The role of religion in modern European history. Ed. by S.A. Burrell. New York, 1964. p. 37—44) (Main themes in European history, 1).

COLESON, Edward. Weber revisited; the reformation and economic development today. **Fides et historia,** 4: 73—84, 1972.

DEMARCHI, Franco. Calvinismo e capitalismo. **Protestantesimo,** 14: 225—230, 1959.

DIEPENHORST, Pieter Arie. De reformatie en het economisch leven. **Stemmen des tijds [Ref. nummer]** p. 146—174, 1917.

GEORGE, Charles H. English Calvinist opinion on usury, 1600—1640. **Journal of the history of ideas,** 18: 455—474, 1957.

GERRISH, Brian Albert. Capitalism and the decline of religion. **Maccormick quarterly,** 18: 12—19, 1965.

HUDSON, Winthrop Still. Weber thesis reexamined. **Church history,** 30: 88—102, 1961.

HYMA, Albert. The economic view of the Protestant Reformation **(In:** Green, Robert W., ed. Protestantism and its critics. Boston Health [1959]) (Problems in European civilization).

KINGDON, Robert McCune. Economic behaviour of ministers in Geneva in the middle of the sixteenth century. **Archiv für Reformationsgeschichte,** 50 (1) 33—39, 1959.

KOLKO, G. Critique of Max Weber's philosophy of history. **Ethics,** 70: 21—36, 1959.

KUCERA, John. Calvinism and the economic order. New York, 1926. 34 1. Thesis—Union Theological Seminary, New York.

LITTLE, David. Max Weber revisited; the Protestant ethic and the Puritan experience of order. **Harvard theological review,** 59: 415—428, 1966.

LOMBARDI, Franco. Galilei, Calvino, Rousseau; tre antesignani del tempo moderno. Firenze, Sansoni (1968) "Max Weber": p. 115—136. (**His** Soritti: saggi, 13).

LÜTHY, Herbert. Nochmals "Calvinismus und Kapitalismus." Über die Irrwege einer sozialhistorischen Diskussion. **Schweizerische Zeitschrift für Geschichte,** 17: 175—187, 1961; **Revue Suisse d'histoire,** 9: 129—156, 1961.

LÜTHY, Herbert. Le passé présent; combats d'idées de Calvin à Rousseau. Monaco, Du Rocher (1965) 269 p. (Collection "preuves") Also published in Spanish, by Il Malino, Bologna, 1971.

LÜTHY, Herbert. Protestantismus und Kapitalismus; die These Max Webers und die Folgen. **Merkur,** 19 (2) 101—119; (3) 226—242, 1965.

MANDROU, Renée. Capitalisme et protestantisme; la science et le mythe. **Revue historique,** 235 (1) 101—107, 1966.

MEYLAN, Henri. Un financier protestant à Lyon, ami de Calvin et de Bèze, Georges Obrecht, 1500—1569. **Bulletin philologique et historique,** 1964: 213—220.

MIEGGE, Mario. Etica protestante e "spirito" del capitalismo. **De Homine,** 19—20; 73—92, 1966.

MITCHELL, Robert M. The Weber thesis as tested by the writings of John Calvin and the English Puritans of the sixteenth and seventeenth centuries. Ann Arbor, Mich., 1969. 310 1. Thesis—Michigan State Univ.

NORWOOD, Frederick Abbott. The economic life and influence of the Protestant refugees during the sixteenth century. New Haven, 1941. 410 1. Thesis—Yale Univ., New Haven.

NORWOOD, Frederick Abbott. The reformation refugees as an economic force. Chicago, American Society for Church History, 1942. 205 p. (Studies in church history, 5).

O'BRIEN, George Augustine Thomas. An essay on the economic effects of the Reformation. New York, Kelley, 1970 (1923) 194 p. (Reprints of economic classics).

PAUL, Robert S. Weber and Calvinism; the effects of a "calling." **Canadian journal of theology,** 11: 25—41, 1965.

PEW, J. Howard. Our Reformed heritage. **Christian economics,** 14 (19) 1; 3, 1962; 16 (19) 1; 3, 1964.

RIEMERSMA, Jelle Coenraad. Religious factors in early Dutch capitalism, 1550—1560. The Hague, Mouton, 1968. 100 p. (Studies in the social sciences, 2).

ROBERTSON, Hector Menteith. Aspects of the rise of economic individualism; a criticism of Max Weber and his school. New York, Kelley & Millman, 1959. 223 p.

ROBINSON, Chalfant. Some economic results of the Protestant Reformation doctrines. **Princeton theological review,** 15: 623—644, 1917.

RYSKAMP, Henry J. Calvinism and economic life. **The Banner,** 94 (33) 9; 20, 1959.

SAMUELSSON, Kurt. Religion and economic action; a critique of Max Weber. Tr. from the Swedish by E. Geoffrey French. Ed. and with an introd. by D. C. Coleman. New

York, Harper & Row (1964) 156 p. (Researches in the social cultural and behavioral science) Original title: Ekonomi och religion.

SCHARF, Betty R. The sociological study of religion. London, Hutchinson Univ. Library, 1970. "Webers' sociology of religion": p. 132—157.

SOLT, Leo F. Puritanism, capitalism, democracy and the new science. **American historical review,** 73: 18—29, 1967.

STARK, Werner. Max Weber's sociology of religious belief. **Sociological analysis,** 25: 41—49, 1964.

STAUFFENEGGER, Roger. Réforme, richesse et pauvreté. **Revue d'histoire de l'église de France,** 52: 47—58, 1966.

STEWART, Herbert L. The business morals of the middle class — what do they owe to the Reformation. **Hibbert journal,** 40: 156—165, 1942.

TREVOR-ROPER, Hugh Redwald. The reformation and economic change. **(In:** Historical studies. London, Bowes & Bowes, 1961. v. 4, p. 19—29). **(Also in:** Capitalism and the reformation, ed. by M. J. Kitch. London, Longmans, 1967 and New York, Burnes & Noble, 1968. p. 24—36. (Problems and perspectives in history).

TROELTSCH, Ernst. The economic ethic of Calvinism **(In:** Green, Robert W., ed. Protestantism and capitalism; the Weber thesis and its critics. Boston, Heath, 1959. p. 21—28).

URBAN, Rudolf. Der ältere Calvinismus und der Kapitalismus. Marburg, Euker, 1931.

WEBER, Max. Die protestantische Ethik (2. durchges. und erw. Aufl., hrsg. von Johannes Winckelmann) München, Siebenstern Taschenbuch Verl. (1969; c1920) v. (Siebenbuch Taschenbuch, 53/54).

WEMYSS, Alice. Calvinismus et capitalisme. **Societé de l'histoire du protestantisme français. Bulletin,** 102: 33—36, 1956.

WIESENMÜLLER. Wirtschaftsethik Thomas von Aquins, Luthers und Calvins und das deutsche Unternehmertun des Vor- und Frühkapitalismus. [Erlangen-Neurenberg] c1968. 371 l. Thesis—Erlangen-Neurenberg.

England and Wales: General.

APPERSON, George Marshall, Jr. The problem of ecclesiastical authority in England, 1559—1589. Richmond, Va., 1964. 252 l. Thesis—Union Theological Seminary, Richmond, Va.

BAN, Joseph D. English Reformation: product of king or minister? **Church history,** 41 (2) 186—197, 1972.

BRASS, Maynard Fay. Moderate episcopacy, 1640—1662. Iowa City, Iowa, 1962. 372 l. Thesis—University of Iowa.

BRUSEN RASMUSSEN, Jens Jorgen. Den engelske kirke under Hendrik VIII og Edward, 1534-'53. **Dansk teologisk tidsskrift,** 28: 14—32, 1965.

BRUSEN RASMUSSEN, Jens Jorgen. Udforskningen af Englands kirkehistorie under Edward VI og Mary Tudor. **Dansk teologisk tidsskrift,** 24: 220—239, 1961.

BRUSEN RASMUSSEN, Jens Jorgen. Udforskningen af Englands kirkehistorie under Hendrik VIII. **Dansk teologisk tidsskrift,** 23: 90—114, 1960.

CARLSON, Arvid John. The bishops and the Queen; a study of "Puritan" Episcopal activity in early Elizabethan England, 1558—1566. (Ann Arbor) 1962. 324 p. Thesis—Princeton Univ.

CARRUTHERS, Samuel William. The everyday work of the Westminster Assembly. With a foreword by Thos. C. Pears, jr. Philadelphia, Presbyterian Historical Society, 1943. 210 p.

CARTER, Charles Sydney. The English church and the Reformation; 2nd ed. London, Longmans, 1925. 150 p.

COULTON, C. G. The Reformation and British freedom. **Modern churchman,** 25 (?) 512—528, 1935.

CREMEANS, Charles Davis. The reception of Calvinistic thought in England. Urbana, University of Illinois Press, 1949. 127 p. (Illinois studies in the social sciences, v. 31 no. 1).

DAMBORIENA, Prudencio. Fe catolica e iglesias y sectas de la Reforma. Madrid, Razon y Fe, 1961. "Cisma y herejia en Inglaterra": p. 139—192.

DANNENFELDT, Karl H. The church of the Renaissance and Reformation; decline and reform from 1300 to 1600. Saint Louis, Concordia (c1970) "The English and Scottish Reformations": p. 91—103.

DAVIES, Godfrey. English political sermons, 1603—1640. **Huntington library quarterly,** 3: 1—22, 1939/40.

DEWAR, Michael Willoughby. How far is the Westminster Assembly an expression of seventeenth-century Anglican theology? Belfast, 1960. 301 p. Thesis-Queens Univ., Belfast.

DICKENS, Arthur Goeffrey. The English Reformation. London, Batsford [1968] 374 p.

DUGMORE, Clifford William. The mass and the English Reformers. London, Macmillan, 1958. 262 p.

FLETCHER, Joseph Smith. The Reformation in Northern England; six lectures. Port Washington, N.Y., Kennikat Press (1971, 1925) 191 p.

GEORGE, Charles H. & GEORGE Katherine. The protestant mind of English reformation, 1570—1640. Princeton, N. J., University Press, 1961. 452 p.

GULLEY, Frank. The influence of Heinrich Bullinger and the Tigurine tradition upon the English church in the sixteenth century. Nashville, Tenn., 1961. 303 1. Thesis—Vanderbilt Univ., Nashville, Tenn.

HALL, Thomas Cuming. Continental Protestantism and English dissent. **Hibbert journal**, 33: 413—420, 1935.

HARGRAVE, O. T. The doctrine of predestination in the English reformation. Nashville, Tenn., 1966. 287 1. Thesis—Vanderbilt Univ., Nashville, Tenn.

HAUGAARD, William P. Elizabeth and the English reformation; the struggle for a stable settlement of religion. Cambridge, University Press, 1968. 392 p.

HEXTER, Jack H. The problem of the Presbyterian independents. **American historical review,** 44: 29—49, 1938/39.

HILL, Christopher. Die gesellschaftlichen und ökonomischen Folgen der Reformation in England (**In:** Beiträge zum neuen Geschichtsbild; zum 60. Geburtstag von Alfred Meusel. Hrsg. von Fritz Klein und Joachim Streisand. Berlin, Rutten & Loening, 1956, p. 88—104).

HOE, Yung Chi. The origin of parliamentary sovereignty or "mixed" monarchy; being a study of the political implications of Calvinism and Bodenism, from the mid-sixteenth to the mid-seventeenth century, chiefly in France and England. Shangai, Commercial Press, 1935. "Calvin in Britain": p. 124—177.

HUDSON, Winthrop Still. The Scottish effort to Presbyterianize the Church of England during the early months of the Long Parliament. **Church history,** 8: 255—282, 1939.

HUEHNS, Gertrude. Antinomianism in English history with special reference to the period 1640—1660. London, Cresset Press, 1951. 199 p. Thesis—London.

HUELIN, G. Peter Martyr and the English Reformation. London, 1954. Thesis—London University.

KNECHT, R. J. The early Reformation in England and France; a comparison. **History,** 57 (2) 1—16, 1972.

KNOX, S. J. A study of the English Genevan exiles and their influence on the rise of Nonconformity. Dublin, 1952. Thesis—Trinity College, Dublin.

KRESSNER, Helmut. Schweizer Ursprünge des anglikanischen Staatskirchentums. Gütersloh, Bertelsman, 1953. 135 p. (Schriften des Vereins für Reformationsgeschichte, 170, Jg. 59).

MCDILL, Joseph Moody. Milton and the pattern of Calvinism. [Nashville] 1942, 432 1. Thesis—Vanderbilt Univ., Nashville, Tenn.

MCGILL, John. Anglican attitudes towards Continental Protestantism in the reign of Elizabeth. New Haven, Conn., 1948. 304 1. Thesis—Yale Univ.

MESSENGER, E. C. The Reformation, the mass and priesthood; a documented history with special reference to the question of Anglican orders. London, Longmans, Green (1936—37) 2v.

PALLISER, D. M. The reformation in York, 1534—1553. York, St. Anthony's Press, 1971. 32 p. (Univ. of York. Borthwick Institute of Historical Research. Borthwick Papers. No. 40).

PARKER, Thomas Henry Louis. The Church of England and Calvin. **Theology,** 53: 91—94, 1950.

PARKER, Thomas Maynard. The English Reformation to 1558; 2nd ed. London, Oxford Univ. Press, 1966. 168 p. (Oxford paperbacks university series, 2).

PAUCK, Wilhelm. Das Reich Gottes auf Erden. Utopie und Wirklichkeit; eine Untersuchung zu Butzers "De regno Christi" und zur englischen Staatskirche des 16. Jahrhunderts. Berlin, De Gruyter, 1928. 208 p. (Arbeiten zur Kirchengeschichte, 10).

PETRI, Frederick Charles. The Presbyterian doctrine of the Lord's Supper for today. Nashville, Tenn., 1964. "The doctrine of the Lord's Supper in the Westminster standards": p. 2—24. Thesis—Vanderbilt Univ., Nashville, Tenn.

PILL, David Halton. The English Reformation, 1529—58. Totowa, N. J. Rowman and Littlefield; London, Univ. of London Press, 1973. 224 p.

PORTER, Harry Culverwell. Reformation and reaction in Tudor Cambridge. Cambridge, University Press, 1958. 461 p.

POWICKE, **Sir** Frederick Maurice. The Reformation in England. London, Oxford Univ. Press, 1961. 153 p. (Oxford paperbacks, no. 24)

REID, William Stanford. Knox's attitude to the English Reformation. **Westminster theological journal,** 25: 1—32, 1963/64.

ROGERS, Jack Bartlett. Scripture in the Westminster Confession; a problem of historical interpretation for American Presbyterianism. Kampen, Kok, 1966. 475 p. Thesis—Vrije Univ., Amsterdam. Also published by Eerdmans, Grand Rapids, 1967.

RUPP, Ernst Gordon. Studies in the making of the English Protestant tradition, mainly in the reign of Henry VIII. Cambridge, University Press, 1966 (1947) 220 p.

SATGÉ, J. C. de The composition of the Articles **(In:** The Articles of the Church of England, with an introd. by H. E. W. Turner. London, Mowbray, 1964. p. 1—24) (Star books).

SIMON, Joan. The Reformation and English education. **Past and present,** 11: 48—65, 1957.

SLAVIN, Arthur Joseph, **ed.** Humanism, reform, and reformation in England. New York, Wiley (c1969) 229 p. (Major issues in history).

SMITH, Herbert Maynard. Henry VIII and the Reformation. London, Macmillan, 1962. 480 p.

SMITHEN, Frederick James. Continental Protestantism and the English Reformation. London, Clarke (1927) 256 p.

SOBERS, Sharon Jo. George Herbert and seventeenth-century English Calvinism. Cincinnati, Ohio, 1972. Thesis—University of Cincinnati.

SOLT, Leo F. Revolutionary Calvinist parties in England under Elizabeth I and Charles I. **Church history,** 27 (3) 234—239, 1958.

SUTHERLAND, Nicola Mary. The origins of Queen Elizabeth's relations with the Huguenots, 1559-'62. **Huguenot Society of London. Proceedings,** 20 (6) 626—648, 1964/65.

SYKES, Norman. Old priest and new presbyter [Episcopacy and Presbyterianism since the Reformation with especial relation to the Churches of England and Scotland; being the Gunning lectures delivered in the University of Edinburgh 1953—54 and the Edward Cadbury lectures in the University of Birmingham, 1954—55]. Cambridge, Cambridge Univ. Press, 1956. 266 p.

TAYLOR, F. J. The Holy Spirit in the thought of the English reformers. **Churchman,** 64: 16—27, 1950.

THOMPSON, W. D. J. C. The two regiments; a study of the development of the theory of church and state during the Reformation, with particular reference to England. Cambridge, [1959/60?] Thesis—Cambridge Univ.

USHER, Roland Greene, **ed.** The Presbyterian movement in the reign of Queen Elizabeth as illustrated by the minute book of the Dedham Classis, 1582—1589 (Comp. by R. Parker) London, Historical Society of Great Britain, 1905. 105 p. (Camden third ser., 8).

WALZER, Michael. The revolution of the saints; a study in the origins of radical politics. Cambridge, Mass. Harvard Univ. Press, 1965. "The Marian exiles": p. 92—113.

WARFIELD, Benjamin Breckinridge. The Westminster Assembly and its work. New York, Oxford Univ. Press, 1931. 400 p.

WERRELL, Ralph S. Church and state in Reformation England. **Evangelical quarterly,** 38: 219—232, 1966.

WESTMINSTER Divines; the form of presbyterial church government (**In:** The Reformation of the church; a collection of Reformed and Puritan documents on church issues. Selected with introd. notes by Iain Murray. London, Banner of Truth Trust 1965. p. 207—233).

WILCOX, Thomas. The necessity for Reformation; the admonition to Parliament, 1572. (**In:** The Reformation of the church; a collection of Reformed and Puritan documents on church issues. Selected, with introd. notes by Iain Murray. London, Banner of Truth Trust, 1965. p. 85—98).

WILLIAMS, G. W. Reformation views of church history. London, Lutterworth, 1970. 85 p.

WILLIAMS, Glanmor. Welsh Reformation essays. Cardiff, University of Wales Press, 1967. 219 p.

WILSON, Derek A. A Tudor tapestry; men, women and society in Reformation England. [Pittsburgh] University of Pittsburgh Press [1972] (Also published by Heineman, London) 287 p.

WOODHOUSE, Hugh Frederick. The doctrine of the church in Anglican theology, 1547—1603. London, S. P. C. K., 1954. 233 p. Thesis—University of Dublin. Also published by Macmillan, New York.

YOST, John K. The Christian humanism of the English reformers, 1525—1555; a study in English Renaissance humanism. Durham. N. C., 1965. 510 1. Thesis—Duke Univ., Durham, N.C.

YULE, George. The independents; decentralised Calvinism in 17th century England. **Reformed theological review,** 15 (2) 38—49, 1956.

ZIA, Daniel Z. V. The causes of the Anglican Reformation under Henry VIII. Nashville, Tenn., 1928. 111 1. Thesis—Vanderbilt Univ., Nashville, Tenn.

England: Bible.

ALEXANDER, J. D. The Genevan version of the Bible: its origin, translation and influence. Oxford, 1957. Thesis—Christ College, Oxford University.

BUTTERWORTH, Charles C. The English primers, 1529—1545; their publication and connection with the English Bible and the Reformation. Repr. of the 1953 ed. New York, Octagon Press, 1971. 353 p.

BUTTERWORTH, Charles C. & CHESTER, Allan G. George Joye, 1495?—1553; a chapter in the history of the English Bible and the English Reformation. Philadelphia, University of Pennsylvania Press, 1962. 293 p.

CRAIG, H. jr. Geneva Bible as a political document. **Pacific historical review,** 7: 40—49, 1938.

DANNER, Dan Gordon. The theology of the Genevan Bible of 1560; a study in English Protestantism. (Iowa City) 1969 (c1970) 223 1. Thesis—Univ. of Iowa.

LIDGETT, J. Scott. The reformation and the English Bible. **Contemporary review,** 70: 562—569, 1935.

LUPTON, Lewis Frederick. A history of the Geneva Bible. London. Fauconberg Press, 1966- v.

METZGER, B. M. The Geneva Bible of 1560. **Theology today,** 17: 339—352, 1960.

MORRISON, Stanley. The Geneva Bible: die Genfer Bibel der Engländer. **Atlantis,** 26 (7) 313—319, 1954.

RYRIE, Charles Caldwell. Calvinistic emphases in the Geneva and

Bishop's Bibles. **Bibliotheca sacra,** 122: 23—30, 1965.

England: Thomas Cranmer.

BOURNE, E. C. E. Cranmer and the liturgy of 1552. **Church quarterly review,** 80 (?) 382—390, 1954.

BROMILEY, Geoffrey William. Cranmer **(In:** Gerrish, Brian Albert, **ed.** Reformers in profile. Philadelphia, Fortress Press [1967] p. 165—191).

BROMILEY, Geoffrey William. Thomas Cranmer, archbishop and martyr. London, Church Book Room Press [1956] 126 p.

BROMILEY, Geoffrey William. Thomas Cranmer; theologian. London, Lutterworth [1956] 108 p. Also published by Oxford Univ. Press, New York, 1956.

BROOKS, Peter. Thomas Cranmer's doctrine of the eucharist; an essay in historical development. New York, Seabury [1965] 134 p.

BROOKS, Peter. Thomas Cranmer's doctrine of the sacraments. [Cambridge, 1959/60?] Thesis—Cambridge Univ.

COATES. R. J. The origin and development of Archbishop Cranmer's eucharistic doctrine. Bristol, 1957. Thesis—Bristol Univ.

COX, G. S. R. Thomas Cranmer **(In:** Puritan and Reformed studies. Conference, 16th, London, 1965. Approaches to Reformation of the Church. [n.p.] 1966. p. 34—45).

CRANMER, Thomas. **Abp. of Canterbury.** Selected writings; with an introd. and bibliography by Carl S. Meyer. London, S. P. C. K., 1961. 109 p. (Seraph series).

CRANMER, Thomas. **Abp. of Canterbury.** The work of Thomas Cranmer. Introduced by J. I. Packer. Ed. by G. E. Duffield. Appleford, Berkshire, Sutton Courtenay Press (1964) 370 p. (Courtenay library of Reformation classics, 2).

DAVIES, Horton. From Cranmer to Hooker, 1534—1603; worship and theology in England. Princeton, Princeton Univ. Press, 1969. 482 p.

DE ZEEUW, Pieter. Thomas Cranmer, 21 Maart 1556. **Belijden en beleven,** 19 (43/44) 6, 1962.

DIX, Gregory. Dixit Cranmer et non timuit. **Church quarterly review,** 74 (?) 45—76, 1948. 75 (?) 44—60, 1948.

DU BOULAY, F. R. H. Archbishop Cranmer and the Canterbury temporalities. **English historical review,** 67: 19—36, 1952.

FORMAN, John P. Cranmer, Tudor diplomacy and primitive discipline **(In:** Sixteenth century essays and studies, 1971. v. 2, p. 108—118).

HUTCHINSON, Francis Ernest. Cranmer and the English Reformation. London, English Universities Press [1961] 188 p. (Teach yourself history.)

LLEWELLIN, Frederick George. Reformers and the Reformation. London, Jakeman & Carner, 1921. "Cranmer": p. 142—167.

LOANE, Marcus L. Masters of the European Reformation. London, Church Book Room Press, 1954. "Cranmer": p. 179—241.

McGEE, E. K. Cranmer and nominalism. **Harvard theological review,** 57: 189—216, 1964.

MCLELLAND, Joseph C. Reformation and its significance today. Philadelphia, Westminster Press [1962] "Thomas Cranmer and our common prayer": p. 79—90.

ODENDAAL, A. A. Die reformatoriese standpunt van Thomas Cranmer. **Nederduitse Gereformeerde teologiese tydskrif,** 9 (1) 8—28, 1968.

POLLARD, Albert Frederick. Thomas Cranmer and the English Reformation, 1489—1556. [London] Cassel, 1965 (1905) 384 p.

PRUETT, Gordon Earl. Thomas Cranmer and the eucharistic controversy in the Reformation. Princeton, N.J., 1968. 401 1. Thesis—Princeton Theological Seminary.

RATCLIFF, E. C. The liturgical work of archbishop Cranmer. **Journal of ecclesiastical history,** 7 (2) 189—203, 1957.

RICE, H. A. L. Thomas Cranmer. **History today,** 6: 478—485, 1956.

RICHARDSON, C. C. Zwingli and Cranmer on the eucharist (Cranmer dixit et contradixit) Evanston, 1949.

RIDLEY, Jasper Godwin. Thomas Cranmer. Oxford, Clarendon Press, 1962.

SMYTH, Charles Hugh Egerton. Cranmer and the Reformation under Edward VI. Westpost, Conn., Greenwood Press (1970, 1926) 315 p.

TIMMS, G. B. Dixit Cranmer; a reply to Dom Gregory. London, 1947. **(Also in: Church quarterly review,** 143: 217—234, 1946; 144: 35—51, 1947).

WARNER, C. A. F. In defence of Cranmer. **Churchman,** 83 (4) 277—283, 1969.

England: Oliver and Thomas Cromwell.

ABBOT, Wilbur Cortez, **ed.** The writings and speeches of Oliver Cromwell. Cambridge, Harvard Univ. Press, 1937—45. 3v.

ASHLEY, Maurice Percy. The greatness of Oliver Cromwell. New York, Collier, 1962 (c1957) 383 p.

BEER, Gil L. Cromwell's policy in its economic aspects. **Political science quarterly,** 17 (1) 46—70, 1902.

BOYER, Richard E. **ed.** Oliver Cromwell and the Puritan revolt; failure of a man or a faith? Lexington, Mass., Heath, 1966. 90 p. (Problems in European civilization).

BUCHAN, John. Oliver Cromwell. London, Hodder and Stoughton, 1934. 458 p.

DICKENS, Arthur Geoffrey. Thomas Cromwell and the English Reformation. London, English Universities Press [1959] 192 p. (Teach yourself history).

DRAKE, G. Ideology of Oliver Cromwell. **Church history**, 35: 259—272, 1966.

ELTON, Geoffrey Rudolph. King or minister?; the man behind the Henrician reformation **History,** 39 (137) 216—232, 1955.

ELTON, Geoffrey Rudolph. Policy and police; the enforcement of the Reformation in the age of Thomas Cromwell. Cambridge, University Press, 1972. 446 p.

ELTON, Geoffrey Rudolph. The political creed of Thomas Cromwell. **Royal historical society. Transactions,** 1956: 69—92.

ELTON, Geoffrey Rudolph. Thomas Cromwell; the moving spirit of the English reformation. **History today,** 6: 528—535, 1956.

GAGNEBIN, Bernard. Cromwell, protecteur d'Angleterre. Pref. de E. Rossier. Genève, Editions Labor,

1941. 184 p. (Collection les Vainquers, 6).

GROSHEIDE, Daniël. Cromwell naar het oordeel van zijn Nederlandse tijdgenoten. Amsterdam, Noord-Hollandse Uitg. Mij., 1951. 270 p. Thesis—Vrije Univ.

MATRAT, J. Oliver Cromwell. Paris, Hachette, 1970. 248 p.

PETTIT, Paul Warsh. The religion of Oliver Cromwell, with special reference to his conception of providence. Edinburgh, 1952. 307 p. Thesis—Univ. of Edinburgh.

SILBERDICK, Barbara Jane. The political thought of Oliver Cromwell; the search for a stable constitutional order. New Haven, 1962. 276 1. Thesis—Yale Univ., New Haven.

SOLT, Leo F. Saints in arms: Puritanism and democracy in Cromwell's army. Stanford, Calif, Stanford University Press, 1959. 150 p. (Stanford, Calif, Stanford studies in history, economics and political science, 18).

TOWSE, M. W. The preservation of public order in Cromwellian London. [Cambridge? 1965/66?] Thesis—Cambridge Univ.

WEDGWOOD, Cicely Veronica. Oliver Cromwell. London, Duckworths [1939] 144 p. (Great lives [82]).

England: Puritans, etc.

BATSEL, John David. The development of the doctrine of conversion in English Puritanism from Thomas Cartwright to Richard Baxter. Nashville, Tenn., 1962. 114 1. Thesis—Vanderbilt Univ., Nashville, Tenn.

BRAUER, Jerald C. Reflections on the nature of English Puritanism. **Church history,** 23 (6) 99—108, 1954.

BRESLOW, Marvin Arthur. A mirror of England; English Puritan views of foreign nations, 1618—1640. Cambridge, Mass., Harvard University Press, 1970. 178 p.

BYINGTON, Ezra Hoyt. The Puritan in England and New England. Boston, Little, Brown, 1900. 457 p.

COLLINSON, Patrick. The Elizabethan Puritan movement. London, Cape, 1967. 528 p.

CUDDIGAN, John D., **S.J.** Three Puritan peers: their religious beliefs and activities in the Puritan revolution. Minneapolis, Minn., 1969. 320 l. Thesis—University of Minnesota.

DAVIES, Horton. The worship of the English Puritans. Westminster, Dacre Press, [1948] 304 p. Thesis—Oxford Univ.

EUSDEN, John Dykstra. Puritans, lawyers and politics in early seventeenth-century England. Hamden, Archon Books, 1968 (c1958) 238 p.

FLYNN, John Stephen. The influence of Puritanism on the political and religious thought of the English. London, Murray, 1920. 257 p.

FOSTER, Herbert Darling. Polical theories of Calvinists before the Puritan exodus to America. **American historical review,** 20: 481—503, 1916.

GARDINER, Samuel Rawson. **ed.** The constitutional documents of the Puritan revolution. 1625—1660. Oxford, Clarendon Press, 1906. 476 p.

GARRETT, Christina Hallowell. The Marian exiles; a study in the origins of Elizabethan Puritanism. Cambridge, University Press, 1966 (1938). 388 p.

GEORGE, Charles H. A social interpretation of English Puritanism. **Journal of modern history, 25 (12)** 327—342, 1953.

GIBSON, Richard Merritt. John Rogers: religion and politics in the life of a Puritan saint. Columbus, Ohio, 1973. 294 l. Thesis- Ohio State University.

HALLER, William. Liberty and reformation in the Puritan revolution. New York, Columbia Univ. Press, 1955. 410 p.

HALLER. William. The rise of Puritanism; or, The way to the New Jerusalem as set forth in pulpit and press from Thomas Cartwright to John Lilburne and John Milton, 1570—1643. New York, Columbia Univ. Press, 1938. 464 p.

HENSON, Herbert Hensley. Puritanism in England. London, Hodder and Stoughton, 1912. 294 p.

HILL, Christopher. Society and puritanism in prerevolutionary England. London, Secker and Warburg, c1964. 520 p.

JAMES, Margaret. Social problems and policies during the Puritan revolution, 1640—1660. London, Routledge, 1930. 430 p. (Studies in economic and social history).

KNAPPEN, Marshall Mason. Tudor Puritanism, a chapter in the history of idealism. Chicago, University of Chicago Press, 1939. 555 p.

LITTLE, David. The logic of order; an examination of the sources of the Puritan-Anglican controversy and of their relation to prevailing legal conceptions of corporation in the late 16th and 17th century in England. Cambridge, Mass., 1963. 328 1. Thesis—Harvard Univ., Cambridge, Mass.

MACLEAR, James Fulton. The Puritan Party, 1603—1643; a study in a lost Reformation. Chicago, 1947. 340 1. Thesis—Univ. of Chicago.

MITCHELL, Robert M. The Weber thesis as tested by the writings of John Calvin and the English puritans of the sixteenth and seventeenth centuries. East Lansing, Mich., 1969. Thesis—Michigan State Univ. **(Excerpts in: Fides et historia,** 4: 55—72, 1972).

MORGANS, John Ivor. The national and international aspects of Puritan eschatology, 1640—1660; a comparative study. Hartford, Conn., 1970. 357 l. Thesis—Hartford Seminary Foundation.

NEW, John F. H. Anglican and Puritan; the basis of their opposition, 1558—1640. London, Black, 1964. 140 p.

NEWTON, J. A. Puritanism in the diocese of York (excluding Nottinghamshire), 1603—1640 London, 1956. Thesis—Univ. of London.

PACKER, James Inneil. The Puritan treatment of justification. **Evangelical quarterly,** 24: 131—143, 1952.

PEARSON, Andrew Forrett Scott. Church and state; political aspects of sixteenth century Puritanism. Cambridge, University Press, 1928. 153 p.

PEARSON, Andrew Forrett Scott. Thomas Cartwright and Elizabethan Puritanism, 1535—1603. Cambridge, University Press, 1925. 511 p.

PRIMUS, John Henry. The role of the convenant doctrine in the Puritanism of John Hooper. **Nederlands archief voor kerkgeschiedenis,** N.S., 48 (2) 182—196, 1968.

PURITANISM in East Devon and the New England emigrants, 1625—1630. **Devon and Cornwall notes and queries,** 18 (?) 86—90, 1934.

PURITANISM: a panel [Contains: Brauer, J. C. Reflections on the nature of English Puritanism. Mosse G. L.: Puritan political thought and the "cases of conscience". Simpson, A.: Saints in arms; English Puritanism as political utopianism). **Church history,** 23: 99—125, 1954.

ROGERS, Richard & WARD, Samuel. Two Elizabethan Puritan diaries. Ed., with introd. by M. M. Knappen. Chicago, American society of church history [c1933] 148 p. (Studies in church history, 7)

SCHNEIDER, Herbert W. The Puritan mind. Ann Arbor, Mich., University of Michigan Press, 1958. 267 p.

SCHNUCKER, Robert Victor. Views of selected Puritans, 1560—1630, on marriage and human sexuality. Iowa City, Iowa, 1969. 736 l. Thesis—University of Iowa.

SCHOLES, Percy A. Those dreadful Puritans [re: music]. **Musical opinion,** 58: 210—212, 1934.

SIMPSON, Alan. Puritanism in Old and New England. Chicago, University of Chicago Press (1955) 125 p. (Charles R. Walgreen Foundation lectures).

STEINMETZ, David Curtis. Reformers in the wings. Philadelphia, Fortress Press (1971) "John Hooper; the birth of the Puritan spirit": p. 143—150.

TATHAM, Geoffrey Bulmer. The Puritans in power; a study in the history of the English church from 1640 to 1660. Cambridge, University Press, 1913. 282 p.

TIPSON, Lynn Baird. The development of a Puritan understanding of conversion. New Haven, Conn., 1972. 368 l. Thesis—Yale University.

TOON, Peter. Puritan eschatology (**In:** Puritan and Reformed Studies Conference, 19th, London 1968. The manifold grace of God. Papers. [London?] 1968. p. 49—60).

TOON, Peter. Puritans and Calvinism. Swengel, Pa., Reiner, 1973. 110 p.

TRINTERUD, Leonard J. The origins of Puritanism. **Church history,** 20 (3) 37—57, 1951.

VANDERMOLEN, Ronald Jay. Anglican against Puritan; ideological origins during the Marian exile. **Church history,** 42 (1) 45—57, 1973.

YULE, George. Theological developments in Elizabethan Puritanism. **Journal of religious history,** 1 (1/6) 16—25, 1960.

England: Reformers.

BARKER, William Shirmer. John Bradford's writings; an example of English reformation piety. Nashville, Tenn., 1970. 321 1. Thesis—Vanderbilt Univ., Nashville, Tenn.

BREWARD, Ian. William Perkins and the ideal of the ministry in the Elisabethan church. **Reformed theological review,** 24 (3) 1965.

BREWARD, Ian. **ed.** The work of William Perkins. Appleford, Courtenay Press (n.d.). 662p. (Courtenay library of Reformation classics).

CARTWRIGHT, Thomas. Cartwrightiana; ed. by Albert Peel and Leland H. Carlson. London, Published for the Sir Halley Stewart Trust [by] Allen and Unwin (1951) 268 p. (Elizabethan nonconformist texts v. 1).

CHALKER, William Houston. Calvin and some seventeenth century English Calvinists; a comparison of their thought through an examination of their doctrines of the knowledge of God, faith and assurance. Durham, N.C., 1961. 312 p. Thesis—Duke Univ., Durham, N. C.

DEIBLER, Edwin Clyde. Bishop John Hooper, a link connecting the Reformation thought of Ulrich Zwingli and the Zurich tradition with the earliest English pietistic Puritanism, Philadelphia, Penn. 1970. 586 l. Thesis—Temple University.

DEWAR, Michael Willoughby. Bishop Joseph Hall, 1574—1656; an ecumenical calvinist churchman. **Churchman,** 80: 194—199, 1966.

DEWAR, Michael Willoughby. An ecumenical Calvinist churchman: Bishop Joseph Hall, 1574—1656. **Evangelical quarterly,** 40: 111—128, 1968.

DUFFIELD, Gervase E., **ed.** The work of William Tyndale. Appleford, Courtenay Press (n.d.) 446 p. (Courtenay library of Reformation classics).

HAUGAARD, William P. John Calvin and the Catechism of Alexander Nowell. **Archiv für Reformationsgeschichte,** 61 (1) 35—49, 1970.

HUGHES, Philip Edgecumbe. Theology of the English Reformers. Grand Rapids, Eerdmans, 1965. 283 p. Also published by Hodder & Stoughton, London, 1966.

HUTCHINS, C. H. Nicholas Ridley; English reformator, theologian and martyr. **Evangelical quarterly,** 41: 232—237, 1969.

JOHNSTON, Philip F. The life of John Bradford, the Manchester martyr, c.1510—1555. Oxford, 1964. Thesis—Oxford Univ.

KIRBY, Ethyn Williams. William Prynne; a study in Puritanism. Cambridge, Harvard Univ. Press, 1931. 228 p.

KNAPPEN, Marshall Mason. William Tyndale, first English Puritan. **Church history,** 5: 201—215, 1936.

MAYOR, Stephen. Teaching of John Owen concerning the Lord's Supper. **Scottish journal of theology,** 18: 170—181, 1965.

MORRELL, George William. The systematic theology of Richard Hooker. 1969. 178 l. Thesis—Pacific School of Religion.

MULLER, James Arthur. Stephen Gardiner and the Tudor reaction. New York, Octagon Books, 1970 (1926) 429 p.

NUCKOLS, Thomas W. A holy commonwealth; the political thought of Richard Baxter. Durham, N. C., 1968. 261 1. Thesis—Duke Univ., Durham, N. C.

PACKER, James Innell. The redemption and restoration of man in the thought of Richard Baxter. Oxford, 1955. Thesis—Balliol, Oxford Univ.

PERKINS, William. The work of William Perkins. Introd. and ed. by Ian Breward. Appleford, Courtenay, 1970. 646 p. (Courtenay library of Reformation classics).

PHILLIPS, James McJunkin. Between conscience and the law; the ethics of Richard Baxter, 1615—1691. Princeton, N. J. 1959. 381 1. Thesis—Princeton University.

POWICKE, Frederick J. A life of the Reverend Richard Baxter, 1615—1691. Boston, Houghton Mifflin, 1924. 326 p. Also published by: Cape, London.

PRIEBE, Victor Lewis. The covenant theology of William Perkins. Madison, N. J., 1967. 290 l. Thesis—Drew University.

REES, Augustus Herbert. The doctrine of justification in the Anglican Reformers. **Theology,** N.S., 2, 1939.

ROSS, Don Smith. The role of John Hooper in the religious controversies of the reign of Edward VI in England. (Iowa City) 1968 (c1969) 234 l. Thesis—Univ. of Iowa.

RUPP, Ernest Gordon. John Bradford, martyr; ob. 1 July 1555. **London quarterly & Holborn review,** 188 (1) 50—55, 1963.

WALLACE, Dewey D. The life and thought of John Owen to 1660; a study of the significance of Calvinist theology in English Puritanism. Ann Arbor, 1965. 336 l. Thesis—Princeton Theological Seminary.

WEST, William Morris S. John Hooper and the origins of Puritanism. **Baptist quarterly,** 15 (8/10) 346—368, 1954; 16 (1/1) 22—46; (2/4) 67—88, 1955.

WEST, William Morris S. A study of John Hooper, with special reference to his contact with Henry Bullinger. Zürich, 1955. 230 l. Thesis—Zürich Univ.

WRIGHT, Louis B. William Perkins; Elizabethan apostle of "Practical divinity". **Huntington library quarterly,** 3 (1) 171—196, 1940.

England: Strangers' churches.

COWELL, Henry J. The 16th century English-speaking refugee churches at Geneva and Frankfort. **Huguenot Society of London. Proceedings,** 16: 209—230, 1937/41.

COWELL, Henry J. Strasbourg Protestant refugees in England, 1547—1553. **Huguenot Society of London. Proceedings,** 14: 333—384, 1929/33.

CRAMER, W. Die Londoner Fremdengemeinde von 1550—1553. **Reformierte Kirchenzeitung,** 64: 50—; 58—; 65—; 73—; 81—, 1914.

FIRPO, Luigi. La comunità evangelica italiani a Londra nel XVI secolo ed i suoi rapporti con Ginevra **(In:** Roma, Facolta Valdesi di Teologica. Ginevra et l'Italia; recolta di studi promosa dalla Facolta Valdesi di Teologica di Roma a cura Delio Cantimori Firenze, Sansoni [et al. 1959] p. 307—412) (Bibliotheca storica Sansoni, 34).

Die FRANZÖSISCH-REFORMIERTEN. Flüchtlings- oder Huguenottenstiftungen in England. **Der deutsche Hugenott,** 26: 23—26, 1962.

HAUBEN, Paul J. A Spanish Calvinist church in Elisabethan London, 1559-'65. **Church history,** 34 (1) 50—56, 1965.

KINDER, Gordon. Two unpublished letters of Charles Censin, minister of the Threedneedle church concerning the affair of Cassiodora de Rena. **Huguenot Society of London. Proceedings,** 22 (1) 51—59 [n.d.].

NORWOOD, Frederick Abbott. The Strangers' Model Churches in 16th Century England **(In:** Reformation studies; essays in honour of R. H. Bainton. Ed: F. H. Littell. Richmond, Knox [c1962] p. 181—198).

SLADE M. W. John a Lasco and the English Reformation. Bristol, 1953. Thesis—Bristol University.

France: General; studies on certain places.

ALBARIC, Ernest. Essai sur l'esprit national du protestantisme français au 16e et au 17e siècle. Genève, Slatkine Reprints, 1969 (1853) 56 p. Thesis—Strasbourg.

ARMSTRONG, Brian G. Calvinism and the Amyraut heresy; Protestant scholasticism and humanism in seventeenth-century France. Madison, University of Wisconsin Press, 1969. 330 p.

ARNAUD, Eugène. Histoire de protestants du Dauphiné aux 16e, 17e et 18e siècles. Genève, Slatkine Reprints, 1970. 3 v.

AUTIN, Albert. L'echec de la Réforme en France au XVIe siècle. Contribution à l'histoire du sentiment religieux. Paris, Colin, 1918. 286 p.

BEAME, E. M. The limits of toleration in sixteenth-century France. **Studies in the renaissance,** 13: 250—265, 1966.

BELS, Pierre. Le mariage des protestants français jusqu'en 1685. Fondements doctrinaux et pratique juridique. Paris, Pichon et Durand-Auzias, 1968. 264 p. (Bibliothèque d'histoire du droit et droit romain, 12).

BOISSET, Jean. Orientations naturelles du protestantisme français. **Annales,** 19 (4) 717—730, 1964.

BORNARD, Roger. La Réformation dans le Pays de Vaud. **Almanach Jean Calvin,** 1936: 24—27.

BOSC, Henri. Der französische Protestantismus im Jahre 1561. **Der deutsche Hugenott,** 28: 46—52, 1964.

BOSC, Henri. Les grandes heures du Protestantisme à Montpellier. Pref.: J. Germain. Montpellier, Reschly, 1957. 124 p.

BOSC, Henri. Der Protestantismus im Jahre 1561, das Julie-Edikt und das Colloquium von Poissy. **Der deutsche Hugenott,** 27: 83—90; 122—125, 1963.

BOURGUET, Pierre. Le IVe jubilé centenaire de l'église réformée de France. **Cahiers français,** 39: 6—8, 1959.

CAILLIET, Emile. The reformed tradition in the life and thought of France. **Theology today,** 1 (3) 349—360, 1944.

CARBONNIER, Jean. Le colloque de Poissy. **Foi et vie,** 60 (5/6) 43—52, 1961.

COURTHIAL, Pierre. Die Calvinisme in Frankryk. **Die Kerkblad,** 67 (1772) 5—6, 1964.

COWIE, Leonard W. The Reformation of the sixteenth century. New York, Putnam, 1970. "Calvinism in France and the Netherlands" p. 47—60. Also published by Longmans, Toronto.

DALE, J. A. Persecuted Calvinists of Sarlat. **Hibbert journal,** 37: 311—321, 1939.

DE FRENNE, M. Die protestantische Reformation in Guînes im 16. und 17. Jahrhundert. **Der deusche Hugenott,** 33 (2) 39—50; (3) 66—76; (4) 103—108, 1969.

DESGRAVES, Louis. Aspects des controverses entre catholiques et protestants dans le Sud-Ouest, entre 1580 et 1630. **Annales du Midi,** 76: 153—187, 1964.

EVENNETT, Henry Outram. The cardinal of Lorraine and the colloquy of Poissy. **Cambridge historical journal,** 2: 133—150, 1927.

FAGUET, Emile. La tragédie du française au XVIe siècle, 1550—1600. Paris, 1968, 1912. Thesis—Paris.

FERMAUD, Jean Claude. Le Protestantisme dans l'arondissement de Draguignan, de 1540 à 1715. Saint-Raphaël, Association culturelle de l'église réformée, 1965. 64 p.

FOLTZ, Magdalene. Begründung, Auftrag und Bestand der Bibliothek über den französischen Protestantismus in Speyer. **Blätter für pfälzische Kirchengeschichte und religiöse Volkskunde,** 31: 82—85, 1964.

FRANCE. Laws, 1589—1610 (Henri IV) Das Edikt von Nantes. Das

Edikt von Fontainebleau. Deutsche ungekurzte Ausg., hrsg. vom Deutschen Hugenottenverein, mit einem Vorw. von Ernst Mengin. Flensburg, Gross, 1963. 93 p. (Rechts-Urkunden zur Geschichte der Hugenotten).

FROMENTAL, Jacques. La Réforme en Bourgogne aux XVIe et XVIIe siècles. Paris, les Belles lettres, 1968. 189 p. (Publications de l'Université de Dijon, 41).

GARRISSON, Robert. Quelques notes sur l'église réformée de Bruniquel, 1561—1685. **Societé de l'histoire du protestantisme française. Bulletin,** 111 (7—9) 240—249, 1965.

HEMPSALL, David S. The Languedoc 1520—1540; a study of pre-Calvinist heresy in France. **Archiv für Reformationsgeschichte,** 62: 225—243, 1972.

HÉRANCOURT, Wilhem. Ein Bild des Gemeindelebens aus den ersten 50 Jahren der französisch-reformierten Kirche. **Der deutsche Hugenott,** 22: 46—56; 57—84; 105—112, 1958.

HOE, Yung Chi. The origin of parliamentary sovereignty or "mixed" monarchy; being a study of the political implications of Calvinism and Bodenism, from the mid-sixteenth to the mid-seventeenth century, chiefly in France and England. Shangai, Commercial Press, 1935. "Calvin in France": p. 58—123.

HOFFMAN, Glen J. French Calvinism; a subversive movement in the sixteenth century. **Northwestern Missouri State College Studies,** 18: 11—36, 1954.

HOFFMAN, Glen J. French Calvinism; a "subversive" movement in the Spanish Netherlands **(In:** The Dawn of modern civilization; studies in Renaissance, Reformation and other topics, presented to honor Albert Hyma. Ed. by **Kenneth** A. Strand. Ann Arbor, Mich., Ann Arbor Publications [1962] p. 197—221).

HOFFMANN, Gottfried. Eine biblisch-theologische Begründung der Liturgie im französischen Calvinismus. **Liturgisches Jahrbuch,** 6B: 68—75, 1956.

KELLER, H. E. Castellios Übertragung der Bible ins Französische. **Romanische Forschungen,** 71: 383—403, 1959.

KELLY, Caleb Guyer. French Protestanism, 1559—1562. Baltimore, Johns Hopkins Univ., 1918. 185 p. (Johns Hopkins University studies in historical and political science, ser. 36, no. 4).

KINGDON, Robert McCune. Calvinism and democracy; some political implications of debates on French reformed church government, 1562—1572. **American historical review,** 69: 393—401, 1964.

KINGDON, Robert McCune. Démocratie et l'église; aspects de la querelle disciplinaire chez les calvinistes au XVIe siècle. **Bollettino della Società di Studi Valdesi,** 87: 47—53, 1966.

KINGDON, Robert McCune. The political resistance of the Calvinists in France and the low Countries. **Church history,** 27 (3) 220—233, 1958.

KINGDON, Robert McCune. Some French reactions to the Council of Trent. **Church history,** 33: 149—156, 1964.

KOENIGSBERGER, Helmut Georg. The organization of revolutionary parties in France and the Netherlands during the sixteenth century. **Journal of modern history,** 27: 335—351, 1955.

LARDANS, Daniel R. La réforme à Luneray 1557—1957 [Conférence prononcée au Temple du Luneray le 15 Juin 1957, lars du IVe centenaire de la fondation de l'église] Luneray, 1957. 24 1.

LART, Charles Edmund. Protestant churches of Angers and Saumur, **Huguenot Society of London. Proceedings**. 15: 36—45.

LECERF, Auguste. Études calvinistes, recueillies et introduities par André Schlemmer. Neuchâtel, Delachaux et Niestle [c1949] "Les destinées du calvinisme dans le protestantisme français": p. 125—134; "Inspiration et grammaire d'après les théologiens protestants du XVIIe siècle": p. 135—148. (Série théologique de l'actualité protestante).

LECERF, Auguste. The Reformed faith in France; a historical survey (**In:** International Conference of Calvinists. 1st, London, 1932. The reformed faith commonly called Calvinism. Report of the International Conference held in May, 1932. London, Sovereign Grace Union [1932] p. 45—53).

LÉONARD, Emile G. Les origines de la Réforme en France. **Revue de théologie et d'action evangeliques,** 3: 291—309, 1943 (**Also in:** Bourilly, E. Calvin et la Réforme en France [No. special de la revue Etudes evangeliques, 1946] Aix-en-Provence [n.d.] p. 23—41).

LIGOU, Daniel. Le Protestantisme en France de 1598 à 1715. Paris, Société d'édition d'enseignement supérieur, 1968. 277 p. (Regards sur l'histoire, II: Histoire générale).

MENGIN, Ernst. Die vierzehn Märtyrer von Meaux; ein Beitrag zur Frühgeschichte der Reformation in Frankreich. **Der deutsche Hugenott,** 34 (1) 3—17; (3) 34—41, 1970.

MEYLAN, Henri. Problèmes de discipline ecclésiastique au 16. siècle. Une ordonnance du comte de Montmayeur pour le Chablais protestant (**In:** Festschrift Oskar Vasella zum 60. Geburtstag am 15. Mai 1964, überreicht vom Schülern und Freunden. Freiburg, Schweiz, 1964. p. 272—285).

MOOTE, A. L. French crown versus its judicial and financial officials, 1615—'83. **Journal of modern history.** 34: 146—160, 1962.

MOREAU, Gérard. Un colporteur calviniste en 1563. **Sociéte de l'histoire du protestantisme français. Bulletin,** 118: 1—31, 1972.

MOUDY, James M. Boussuet and the Protestants; a chapter in the seventeenth-century struggle for religious alliance in France. Durham, 1953. 349 1. Thesis—Duke Univ., Durham.

MOURS, Samuel. Des églises réformées en France; tableaux et cartes. Pref. de P. Bourguet. Paris, Librairie Protestante, 1958. 236 p.

MOURS, Samuel. Le Protestantisme en France. Paris, Librairie Protestante, 1959- v.

MOUSSEAUX, M. Des origines françaises de la réforme. **Societé de l'histoire du protestantisme français. Bulletin,** 107: 146—165, 1961.

MURALT, Leonhard von. Der Historiker und die Geschichte; ausgewählte Aufsätze und Vorträge. Zurich, 1960. "Über den Ursprung der Reformation in Frankreich": p. 219—227.

NAUTA, Doede. Godsdienstgesprek te Poissy, 1561. **Centraal weekblad voor de Gereformeerde Kerken in Nederland,** 9 (38) 323, 1961.

PATTERSON, W. Brown. James I and the Huguenot synod of Tonneins of 1614. **Harvard theological review,** 65: 241—270, 1972.

PERRIRAZ, Louis. Histoire de la théologie reformée française. Neuchâtel, Messeiler, 1961. [Calvin in France] p. 36—77.

PINEAUX, Jacques. La poésie des Protestants de langue française, 1559—1598. Paris, Klincksieck, 1971. 523 p.

POLENZ, Gottlob von. Geschichte des französischen Calvinismus zum Gnadenedikt von Nîmes im Jahre 1629. Aalen, Scientia Verl., 1964. 5 v.

POPKIN, Richard Henry. Scepticism and the counter-reformation in France. **Archiv für Reformationsgeschichte,** 51 (1) 58—89, 1960.

RABELON, Jean Pierre. Les débuts de la Réforme en France; commémorés aux archives nationales. **Societé de l'histoire du protestantisme français. Bulletin,** 105: 145—151, 1959.

RICHARD, Michel. La vie quotidienne des protestants sous l'Ancien Régime. Paris, Hachette, 1967.

RICHARD, Willy. Untersuchungen zur Genesis der reformierten Kirchenterminologie der Westschweiz und Frankreichs mit besonderer Berücksichtigung der Namengebung. Bern, Francke, 1959. 260 p. (Romanica Helvetica, v. 57).

ROELKER, Nancy Lymon. The appeal of Calvinism to French noblewomen in the 16th century; a study in psychohistory. **Journal of interdisciplinary history,** 2: 1972.

ROESSLER, Hellmuth. Der Calvinismus; Versuch einer Erfassung und Würdigung seiner Grundlagen und Wirkungen. Bremen, Schünemann [195?-] "Frankreich und die Geistordnung Calvins": p. 9—20. (Schriften der Wittheit zu Bremen. Reihe D: Abhandlungen und Vorträge, Bd. 19, Hft. 3).

ROMANE-MUSCULUS, Paul. Les abjurations de protestants à Toulouse entre l'Edit de Nantes et la Révolution. **Annales du Midi,** 71 (47) 283—295, 1959.

ROMANE-MUSCULUS, Paul. Baptêmes en l'église Saint Pierre des Cuisines de Toulouse de Réformes ayout abjuré. **Annales du Midi,** 72 (51) 325—337, 1960.

ROMANE-MUSCULUS. Paul. L'-Eglise réformée de Pouzauges des origines à L'Edit de Nantes. **Societé de l'histoire du protestantisme français Bulletin,** 109: 65—81, 1963.

ROMANE-MUSCULUS, Paul. Les protestants de Toulouse en 1568. **Societé de l'histoire du protestantisme français. Bulletin,** 107: 69—93, 1961.

ROMANE-MUSCULUS, Paul. Les Protestants de Toulouse en 1574. **Societé de l'histoire du protestantisme français. Bulletin,** 110: (10—12) 272—283, 1964.

SCHNETZLER, Jacques. L'evolution religieuse d'une communauté cévenole aux temps modernes. Les Vans. **Cahiers d'histoire,** 11: 37—47, 1966.

SIMPSON, Lesley Byrd. The struggle for Provence, 1593—1596. Berkeley, Calif, 1929. 23 p. (University of California publications in history, 17, 1).

SOCIETE DE L'HISTOIRE DU PROTESTANTISME FRANÇAIS. Les réformés à la fin du XVIe siècle; relevés de documents dans les fonds d'archives. Paris, 1972.

SOMAN, A. Armininiasm in France; the D'Huisseau incident.

Journal of the history of ideas, 28: 597—600, 1967.

STEPHAN. Raoul. Gestalten und Kräfte des französischen Protestantismus [übers. von] Gerda Onken-Joswish und Franz Oesterwitz. Vorw. von Marc Boegner. München, Claudius, 1967. 369 p. Original title: Histoire du protestantisme français.

SYPHER, George Wylie. La Popeliniere's Histoire de France; a case of historical objectivity and religious censorship. **Journal of the history of ideas,** 24: 41—54, 1963.

TAYLOR, Henry Osborn. Thought and expression in the sixteenth century; 2nd rev. ed. New York, Ungar, 1962. v. 1, book 3: "The French mind".

TROCMÉ, Etienne. L'église réformée de la Rochelle jusqu'en 1628. **Societé de l'histoire du protestantisme français. Bulletin,** 99 (7—9) 113—199, 1952.

VAN DER WOUDE, Cornelis. Reformatie in Frankrijk [Calvin and France in his letters] **Gereformeerd weekblad,** 28 (5/6) 18—19, 1972.

VIÉNOT, John. Histoire de la Réforme Française des origines à l'Edit de Nantes. Paris, Fischbacher, 1925. 478 p.

VIERHUNDERT-JAHRFEIER der reformierten Kirche Frankreichs, 1559—1959. **Der deutsche Hugenott,** 23 (2—4) 68—72, 1959.

VOELTZEL, René Frédéric. Vraie et fausse église selon les théologiens protestants français du XVIIe siècle. Paris, Presses Universitaires de France, 1956. 180 p. (Etudes d'histoire et de philosophie religieuses, 44).

WALDER, Ernst. Religionsvergleiche des 16. Jahrhunderts; 2. durchges. und erw. Aufl. Bern, Lang, 1960-'61. 71 p. (Quellen zur neueren Geschichte, 7, 8).

WEBER, B. C. Conference of Bayonne 1565; an episode in Franco-Spanish diplomacy. **Journal of modern history,** 11: 1—22, 1939.

WEIGERT, Roger-Armand. Cent ans d'erudition nationale; la Société de l'histoire du protestantisme français, 1852—1952. **Société de l'histoire du protestantisme français. Bulletin,** 99 (10—12) 219—250, 1952.

WHITE, Janet. French protestant poetry of the 16th and early 17th centuries. **Huguenot Society of London. Proceedings,** 19 (6) 295—312, 1959.

France: Huguenots; wars; events; Bartholomew's massacre.

AIRO-FARULLA, Joseph Anthony. The political opposition of the Huguenots to Henry IV, 1589 to 1598. (Seattle, c1969) 206 l. Thesis—Univ. of Washington.

BALESTIÉ, Francis. Le Montalbanais, des dragonnades au réveil. Montauban, Lormand, 1971. 159 p.

BERNOULLI, Wilhelm. Das Diakonenamt bei den Hugenotten. Greifensee, Schweizerische Reformierte Diakonenhaus, 1965—1968. 3 v.

BOURGUET, Pierre. La croix huguenote. Genève, Labor et Fides, 1966. 65 p. Also published by Les Berges et les Mages, Paris.

BOURGUET, Pierre. Huguenots; le soubriquet mystérieux. Paris, Les Berges et les Mages (1959) 87 p.

BRONOWSKI, Jacob & MAZLISH, Bruce. The Western intellectual tradition, from Leonardo to Hegel. Freeport, Books for Libraries Press,

1971. "The French Huguenots": p. 99—106.

CANTALOUBE, C. La réforme en France vue d'un village cévenol; Saint-Laurent-le-Minier, une petite paroisse du diocèse de Nîmes. Paris, du Cerf, 1951. 309 p. (Unam sanctam, 22).

CARDAUNS, Ludwig. Die Lehre vom Widerstandsrecht des Volkes gegen die rechtmässige Obrigkeit im Luthertum und im Calvinismus des 16. Jahrhunderts. Darmstadt, Wissenschaftliche Buchgesellschaft 1973. 123 p. (Thesis—1903). „Die Theorie vom Widerstandsrecht in der Zeit der französischen Religionskriege", p. 49—111.

CORDEWIENER, André. Prêche calviniste à Boeschepe. **Societé de l'histoire du protestantisme français. Bulletin,** 112 (4—6) 105—120 1966.

COUDY, Julien. Les guerres de religion; il y a toujours un reporter, avec deux prèf. par le H. Bosc et A. M. Roguet. Paris, Julliard, 1962. 442 p.

COUDY, Julien. The Huguenot wars. Tr. by Julie Kernan. Philadelphia, Chilton, 1969. 405 p.

DAVIS, Natalie Zemon. Strikes and salvation at Lyons. **Archiv für Reformationsgeschichte,** 56: 48—64, 1965.

DUFOUR, Alain. L'affaire de Maligny, Lyon, 4—5 Septembre 1560, vue à Fravers la correspondance de Calvin et de Bèze. Lyon, Faculté des lettres, 1963. From: **Cahiers d'histoire,** 8 (3) 269—280, 1963.

DURAND, C. Die Bartholomäus-Nacht; in heutiger Sicht. **Der deutsche Hugenott,** 22 (1) 6—14, 1958.

ENGLAND, Sylvia Lennie. The massacre at Saint Bartholomew. London, Long, 1938. 284 p.

ERLANGER, Philippe. Le massacre de la Saint-Barthélemy. Paris, Gallimard, 1960. 322 p. (Trente journées qui ont fait la France, 12).

GAGG, Robert P. Kirche im Feuer; das Leben der südfranzösischen Hugenottenkirche nach dem Todesurteil durch Ludwig XIV. Zurich, Zwingli [1961?] 387 p.

GOTHIE, P. Remontrance et supplication de ceux de l'église réformée de Valenciennes 1567. **Societé de l'histoire du protestantisme français. Bulletin,** 108: 22—24, 1962.

Les GUERRES de religion. (Paris) Delpire [1968?] Documents (in portfolio) (Documents, no. 9).

HÉRITIER, Jean. Catherine de Medici. Tr. by Charlotte Haldane. New York, St. Martin's Press (1963). 480 p.

KEMPFF, Dionysius. Frankryk is daardeur berowe [Bartholomeusnag] **Die Kerkblad,** 75 (2164) 3, 1972.

LONG, Jean-Denis. La Réforme et les guerres de religion en Dauphiné de 1560 à l'édit de Nantes, 1598. Genève, Slatkine Reprints, 1970 (1856) 319 p.

MANOURY, Karl. Die Belagerung von La Rochelle, 1572-'73. **Die Hugenottenkirche,** Beiheft März—Mai 1961: 1—12.

MANOURY, Karl. Hintergründe der Bartholomaüsnacht. **Die Hugenottenkirche,** 15: 25—26, 1962.

NEALE, John Ernest. The age of Catherine de Medici. London, Cape, 1943. 111 p.

NOGUÈRES, Henri. The massacre of Saint Bartholomew; tr. by Claire

Elaine Engel. London, Allen & Unwin, 1962. 168 p.

PABLO, Jean de. Die Armee von La Rochelle. **Die Hugenottenkirche, Beiheft,** 22 (5—6) 1—7, 1969.

PALM, Franklin Charles. Calvinism and the religious wars. New York, Fertig, 1971 (c1932) 117 p. "Calvinism and the religious wars in France": p. 34—64.

PONT, A. D. By die herdenking van die Bartholomeusnag-bloedbad in Parys, 24 Augustus 1572. **Die Hervormer,** 59 (5) 10—11, 16; 18, 1968.

ROMIER, Lucien. Les protestants français à la veille des guerres civiles. **Revue d'histoire,** 124: 1—51; 226—286, 1917.

ROTHROCK, George A. Jr. Some aspects of early Bourbon policy toward the Huguenots. **Church history,** 29: 17—24, 1960.

SALMON, John Hearsey McMillan, **ed.** The french wars of religion; how important were religious factors? Ed. with introd. Boston, Heath, 1967. 104 p.

SAVORY, D. L. Pope Gregory XIII and the massacre of St. Bartholomew. **Huguenot Society of London. Proceedings** 17 (2): 93—109.

SEGOND, A. Une histoire romantique des Camizards. **Société de l'histoire du protestantisme française. Bulletin,** 108 (7—9) 166—169, 1962.

SUTHERLAND, Nicola Mary. Calvinism and the conspiracy of Amboise. **History,** 47: 111—138, 1962.

SUTHERLAND, Nicola Mary. The massacre of St. Bartholomew and the European conflict 1559—1572. London, Macmillan, 1973. 373 p.

THOMPSON, James Westfall. The wars of religion in France, 1559—1576; the Huguenots, Catherine de Medici and Philip II. Chicago, University of Chicago Press, 1909. 635 p.

TILLEY, Arthur Augustus. The French wars of religion. London, Society for Promoting Christian Knowledge, 1919. 54 p. (Helps for the students of history, no. 8).

TREVOR-ROPER, Hugh Redwald. Pogrom [re: Bartholomew's massacre] **New statesman,** 64: 230—231, 1962.

VAN DER VYVER, Gert Christoffel Petrus. Die Bartholomeüsnag, 23—24 Augustus 1572. **Die Kerkblad,** 75 (2163) 11, 13; (2164) 10, 1972.

VAN DER WOUDE, Cornelis. St. Bartholomeus-nacht, 1572- 24 Augustus 1972. **Gereformeerd weekblad,** 28 (7—8) 27—28, 1972.

WALZER, Michael. The revolution of the saints; a study in the origins of radical politics. Cambridge, Mass., Harvard Univ. Press, 1965. "The Huguenots": p. 68—91.

WILKINSON, Maurice. A history of the League or Sainte Union 1576—1595. Glasgow, Jackson & Wylie, 1929. 223 p.

WILKINSON, Maurice. The last phase of the League in Provence, 1588—1598. London, Longmans, Green, 1909. 84 p.

France: Important personalities.

AMBERT, Joachim Marie Jean Jacques Alexandre Jules. Du Plessis-Mornay; ou, Études historiques et politiques sur la situation de la France de 1549 à 1623 (Reimpr. de l'ed. de Paris, 1848) Genève, Slatkine Reprints, 1970. 562 p.

ANSERMIN, Silvia Laura. La poésie religieuse de Marguerite de Navarre et Vittoria Colonna. Boulder, Col., 1966. 200 l. Thesis—University of Colorado.

BERTHAULT, E. A. Mathurin Cordier et l'enseignement chez les premiers calvinistes (Réimpr. de l'-ed. de Paris, 1876) Genève, Slatkine Reprints, 1970. 89 p.

BIRON, Armand de Gontaut, **baron** de. The letters and documents of Armand de Gontaut, Baron de Biron, Marshal of France, 1524—1592. Collected by Sidney Hellman Ehrman; ed., with an introd., by James Westfall Thompson. Berkeley, Calif., University of California Press, 1936. 2v.

BLOT, Georges. Le dernier jour chez Coligny. Piece et quatre actes et en deux parties représentée pour la première fois à Lyon le 23 avril 1925 a l'occasion de la "Semaine Protestante". 3e ed. Carrières-sous-Poissy, La Cause [1971].

BOISSET, Jean. La religion de Clément Marot. **Societé de l'histoire de protestantisme française. Bulletin,** 114 (9—12) 487—506, 1968.

BOSC, P. Henry. Der Admiral Gaspard de Coligny. **Der deutsche Hugenott,** 36 (4) 121—129, 1972 [et al].

BUISSON, F. Note additionelle sur la Réforme française; les apôtres de la tolérance **(In:** Etudes sur la Réforme; a propos du quatrième centenaire de la Réforme. Paris, Colin, 1919, p. 707—718).

BUYS, Pieter Willem. Waarom die sluipmoord op Gaspard de Coligny. **Die Kerkblad,** 75 (2164) 8—9, 1972.

CALLOT, Pierre-Simon. Jean Guiton, maire de La Rochelle, et le siège de 1628. Introd. par Olga de Saint-Affrique. Réimpr. de l'edition de 1880 accompagnée de plusiers documents. La Rochelle, Quartier Latin, 1967. 135 p.

CHRISTOL, Marguerite. La dépouille de Gaspard de Coligny. **Société de l'histoire du protestantisme français. Bulletin,** 111 (4—6) 136—141, 1965.

COLIGNY; protestants et catholiques en France au XVIe siècle. [Paris] Archives nationales [1972] 142 p. [Catalogue of an exhibition held Oct. 1972 — Jan. 1973 at the Hôtel de Rohan].

COWELL, Henry J. Gaspard de Coligny. **Huguenot Society of London. Proceedings,** 18: 140—149.

DE ZEEUW, Pieter. Casper de Coligny, 24 Aug. 1572. **Belijden en beleven,** 19 (52) 6, 1962.

ELTZ-HOFFMANN, Lieselotte. Protestanten aus romanischen Ländern; sechs Lebensbilder [Von Lieselotte Hoffman] Basel, Reinhardt [1956] "Gaspard de Coligny": p. 9—38.

ENGEL, Claire Élaine. L'Amiral de Coligny. Genève, Labor et Fides, 1967. 330 p.

GUGGENHEIM, Ann H. Calvinism and the political elite of sixteenth century Nimes. [New York? n.d.] 352. p. Thesis—New York Union Graduate School.

GUGGENHEIM, Ann H. The Calvinist notables of Nimes during the era of the religious wars. **The sixteenth century journal,** 3: 80—96, 1972.

GUILLAUME, Paul. Les Du Tillet, seigneurs de La Bussière. Gien, Jeanne d'Arc [n.d.] 8 p.

HELLER, H. Marguerite of Navarre and the Reformers of Meaux. **Bibliotheque d'humanisme et renaissance,** 33 (2) 271—310, 1971.

HEMARDINQUER, Jean-Jacques. Les protestants de Grenoble au XVIe siècle d'après des études récentes. **Societé de l'histoire du protestantisme français. Bulletin,** 111 (1—3) 15—23, 1965.

HIGMAN, Francis Montgomery. A lost letter by Charles de Jonvelliers. **Bibliotheque d'humanisme et renaissance,** 23: 556—566, 1961.

HURST, Quentin. Henry of Navarre. London, 1938. 319 p.

JENKINS-BLAISDEL, Charmarie. Renée de France between Reform and Counter-Reform. **Archiv für Reformationsgeschichte,** 63: 196—225, 1972.

LEFANU, William Richard. Thomas Vantrollier, printer & bookseller. **Huguenot Society of London. Proceedings,** 20 (1) 12—25, 1959.

MORNAY, Charlotte Arbaleste de. A Huguenot family in the 16th century; the memoirs of Phillippe de Mornay, sieur du Plessis Marly, written by his wife. Tr. by Lucy Crump, with an introd. London, Routledge [1926?] 300 p. (Broadway translation).

MORNAY, Philippe de, **seigneur du Plessis-Marly called du Plessis-Mornay.** Memoires et correspondence, pour servir à l'histoire de la Réformation et des guerres civiles et religieuses en France, 1571—1623. Ed. complète publiée sur les manuscrits originaux, par A.-D. de la Fontenelle de Vaudoré et P.-R. Auguis. Paris, 1969 (1824-'25) 12 v. (6863 p.).

MOUSSIEGT, P. Hotman et Du Plessis-Mornay; théories politques des réformés au 16e siècle; réimpr. de l'ed. de 1899. Genève, Slatkine Reprints, 1970. 71 p.

MURET, Ph. François Varlut et Alexandre Dayke, martyrs calvinistes a tournai en 1562. **Societé de l'histoire du protestantisme français. Bulletin,** 110 (1—3) 19—53 1964.

NABONNE, Bernard. Jeanne d'Albret; reine des Huguenots. Paris, Hachette, 1945. 284 p.

PABLO, Jean de. Gaspard de Coligny als Feldherr. **Die Hugenottenkirche. Beiheft,** 6 (6) 1—48, 1961—62; 23 (10) 12, 1970; 24 (1) 1—14, 1971.

PALM, Franklin Charles. Politics and religion in sixteenth-century France; a study of the career of Henry of Montmorency-Damville, uncrowned king of the South. Gloucester, Mass., Smith, 1969 (c1927) 299 p.

PATRY, Raoul. Philippe du Plessis-Mornay. **Almanach Jean Calvin,** 1935.

PATRY, Raoul. Philippe du Plessis-Mornay; un huguenot homme d'état, 1539—1623. Paris, Fishbacher, 1933. 655 p.

PEARSON, Hesketh. Henry of Navarre. London, Heinemann, 1963. 249 p.

RICHTER, Mario. Il discours de la vie et de la mort de Philippe Du Plessis-Mornay. Milano, Vite e pensiero, 1964. 85 p.

ROELKER, Nancy Lyman. Queen of Navarre; Jean d'Albret. Cambridge, Harvard Univ. Press, 1968. 503 p.

ROELKER, Nancy Lyman. The role of noblewomen in the French Reformation. **Archiv für Reformationsgeschichte,** 63: 168—195, 1972.

RUSCITO, Enrico. Renée de France, duchesse de Ferrare et ses relations avec Jean Calvin. Genève, 1965. 151 p. Thesis—Genève.

SALLEY, Claudia Louise. Jacques Lefevre d'Étaples; heir of the Dutch Reformers of the fifteenth century (**In:** The Dawn of modern civilization; studies in Renaissance, Reformation and other topics, presented to honor Albert Hyma. Ed. by Kenneth A. Strand. Ann Arbor, Mich., Ann Arbor Publications [1962] p. 75—124).

SAULNIER, Verdun L. La correspondance de Marguerite de Navarre; complément au répertoire. **Bibliotheque d'humanisme et renaissance,** 33 (3) 571—604, 1971.

SAULNIER, Verdun L. Martin Pontus et Marguerite de Navarre; la réforme lyonnaise et les sources de l'Heptaméron. **Bibliotheque d'humanisme et renaissance,** 21: 557—594, 1959.

SCHMIDT, Charles Guillaume Adolphe. Gérard Roussel, prédicateur de la reine Marguerite de Navarre. Mémoire servant à l'histoire des premières tentatives faites pour introduire la Réformation en France. (Réimpr. de l'ed. de Strasbourg, 1845). Genève, Slatkine Reprints, 1970. 246 p.

SEDGWICK, Henry Dwight. Henry of Navarre. Indianapolis, Bobbs-Merrill, 1930. 324 p.

SEDGWICK, Henry Dwight. The house of Guise. Indianapolis, N.Y., Bobbs-Merrill (c1938). 324 p.

SHIMIZU, Junko. Conflict of loyalties: religion in the career of Gaspard de Coligny, Admiral of France, 1519—1572. Medford, Mass., 1969. 325 l. Thesis—Tufts University.

SICHEL, Edith Helen. Catherine de' Medici and the French Reformation. London, Dawsons, 1969 (1905) 329 p.

SICHEL, Edith Helen. The later years of Catherine de Medici (repr.) London, Dawsons, 1969 (1908) 445 p.

SMITH, David Baird. François Hotman [Life and writings]. **Scottish historical review,** 13: 328—365, 1916.

STROHL, Henri. De Marguerite de Navarre à Louise Scheppler; quelques étapes de l'evolution de la pieté protestante en France. Strasbourg, Librairie évangélique, 1926. 126 p.

TAIT, Leslie Gordon. Pierre de Moulin, 1568—1658, Huguenot theologian. Edinburgh, 1955. 272 l. Thesis—Edinburgh Univ.

WALTHER, Daniel. Marguerite d'Angoulême and the French Lutherans; a study in pre-Calvin reformation in France. **Andrews university seminary studies,** 2: 137—155, 1964; 3: 49—65, 1965.

WEBB, Charmarie Jenkins. Royalty and reform; the predicament of Reneé de France, 1510—1575. [Medford, Mass.] 1969. 655 p. Thesis—Tufts Univ.

WHITEHEAD, Arthur Whiston. Gaspard de Coligny, Admiral of France. London, Methuen, 1904. 387 p.

France: Synods & confessions

ARMOGATHE, J. R. Quelques réflexions sur la confession de foi de la Rochelle. **Societé de l'histoire du protestantisme français. Bulletin,** 117 (4—6) 201—213, 1971.

BAKHUIZEN VAN DEN BRINK, Jan Nicolaas. La Confession de foi des églises réformées de France, de 1559, et la Confession des Pays-Bas, de 1561. **Commission de l'histoire des eglises Wallone. Bulletin,** 5 (6) 3—28, 1959.

BAKHUIZEN VAN DEN BRINK, Jan Nicolaas. Ecclesia II: een bundel opstellen; uitg. ter gelegenheid van zijn afscheid als hoogleraar der Rijksuniversiteit te Leiden. Leiden, Nijhoff, 1966. "La Confession de foi des églises réformées de France, de 1559, et la Confession des Pays-Bas, de 1561": p. 309—335.

DEDDENS, D. De eerste Synode der Franse Gereformeerde kerken te Parys. **Lucerna,** 1 (3) 99—120, 1959.

HALASKI, Karl. Studien zur Überlieferungsgeschichte der Confession de foi von 1559. **Reformierte Kirchenzeitung,** 106: 51—54, 1965.

JAHR, Hannelore. Studien zur Überlieferungsgeschichte der Confession de foi von 1559. (Neukirchen-Vluyn) Verlag des Erziehungsvereins, 1964. 162 p. (Beiträge zur Geschichte und Lehre der Reformierten Kirche, 16. Bd.).

KEMPFF, Dionysius. La Rochelle, 2—11 April 1571; Hervorming en Frankryk. **Die Kerkblad,** 74 (2123) 6—7, 1971.

LÉONARD, Emile. G. Légende et histoire du Synode de 1559. **Etudes evangéliques,** 19: 12—27, 1959.

LONGEIRET, Maurice. Le synode de 1559 et les églises réformées évangéliques. **Etudes evangéliques,** 2: 58—67, 1959.

MÉJAN, F & ROBERT, D. La quatrième centenaire de la confession de foi de La Rochelle. **Societé de l'histoire du protestantisme français. Bulletin,** 117 (4—6) 317—320, 1971.

POUJOL, Jacques. De la Confession de foi de 1559 à la Conjuration d' Amboise. **Société de l'histoire du protestantisme français. Bulletin,** 119: 158—177, 1973.

REULOS, Michel. L'organisation des églises réformées françaises et le synode de 1559. **Societé de l'histoire du protestantisme français. Bulletin,** 105: 9—24, 1959.

SAVIGNAC, Jean de. Confession de la Rochelle. **Les cahiers calvinistes,** 11 (3) 3—5, 1962.

STAUFFER, Richard. Brève histoire de la Confession de la Rochelle. **Societé de l'histoire du protestantisme français. Bulletin,** 117 (7—9) 355—366, 1971.

VAN ITTERZON, G. P. De eerste nationale synode van Parijs. **Hervormd weekblad — de Geref. Kerk,** 70: 300—302, 1958/59. **(Also in:** Belijnd belijden. Kampen, Kok, 1971. p. 30—36).

Geneva see Switzerland.

Germany and Austria.

ADAM, Johann. Evangelische Kirchengeschichte der Stadt Strassburg bis zur französischen Revolution. Strassburg, Heitz, 1922. 496 p.

ANRICH, Gustav. Die strassburger Reformation nach ihrer religiösen Eigenart und ihrer Bedeutung für den Gesamtprotestantismus. **Die Christliche Welt,** 19: 583—587; 602—606; 630—634, 1905.

ANRICH, Gustav. Die strassburger Reformation nach ihrer religiösen Eigenart und ihrer Bedeutung für den Gesamtprotestantismus. **Die christliche Welt,** 19: 583; 602; 630, 1905.

BARON, Hans. Religion and politics in the German imperial cities during the Reformation. **English historical review,** 52: 405—419, 614—633, 1937.

BENRATH, Gustav Adolf. Reformierte Kirchengeschichtsschreibung an der Universität Heidelberg im 16 und 17. Jahrhundert. Heidelberg, 1959. 150 p. Thesis—Heidelberg. Also published in the series: Veröffentlichungen des Vereins für pfälzische Kirchengeschichte, Bd. 9.

BERNOULLI. Wilhelm. Das Diakonenamt bei Kurfürst Friedrich dem Frommen von der Pfalz. Greifensee, Schweizerisches Reformierte Diakonessenhaus, 1960. 22 p.

BESSER, Gustav Adolf. Geschichte der frankfurter Flüchtlingsgemeinden 1554—1558. Halle, Karras, 1906. 30 p. Thesis—Vereinigte Friedrichs-Universität,, Halle-Wittenberg.

BRADY, T. A. jr. Jacob Sturm of Strasbourg and the Lutherans at the Diet of Augsburg, 1530. **Church history,** 42: 183—202, 1973.

BRESCH, Frédéric. Strasbourg et la querelle sacramentaire. Montauban, Granié, 1902. 100 p.

CAVELL, Henry J. English protestant refugees in Strasbourg, 1553—1558. **Huguenot Society of London. Proceedings,** 15: 69—120.

CELLARIUS, Helmut. Die Bedeutung der Hugenotten für Deutschland, besonders für Hessen und Nassau. **Verein für nassauische Altertumskunde. Annalen,** 77: 46—57, 1966.

CHRISMAN, Miriam Usher. Strasbourg and the Reform; a study in the process of change. New Haven, Yale University Press, 1967. 351 p. (Yale historical publications. Miscellany, 87).

CHRISMAN, Miriam Usher. Women and the Reformation in Strasbourg, 1490—1530. **Archiv für Reformationsgeschichte,** 63: 143—167, 1972.

CLASEN, Claus-Peter. The Palatinate in European history, 1555—1618 (rev. ed.) Oxford, Blackwell, 1966, 1963. 48 p.

COENEN, Dorothea. Die Kirche am Niederrhein im Jahrhundert der Reformation, von begin des 16 Jahrhunderts bis zum Jahre 1614 **(In:** Niederrheinische Kirchengeschichte. In Zusammenarbeit mit Kurt Abels und Paul Dyckmans hrsg. von Gregor Hövelmann. Kevelaer, Butzon u. Bercker [1965] p. 80—97).

COURVOISIER, Jaques. Les Catéchismes de Genève et de Strasbourg. **Société de l'histoire du protestantisme français. Bulletin,** 84: 105—121, 1935.

COWELL, Henry J. The 16th century English-speaking refugee churches at Geneva and Frankfort. **Huguenot Society of London, Proceedings,** 16: 209—230.

COWELL, Henry J. Sixteenth-century French-speaking and English-speaking refugee churches at Frankfort. **Huguenot Society of London. Proceedings,** 14: 62—95.

DE HAAN, Hugo. Frühe Beziehungen der kalvinischen Reformatoren mit Studenten aus Österreich. **Bibliotheque d'humanisme et renaissance,** 26 (2) 432—438, 1964.

DIEHL, Wilhelm. Entstehung der evangelisch-protestantische Kirche in Rheinhessen. **Hessische Chronik,** 15: 52—62; 83—93, 1929.

DIEHL, Wilhelm. Geschichte der kalvinistischen Reformation der Kurfürsten Friedrich III von der Pfalz. **Hessische Chronik,** 15: 20—32; 42—44, 1929.

DOLLINGER, R. Calvinisten im lutherischen Regensburg, 1610 und 1611. **Zeitschrift für bayerische Kirchengeschichte,** 24: 35—47, 1955.

FORSTHOFF, H. Die Eigenart des rheinische Calvinismus. **Monatshefte für rheinische Kirchengeschichte,** 26: 161—, 1932.

FORSTHOFF, H. Zur Geschichte der Reformation am Niederrhein. **Monatshefte für rheinische Kirchengeschichte,** 16: 33—55; 17: 34—61, 1922.

GERCKEN, E. Ein lübecker Hugenottengeschlecht; die Familie Sonchay. **Lübeckische Blätter,** 128 (21) 277—278, 1968.

GÖTZ, Johann Baptist. Die erste Einführung des Kalvinismus in der Oberpfalz, 1559—1576. Auf Grund urkundlicher Forschungen. Münster i.W., Aschendorff, 1933. 160 p. (Reformationsgeschichtliche Studien und Texte, Hft. 60).

GÖTZ, Johann Baptist. Die religiösen Wirren in der Oberpfalz von 1576 bis 1620. Münster i.W., Aschendorff, 1937. 371 p. (Reformationsgeschichtliche Studien und Texte, Hft. 66).

GUMBEL, Hermann. Humanitas alsatica. Strassburger Humanismus von Jakob Wimpfelung zu Johann und Jakob Sturm. **Elsass-Lotharingisches Jahrbuch,** 17: 1—36, 1938.

HANCOCK, Alton Odell. Philip of Hesse's view of the relationship of prince and church. **Church history,** 35: 157—169, 1966.

HANCOCK, Alton Odell. The Reformation in Hesse to 1538; a study of the encounter of differing reformation points of view. Atlanta, Ga., 1962. 274 1. Thesis—Emory University, Atlanta.

HANLE, Gisela (Wallau). Graf Wolfgang Ernst von Ysenburg und die Einführung des Calvinismus in der Grafschaft Büdingen; Ursachen, Art und Auswirkungen. Mainz, 1965. 160 p. Thesis—Mainz.

HASHAGEN, J. Kalvinismus und Kapitalismus am Rhein. **Schmollers Jahrbuch,** 47: 49—72, 1924.

HEMMERLE, Josef. Die calvinische Reformation in Böhmen. **Stifter-Jahrbuch,** 8: 243—276, 1964.

HILLERBRAND, Hans Joachim. Landgrave Philipp of Hesse, 1504—67; religion and politics in the Reformation. St. Louis, Foundation for Reformation Research, 1967. 40 p. (Reformation essays & studies, 1).

HOLLWEG, Walter Wilhelm. Der Augsburger Reichstag von 1566 und seine Bedeutung für die Entstehung der Reformierten Kirche und ihres Bekentnissen. [Neukirchen-Vluyn] Neukirchener Verlag des Erziehungsvereins, 1964. 419 p. (Beiträge zur Geschichte und Lehre der Reformierten Kirche, Bd. 17).

Die HUGENOTTEN und Berlin-Brandenburg. Hrsg. zum Hugenottentreffen 1971 in Berlin [Herausgeber: B. Botta, u.a.] Berlin, Haude & Spener [1971] 160 p.

HULSHOF, Abram. Geschiedenis van de Doopsgezinden te Strassburg van 1525 tot 1557. Amsterdam, Clausen, 1905. 260 p. Thesis—Amsterdam.

HUPFELD, Renatus. Der Calvinismus in Heidelberg (**In:** Marianne Weber-Kreis. Festgabe für Georg Poensgen zu seinem 60. Geburtstag am 7. 12. 1958. Heidelberg, 1958. p. 40—42).

JUNG, R. Die englische Flüchtlingsgemeinde in Frankfurt-am-Main, 1554—1559. Herausgeber: R. Küntzel. Frankfurt a.M., 1910. 66 p. (Frankfurter historische Forschungen, Hft. 3).

KANTZENBACH, Friedrich Wilhelm. Die Reformation in Deutshland und Europa. Gütersloh, Mohn [1965] 160 p.

KAUTZ, Walter. Zwei reformierte Strassburger Bekenntnisse aus den

Jahren 1533 und 1539. **Reformierte Kirchenzeitung,** 81: 201—204; 207, 211, 1931.

KAYSER, Christine Roma. Calvinism and German political life. Radcliffe, 1961. "Johann Sigismund's conversion and the repercussions": p. 84—88; "The Calvinism of the Hohenzollerns": p. 88—96. Thesis—Radcliffe.

KLAUSTERMEYER, William Henry. The role of Matthew and Catherine Zell in the Strassburg Reformation. Stanford, Calif., 1965. 278 l. Thesis—Stanford University.

KOHLS, Ernst-Wilhelm. Die theologische Lebensaufgabe des Erasmus und die oberrheinischen Reformatoren, zur Durchdringung von Humanismus und Reformation. Stuttgart, Calwer, 1969. 45 p. (Arbeiten zur Theologie. Reihe 1, Hft. 39).

KRAWARIK, Hans. Das Jahr 1549; über die Anfänge des Protestantismus im südlichen Oberösterreich. **Gesellschaft für die Geschichte des Protestantismus im Österreich. Jahrbuch,** 84: 97—107, 1968.

KREIDER, R. The Anabaptists and civil authorities of Strasbourg, 1525—55. **Church history,** 24: 99—118, 1955.

KUHN, Karl. Wesen und Werden des niederrheinischen Calvinismus. **Reformierte Kirchenzeitung,** 113: 120—122, 1972.

LANGSDORFF, Karl Georg Wilhelm von. Die deutsch-protestantische Politik Jakob Sturms von Strassburg. Heidelberg, 1904. 42 p. Thesis.

MAASS, Carl. Die ältesten Tauf- und Traueregister der französisch-reformierten Kirche in Emden. **Quellen und Forschungen zur ostfriesischen Familien- und Wappenkunde,** 8: 13—17, 1959.

MESNARD, Pierre. La Piètas litterata de Jean Sturm et le developpement à Strasbourg d'une pédagogie oecuménique, 1538—1581. **Société de l'histoire du protestantisme française. Bulletin,** 111 (10—12) 281—302, 1965.

MOLTMANN, Jürgen. Christoph Pezel, 1539—1604, und der Calvinismus in Bremen. Bremen, Einkehr, 1958. 192 p. illus. (Hospitium Ecclesiae Forschungen zur bremischen Kirchengeschichte, Bd. 2).

MOLTMANN, Jürgen. Johannes Molanus, 1510—83, und der Übergang Bremens zum Calvinismus. **Wittheit zu Bremen. Jahrbuch,** 1: 119—141, 1957.

MOLTMANN, Jürgen. Ursprung und Gestalt der Reformierten Kirche in Deutschland. **Der deutsche Hugenott,** 23: 79—84, 1959.

MÜLHAUPT, Erwin Friedrich. Eigenart und Bedeutung der Reformation im Rheinland. **Monatshefte für evangelische Kirchengeschichte des Rheinlandes,** 13: 33—58, 1964.

MÜLLER, Dieter. Beginn und Verlauf der Reformation am Rhein. **Monatshefte für evangelische Kirchengeschichte des Rheinlandes,** 5: 53—58, 1956.

MÜLLER, Dieter. Der Calvinismus am Rhein; seine Entstehung und Bedeutung. **Monatshefte für evangelische Kirchengeschichte des Rheinlandes,** 3: 97—105, 1954.

MÜLLER, Heinrich. Die Eigenart des rheinischen Calvinismus. **Rheinische wissenschaftliche Prediger-Verein. Theologische Arbeiten, N.F.** 26: 23—77, 1935.

MÜLLER, Heinrich. Missglückter Vorstoss der Calvinismus am Niederrhein während des 30 jährigen

Krieges. **Monatshefte für rheinische Kirchengeschichte,** 27: 353—372, 1933.

MÜLLER, M. Werden des rheinische Calvinismus. **Monatshefte für rheinische Kirchengeschichte,** 26: 225—233, 1932.

MÜLLER-DIERSFORDT, D. Der Calvinismus am Rhein; seine Entstehung und Bedeutung. **Monatshefte für evangelische Kirchengeschichte des Rheinlandes,** 3: 34—40; 65—76; 97—105, 1954; 4: 1—10; 114—121, 1955.

MUTH, Heinrich. Der pfälzische Kalvinismus und die brandenburgische Geheimratsordnung von 1604. **Zeitschrift für die Geschichte des Oberrheins,** 107: 400—467, 1959.

OESTREICH, Gerhard. Calvinismus, Neustoizismus und Preussentum; eine Skizze. **Jahrbuch für Geschichte Mittel- und Ostdeutschlands,** 5: 157—181 1956.

PETRI, Franciscus. Strassburgs Beziehungen zu Frankreich während der Reformationszeit. **Elsass-Lotharingisches Jahrbuch,** 8: 134—165, 1929; 10: 123—192, 1931.

PIXBERG, Hermann. Der deutsche Calvinismus und die Pädagogik. Gladbeck, Heilmann, 1952. "Calvinismus in der Pfalz": p. 20—28.

PRESS, Volker. Calvinismus und Territorialstaat; Regierung und Zentralbehörden der Kurpfalz, 1559—1619. Stuttgart, Klett (c1970) 543 p. (Kieler historische Studien, Bd. 7).

PRIVAT, E. C. Die geistige Kräfte des Calvinismus; besonders im Hinblick auf die Hugenottenkolonie Friedrichsdorf. **Der deutsche Hugenott,** 14 (3) 69—82, 1950.

RICHARDS, George W. Calvinism in the Reformed churches of Germany. **Reformed Church review,** 4 (13/2) 316—345, 1909.

ROSENKRANZ, Albert. Eine bedeutsame Gemeindeversammlung in Düsseldorf, am 19. Januar 1614. Erinnerungsblatt aus der Frühgeschichte der dortigen reformierten Gemeinde. **Monatshefte für evangelische Kirchengeschichte des Rheinlandes,** 11: 63—71; 100—103, 1962.

SCHELP, Robert. Die Reformationsprozesse der Stadt Strassburg am Reichskammergericht zur Zeit des Schmalkaldischen Bundes (1524) 1531—1541 (1555) Erw. Ausg. Mit einem Geleitwort von Philippe Dollinger. Kaiserslautern, Schmidt, 1965. 287 p.

SCHMIDT, Charles. La vie et les travaux de Jean Sturm (repr.) Nieuwkoop, De Graaf, 1970 (1855) 335 p.

SCHMIDT, Heinrich. Über die ostfriesische Reformationsgeschichte. **Ostfriesland,** 4: 9—14, 1961.

SCHOEMAKER, J. Geschiedenis der Oud-Gereformeerde kerk in het Graafschap Bentheim en het Vorstendom Ostfriesland. [n.p., n.d.]

SCHULZE, Ludolf Ferdinand. Straatsburg; stad van die Reformasie. **Die Kerkblad,** 71 (1961) 8—9, 1968.

SEELING, Werner. Der sogenannte Calvinismus in der Pfalz. Versuch einer Klärung, 1. Teil. **Blätter für pfalzische Kirchengeschichte und religiöse Volkskunde,** 37/38: 267—294, 1970/71 [**Also in:** Festgabe für Prof. D. Theodor Schaller zum 70. Geburtstag vom Verein für pfalzische Kirchengeschichte].

SEMMELROTH, R. Der gewaltsame Einführung der Calvinismus in die lutherische Grafschaft Sayn. **Monatshefte für rheinische Kirchengeschichte,** 24: 161—192, 1930.

SIEGMUND-SCHULTZE, Ernst. Kryptocalvinismus in den schlesischen Kirchenordnung. **Schlesische Friedrich-Wilhelms Universität zu Breslau. Jahrbuch,** 5: 52—68, 1960.

SOHM, Walter. Die Schule Johann Sturms und die Kirche Strassburgs in ihrem gegenseitigen Verhältnis, 1530—1581; ein Beitrag zur Geschichte deutscher Renaissance. München, Oldenbourg, 1912. 317 p. (Historische Bibliothek, Bd. 27).

STROHL, Henri. Bâle et Strasbourg au siècle de la Réforme. **Revue d'histoire et de philosophie religieuses,** 9: 140—148, 1929.

STROHL, Henri. Le protestantisme en Alsace. Strasburg. Oberlin, 1950. 510 p.

STROHL, Henri. Théologie et Humanisme à Strasbourg ou moment de la création de la Haute-École. **Recherches théologiques,** 2: 35—56, 1938.

STROHL, Henri. La théorie et la pratique des quatre ministères à Strasbourg avant l'arrivée de Calvin. **Société de l'histoire du protestantisme français. Bulletin,** 84: 123—144, 1935.

STUPPERICH, Robert. Glaube und Politik in der westfälischen Reformationsgeschichte. **Verein für westfalische Kirchengeschichte. Jahrbuch,** 45/46: 97—121, 1952/53.

STUPPERICH, Robert. Strassburgs Stellung im Beginn des Sakramentsstreits, 1524—5. **Archiv für Reformationsgeschichte,** 38: 249—272, 1941.

STUPPERICH, Robert. 450 Jahre Reformation; ein Bericht über die Gedenkfeiern in Westfalen. **Verein für westfalische Kirchengeschichte. Jahrbuch,** 61: 165—167, 1968.

TAYLOR, M. W. The educational doctrine of Johannes Sturm. Glasgow, 1959. Thesis-Univ. of Glasgow.

THOMPSON, Bard. Palatinate church order of 1563. **Church history,** 23: 339—354, 1954.

THOMPSON, Bard. The Reformed Church in the Palatinate **(In:** Essays on the Heidelberg Catechism, by Bard Thompson [a.o.] Philadelphia, United Church Press, 1963. p. 31—52).

VAN DER LINDE, Simon. De betrekkingen tussen Nederland en de Palts, 1562—1962. **Theologia reformata,** 5: 125—135, 1962.

VAN DOOREN, P. Kirchliche Beziehungen zwischen den Pfalz und den Niederlanden. **Blätter für pfalzische Kirchengeschichte und religiöse Volkskunde,** 37/38: 444—451, 1970/71. **(Also in:** Festgabe für Prof. D. Theodor Schaller zum 70. Geburtstag vom Verein für Pfalzische Kirchengeschichte).

VIOLET, Kurt. Über die Geschichte der französisch-reformierten Gemeinde in Hamburg. **Der deutsche Hugenott,** 28: 3—6, 1964.

WEBER, Otto. Eigenart und Bedeutung niederhessisch-reformierten Kirchentums **(In:** Staatsverfassung und Kirchenordnung. Festgabe für Rudolf Smend zum 80. Geburtstag am 15.1.1962. Tübingen, 1962. p. 377—399).

WEIGEL, M. Anfänge des Calvinismus in der Oberpfalz. **Zeitschrift für bayrische Landesgeschichte,** 8: 101—108, 1935.

WENDEL, Francois. L'église de Strasbourg; sa constitution et son organization, 1532—5. Paris, 1942. (Etudes d'histoire et de philosophie religieuses publiées par la Faculté de Théologie Protestante de l'Université de Strasbourg, 38).

WENDEL, François. Le mariage à Strasbourg à l'époque de la Réforme, 1520—1692. Strasbourg, 1928. (Collection d'études sur l'histoire du droit et des institutions de l'Alsace, 4).

WILL, Robert. Les origines de la liturgie protestante de Strasbourg. **Revue d'histoire et de philosophie religieuses,** 9: 479—486; 1929; 11: 521—537, 1931.

YOUNG, Clyde William. School music in sixteenth century Strasbourg. **Journal of the research of music education,** 10: 129—136, 1962.

ZEEDEN, Ernst Walter. Calvinistische Elemente in der kurpfalzischen Kirchenordnung von 1563 **(In:** Existenz und Ordnung. Festschrift für Erik Wolf zum 60. Geburtstag. Frankfurt a.M., 1962. p. 183—214).

ZEEDEN, Ernst Walter. Die kurpfälzische reformierte Zuchtordnung von 1570 **(In:** Festschrift Dr. I. E. Lichtigfeld, Landesrabbiner von Hessen, zum 70. Geburtstag. Hrsg. von Emil Roth, unter Mitwirkung von Fr. Bloch. Frankfurt a.M. 1964. p. 286—300).

ZINS, H. The political and social background of the early Reformation in Ermeland. **English historical review,** 75 (297): 589—600, 1960.

Heidelberg Catechism and its authors.

BENRATH, Gustav Adolf. Briefe des Heidelberger Theologen Zacharias Ursinus, 1534—1583 [Letters to Bullinger] **Heidelbergische Jahrbücher,** 8: 93—141, 1964.

BENRATH, Gustav Adolf. Zacharias Ursinus (1534—1583). **Blätter für pfalzische Kirchengeschichte und religiöse Volkskunde,** 37/38: 202—215, 1970/71.

BERKHOF, Hendrikus. The Catechism as an expression of our faith **(In:** Essays on the Heidelberg Catechism, by Bard Thompson [a.o.] Philadelphia, United Church Press, 1963. p. 93—122).

BERKHOF, Hendrikus. The Catechism in historical context **(In:** Essays on the Heidelberg Catechism, by Bard Thompson [a.o.] Philadelphia, United Church Press, 1963. p. 79—92).

BERKHOF, Hendrikus. De Heidelbergse Catechismus, 1563—1963. **In de waagschaal,** 18 (8) 151—158, 1963.

BERNOULLI, Wilhelm. Das Diakonenamt bei die Heidelberger Theologen Ursin, Tossin und Olevian. Greifensee, Schweizerisches Reformierte Diakonessenhaus, 1963. 29 p.

BOUWMEESTER, G. Caspar Olevianus en Zacharias Ursinus; hoofdopstellers van de Heidelbergse Catechismus. **Centraal weekblad voor de Gereformeerde Kerken in Nederland,** 11 (2) 6, 1963.

BOUWMEESTER, G. Caspar Olevianus en zijn reformatorische arbeid. 's-Gravenhage, Willem de Zwijgerstichting, 1954. 65 p.

BRONKHORST, Alexander Johannes. De omlijsting van de Heidelbergse Catechismus. **Kerk en theologie,** 14: 1—17, 1963.

CADIER, Jean. Le catechisme de Heidelberg. **Les cahiers calvinistes,** 17 (8) 1—7, 1963.

CARSON, John T. The Heidelberg Catechism and the Shorter Catechism compared. **Evangelical quarterly,** 18: 286—296, 1946.

CRAMER, H. De Heidelbergse Katechismus. **In de Waagschaal,** 17 (21) 412; (23) 450—451; (24) 468, 470; (25) 476—479, 1962.

DAHLMANN, A. E. The theology of the Heidelberg Catechism. **Reformed church review,** 2: 167—181, 1913.

DE JONG, E. Jubileumviering van catechismus in Heidelberg. **Centraal weekblad voor de Gereformeerde Kerken in Nederland,** 11 (25) 8, 1963.

DENKS, Hans. Was bedeutet der Heidelberger Katechismus für die Leitung der Gemeinde. **Reformierte Kirchenzeitung,** 103: 490—501, 1962.

DREYER, Johannes Gerhardus Martinus. Vierhonderd jaar Heidelbergse Kategismus. **Die Hervormer,** 53 (10) 1—2, 1963.

ENGELBRECHT, Barend Jacobus. Enkele opmerkings by die vierde eeufees van die Heidelbergse Kategismus. **Die Hervormer,** 53 (10) 5—10, 1963.

FRENZEL, O. Zur katechetischen Unterweisung im Zeitalter der Reformation und Orthodoxie. Leipzig. Hinrichs, 1915. 60 p.

GOOD, James Isaac. The Heidelberg Catechism and its 350th anniversary. **Presbyterian historical society. Journal,** 7: 96—104, 1013/14.

GOOD, James Isaac. New light on the Heidelberg Catechism. Tiffin, Ohio, 1907. Inauguration — Central Theological Seminary.

GRAAFLAND, Cornelis. De zekerheid van het geloof; een onderzoek naar de geloofsbeschouwing van enige vertegenwoordigers van reformatie en nadere reformatie. Wageningen, Veenman, 1961. Olevianus: p. 102—118; Ursinus: p. 119—127.

HARTVELT, Gerrit Pieter. Patronen van interpretatie. Kampen, Kok [1966?] 34 p.

HARTVELT, Gerrit Pieter. Vierhonderd jaar Heidelbergse Catechismus. **Gereformeerd weekblad,** 18 (19) 140; (19) 149; (20) 156; (21) 164; (22) 173, 1962.

HEIDELBERG CATECHISM. English. The Heidelberg Catechism with commentary; 400th anniversary ed., 1563—1963. Tr. by Allen O. Miller and M. Eugene Osterhaven. Philadelphia, United Church Press (1963) 224 p.

A HEIDELBERGI káté története Magyarországon. Bartha Tibor elöszavával és szerkesztésében irták Bucsay Mihály [et al] Budapest, Magyarországi Református Egyház. Zsinati Irodájának Sajtóosztálya, 1965. 337 p. (Tanulmányok a Magyarországi Református Egyhaz négyszázéves történetéböl, 1).

HEYNS, Johan Adam. Die Heidelbergse Kategismus, 1563—1963. **Die Kerkbode,** 91 (18) 598—602, 1963.

HINKE, William J. The origin of the Heidelberg Catechism. **Reformed church review,** 2: 152—166, 1913.

HOLLWEG, Walter Wilhelm. Neue Untersuchungen zur Geschichte und Lehre des Heidelberger Katechismus. Neukirchen, Neukirchener Verl., 1961. 208 p. (Beiträge zur Geschichte und Lehre der Reformierten Kirche, 13).

HOLLWEG, Walter Wilhelm. Neue Untersuchungen zur Geschichte und Lehre des Heidelberger Katechismus; zweite Folge. Neukirchen, Neukirchener Verl., 1968. 120 p. (Beiträge zur Geschichte und Lehre der reformierten Kirche, 28).

HOLTMANN, Wilhelm. Vorschlag für ein allgemeines Konzil von

Zacharias Ursinus. **Reformierte Kirchenzeitung,** 105: 63; 74—75, 1964.

JACOBS, Paul. Heidelberger Katechismus; reformatorische Bekenntnis (**In:** Warum wirst du ein Christ genannt? Vorträge und Aufsätze zum Heidelberger Katechismus im Jubiläumsjahr 1963. Hrsg. von Walter Herrenbrück und Udo Smidt. [Neukirchen] Verlag des Erziehungsvereins, 1965. p. 40—47).

JONKER, Willem Daniël. Die Heidelbergse Kategismus; van waar dit kom en wat dit leer. **Die Voorligter,** 27 (1) 27; 29, 1963.

KIEFER, J. Spangler. An appreciation of the Heidelberg Catechism. **Reformed church review,** 2: 133—151, 1913.

KLOOSTER, Fred H. The Heidelberg Catechism; an ecumenical creed? **Torch and trumpet,** 15 (2) 16—18; (3) 13—15, 1965; **Evangelical Theological Society. Bulletin,** 8 (1) 23—33, 1965.

KOHLS, Ernst-Wilhelm, **ed.** Evangelische Katechismen der Reformationszeit vor und neben Luthers kleinem Katechismus. Gütersloh, Mohn (1971) 75 p. (Texte zur Kirchen- und Theologiegeschichte, 16).

KRAAN, E. D. Les origines du Catéchisme de Heidelberg. **Etudes evangéliques,** 23: 9—17, 1963.

KÜTHER, Waldemar. 400 Jahre Heidelberger Katechismus. **Reformierte Kirchenzeitung,** 104: 134—137; 149—151; 165—167; 176—178, 1963. **Reformatio,** 12: 163—169; 225—229, 1963.

LANG, August. Der Heidelberger Katechismus; zum 350-jahrigen Gedächtnis seiner Entstehung. Leipzig, Verein für Reformationsgeschichte, 1913. 68 p. (Schriften des Vereins für Reformationsgeschichte, 31. Jg., 1. Stück, Nr. 113).

MANOURY, Karl. Die Calvinische im Heidelberger Katechismus. **Die Hugenottenkirche,** 16 (6) 26—28, 1963.

MASSELINK, Edward J. The Heidelberg story; the Heidelberg Catechism. **The Banner,** 97 (41) 16—17; (43) 16—17; (45) 16—17; (47) 16—17; (49) 16—17; (51) 16—17 1962. Also: Grand Rapids, Mich., Baker, 1964. 121 p.

MATTER, Hendrik Margienus. Heidelberg et son catéchisme. **Etudes evangéliques,** 23: 3—8, 1963.

MATTER, Hendrik Margienus. L'eocuménisme du catéchisme du Heidelberg. **Etudes evangéliques,** 23: 18—29, 1963.

METZ, Wulf. Necessitas satisfactionis? Eine systematische Studie zu den Fragen 12—18 des Heidelberger Katechismus und zur Theologie des Zacharias Ursinus. Stuttgart, Zwingli-Verl., 1970. 26 p.

MILLER, Allen O. & OSTERHAVEN, Maurice Eugene. Heidelberg Catechism, 1563—1963. **Theology today,** 19 (4) 536—550, 1963.

NAUTA, Doede. De Heidelbergse Catechismus, 1563—1963. **Centraal weekblad voor de Gereformeerde Kerken in Nederland,** 11 (2) 1; 3, 1963.

NAUTA, Doede. De verbreiding van de Heidelberger. **Centraal weekblad voor de Gerformeerde Kerken in Nederland,** 11 (2) 3, 1963.

NÉMETH, Balàzs. Die Geschichte des Heidelberger Katechismus in Ungarn. **Reformierte Kirchenzeitung,** 104: 265—268, 1963.

NEUSER, Wilhelm Heinrich. Der Briefwechsel Ursins mit dem wittenberger kryptocalvinisten Christoph Pezel im Jahre 1572. **Blätter für pfalzische Kirchengeschichte**

und religiöse Volkskunde, 37/38: 216—222, 1970/71.

NEUSER, Wilhelm Heinrich. Das Stammbuch des Zacharias Ursinus, 1553—1563 und 1581. **Blätter für pfalzische Kirchengeschichte und religiöse Volkskunde,** 31: 101—155, 1964.

NIJENHUIS, Willem. Coornhert en de Heidelbergse Catechismus; moment in de stryd tussen Humanisme en Reformatie. **Nederlands theologisch tijdschrift,** 18: 271—288, 1963/64.

PENNINGS, Burrell. A comparison of the Heidelberg Catechism with the Westminster Confession and the Augsburg Confession. **Reformation review,** 9: 26—38, 1955.

PONT, A. D. Iets oor die ontstaan van die Heidelbergse Kategismus. **Die Hervormer,** 53 (10) 22—24, 1963.

PRAAMSMA, Louis. Het symbolisch karakter van de Heidelbergse Catechismus. **De Wachter,** 96 (11) 4—5; (12) 4—5; (13) 5, 13; (14) 5; 15, 1963.

RAWLINS, A. J. B. Heidelbergse Kategismus vier eeue oud. **Die Voorligter,** 26 (11) 29, 1963.

RICHARDS, George W. A comparative study of the Heidelberg Catechism, Luther's Smaller and the Westminster Shorter Catechism. **Reformed church review,** 2: 193—212, 1913.

RIDDERBOS, Herman Nicolaas. Na 400 jaar. **Gereformeerd weekblad,** 18 (28) 48, 1963.

SCHMITZ, Otto. Die Botschaft des Heidelberger Katechismus 1563 und 1963 **(In:** Warum wirst du ein Christ genannt? Vorträge und Aufsätze zum Heidelberger Katechismus im Jubiläumsjahr 1963. Hrsg. von Walter Herrenbrück und Udo Smidt. [Neukirchen] Verlag des Erziehungsvereins, 1965. p. 156—165).

SCHULZE, Ludolf Ferdinand. Die klein Heidelbergse Kategismus. **Die goue kandelaar,** 10: 61—62, 1971.

STAEDTKE, Joachim. Entstehung und Bedeutung des Heidelberger Katechismus **(In:** Warum wirst du ein Christ genannt? Vorträge und Aufsätze zum Heidelberger Katechismus im Jubiläumsjahr 1963. Hrsg. von Walter Herrenbrück und Udo Smidt. [Neukirchen] Verlag des Erziehungsvereins, 1963. p. 11—23).

STURM, Erdmann K. Der junge Zacharias Ursin; sein Weg vom Philippismus zum Calvinismus, 1534—1562. Neukirchen-Vluyn, Neukirchener Verl., 1972. 323 p. (Beiträge zur Geschichte und Lehre der reformierten Kirche, Bd. 33) Thesis—Münster (Westf.) Univ.

SYMPOSIUM on the Heidelberg Catechism. **Reformed church review,** 2: 213—249, 1913.

TANIS, James. The Heidelberg Catechism in the hand of the Calvinistic pietists. **Reformed review,** 24: 154—161, 1970/71.

THOMPSON, Bard. Historical background of the Catechism **(In:** Essays on the Heidelberg Catechism, by Bard Thompson [a.o.] Philadelphia, United Church Press, 1963. p. 8—29).

VAN BAALEN, Jan Karel. De Heidelbergse Catechismus; een kritische bijdrage. **De Wachter,** 96 (23) 4—5, 13; (24) 5; (25) 5; 14, 1963.

VAN DER LINDE, Simon. De Heidelbergse Catechismus in het kader van het Gereformeerd protestantisme. **Theologia reformata,** 6: 5—23, 1962.

VAN DER VYVER, Gert Christoffel Petrus. Die Heidelbergse Kategismus. **Die Kerkblad,** 65 (1676) 9—10; (1685) 8, 10; (1686) 11—12; 14, 1962; 66 (1693) 7—9; (1966) 8—13; (1702) 6—9, 1963.

VAN HALSEMA, Emo. Onze Catechismus, 1563—1963. **De Wachter,** 96 (4) 4—5, 11; (5) 4—5; (7) 4—5, 15; (9) 4; (10) 4—5, 15; (23) 4, 1963.

VAN RONGEN, G. Jubilerende vertroosting [re: Heidelberg Catechism] **De Reformatie.** 38 (16) 125—126; (17) 133—134, (18) 141—142; (19) 149—150; (20) 157—158, 1963.

WARUM wirst du ein Christ genannt? Vorträge und Aufsätze zum Heidelberger Katechismus im Jubiläumsjahr 1963. Hrsg. von Walter Herrenbrück und Udo Smidt. [Neukirchen] Verlag des Erziehungsvereins, 1965. 220 p.

WEBER, Otto. Analytische Theologie **(In:** Warum wirst du ein Christ genannt? Vorträge und Aufsätze zum Heidelberger Katechismus im Jubiläumsjahr 1963. Hrsg. von Walter Herrenbrück und Udo Smidt. [Neukirchen] Verlag des Erziehungsvereins, 1965. p. 24—39).

WEBER, Otto. Der Heidelberger Katechismus und die Predigt. **Reformierte Kirchenzeitung,** 103: 468—472, 1962.

WEBER, Otto. Die Treue Gottes in der Geschichte der Kirche. Neukirchen, Neukirchener Verl. des Erziehungsvereins, 1968. "Analytische Theologie; zum geschichtlichen Standort des Heidelberger Katechismus": p. 131—146. (Beiträge zur Geschichte und Lehre der reformierten Kirche, 29).

WESSENDORFT, K. Luther im Heidelberger Katechismus. **Reformierte Kirchenzeitung,** 106: 71—73, 1965.

WOLTHUIS, Enno. It happened 400 years ago [re: Heidelberg Catechism] **Torch and trumpet,** 13 (6) 18—20; (7) 14—15; (8) 22—23; (9) 16—17; (10) 17—18, 1963.

ZEEDEN, Ernst Walter. Calvinistische Elemente in der kurpfälzischen Kirchenordnung von 1563 **(In:** Existenz und Ordnung. Festschrift für Erik Wolf. Frankfurt a.M., Klostermann, 1962. p. 183—214).

ZEEDEN, Ernst Walter. Staatskirchentum und calvinische Gemeindeordnung in der pfälzischen Reformationsgeschichte. **Oberrheinische Pastoralblatt,** 67 (3) 72—82, 1966.

Huguenots: General.

ALAND, Kurt. Der Weg zur "Kirche der Wüste"; vor vierhundert Jahren begannen die Hugenottenkriege. **Der Evangelist,** 113: 189—190, 1962.

ALLIER, Jacques. A la mémoire des Huguenots français émigrés en Afrique du Sud. **Societé de l'histoire du protestantisme français. Bulletin,** 113 (1—3) 11—23, 1967.

AMBURGER, Erik. Hugenottenfamilien in Russland. **Die Herold,** 5 (6/7) 125—135,1964.

L'ASSOCIATION des Huguenots allemands. **Societé de l'histoire du protestantisme français. Bulletin,** 106: 54—55, 1960.

BEULEKE, Wilhelm. Die Hugenottengemeinde Braunschweig. **Braunschweigisches Jahrbuch,** 42: 99—124, 1961; 43: 102—130, 1962; 44: 85—118, 1963; 46: 24—77, 1965.

BEULEKE, Wilhelm. Die Hugenottengemeinde Prenzlau. **Genealogie,** 141 (7/2) 416—421, 1965.

BEULEKE, Wilhelm. Die Hugenottenkolonie Kelze. **Verein für hes-**

sische Geschichte und Landeskunde. Zeitschrift, 69: 150—173, 1958.

BEULEKE, Wilhelm. Eine lebhaft sprudelnde Fehlerquelle der Hugenottenforschung; von der Gleichsetzung urkundlicher Heimatbelege mit den althergebrachten Landschaftsbezeichnungen und den heutigen Ortsnamen. **Archiv für Sippenforschung,** 33 (28) 281—300, 1967.

BOLHUIS, H. H. La Hollande et les deux Refuges. **Societé de l'histoire du protestantisme français. Bulletin,** 115: 407—409, 1969.

BOURGUET, Pierre. La croix huguenote; 2. éd. Paris, Les Bergers et les Mages [1966?] 64 p. (Les bergers et les mages, 30).

CELLARIUS, Helmut. Aspekte der Hugenottenforschung. **Der deutsche Hugenott,** 30 (1) 4—16; (2) 43—48, 1966.

CELLARIUS, Helmut. Die Bedeutung der Hugenotten für Deutschland, besonders für Hessen und Nassau. **Verein für nassauische Altertumskunde Annalen,** 77: 46—57, 1966.

CELLARIUS, Helmut. Einführung in Wege und Probleme der Hugenottenforschung. **Archiv für Sippenforschung,** 33 (28) 252—267, 1967.

CLARKE, Alison. Jean Loiseau de Tourval; a Huguenot translator in England, 1603—1631. **Huguenot Society of London. Proceedings,** 20 (1) 36—59, 190.

COLEMAN, D. C. The early British paper industry and the Huguenots. **Huguenot Society of London. Proceedings,** 19 (5) 210—225.

COLLIN, W. Das Hugenottentum des 16. und 17. Jahrhunderts. **Der deutsche Hugenott,** 25: 66—76, 1961.

DAWIN, F. Der Hugenottensturm in Karlshafen. **Der deutsche Hugenott,** 27: 24—27, 1963.

DE FAYE, W. E. Huguenots in the Channel Islands. **Huguenot Society of London. Proceedings,** 19: 28—40.

DIETZ, B. The Huguenot and English corsairs during the 3rd civil war in France, 1568—1570. **Huguenot Society of London. Proceedings,** 19: (6) 278—294.

DODGE, Guy Howard. The political theory of the Huguenots of the dispersion, with special reference to the thought and influence of Pierre Jurieu. With a new pref. (Repr.). New York, Octagon Books, 1972 (c1947) 287 p.

EBRARD, Friedich. Das Flüchtlingsschicksal der Hugenotten in der Sicht unserer Zeit. **Archiv für Sippenforschung,** 33 (28) 241—246, 1967.

Die FLÜCHTLINGE aus Frankreich; in Soest und Lippstadt, durch König Ludwig XIV aus ihrem Vaterland vertrieben. **Heimatblätter,** 43: 91—92, 1962.

Die FRANZÖSISCH-REFORMIERTEN Flüchtlings- order Hugenottenstiftungen in England. **Der deutsche Hugenott,** 26: 23—26, 1962.

GAGG, Robert P. Hugenottenprediger vor Gericht. **Reformatio,** 15 (2) 75—85, 1966.

GAGG, Robert P. Zum Menschenbild des Hugenotten. **Reformatio,** 18 (1) 26—33, 1969.

GARRISSON, Robert. Images et visages du vieux Montauban huguenot, 1559—1659. **Societé de l'histoire du protestantisme français. Bulletin.** 106: 69—86, 1960.

GIEBEL, Alfred. Die Bedeutung der Hugenotten für Hessen- Kassel.

Der deutsche Hugenott, 23: 112—119, 1959; 24: 20—25, 1960.

GINOLAT, M. 375 Jahre Edikt von Potsdam. **Der deutsche Hugenott,** 24: 98—109, 1960.

GINOLAT, M. Die Einwanderung in der Südpfalz. **Der deutsche Hugenott,** 23 (1) 25—27, 1959.

GINOLAT, M. Von der Hugenotten-Strasse zum Calvin-Platz in Neu-Isenburg. **Der deutsche Hugenott,** 25: 103—107, 1961.

GIROUARD, Mark. Alien craftsmen. **Huguenot Society of London. Proceedings,** 20 (1) 26—35, 1960.

GOETZEL, W. Rückerstattungsrecht zu Gunsten hugenottischer Réfugies. **Der deutsche Hugenott,** 23 (1) 27—31, 1959.

GRANDIJOL, J. Der Kampf der Louisendorfer um die Reinhaltung des franzosischen Charakters ihrer Siedlung. **Der deutsche Hugenott,** 27: 11—16, 1963.

GRANT, Arthur James. The Huguenots. (Hamden, Conn.) Archon, 1969. 255 p.

HARRIS, G. T. Rev. James Fontaine; Huguenot refugee in Devon. **Devon & Cornwall notes and queries,** 16: 364—370, 1931.

HAUSER, E. O. Durable Huguenots. **Saturday evening post,** 235: 68—70, 1962.

HÉMARDINQUER, Jean-Jacques. Droit et histoire [re:Huguenots] **Annales,** 15 (6) 1155-1167, 1960.

HÉRISSON, Charles D. La contribution des Huguenots français et de leurs descendants à la vie nationale Sud-Africaine. **Societé de l'histoire du protestantisme français. Bulletin,** 97: 69—90, 1951.

HÉRISSON, Charles D. Les réfugiés Huguenots du XVIIe siècle et la survivance française en Afrique du Sud. **Societé de l'histoire du protestantisme français. Bulletin,** 99 (4—6) 57—93, 1953.

Die HUGENOTTEN in Holland. **Der deutsche Hugenott,** 27: 59, 1963.

Die HUGENOTTENGEMEINDE Ludweiler. **Der deutsche Hugenott,** 25: 56—59, 1961.

HUGO, André Malan. Op soek na ons stamouers in die argiewe van Frankryk. **Familia,** 1: 7—11, 1964/65.

Ein INTERESSANTER Fund in Frankreich; Bittschrift der Hugenotten an den Grossen Kurfürsten. **Der deutsche Hugenott,** 24: 36—45, 1960.

JACOBS, Paul. Das hugenottische Bekenntnis. **Evangelische Theologie,** 19: 203—208, 1959.

KLEBER, L. C. Spain and France in Florida [re: Huguenot colony, 1562—1565] **History today,** 18: 487—494, 1968.

KLEE, Franz. Die Hugenotten im Elsass. **Archiv für Sippenforschung,** 28: 254—259, 329—336, 1962.

KNODT, H. Wann und wohin flüchteten die Hugenotten? **Hessische Familienkunde,** 8 (6) 344—345, 1967.

KRIEG, Martin. Die Hugenotten in Minden; ein Flüchtlingsproblem. Die Gründung einer französischen Gemeinde in unserer Stadt. **Heimatblätter,** 33: 89—93, 1961.

LANGDON, C. S. They took their gardens with them. **Flower grower,** 49:42—45, 1962.

LEFANU, William Richard. Huguenot refugee doctors in England. **Huguenot Society of London. Proceedings** 19 (4) 113—127.

LEFANU, William Richard. Cities of refuge [towns in England other than London where Huguenot refugee congregations were established in the 16th—17th centuries] **Huguenot Society of London. Proceedings,** 19 (6) 270—277, 1959.

LEWIS, M. The Huguenot navy, 1568-'70. **Mariner's mirror,** 46 (1) 67—68, 1960.

LILLINGSTON, E. B. C. Huguenots of the house of Orange-Nassau. **Huguenot Society of London. Proceedings** 18: 150—157.

LINDENBORN, E. Der brennende Dornbusch. **Der deutsche Hugenott,** 25: 2—20, 1961.

LINDENBORN, E. Unser Glaube ist der Sieg; Gottesdienst gehalten am Refugefest. **Der deutsche Hugenott,** 24: 109—123, 1960.

LÜTHY, Herbert. Hugenotten als Bankiers. **Kirchenblatt für die reformierte Schweiz,** 116: 106—107, 1960.

MAIZIÈRE, Clemens de. Einige Bemerkungen zur Soziologie der Hugenotten (Auszug aus einem Vortrag aus Anlass des Refugefestes, 1967) **Die Hugenottenkirche,** 21 (6) 31—33, 1968.

MALBRANC, Gabriele. Vom Leben in der französisch-reformierte Gemeinde zu Stettin **Der deutsche Hugenott,** 28: 36—39, 1964.

MANCHÉE, William Henry. Huguenot London; the city of Westminster: Soho. **Huguenot society of London. Proceedings** 14: 144—190.

MANDROU, Robert. Les protestants français réfugiés à Genève après la St. Barthélémy. **Schweizerische Zeitschrift für Geschichte,** 16 (2) 243—249, 1966.

MATHIEU, N. Ch. Hugenottenausstellung in Erlangen. **Der deutsche Hugenott,** 30 (2) 57—58, 1966.

MENGIN, Ernst. Die Bedeutung der Hugenotten für Deutschland und für die Welt. **Der deutsche Hugenott,** 29 (4) 106—115, 1965.

MENGIN, Ernst. Die Hugenotten und ihre Nachkommen in der französischen Gesetzgebung. **Der deutsche Hugenott,** 25: 98—103, 1961.

MENGIN, Ernst. Ursprung und Etymologie des Wortes "Hugenotten". **Der deutsche Hugenott,** 30 (4) 120—124, 1966; 31 (1) 13—18; (2) 53—56; (3) 80—85; 108—115, 1967; 32 (1) 11—18; (2) 41—49; (3) 76—87; (4) 121—124, 1968; 33 (1) 9—17; (2) 34—39, 1969.

MINET, S. Huguenot [church] ministers in Great Britain [alphabetical list] **Huguenot society of London. Proceedings** 19 (4) 170—187.

MOBBS, Arnold. Das hugenottische Genf. **Der deutsche Hugenott,** 18 (1) 8—11, 1954.

MORRALL, John B. The Huguenots; a study of a minority. **History today,** 11: 191—198; 271—277, 1961.

MÜLLER-MULOT, Wolfgang. Assis-sur-serre im 17. Jahrhundert; eine Studie des protestantisch-hugenottischen Lebens in Lannois. **Der deutsche Hugenott,** 27: 16—22, 1963.

PASCH, G. Note sur une pavillon rouge des marins Huguenots. **Societé de l'histoire du protestantisme français. Bulletin,** 107 (10—12) 218—221, 1961.

PATTERSON, W. Brown. James I and the Huguenot Synod of Tonneins of 1614. **Harvard theological review,** 65 (2): 241—270, 1972.

PIENAAR, W. J. B. Huguenots as free burghers. **Hugenote-Vereniging van Suid-Afrika. Bulletin,** 3: 15—17, 1965.

PILASKY. L.v. Hugenotten in Rusland. **Der deutsche Hugenott,** 24: 17—20, 1960.

PINETTE, G. L. Freedom in Huguenot doctrine. **Archiv für Reformationsgeschichte,** 50: 200—234, 1959.

POÈTS huguenots du XVIIe siècle. **Cahiers internationaux de sociologie,** 45: 320—340, 1961.

PREETZ, M. Die Privilegien für die deutschen Hugenotten. **Der deutsche Hugenott,** 25: 76—86, 1961; 26: 7—23, 1962.

PRIVAT, E. C. Brauchen wir einen Hugenotten-Verein? **Der deutsche Hugenott,** 22 (1) 2—6, 1958.

PRIVAT, E. C. Die Hugenotten in Südafrika. **Der deutsche Hugenott,** 30 (4) 99—101, 1966.

PRIVAT, E. C. Die Hugenottenkriege in Augenzeugenberichten. **Der deutsche Hugenott,** 29 (2) 34—44, 1965.

PRIVAT, E. C. Den Nachkommen der Hugenotten-Familien kommt im Rahmen der Versöhnung mit Frankreich eine besondere Rolle zu. **Der deutsche Hugenott,** 27: 98—103, 1963.

QUATRE poétes huguenots du XVIe siècle. **Les cahiers protestants,** 43: 238—255, 1959.

RAIMAR, Jos A. Die Wallonen-und Hugenotten-Gemeinde Heidelberg. **Der deutsche Hugenott,** 33 (4) 119—120, 1969.

RAINER, E. Im Banne einer Utopie. **Der deutsche Hugenott,** 23 (1) 84—86, 1959.

REAMAN, George Elmore. Huguenots around the world. **Zeitschrift für Kulturaustauch,** 12 (4) 318—319, 1962.

REGULA, F. Die Hugenotten in Annweiler. **Der deutsche Hugenott,** 23 (1) 39—44, 1959.

REGULA, H. Heimat und Auszug der Anweilerer Huguenotten. **Der deutsche Hugenott,** 24: 46—52, 1960.

RIEMENS, Kornelis Jacobus. Une tentative de colonisation huguenote à Rio, de 1555 à 1560. **Commission de l'histoire des eglises Wallone. Bulletin,** 5 (5) 6—9, 1955.

ROON, Albrecht von. Eine bemerkenswerte frankfurter Hugenottenfamilie. **Der deutsche Hugenott,** 32 (1) 2—11, 1968.

SAVORY, D. L. The Huguenot-Palatine settlements in the countries of Limerick, Kerry and Tipperary. **Huguenot society of London. Proceedings,** 18: 111—133.

SCHULTZE, Karl-Egbert. Die Vorläufer der Hamburger Hugenotten; Bausteine zu einer wahren Geschichte der Hamburger französisch-reformierten Gemeinde. **Archiv für Sippenforschung,** 33 (28) 267—281, 1967.

SUTHERLAND, Nicola Mary. The origins of Queen Elizabeth's relations with the Huguenots, 1559-'62. **Huguenot society of London. Proceedings,** 20 (6) 626—648, 1964/65.

THEIR home was the green Cape valleys. **South African Panorama,** 11 (4) 12—15, 1966.

THORNTON, Peter & ROTHSTEIN, Natalie. Importance of the Huguenots in the London silk industry. **Huguenot society of London. Proceedings,** 20 (1). 60—88, 1960.

UYS, C. J. Settler country. **Farmer's weekly,** 111: 56—57, May 25, 1966.

VOGLER, Bernard. Les contacts culturels entre huguenots français et protestants palatins au XVIe siècle. **Societé de l'histoire du protestantisme français. Bulletin,** 115 (4) 29—42, 1969.

VOR 275 Jahren; Hugenotten fanden neue Heimat in Brandenburg. **Tradition und Leben,** 12 (139) 7—9, 1960.

WAGNER, F. Die Hugenotten; ein europäisches Schicksal. **Der deutsche Hugenott,** 27: 103—116, 1963.

Die WALLONISCHEN und französischen Kolonien in der Pfalz aus dem 16., 17 und 18. Jahrhundert. **Der deutsche Hugenott,** 26: 34—37, 1962.

WESCHE, Richard. Welttreffen der Hugenotten in Nîmes. **Der deutsche Hugenott,** 32 (1) 18—19, 1968.

WESHALB verliessen die Refugies Frankreich? **Der deutsche Hugenott,** 26: 52—62, 1962.

ZOFF, Otto. The Huguenots; fighters for God and human freedom. Tr. by E. B. Ashton and J. Mayo. New York, Fischer, 1942. 340 p.

Huguenots in France see France

Huguenots in North America see America.

Italy and Spain.

BAKHUIZEN VAN DEN BRINK, Jan Nicolaas. Juan de Valdès réformateur en Espagne et en Italie, 1529—1541. Genève, Droz, 1969. 119 p. (Études de Philologie et d'histoire, 11).

BALMAS, Enea Henri. Ginevra e l'Italia. **Protestantesimo,** 16: 81—91, 1961.

BROWN, George Kenneth. Italy and the Reformation to 1550 (repr.) New York, Russel & Russel [1971] (1933) 331 p.

CANTIMORI, Delio. Spigolature per la storia del nicodemismo italiano (**In:** Roma, Facolta Valdesi di Teologica. Ginevra et l'Italia; recolta di studi promossa dalle Facolta Valdesi di Teologica di Roma a cura Delio Cantimori [et al] Firenze, Sansoni [1959] p. 177—190) (Bibliotheca storica Sansoni, 34).

CAPONETTO, S. Ginevra e la Riforma in Sicilia. (**In:** Roma, Facolta Valdesi di Teologica. Ginevra et l'Italia; recolta di studi promossa dalla Facolta Valdesi di Teologica di Roma a cura Delio Cantimori [et al] Firenze, Sansoni [1959] p. 287—306) (Bibliotheca storica Sansoni, 34).

CHIMINELLI, Piero. Bibliografia della storia della riforma religiosa in Italia; contributo alla storiografia religiosa italiana. Roma, Bilychnis, 1921. 301 p. (Biblioteca di studi religiosi, n. 10).

CHIMINELLI, Piero. The contribution of Italy to the European reformation. Louisville, Ky., 1923. Thesis—Southern Baptist Theological Seminary, Louisville.

CHIMINELLI, Piero. Il contributo dell' Italia alla riforma religiosa in Europa. Roma, Bilychnis, 1924. 219 p. (Biblioteca di studi religiosi, n. 16).

CHURCH, Frederic Corss. The Italian reformers, 1534—1564. New York, Octagon Books, 1974 [c1932] 428 p. Reprint ed. by Columbia Univ. Press., New York.

ELTZ-HOFFMANN. Lieselotte. Protestanten aus romanischen Ländern; sechs Lebensbilder [Von Lieselotte Hoffmann] Basel, Reinhardt, [1956] "Bernardo Occhino": p. 63—86; "Julia Gonzaga": p. 87—107.

GONNET, Giovanni. I rapporti tra i Valdesi franco-italiani e i riformati d'Oltralpe prima di Calvino **(In:** Roma, Facolta Valdesi di Teologica. Ginevra et l'Italia; recolta di studi promossa dalla Facolta Valdesi di Teologica di Roma a cura Delio Cantimori [et al] Firenze, Sansoni [1959] p. 1—64) (Bibliotheca storica Sansoni, 34).

HAGGARD, Theodore Merrill. The church and the sacraments in the theological writings of Juan de Valdés. Atlanta, Ga., 1971 284 1. Thesis —Emory University.

LÓPEZ MICHELSEN, Alfonso. La estirpa calvinista de nuestras instituciones politicas. Prólogo por Carlos José Romero. [Bogotá] Ediciones Tercer Mundo [1966] 90 p. (El Dedo en la herida, 2. Politica).

McNAIR, P. M. J. The life and work of Pietro Martire Vermigli in Italy. Oxford 1963. Thesis—Christ College, Oxford University.

MENDES, S. La reformation espagnole au XVIe siècle. **Les cahiers calvinistes** 14 (12) 3—31, 1962.

NIETO, Jose C. Juan de Valdès and the origins of the Spanish and Italian reformations. Genève, Droz, 1970. 355 p. (Travaux d'humanisme et renaissance, 58).

NIETO, José C. Juan de Valdes, 1509 (?) —1541; background, origins and development of his theological thought with special reference to knowledge and experience. Princeton, N.J., 1967. 705 l. Thesis—Princeton Theological Seminary.

OLIVIERI, Achille. Alessandro Trissino e il movimento calvinista vicentino nel Cinquecento. **Rivista di storia della chiesa in Italia,** 21: 54—117; (3) 361—366, 1967.

PASCAL, Arturo. Il marchesato di Saluzzo e la Riforma protestante; durante il periodo della dominazione Francese, 1548—1588. Florence, Sansoni, 1960. 659 p. (Biblioteca Storica Sansoni, N.S., 36).

PEYROT, Giorgio. Influenze franco-ginevrine nella formazione delle discipline ecclesiastiche valdesi alla meta del XVI secolo **(In:** Roma, Facolta Valdesi di Teologica. Ginevra et l'Italia; recolta di studi promossa dalla Facolta Valdesi di Teologica di Roma a cura Delio Cantimori [et al] Firenze, Sansoni [1959] p. 215—286) (Bibliotheca storica Sansoni, 34).

VINAY, Valdo. Der Anschluss der romanischen Waldenzen an die Reformation und seine theologische Bedeutung. **Theologische Literaturzeitung,** 87: 89—100, 1962.

VINAY, Valdo. La prima e la seconda Riforma nel passato e nel presente della Chiesa Valdese. **Protestantesimo,** 22: 129—147, 1967.

Music and Huguenot Psalter.

ALLIN, Michel. Caractères spécifiques de la musique et possibilités d'une expression musicale de la foi. Paris, 1956. 73 l. Thesis—Faculté libre protestante de Paris.

BOURGEOIS, Loys. Le droiet chemin de musique; ed. P. A. Gaillard. Kassel, Bärenreiter, 1954. (Documenta musicologica, 6).

BOURGEOIS, Loys. Le premier livre des pseaumes; ed. P. A. Gaillard. Kassel, Bärenreiter, 1960. (Schweizerische Musikdenkmäler, 3).

CHAIX, H. Le psautier huguenot; sa formation et son histoire. Genève, 1907. Thesis—Genève.

CLIVE, H. P. The Calvinist attitude to music, and its literary aspects and sources. **Bibliotheque d'huma-**

nisme et renaissance, 19 (1) 80—102; (2) 294—319, 1957; 20 (1) 79—107, 1958.

COFFIN, Henry Sloane. The enduring significance of the Scottish psalter. **Hymn society of America. Paper,** 2, 1950.

DOUEN, Orentin. Clément Marot et le Psautier Huguenot, étude historique, littéraire, musicale et bibliographique, contenant les mélodies primitives des psaumes et des spécimens d'harmonie de Clement Jannéquin, Bourgeois, J. Louis, Jambe-de-Fer, Goudimel, Grassot, Sureau, Servin, Roland de Lattre, Claudin le Jeune, Mareschall, Sweelinck, Stobée, etc. (Repr.) Niewkoop, De Graaf, 1967 (1878-79) 2 v.

ERGEBNISSE der Forschungen um den Hugenottenpsalter **(In:** Kirchenmusik in ökumenischer Schau. 2. Internationale Kongress für Kirchenmusik in Bern, 22—29 Sept. 1962. Kongresbericht. Bern, Schweizerische Musikforschende Gesellschaft, 1964. p. 51—55).

FORNAÇON, Siegfried. L'Estocart und sein Psalter. **Die Musikforschung,** 13: 188—191, 1960.

FRANÇON, Marcel. Clement Marot and popular songs. **Speculum,** 25: 247—248, 1950.

GEROLD, Théodore. Les péres de l'église et la musique. Paris, Alcan, 1931. 222 p. (Etudes d'histoire et de philosophie religieuses, 25).

GEROLD, Théodore. Les plus anciennes mélodies de l'église protestante de Strasbourg et leurs auteurs, par Théodore Gerold, avec la collaboration de M.E. Wagner. Paris, Alcan, 1928 80 p. (Cahiers de la Revue d'histoire et de philosophie religieuses, 18).

GOUDIMEL, Claude. Oevres complètes. Publiées par H. Gagnebin, R. Häusler et E. Lawrey, sous la dir. de L. A. Dittmer et P. Pidoux. I. Premier livre des psaumes en forme de motets d'après l'edition de 1557. Transcription de Henri Gagnebin. New York, 1967. 144 p. (Collected works of the Institute of medieval music).

HAEIN, Emmanuel. Le problème du Chant Choral dans les églises réformées et le trésor liturgique de la cantilène huguenote. Montpellier, 1926. 100 p. Thesis—Univ. Montpellier.

HAGEMAN, Howard G. Can church music be reformed? **Reformed review,** 14 (12) 19—28, 1960.

HARMS, John Kenwood. Message or medium? The theological crisis in sixteenth century church music. St. Paul, Minn., 1971. Thesis—Luther Theological Seminary.

HENKING, Bernhard. Der Hugenottenpsalter. **Reformatio,** 8: 350—356, 1959.

KNIGHT, George Litch. The significance of the Genevan psalter of 1551. **Hymn society of America. Paper,** 5, 1951.

LAWRY, Eleanor McChesny. The Psalm motets of Claude Goudimel. New York, 1954. Thesis—New York University.

LE HURAY, Peter. Music and the reformation in England, 1549—1660. London, Jenkins (1967) 454 p. (Studies in church music).

LENSELINK, Samuel Jan. Les psaumes de Clement Marot. Ed. critique du plus ancien texte, avec toutes les variantes des manuscrits et des plus anciennes éditions jusquá 1543, accompagnée du texte définitif de 1562 et précédée d'une étude. Assen, Van Gorcum, 1969. 247 p.

L'ESTOCART, Pascal de. Cent cinquante pseaumes de David, ed. Hans Holliger und Pierre Pidoux. Kassel, Bärenreiter, 1954. (Documenta musicologica, 7).

LESURE, François. Claude Goudimel, étudiant, correcteur, et editeur parisien. **Musica disciplina,** 2: 225, 1948.

MCALL, Reginald Ley. The story of the music of the Genevan psalter. **Hymn society of America. Paper,** 2, 1950.

MACMILLAN, John Buchanan. The Calvinistic psalmody of Claude le Jeune, with special reference to the Dodecacorde of 1598. (New York) 1966. 3 v. Thesis—New York Univ.

PIDOUX, Pierre. Le psaumes d'Antoine de Mornable, Guillaume Morlaye, et Pierre Certon. **Annales musicologiques,** 5: 179—199, 1957.

PIDOUX, Pierre. Le psautier huguenot du XVIe siècle; mélodies et documents. Bâle, Baerenseiter, 1962. 2v.

PIDOUX, Pierre. Über die Melodien des Hugenotten Psalters. **Jahrbuch für Liturgik und Hymnologie,** 1: 113—114, 1956.

POINCENOT, Ph. Essai sur les origines des cantiques français. Paris, 1908. 98 p. Thesis—Montpellier.

PRATT, Waldo Selden. The importance of the early French Psalter. **Musical quarterly,** 21: 25—32, 1935.

PRATT, Waldo Selden. The significance of the Old French psalter. New York, **Hymn society of America. Paper,** 1933. 16 p.

REUSS, R. Une enquête sur l'origine des Cantiques français usités à Strasbourg et en Allemagne. Montbéliard, 1908.

ROKSETH, Yvonne. Les premiers chants de l'église calviniste. **Revue de musicologie,** 36: 7—20, 1954.

ROPER, Cecil Mizelle. The Strasbourg French psalters, 1539—1553. Los Angeles, Cal., 1972. 437 l. Thesis—University of Southern California.

RUUT, August. The Genevan Psalm melodies set by Claude Goudimel in chordal style. New York, 1962. Thesis—New York Univ.

STERNFELD, Frederick W. Music in the schools of the Reformation. **Musica disciplina,** 1: 99—121, 1948.

SUGGESTIONS for observing the Genevan psalter anniversary, 1551—1951. **Hymn society of America. Paper,** 1951.

TEUBNER, Ulrich. Notes sur la rédaction musicale du psautier genevois. **Annales musicologiques,** 4: 113—128, 1956.

THOMPSON, Robert Ellis. The Psalmbook of the Reformed churches. **Presbyterian historical society. Journal** 5: 311—339, 1909/10.

VAN AMSTEL, Piet. De Geneefse psalmmelodieën Anno 1562 en de vraag naar hun mogelijk verband met oud-kerklijke zangwijzen. **Het orgel,** 58, 1962; 59: 7—18, 1963.

WOODWARD, G. R. The Genevan psalter of 1562, set in four-part harmony by Claude Goudimel in 1565. **Musical association, 44th session,** 1917—18. **Proceedings,** 44: 167-, 1918.

Netherlands: General.

BEINS, Ernst. Die Wirtschaftsethik der calvinistischen Kirche der Niederlande, 1565—1650. s'-Gravenhage, Nijhoff, 1931. 73 p.

BOLHUIS, H. H. La hollande et les deux Refuges. **Societé de l'histoire du protestantisme français. Bulletin,** 115: 407—409, 1969.

BRUINSMA, Henry. The organ controversy in the Netherlands reformation to 1640. **American Musicological Society. Journal,** 7: 205—212, 1955.

BRUINSMA, Henry. The Souterliederkens and its relation to psalmody in the Netherlands. Ann Arbor, 1948. Thesis—University of Michigan, Ann Arbor.

CISTOZVONOV, A. N. Die Rolle des Kalvinismus in der niederländischen bürgerlichen Revolution des 16. Jahrhunderts **(In:** Weltwirkung der Reformation. Internationales Symposium anlässlich der 450. Jahr-Feier der Reformation in Wittenberg von 24. bis 26. Oktober 1967. Referate und Diskussionen. Hrsg. von Max Steinmetz und Gerhard Brendler. Berlin, VEB Deutsch-verl. der Wissenschaften, 1969. p. 104—128).

CONRING, Enno. Kirche und Staat nach der Lehre der niederländischen Calvinisten in der ersten Hälfte des 17. Jahrhunderts. (Neukirchen) Neukirchener Verl., 1965. 197 p. (Beiträge zur Geschichte und Lehre der reformierten Kirche, Bd. 18).

COWIE, Leonard W. The Reformation of the sixteenth century. New York, Putnam, 1970. "Calvinism in France and the Netherlands": p. 47—60. Also published by Longmans, Toronto, 1970.

DANKBAAR, Willem Frederik. Die Reformation in den Niederlanden. **Der deutsche Hugenott,** 24: 6—10, 1960.

DE BOER, Johannes. De verzegeling met de Heilige Geest, volgens de opvatting van de nadere reformatie. Rotterdam, Bronder-Offset, 1968. 204 p. Thesis—Theologische Hogeschool, Kampen.

DE JONG, Peter Ymen. Can political factors account for the fact that Calvinism rather than Anabaptism came to dominate the Dutch Reformation? **Church history,** 33: 392—417, 1964.

DE JONG, Peter Ymen. Christian missions in the days of Dort. **Torch and trumpet,** 18 (5) 26—32, 1968.

DE JONG, Peter Ymen. Secrets of Calvinist success in the Netherlands. **Torch and trumpet,** 14 (8) 4—7; 14, 1964.

DE RIDDER, J. G. De kerkhistorie van het Westland; 400 jaren protestantisme in het Westland, 1566—1966. Zaltbommel, Europese Bibliotheek, 1967. "Het Calvinisme": p. 41—48.

DUKE, Alastair C. A footnote to "Marrano Calvinism" and the troubles of 1566-'67 in the Netherlands. **Bibliotheque d'humanisme et renaissance,** 30 (1) 147—148, 1968.

DU TOIT, Hendrik Daniël Alphonso. Die vierde eeufees van ons kerkboek. **Die Kerkbode,** 95 (35) 1094—1096, 1965.

HOUBEN, P. J. Marcus Térez and Marrano Calvinism in the Dutch revolt and the reformation. **Bibliotheque d'humanisme et renaissance,** 29 (1) 121—132, 1967.

Die HUGENOTTEN in Holland. **Der deutsche Hugenott,** 27: 59, 1963.

KEMPFF, Dionysius. Die oorlog van tagtig jaar. **Die Kerkblad,** 71 (1978) 2—4, 1968.

KEMPFF, Dionysius. Stryd; in

die verlede en toekoms. **Die Kerkblad,** 69 (1872) 2—4, 1966.

KINGDON, Robert McCune. Political resistance of the Calvinists in France and the Low Countries. **Church history,** 27: 220—233, 1958.

KOCH, A. C. F. De reformatie te Deventer in 1579—1580 **(In:** Postillen over kerk en maatschappy in de vijftiende en zestiende eeuw. Aangeboden aan Prof. Dr. R. R. Post bij zijn afscheid als hoogleraar aan de Katholieke Universiteit te Nijmegen. Utrecht, Dekker en Van de Vegt, 1964).

KUYPER, H. H. De Reformatie in Nederland. **Stemmen des tijds,** Reformatie-nummer: 22—43, 1917.

LAGERWEY, Walter. Calvinism in the Netherlands. **The Banner,** 94 (14) 9, 29; (16) 9; 29, 1959.

NAUTA, Doede. Beeldenstorm; 400 jaar geleden. **Centraal weekblad voor de Gereformeerde Kerken in Nederland,** 14 (32) 3, 1966.

NAUTA, Doede. Hagepreken; Juni 1566. **Centraal weekblad voor de Gereformeerde Kerken in Nederland,** 14 (22) 3, 1966.

NAUTA, Doede. Nu of nooit, herwinnen of sterven [The battle of Heiligerlee] **Centraal weekblad voor de Gereformeerde Kerken in Nederland**, 16 (20) 5, 1968.

NAUTA, Doede. Het smeekschrift der edelen. **Centraal weekblad voor de Gereformeerde Kerken in Nederland,** 14 (13) 3—4, 1966.

NEDERBRAGT, Johan Alexander, Kalvinismus; Studien und Skizzen. Budapest, Sylvester, 1938. "Kalvinismus in Holland": p. 11—96.

NOBBS, Douglas. Theocracy and toleration; a study of the disputes in Dutch Calvinism from 1600 tot 1650. Cambridge, University Press, 1938. 280 p.

PETRI, Franz. Mass und Bedeutung der reformatorische Strömungen in den niederländischen Maaslanden im 16. Jahrhundert **(In:** Reformation und Humanismus, R. Stupperich zum 65. Geburtstag, hrsg. [von] M. Greschat [und] J. F. Gerhard Goeters. Witten, 1969. p. 212—224).

QUATRIÈME centenaire de la Requête des nobles, 5 avril 1566. **Les cahiers calvinistes,** 7 (27/3) 1—12, 1966.

ROELINK, Jan. Een drietal vragen bij de geschiedenis van het vroegste Nederlandse Calvinisme. **Bijdragen van de geschiedenis der Nederlanden,** 3: 222—230, 1960.

SMITSKAMP, Hendrik. Calvinistisch nationaal besef in Nederland vóór het midden der 17de eeuw. 's-Gravenhage, Daamen, 1947. 32 p.

SPRUNGER, K. L. Dutch career of Thomas Hooker. **New England quarterly,** 46: 17—44, 1973.

STEARNS, Raymond Phineas. Congregationalism in the Dutch Netherlands; the rise and fall of the English Congregational classis, 1621—1635. Chicago, American Society of Church History, 1940. 151 p. (Studies in church history, IV).

TEN DOORNKAAT, Hans. Der Calvinismus in den Niederlanden. **Neue zürcher Zeitung,** 59 (2230) 4, 1964.

VAN GELDER, Herman Arend Enno. Aantekening naar aanleiding van drie vragen omtrent het vroegste Nederlandse Calvinisme gesteld door J. Roelink. **Bijdragen van de geschiedenis der Nederlanden,** 1: 58—63, 1961.

VAN ITTERZON, G. P. Christelijk geloven en leven in het begin van de Reformatie in Nederland. **Hervormd weekblad—de Geref. Kerk,** 76: 122; 130; 138, 1964/65.

VAN RHYN, Elmer L. Catholics, Calvinists and Philip II; the patriotic movement and patriotic propaganda in the revolt of the Netherlands from 1576 to 1581 **(In:** The Dawn of modern civilization; studies in Renaissance, Reformation and other topics, presented to honor Albert Hyma, Ed. by Kenneth A. Strand. Ann Arbor, Mich., Ann Arbor Publications [1962] p. 225—236).

WENSINCK, Arent Jan. De Nederlandsch-Hervormde Kerk en de gemeente van Christus; gedachten naar aanleiding van de reorganisatiebeweging. Rotterdam, Voorhoeve [193-?] 47 p.

WIERSINGA, Albertus. Een vijftal lezingen. Middelburg, Gereformeerd traktaatgenootschap "Filippus," F. P. D'Huij, 1900. "De strijd tussen Calvinisten en libertijnen tydens de opkomst onzer republiek": p. 86—102.

WOLTJER, Jan Juliaan. Friesland in hervormingstyd. Leiden, 1962. 354 p. Thesis—Leiden.

Netherlands: Belgic Confession **see Belgic Confession.**

Netherlands: Outstanding personalities.

BOS, F. L. De vergeten martelaar [Adriaan Corneliszoon van Haamsteck] 's-Gravenhage, Willem de Zwyger-Stichting, 1960. 76 p. (Reformatorische Stemmen).

CAZAUX, Yves. Guillaume le Taciturne; de la "Généralité" de Bourgogne à la Republique des Sept Provinces-Unies. Paris, Michel, 1970. 384 p.

CRAMER, J. A. Guillaume d'Orange. **Almanach Jean Calvin,** 1935: 1—2.

DE GRAAFF, B. J. W. Jacobus Trigland. Vianen, De Banier, 1970. 180 p. (Banier bibliotheek voor het gezin).

DE ZEEUW, Pieter. Brekers, bouwers en bewaarders; geestelijke leiders in de 17e en 18e eeuw [Plancius, Johannes W. ten Bogaert, Arminius, Gomarus, Bogerman, Episcopius, Trigland, Camhuysen, Revius] **Belijden en beleven,** 20 (4) 6; (5) 6; (6) 6; (7) 6; (8) 6; (9) 6; (10) 6; (11) 6; (12) 6, 1962.

DONNELY, M. C. Calvinism in the work of Jacob Jordaens. **Art quarterly,** 4: 356—366, 1959.

DIJKSTRA, S. Dr. Festus Hommius; een groot man uit het kerkelijk leven van de 16e eeuw. **Centraal weekblad voor de Gereformeerde Kerken in Nederland,** 16 (31) 6, 1968.

FABER, Jelle. De reformatorische strijd van Franciscus Gomarus **(In:** Francicus Gomarus; lustrumbundel, ter gelegenheid van het derde lustrum van de Vereniging van Gereformeerde Studenten te Leiden "Franciscus Gomarus". Groningen, De Vuurbaak, 1972).

GEESINK, W. Calvinisten in Holland: Franciscus Junius, 1545—1602, Petrus Plancius, 1552—1622, Cornelius Geselius, 1583—1614, de doleerende kerk van Rotterdam (Herdr.) Genève, Slatkine Repr, 1970 (1887) 294 p.

GRAAFLAND, Cornelis. De zekerheid van het geloof; een onderzoek naar de geloofsbeschouwing van enige vertegenwoordigers van reformatie en nadere reformatie. Wageningen, Veenman, 1961. „Gomarus". p. 85—97.

HARTVELT, Gerrit Pieter. Petrus Boquinus. **Gereformeerd theologisch tijdschrift,** 62: 49—77, 1962.

KAMPHUIS, J. De avondmaalsbrief van Cornelis Koen. **De Reformatie,** 42: 353—354; 361—362; 369—370; 377—378; 385—386, 1967.

KAWERAU, Peter. Die Homiletik des Andreas Hyperius. **Zeitschrift für Kirchengeschichte,** 71 (1/2) 66—81, 1960.

KOK, Arie B. W. M. Dirk Raphaëlz Camphuysen, dichter-theoloog; een vat vol tegenstrydigheden. **Centraal weekblad voor de Gereformeerde Kerken in Nederland,** 13 (35) 4, 1965.

KRAUSE, G. Andreas Hyperius in der Forschung seit 1900. **Theologische Rundschau,** 34 (3) 362—380; (4) 281—341, 1969.

LEEMANS, W. F. Orangeois aux Pays-Bas. **Commission de l'histoire des églises Wallone. Bulletin,** 6 (4) 17—82, 1971.

MULLER, Pieter Johannes. Willem van Oranje. (Baarn, Hollandia, 1914) 44 p. (Onze groote mannen, ser. 1, no. 7).

NAUTA, Doede. Petrus Plancius. **Centraal weekblad voor de Gereformeerde Kerken in Nederland,** 15 (26) 2, 1967.

NAUTA, Doede. Van hoogverraad beschuldigd, 5 Juni 1568; Egmond en Hoorne terechtgesteld. **Centraal weekblad voor de Gereformeerde Kerken in Nederland,** 16 (22) 3, 1968.

NEILSON, George Alexander. Twelve Reformation heroes. London, Pickering & Inglis, 1960. "William, Prince of Orange", p. 81—88.

ORNÉE, Wilhelmus A. Calvinisme en humanisme bij Philips van Marnix, heer van St. Aldegonde. Groningen, Wolters, 1966. (Gelderse leergangen te Arnhem. Voordrachten, no. 16).

UIT DEN BOGAARD, Maximiliaan Theodoor. De Gereformeerden en Oranje tijdens het eerste stadhouderloze tijdperk. Groningen, Wolters, 1954. 258 p. Thesis—Groningen.

VAN WESTHOVE, Jan. Hermanus Faukelius. **Centraal weekblad voor de Gereformeerde Kerken in Nederland,** 17 (33) 6, 1969.

VAN WESTHOVE, Jan. De moeilijke herderspsalm; twee psalmdichters tegenover elkaar [Datheen and Marnix] **Centraal weekblad voor de Gereformeerde Kerken in Nederland,** 17 (22) 5, 1969.

VAN WESTHOVE, Jan. Petrus Dathenus. **Centraal weekblad voor de Gereformeerde Kerken in Nederland,** 17 (11) 8; (12) 6, 1969.

WEDGWOOD, Cicely Veronica. William the Silent, William of Nassau, Prince of Orange, 1533—1584. London, Cape, 1944, 256 p.

Netherlands: Southern parts; Belgium.

ANTWERP. Commissie van de Religionsvrede. Register der Commissie tot onderhoud van de Religionsvrede te Antwerpen (1579—1581) door Fl. Prims. Brussel, Paleis der Academiën, 1954. 259 p.

BAKHUIZEN VAN DEN BRINK, Jan Nicolaas. Le catéchisme de Genève et les eglises Wallones de Pays Bas. **Commission de l'histoire des églises Wallone. Bulletin,** 5 (4) 38—40, 1950.

COLLINET, Robert. Histoire du Protestantisme en Belgique aux XVII me et XVIII me siècles. Bruxelles, Librairie des Eclaireurs Unionistes, 1959. 254 p. (Histoire du Protestantisme en Belgique et au Congo Belge, t.2).

COLLINET, Robert. La Réformation en Belgique au XVIe siècle. 2. éd. Bruxelles, Librairie des Eclaireurs Unionistes, 1958. 156 p. (Histoire du Protestantisme en Belgique et au Congo Belge, t. 1).

DECAVELE, Johan. Jan Hendrickx en het Calvinisme in Vlaanderen, 1560—1564. **Genootschap voor Geschiedenis Gesticht onder de Benaming 'Société d'émulation', Brugge. Handelingen,** 106: 17—32, 1969.

DELMOTTE, M. Het Calvinisme in de verschillende bevolkingslagen te Gent. **Tijdschrift voor geschiedenis,** 76: 145—175, 1963.

DE PATER, Jan Cornelis Hendrik. De opkomst en de ondergang van het Calvinisme in de stad Doornik. 's-Gravenhage, Willem de Zwijger-Stichting [n.d.] 32 p. (Reformatorische Stemmen).

ENKELE cijfers in verband met de bekering van de protestanten te Antwerpen in 1585—1589. **Ons geestelijk erf,** 41 (3) 302—309, 1967.

HALKIN, Léon Ernest. La réforme en Belgique sous Charles-Quint. Bruxelles, La Renaissance du livre, 1957. "Le calvinisme": p. 95—110.

MEYHOFFER, Jean. Les origines du protestantisme belge. Brussels, La Gerbe, 1938. 31 p.

MOREAU, É. de. Histoire de l'église en Belgique. Bruxelles, L'Edition Universelle, 1952. "La Calvinisme et le période des troubles": p. 109—264. (Museum Lessianum. Section historique, 15).

PICHAL, E. Calvin et la Belgique. **Les cahiers calvinistes,** 22 (12) 7—16, 1964.

VERHEYDEN, Alphonse L. E. Geschiedenis der Doopsgezinden in de Zuidelijke Nederlanden in de XVIe eeuw. Brussel, A.W.I.S.K., 1959. 178 p. (Vlaamse Academie voor Wetenschappen, Letteren en Schone Kunsten van België, Brussel. Klasse der Letteren. Verhandelingen, no. 36).

VERHEYDEN, Alphonse L. E. De Hervorming in de Zuidelijke Nederlanden in de XVIe eeuw. Met een inl. door M.C.W. Wegeling. Brussel, Synode van de Protestantse Kerken, 1949. 198 p.

VERHEYDEN, Alphonse L. E. Le martyrologe Protestant des Pays-Bas du Sud au XVI me siècle. Bruxelles, Librairie des Eclaireurs Unionistes, 1960. 285 p. (Histoire du protestantisme en Belgique et au Congo Belge,8).

VERHEYDEN, Alphonse L. E. Le protestantisme à Eupen sous le gouvernement du duc d'Albe, 1567—1573. Plus: Enquête en matière d'hérésie, a Eupen en 1569. **Commission de l'histoire des églises Wallone. Bulletin,** 5 (5) 10—70, 1955.

WIELENGA, D. J. A. Boechout en de hervorming in Vlaanderen II-XX. **De Bazuin,** 103 (12) 1—2; (13) 1—2; (14) 1—2; (15) 3; (16) 2; (17) 2; (18) 2; (19) 1—2; (20) 2; (22) 2—3; (23) 2; (24) 1—2; (25) 2—3; (26) 1—2; (27) 1—2; (28) 3; (29) 1—2; (30) 1—2; (31) 1—2, 1960.

Netherlands: Synods, etc.

BALKENENDE, W. P. Overpeinzingen rondom Emden, 1571. **De Reformatie,** 47 (4) 34—35; (5) 40—42; (7) 56—58; (8) 63—65, 1971.

BOTHA, S. J. Agtergronde van die Convent van Wezel (1568) en die Sinode van Emden (1571). **Hervormde teologiese studies,** 28 (3/4) 113—126.

BRONKHORST, Alexander Johannes. Der Raum der Freiheit und die reformierte Tradition; Vortrag bei der 400-Jahr-Feier der Emder Synode am Mittwoch. **Nederlands theologisch tijdschrift,** 26: 15—31, 1972.

DEDDENS, D. De synode van Emden, 4—13 Oktober 1571. **De Reformatie,** 47 (1) 1, 1971.

DE JONG, Otto J. Die Emdener Generalsynode vor dem Hintergrund der westeuropäischen Reformationsgeschichte. **Gesellschaft für niedersächische Kirchengeschichte. Jahrbuch,** 68: 9—24, 1970.

DE JONG, Otto J. Le synode d'Emden, 1571—1971. **Commission de l'histoire des églises Wallone. Bulletin,** 6 (4) 3—16, 1969—'71.

DE JONG, Peter Ymen. **ed.** Crisis in the Reformed Churches; essays in commemoration of the great Synod of Dort, 1618—1619. Grand Rapids, Reformed Fellowship, 1968. 266 p.

DEWAR, Michael Willoughby. The Synod of Dort, the Westminster Assembly, and the French Reformed Church, 1618-'43. **Huguenot Society of London. Proceedings,** 21: 119—123, 1965/70.

DREYER, Johannes Gerhardus Martinus. Die Dordtse Sinode. **Die Hervormer,** 59 (8) 1—2, 1968.

1571 EMDER SYNODE 1971. Beiträge zur Geschichte und zum 400 jährigen Jubiläum. Bearbeitet und redigiert von Elwin Lomberg. Hrsg. von der Evangelisch- reformierten Kirche in Nordwestdeutschland. Neukirchen—Vluyn, Neukirchener Verslag des Erziehungsverein, 1973.

ENGELBRECHT, Barend Jacobus. Die Dordtse Leerreëls; 'n lofsang tot eer van die soewereine, genadige God. **Die Hervormer,** 59 (8) 2, 1968.

FATIO, O. Nihil pulchrius ordine; contribution a l'étude de l'establissement de la discipline ecclesiastique aux Pays-Bas. Leiden, Brill, 1971.

FOSTER, Herbert Darling. Liberal Calvinism; the remonstrants of the Synod of Dort in 1618. **Harvard theological review,** 16 (1) 1—37, 1923.

FROST, Herbert. Der Konvent von Wesel im Jahre 1568 und sein Einfluss auf das Entstehen eines deutschen evangelischen Kirchenverfassungsrecht. **Savigny-Stiftung für Rechtsgeschichte, kanon. (germ) Abteilung.** Zeitschrift 56: 325—387, 1970.

HANEKOM, Tobias Nicolaas. Die groot sinode; terugblik op Dordrecht. **Die Kerkbode,** 102 (19) 594—595; 609, 1968.

HOEKEMA, Anthony A. The heritage of Dort. **The Banner,** 103 (30) 4—5; (31) 18—19, 1968.

HOENDERDAAL Gerrit Jan. De Kerkordelijke kant van de Dordtse Synode. **Nederlands theologisch tijdschrift;** 23: 349—400, 1968/69.

HOVIUS, Jan. Notities betreffende de synode te Emden, 1571, en haar artikelen. Kampen, Kok, 1972. (Apeldoornse studies, no. 4).

JONKER, Willem Daniël. Belydenis van Gods genade. **Die Kerkbode,** 101 (8) 265—266; 268, 1968.

JOOSTE, Josef Petrus. Dordt en die kategese. **Die Kerkblad,** 71 (1972) 14—17, 1968.

KAMPHUIS, J. Het convent van Wezel, 3 Nov. 1568. **De Reformatie,** 44 (1) 1—2; (2) 9—10; (3) 17—18, 1968.

KEMPFF, Dionysius. Dordt en die Bybel. **Die Kerkblad,** 71 (1972) 2—3, 1968.

KEMPFF, Dionysius. Emden, 5—13 Oktober, 1571; Hervorming en Nederland. **Die Kerkblad,** 74 (2123) 6—7, 1971.

KEMPFF, Dionysius. Die sinode van Dordrecht 1574. **Die Kerkblad,** 77 (2274) 7—8, 1974.

KEMPFF, Dionysius. Konvent van Wezel, 1568. **Die Kerkblad,** 71 (1976) 2—4, 1968.

LOMBARD, Jacobus Christoffel. Rondom Dordrecht; flitse uit die strydperk. **Die Kerkbode,** 102 (20) 630—631, 1968.

MEIJERINK, H. J. Uit de geschiedenis van het ontstaan van de Dordtse Leerregels **(In:** De schat van Christus' bruid, door J. Faber [e.a.] Goes, Oosterbaan & Le Cointre, 1965. p. 7—65).

MULLER, J. J. P. Die Dordtse Kerkorde, 1619. **Hervormde teologiese studies,** 25 (2) 88—97, 1969.

MIJDERWIJK, P. De synode van Dordrecht en Dordtse Leerregels. **De Bazuin,** 103 (53) 1960; 104 (54) 2; (55) 2; (56) 2, 1961.

NAUTA, Doede. Betekenis van de Synode van Dordrecht, 1618—1619. **Centraal weekblad voor de Gereformeerde Kerken in Nederland,** 16 (45) 1, 1968.

NAUTA, Doede. Blik op de Dordtse Synode. **Centraal weekblad voor de Gereformeerde Kerken in Nederland,** 16 (45) 3, 1968.

NAUTA, Doede. Het Convent te Wezel in 1568. **Centraal weekblad voor de Gereformeerde Kerken in Nederland,** 16 (43) 3, 1968.

NAUTA, Doede. Opera minora; kerkhistorische verhandelingen over Calvijn en de geschiedenis van de kerk in Nederland. Kampen, Kok, 1961. "Wezel (1565) en Emden": p. 50—57.

NAUTA, Doede. De Synode van Emden, 1571, en de Hugenoten. **Gereformeerd theologisch tijdschrift,** 73 (2) 76—94, 1973.

NIJENHUIS, Willem. De Synode van Emden, 1571. **Kerk en theologie,** 23 (1) 34—54, 1972.

PONT, A D. Die groot Sinode van Dordrecht, 1618. **Hervormde teologiese studies,** 25 (2) 74—87, 1969.

PONT, A. D. Die kerkorde van Emden 1571. **Hervormde teologiese studies,** 28 (3/4) 148—159.

PONT, A. D. Rondom die Sinode van Dordrecht, 1618—1968. **Die Hervormer,** 59 (8) 9—13, 1968.

SCHULZE, Ludolf Ferdinand. Dordt en die leer. **Die Kerkblad,** 71 (1972) 8—10, 1968.

SWART, Marius Johannes. Die Sinode van Dordt. **Die Voorligter,** 31 (8) 12, 28; (9) 12; 22, 1968.

De SYNODE van Emden, 1571—1971. Een bundel opstellen ter gelegenheid van de vierhonderdjarige herdenking, onder red. van D. Nauta, J. P. van Dooren [en] Otto J. de Jong. Kampen, Kok, 1971.

DE SYNODE van 1574. **De Wekker,** 83 (30) — (39), 1974.

TUKKER, Cornelis Andries. De classis Dordrecht van 1573 tot 1609; bijdragen tot de kennis van in-en extern leven van die Gereformeerde Kerk in de periode van haar organisering. Leiden, Universitaire Pers, 1965. 199 p. (Leidse historische reeks, dl. 10) Thesis—Leiden.

VAN DER LINDE, Gerhardus Philippus Leonardus. Dordt en die kerk-reg. **Die Kerkblad,** 71 (1972) 11—13, 1968.

VAN DER LINDE, Simon. De Dordtse Synode, 1619—1969. **Nederlands theologisch tijdschrift,** 23: 339—348, 1968/69.

VAN DER LINDE, Simon. Van Wezel (1568) naar Emden (1571) **Theologia reformata,** 14 (3) 181—198, 1971

VAN DER LINDE, Simon. Vierhonderd jaar Convent van Wezel, 1568—1968. **Theologia reformata,** 11 (4) 210—225, 1968.

VAN DER VYVER, Gert Christoffel Petrus. Die voorgeskiedenis van Dordt. **Die Kerkblad,** 71 (1972) 6—7, 1968.

VAN DER WOUDE, Cornelis. Synode van Emden. **Gereformeerd weekblad,** 27 (14) 77, 1971

VAN DOOREN, J. P. De synode van Emden 1571. **Act-if** (Actuele informatie van de Stichting Prisma—Lectuurvoorlichting). 7: 3—18, 1971.

VAN RONGEN, G. "Oecumenische" tendenzen in de dagen van "Dordrecht". **De Reformatie,** 44 (13) 101, 1969

WESELER KONVENT. Die Beschlüsse des Weseler Konvents von 1568. Hrsg. und ins Deutsche übertragen von J. F. Gerhard Goeters. Düsseldorf, Presseverband der Evangelische Kirche im Rheinland, 1968. 25 [i.e. 50] p. (Schriftenreiche des Vereins für rheinische Kirchengeschichte, Nr. 30).

Scotland.

AINSLEE, James Lyon. The Scottish reformed church and [its relations with] English Puritanism. **Scottish Church History Society. Records,** 8: 75—95, 1943.

AITKEN, James Macrae. The trial of George Buchanan before the Lisbon inquisition; including the text of Buchanan's defences, along with a tr. and commentary. London, Oliver & Boyd, 1939. 166 p.

BARTH, Karl. Gotteserkenntnis und Gottesdienst nach reformatorischer Lehre; 20 Vorlesungen über das Schottische Bekenntnis van 1560, gehalten an der Universität Aberdeen im Frühjahr 1937 und 1938. Zollikon, Evangelische Buchhandlung, 1938. 226 p. (Gifford lectures).

BURNET, George Bain. The Holy Communion in the Reformed Church of Scotland, 1560—1960. Edinburgh, Oliver & Boyd, 1960. 329 p.

CHEYNE, A. C. The Scottish Reformation. **Scottish journal of theology,** 16: 78—88, 1963.

CLARK, Ivo MacNaughton. A history of church discipline in Scotland. Aberdeen, Lindsay, 1929. 235 p.

DANNENFELDT, Karl H. The church of the Renaissance and Reformation; decline and reform from 1300 to 1600. Saint Louis, Concordia (c1970) "The English and Scottish Reformations": p. 91—103.

d'ASSONVILLE, Victor Edouard. Die bloedstryd ter wille van ouderlinge; uit die geskiedenis van die Skotse „Covenanters." **Die Kerkblad,** 68 (1798) 8—9; (1799) 6—7; (1800) 8—9, 1965.

d'ASSONVILLE, Victor Edouard. Die Skotse kerk 400 jaar van 'n donker wolk verlos. **Die Kerkblad,** 64 (1631) 11; 13; 15, 1961.

DAVIDSON, Donald. The influence of England on the Scottish Reformation. Edinburgh, 1926. 157 l. Thesis—Edinburgh Univ.

DONALDSON, Gordon. 'The example of Denmark' in the Scottish reformation. **Scottish historical review,** 46: 57—64, 1948.

DONALDSON, Gordon. The Scottish reformation. Cambridge, University Press, 1960. 242 p.

DONALDSON, Gordon & HAIRE, J. L. M. The Scottish Reformation. **Scottish historical review,** 40 (130) 161—164, 1961.

DOUGLAS, James Dixon. Light in the north; the story of the Scottish Covenanters. Exeter, Paternoster, 1964. 220 p. (Paternoster Church History, 6).

DOUGLAS, James Dixon. The work of Reformation in Scotland. **International reformed bulletin,** 3 (6) 17—29, 1966.

DREYER, Johannes Gerhardus Martinus. Die vierde eeufees van die kerk van Skotland. **Die Hervormer,** 51 (2) 1—2, 1960.

DUNLOP, A. Ian. Baptism in Scotland after the Reformation **(In:** Reformation and revolution; essays presented to the very reverend principal emeritus Hugh Watt, on the sixtieth anniversary of his ordination. Ed. by Duncan Shaw. Edinburgh, St. Andrew Press, 1967. p. 82—99).

ESSAYS on the Scottish Reformation, 1513—1625 [Essays which appeared in the Innes Review] Ed. by David McRoberts. Glasgow, Burns, 1962. 496 p.

FLEMING, D. Hay. The influence of the Reformation on social and cultured life in Scotland. **Scottish historical review,** 15 (10) 1—29, 1917.

GEHEIM van die Skotse reformasie. **Naweekpos,** 11 (124) 22—23, 1964.

HAGAN, E. J. Sozialethos des schottischen Calvinismus. **Kirche und Welt,** 1: 92—102, 1932.

HAWS, C. H. The Scottish clergy at the Reformation. Glasgow, 1969. Thesis—Glasgow University.

HENDERSON, Henry F. Religion in Scotland; its influence on national life and character. Paisley, Gardner [1920] 236 p. (The Chalmers lectures, 1916—20).

Die HERVORMING in Skotland. **Die Kerkbode,** 86: 548—549, 1960.

HEWAT, Kirkwood. Makers of the Scottish church at the Reformation. Edinburgh, Macniven & Wallace, 1920. 410 p.

'JESUS and no quarter' [The Reformation in Scotland and John Knox] **Times Literary Supplement,** p. 301—303, 1950.

JOHNSTON, George. Scripture in the Scottish reformation; I: historical statement. **Canadian journal of the theology** 8: 249—257, 1962.

KERR, Thomas Angus. John Craig, 1512 [?]-1600; with special reference to his contribution to the upbuilding of the Reformed Church in Scotland. Edinburgh. 1954. 209 l. Thesis—Edinburgh Univ.

KERR, Thomas Angus. John Craig, minister of Aberdeen, and King's Chaplain **(In:** Reformation and revolution; essays presented to the very reverend principal emeritus Hugh Watt, on the sixtieth anniversary of his ordination. Ed. by Duncan Shaw. Edinburg, St. Andrew Press, 1967. p. 100—123).

LEE, Maurice Jr. The Scottish Reformation after 400 years. **Scottish historical review,** 44 (138) 135—147, 1965.

McCOY, Florence Nina. Robert Baillie and the second Scots reformation. 1972. 352 1. Thesis—University of Oregon.

MACDOUGALL, A. G. The keys of the kingdom; an historical and doctrinal study of the power of the keys in the Reformed Church, with special reference to the Church of Scotland in the period 1560—1712. Edinburgh [1963?] Thesis—Edinburgh Univ.

MACGREGOR, Janet Girdwood. The Scottish Presbyterian policy; a study of its origins in the sixteenth century. Edinburgh, Oliver & Boyd, 1926. 144 p. Thesis—Univ. of Edinburgh.

MCMILLAN, William. The worship of the Scottish Reformed Church, 1550—1638. Edinburgh, 1925. 426 1. Thesis—Edinburgh Univ.

MECHIE, Stewart. The principles of the Scottish Reformation. **Expository times,** 71 (12) 356—358, 1960.

MELDRUM, Neil. The General Assembly of the Church of Scotland in the year 1638. A study from contemporary documents of its origin, proceedings and importance. Edinburgh, 1924, 217 1. Thesis—Edinburgh Univ.

MUIR, Thomas. The Scots Confession of 1560; its sources and distinctive characteristics. Edinburgh, 1926. 191 1. Thesis—Edinburgh Univ.

NAUTA, Doede. Vier eeuwen Schotse geloofsbelijdenis. **Centraal weekblad voor de Gereformeerde Kerken in Nederland,** 8 (21) 163, 1960.

PRUGH, J. W. The theory and practice of discipline in the Scottish Reformation. Edinburgh [1959/60?] Thesis—Edinburgh Univ.

REID, J. M. Kirk and nation; the story of the Reformed Church of Scotland. London, Skeffington, 1960. 207 p.

REID, William Stanford. The coming of the Reformation to Edinburgh. **Church history,** 42 (1) 27—44, 1973.

REID, William Stanford. French influence on the first Scots Confession and Book of discipline. **Evangelical theological journal,** 35 (1) 1—14, 1972.

REID, William Stanford. Middle class factor in the Scottish reformation. **Church history,** 16, 137—153, 1947.

RENWICK, Alexander M. Story of the Scottish Reformation; 2nd ed. London, Inter Varsity Fellowship Press (1960) 176 p.

The SCOTS Confession, 1560. Ed. with an introd. by G. D. Henderson, together with a rendering into modern English by James Bulloch. Edinburgh, St. Andrew [1960] 80 p.

SHAW, D. The origin and development of the General Assembly of the Church of Scotland, 1560—1600. Edinburgh [1961/62?] Thesis—Edinburgh Univ.

SHORT, L. B. Challenge to Scottish Calvinism; the Arminian-universalist challenge. **Hibbert journal,** 62: 87—91, 1964.

STRIKWERDA, Earl. Calvinism in Scotland and in England. **The Banner,** 94 (18) 9; 21, 1959.

STUTTERHEIM, J. F. Die „kirk" in ekumeniese perspektief. **Die Hervormer,** 51 (2) 9; 12—13, 1960.

VAN DEN BERG, J. Hervormingsherdenking in Schotland. **Gereformeerd weekblad,** 15 (48) 377—378; (49) 390; (50) 393; (51) 401, 1960.

VIERHUNDERTJAHRFEIER der schottischen Reformation. **Kirchenblatt für die reformierte Schweiz,** 116: 345—346, 1960.

WALLS, Ronald. Scottish survey; the fourth centenary of the Scottish Reformation. **Blackfrairs, 7—8:** 286—290, 1960.

WATKIN, R. N. Jr. The forming of the Southern Presbyterian minister, from Calvin to the American Civil War. Nashville, Tenn., 1969." Scotland and Westminister": p. 79—169. Thesis—Vanderbilt Univ., Nashville.

WEBB, O Kenneth. The political thought of Samuel Rutherford. Durham, N.C., 1964. 242 1. Thesis—Duke Univ., Durham.

WEIR, T. E. Pastoral care in the Church of Scotland in the seventeenth century. Edinburgh [1960/61?] Thesis—Edinburgh Univ.

South Africa and the Huguenots in South Africa.

Die AFRIKAANSE volk se krag is in Calvinisme. **Woord en daad,** 9 (46) 1—3, 1966.

ALLIER, Jacques. A la mémoire des Huguenots français émigrés en Afrique du Sud. **Societé de l'histoire du protestantisme français. Bulletin,** 113 (1—3) 11—23, 1967.

BESSELAAR, Gerrit. The present position in South Africa **(In:** International Conference of Calvinists. 1st, London, 1932. The reformed faith commonly called Calvinism. Report of the International Conference held in May, 1932. London, Sovereign Grace Union [1932] p. 160—169).

Die CALVINISME in Suid-Afrika; 'n waardering en 'n uitdaging. **Woord en daad,** 8 (36) 7—9, 1965.

COETZEE, Johannes Hendrik. Moet Afrikaners juis Calviniste wees? **Die Burger,** 54: (1/5) 14, 1969.

COETZEE, Johannes Hendrik. Must an Afrikaner be a Calvinist? **New nation,** 7—9, 6/1969.

COETZEE, Johannes Hendrik & DU PLESSIS, Hugo. Calvinisme in Afrika. **Potchefstroomse Universiteit vir Christelike Hoër Onderwys. Instituut vir Bevordering van Calvinisme. Studiestuk,** no. 12.

DE KLERK, Willem Johannes. Die Calvinisme in Suid-Afrika; 'n toekomsperspektief. **Potchefstroomse Universiteit vir Christelike Hoër Onderwys. Instituut vir Bevordering van Calvinisme. Studiestuk,** no. 34. ques e Fnrance au XVIe siècle.

DU PLESSIS, Hugo. Die Calvinisme en Afrika. **Die Bondsbode,** 16 (21—22) 48—51, 1965.

DU TOIT, Stefanus. Calvinisme in Suid-Afrika en die betekenis van ons Universiteit in hierdie verband **(In:** Potchefstroomse Universiteit vir Christelike Hoër Onderwys. Instituut vir Bevordering van Calvinisme. Die atoomeeu; in U lig. Potchefstroom, 1969. p. 35—51).

ENGELBRECHT, Barend Jacobus. Die prinsipiële patroon van die Calvinisme in Suid-Afrika. **Potchefstroomse Universiteit vir Christelike Hoër Onderwys. Instituut vir Bevordering van Calvinisme. Studiestuk,** no. 31.

HÉRISSON, Charles — D. La contribution des Huguenots français et de leurs descendants à la vie nationale Sud-Africaine. **Societé de l'histoire du protestantisme français. Bulletin,** 97: 69—90, 1951.

HÉRISSON, Charles — D. Les réfugiés Huguenots du XVIIe siècle et la survivance française en Afrique du Sud. **Societé de l'histoire du protestantisme français. Bulletin,** 99 (4—6) 57—93, 1953.

PIENAAR, W. J. B. Huguenots as free burghers. **Hugenote-Vereniging van Suid-Afrika. Bulletin,** 3: 15—17, 1965.

PRIVAT, E. C. Die Hugenotten in Südafrika. **Der deutsche Hugenott,** 30 (4) 99—101, 1966.

ROSS, Andrew C. Calvinism in an African situation. **Union Seminary quarterly review,** 16: 21—31, 1960.

THEIR home was the green Cape valleys. **South African Panorama,** 11 (4) 12—15, 1966.

TREURNICHT, Andries Petrus. Die praktiese belewing van die Calvinisme in Suid-Afrika. **Potchefstroomse Universiteit vir Christelike Hoër Onderwys. Instituut vir Bevordering van Calvinisme. Studiestuk,** no. 33.

Spain see Italy.

Switzerland and Geneva.

ADAM, G. Der Streit um die Prädestination im ausgehenden 16. Jahrhundert; eine Untersuchung zu den Entwürfen von Samuel Huber und Aegidius Hunnius. Neukirchen, Neukirchener Verlag, 1970. 224 p. (Beiträge zur Geschichte und Lehre der Reformierten Kirche, 30).

AMMANN, Hektor. Oberdeutsche Kaufleute und die Anfänge der Reformation in Genf. **Zeitschrift für württembergische Landesgeschichte,** 13: 150—193, 1954.

BERGIER, Jean François. Commerce et politique du blé à Genève aux XVe et XVIe siècles. **Schweizerische Zeitschrift für Geschichte,** 14 (4) 521—550, 1964.

BERGIER, Jean François. Salaires des pasteurs de Genève au XVIe siècle **(In:** Mélanges d'histoire du XVIe siècle. Offerts à Henri Meylan. Genève, Droz, 1970. p. 159—178) (Travaux d'humanisme et renaissance, 110).

BLANKE, Fritz. Entstehung und Bedeutung des zweiten helvetischen Bekenntnisses. **Reformatio,** 15: 575—582, 1966.

(BORGEAUD, Charles. L'adoption de la Réforme par le peuple de Genève. Genève, 1923.

BORGEAUD, Charles. La conquête religieuse de Genève, 1532—1536. Extrait de "Guillaume Farel" publié par le Comité du Quatrième Centenaire de la Réformation Neuchâteloise. Neuchâtel, Delachaux & Niestlé, 1930. 40 p.

BORGEAUD, Charles. Les étudiants de l'Acedémie de Genève au XVIe siècle **(In:** Gaudeamus; quelques aspects de la vie des étudiants étrangers à Genève.Genève, Kundig, 1959. p. 25—35).

BÜHLER, Hans. 400 Jahre Confessio Helvetica Posterior. **Kirche in der Zeit,** 22 (7) 322—325, 1967.

BUSCARLET, Daniel. Le mur des Réformateurs. Genève, L'eau vive, 1963. 24 p.

BÜSSER, Fritz. Die Arbeit am Institut für schweizerische Reformationsgeschichte. **Theologische Literaturzeitung,** 92 (5) 325—328, 1967.

CHOPARD, Adrien. Genève et les anglais. **Societe d'histoire et d'archeologie de Genève. Bulletin,** 7 (2) 175—280, 1939/40.

COUDY, Julien. **ed.** The Huguenot wars. Tr. by Julie Kernan. Philadelphia, Chilton, 1969. "A Jesuit at the Academy of Geneva": p. 55—58.

COURVOISIER, Jaques. Les Catéchismes de Genève et de Strasbourg. **Société de l'histoire du protestantisme français, Bulletin,** 84: 105—121, 1935.

COURVOISIER, Jaques. La Confession helvétique postérieure. **Revue de theologie et de philosophie, N.S.,** 99 (5) 289—298, 1966.

COWELL, Henry J. The 16th century English-speaking refugee churches at Geneva and Frankfort. **Huguenot Society of London. Proceedings,** 16: 209—230, 1937/41.

COWIE, Leonard W. The Reformation of the sixteenth century. New York, Putnam, 1970. "Calvinism in Switzerland": p. 39—45. Also published by Longmans, Toronto, 1970.

DEONNA, W. Les arts à Genève. Genève, Musee d'Art et d'Histoire, 1942.

DUFOUR, Alain. Histoire politique et psychologie historique. Suivi de deux essais sur Humanisme et Réformation et Le mythe de Genève au temps de Calvin. Genève, Droz, 1966. 133 p.

FOURNIER-MARCIGNY, Fernand. Genève au 16 me siècle; la vie ardente du premier refuge français, 1532—1602. Lettre pref. de Édouard Chapuisat. Genève, Editiones du Mont-Blanc (1942) 280 p.

GABEREL, Jean Pierre. Histoire de l'église de Genève, depuis le commencement de la réformation jusqu'a nos jours [Réimpression] Nieuwkoop, De Graaf, 1970. 4 v.

GANOCZY, Alexandre. La bibliothèque de l'Académie de Calvin; le catalogue de 1572 et ses enseignements. Genève, Droz, 1969. 343 p. (Études de philologie et d'histoire, 13).

GEISENDORF, Paul Frédérik. Métiers et conditions sociales du premier refuge à Genève, 1549—1586 (**In:** Melanges; Antony Babel, v 2. Genève, 1963. p. 239—249).

GENEVA. University. Actes du IVe centenaire, 1559—1959. Genève, Georg, 1963. 297 p.

GENEVA. University. Le livre du recteur de l'Academie de Genève, 1559—1878. Publié sous la direction de S. Stelling-Michaud. Genève, Droz, 1959- v. (Travaux d'humanisme et renaissance, 33-).

GENEVE à l'heure de Calvin, 1509—1559. Préf. de Marc Chenevière, President du Comité du Jubilé calvinien, texte de Paul-F. Geisendorf, photos de Jean-Pierre Landenburg et Jean Mohr. Genève, 1959.

GERMANN, Georg. Der protestantische Kirchenbau in der Schweiz; von der Reformation bis zur Romantik. Basel, 1963. 213 p. Thesis—Basel.

GLAUBEN und Bekennen; vierhundert Jahre Confessio Helvetica Posterior. Beiträge zu ihrer Geschichte und Theologie, hrsg. von Joachim Staedtke. Zurich, Zwingli, 1966. 407 p.

GROB, Rudolf. Calvinisme in Switserland. **Die Kerkblad,** 67 (1772) 6—8, 1964.

HAURI Rudolf. Die Reformation in der Schweiz im Urteil der neueren schweizerischen Geschichtschreibung. Zürich, Leeman, 1945. Thesis.

HISTOIRE de Genève des origines à 1798, par Henri Grandjean [et al.] Genève, Société d'Histoire et d'Archéologie, 1951.

JACOT, L. La dispute de Lausanne. **Schweizerisches Gutenberg Museum/Musée Gutenberg suisse,** 1: 6—11, 1928.

JALLA, Jean. Les Vaudois des Vallées et Genève en 1536. **Almanach Jean Calvin,** 1936: 39—40.

KALSBEEK, L. De unieke verhouding van kerk en staat in Genève.

Hervormd weekblad — de Geref. Kerk, 84: 138—139, 1972/73.

KINGDON, Robert McCune. Geneva and the consolidation of the French Protestant movement, 1564—1572; a contribution to the history of Congregationalism, Presbyterianism, and Calvinist resistance theory. Madison, University of Wisconsin Press, 1967, 241 p.

KINGDON, Robert McCune. Genève et les réformés français; le cas d'Hugues Sureau, dit Du Rosier. **Societé d'histoire et d'archéologie de Genève. Bulletin,** 12: 77—88, 1961.

KOCH, Ernst. Die Theologie der Confessio Helvetica Posterior. (Neukirchen) Neukirchener Verl., 1968. 455 p. (Beiträge zur Geschichte und Lehre der Reformierten Kirche, Bd. 27).

LOCHER, Gottfried Wilhelm. Zur Vierhundertjahrfeier des zweiten Helvetischen Bekenntnisses. **Kirchenblatt für die reformierte Schweiz,** 122 (15) 226—229; (16) 242—245, 1966.

MANDROU, Robert. Les protestants français réfugiés à Genève après la St. Barthélémy. **Schweizerische Zeitschrift für Geschichte,** 16 (2) 243—249, 1966.

MANOURY, Karl. Die Reformation in Genf. **Die Hugenottenkirche. Beiheft:** p. 1—18, 3—8/1971.

MARTIN, Charles. Les protestants anglais réfugiés à Genève au temps de Calvin, 1550—1560—1915. Genève, Droz [n.d.].

MARTIN, Paul Edmond. Trois cas de pluralisme confessionel aux XVIe et XVIIe siècles; Genève-Savoie France. Genève, Jullien, 1961. "Le mandement de Thiez": p. 23—44.

MEYLAN, Henri. Fêter Noël ou pas? Une controverse dans l'église neuchâteloise du XVIe siècle. **Revue d'histoire et de philosophie religieuses,** 54: 49—67, 1974.

MONTER, E. William. Calvin's Geneva. New York, Wiley (c1967) 250 p. (New dimensions in history: historical cities).

MONTER, E. William. Genevan libraries of the early 1600's; magistrate and refuge. **Bibliotheque d'humanisme et renaissance** 27 (2) 523—531, 1965.

MONTER, E. William. The Italians in Geneva, 1550—1600; a new look **(In:** Genève et l'Italie; études publieées à l'occasion du 50e anniversaire de la Societé genevoise d'études italiennes, par Luc. Monnier. Genève, Droz, 1969. p. 53—77).

MONTER, E. William. Studies in Genevan government, 1536—1605. Genève, Droz, 1964. 128 p. (Travaux d'humanisme et renaissance, 62).

MONTER, E. William. Witchcraft in Geneva, 1537—1662. **Journal of modern history,** 43 (2/6) 179—204, 1971.

NAEF, Henri. Les origines de la réforme à Genève. Genève, Droz, 1968. 2 v. (Travaux d'humanisme et renaissance, 1—2).

NAUTA, Doede. De tweede Helvetische geloofsbelijdenis van Maart 1566. **Centraal weekblad voor de Gereformeerde Kerken in Nederland,** 14 (9) 2, 1966.

NIESEL, Wilhelm. Die Bedeutung des 2. Helvetischen Bekenntnissen für die Kirchen der Reformation. **Reformierte Kirchenzeitung,** 108: 150—154, 1967.

PASCAL, Arturo. La colonia piemontese a Ginevra nel sec. XVI **(In:**

Roma Facolta Valdesi di Teologica. Ginevra et l'Italia; recolta di studi promossa dalla Facolta Valdesi di Teologica di Roma a cura Delio Cantimori [et al] Firenze, Sansoni [1959] p. 65—134) (Bibliotheca storica Sansoni, 34).

PFISTER, Rudolf. Ambrosius Blarer in der Schweiz (**In:** Der Konstanzer Reformator Ambrosius Blarer, 1492—1564. Gedenkschrift zu seinem 400. Todestag. Im Auftrag der Evangelischen Kirchengemeinde Konstanz im Gemeinschaft mit Fritz Blanke [u.a.] Hrsg. von Bernd Moeller. Konstanz, Thorbecke, 1964. p. 205—220).

POLLET, Jacques Vincent. Chronique de théologie historique; seizième siècle. Reforme suisse. **Revue des sciences religieuses,** 37: 34—59, 1963.

POTGIETER, Frederick Johannes Mentz. Die Universiteit van Genève. **Die Kerkbode,** 84 (2) 54—57, 1959.

REINHARDT, William Wayne. The Reformation as seen from Basel. Nashville, Tenn., 1963. 102 1. Thesis—Vanderbilt Univ., Nashville.

RISSE, Heinz. Schlangen in Genf. Krefeld, Scherpe, 1951. 93 p.

ROGET, Amédée. Histoire du peuple de Genève depuis la réforme jusqu'a l'escalade, 1536—1568 (Repr.) Nieuwkoop, De Graaf, 1970 (1870-'83).

STAEDTKE, Joachim. Gibt es einen offizielen Text der Confessio Helvetica Posterior? **Theologische Zeitschrift,** 19: 29—42, 1963.

STRASSER, Otto Erich. Bern am Kreuzweg ökumenischer Begegnung zur Reformationszeit. **Zwingliana,** 13: 400—406, 1969/73.

VAN ITTERZON, G. P. De universiteit van Genève. **Hervormd weekblad — de Geref. Kerk,** 70: 292—294, 1958/59. (**Also in:** Belijnd belijden. Kampen, Kok, 1971. p. 24—30).

VORSTER, J. L. Kerke van Petrus; in Rome en Genève. **Die Kerkblad,** 70 (1923) 8—9, 1967.

VUILLEUMIER, Henri. Histoire de l'église réformée du Pays de Vaud sous le régime Bernois. Lausanne, La Concorde, 1927/28. 4 v.

Wales — See England.

LIST OF AUTHORS